MANAGEMENT WISDOM OF LORD KRISHNA

MANAGEMENT WISDOM OF LORD KRISHNA

A Treatise on Unified Concept of Management Performance for the Globalised World

By

Dr. Udai Vir Singh

NEW CENTURY PUBLICATIONS
NEW DELHI, INDIA

New Century Publications,
4852 / 24, Bharat Ram Road,
Ansari Road, Daryaganj,
New Delhi – 110 002 (India)

Tel.: 011- 4358 7398, 4101 7798
E-mail: info@newcenturypublications.com • ncpublications2000@gmail.com

www.newcenturypublications.com

Editorial office:
4832/24, Ansari Road, Daryaganj,
New Delhi – 110 002

Tel.: 011- 4356 0919

Edition: **2026**

ISBN: **978-81-7708-160-2**

First Published: 2008

Published by New Century Publications and printed at Milan Enterprises, New Delhi

Designs: Patch Creative Unit, New Delhi

PRINTED IN INDIA

DEDICATION

This work is dedicated to my late mother who, despite being an unlettered woman in rural work environment, was a wisdom concentrate—a management genius in her own way. Womenfolk, young and old, formed a regular stream of visitors for consultation and advice pertaining to challenges of rural life. Her righteous handling of three daughters-in-law smelt of professionalism of superior order.

FOREWORD

Dr. Udai Vir Singh is an individual with a powerful imagination. He has got much out of life. In his own modest and original way he has given something to life and society.

He has had a chequered career as a corporate guru, industrialist, management consultant and much more. In his latest Avatar, he has turned author. His book entitled **Management Wisdom of Lord Krishna** is certainly an unusual offering. Coming as I do from Braj I am a Krishna Panthi.

I asked Dr. Singh as to why he has asked me to write the foreword for this original book. He replied that my name has a close affinity with Lord Krishna.

In this book Lord Krishna is depicted as a divine super management Guru. The book has nine Parvas (or Chapters) along with attachments, references and index. No aspect of management has been neglected. Lord Krishna is in command in every area and direction. The author has taken a wholly new road to add a modern, technical dimension to the skills of Arjuna's Parthasarthy. He is immortal. He gave us the Gita.

14.09.2007 **K. Natwar Singh**

CONTENTS

ABOUT THE BOOK

In recent years, the Western management education and training citadels such as Harvard, Kellogg, Wharton and several others have experienced persistent failure of their modern management technology to inspire executive trainees and students to stay perpetually motivated in the face of growing challenges posed by economic liberalisation and globalisation trends sweeping across the world. Hence, modern management minds are looking for solutions beyond the reservoir of Western management thoughts and practices. They have examined and experimented with the Japanese and Chinese systems of management. Of late, their focus has shifted to Indian philosophy to find solutions to re-occurring irritants in efficient management practices. As a step in this direction, Western management executives, particularly in USA, are being cajoled to put **purpose before self** during retraining sessions at institutions of management learning. It is Ved Vyasa's **Bhagavad Gita** through which they are attempting to enrich themselves with the **supremacy of action**. They are trying to enrich matter with forces of spirit, realising that the **principle of karma** has invaluable merits.

The present work is an attempt at systematic presentation of the vital management contents as enshrined in **Bhagavad Gita**, the eternal **Song of Wisdom**. The book is a running treatise comprising principles, percepts and practices employed by Lord Krishna to achieve his mission incarnate objectives.

The work is divided into IX Parvas (or Chapters).

Parva I presents the wisdom concentrates of Lord Krishna in the form of brief analysis of selected management-relevant slokas from the **Bhagavad Gita,** the divine **Song of Wisdom.**

Parva II delves on Lord Krishna's approach to dignity of work, commitment appreciation, respect for reality, strategic intervention, efficient facilitation, intense rapport, internal conflict management, talent recognition, superior team management and management of uncertainties.

Lord Krishna was a **man of action,** a unique manifestation of **action warriorism.** His action initiatives, at all stages of his life, are perpetual source of inspiration for productive action. His leadership qualities of divine proportions come alive in Parva III.

Parva IV elaborates the intense t**hought warriorism** of Lord Krishna. His unique thought prowess led him to command people of immense capabilities and diverse interests, with the finesse of a magician. His skills as a power thinker, his practice of thinking ahead, his divine doctrines of **karma, dharma** and **non-material motivation,** are described in this Parva.

Lord Krishna was a true **master of soft skills,** the skills of verbal and non-verbal communication, logic and intellect, through which he managed friends and foes, juniors and seniors, and co-operators and antagonists, with equal ease. The humility and ethicality of his approach, respect for virtue and merit, effective empowerment of subordinates, superior emotion quotient, skillful ego management, total impartiality, and his irresistible **technology of madhura,** are detailed in Parva V.

Parva VI is devoted to Lord Krishna's skills as a teacher and as a guru. He was a guru with a spiritual core, and a guru of rectitude and alternatives. His relevance as a perpetual guru, and also as a management guru, is elaborated with essential brevity.

Finer aspects of management, practised by Lord Krishna are detailed in Parva VII. Energy as a management tool, principle of causality, power of absolute, creative destruction, approach to managing the boss, and more significantly, the **unified concept of management performance** are discussed therein.

Parva VIII presents the **distilled wisdom** of Lord Krishna's management approach and practices. His divine skills of madhura, doctrines of karma and dharma, sanctity of objectives, among others, are discussed here as the **omnipotent technology of management.**

Parva IX entitled as **nectar of management wisdom** covers the essentials of Lord Krishna's management skills, practices, percepts and preaching.

Besides, the book contains a detailed introduction by the author in the form of preface, attachments, references and index.

The work is topical in view of the fast changing business scenario across the world. It is relevant to deal with frequently encountered modern day management requirements and challenges.

AUTHOR'S PROFILE

Dr. Udai Vir Singh is a management consultant, specialising in Productivity Improvement Acceleration (PIA) in corporate work environment. He holds a Ph.D. degree from IARI, New Delhi and a Post-doctorate from CNRA, Versailles, France.

Early in work life, he entered corporate work environment, passing through the varied fields of research and development, product development, marketing, market development, project planning, production, technology upgradation, technology transfer, business diversification and productivity acceleration, earning an intense and varied work experience for over 40 years. In latter part of his career, he concentrated on management training and consultancy work, aimed at collective work output acceleration, for a number of corporates.

He developed and productively employed several of his work and working related thought formulations during his intense and challenging work assignments.

Dr. Singh has travelled widely in India and abroad.

ACKNOWLEDGEMENTS

I express sincere thanks to Pankaj Saran Srivastava, Bhawna Sharma, Qamar Raza and Bhavna Arora for making me computer literate, without which this work would not have seen the light of the day. Further, the multilateral assistance extended by Ainual Abedin, Habitat Library Resource Centre, is most sincerely acknowledged. Special thanks are also due to M/s L.S. Davar & Co., New Delhi for extending their cooperation in getting the copyright registered.

My daughter Udita Singh and daughter-in-law Gayatri Shiveshwarkar Singh, the two wise young ladies, deserve my appreciation and thanks for constantly motivating me to complete this work without any long break. I am also thankful to my wife Jyotsna Singh for her huge collection of books on religion and culture, which helped me, in my initial orientation, to take up this work.

New Delhi
October, 2007

Udai Vir Singh

AUTHOR'S NOTE ON THE BOOK

I am not a devotee of Krishna: in fact, not a devotee of any God or Goddess. Also, I bear no active or passive hostility towards any religion, God, *devas* or deity. I see merit in all religions as circumstances of their origin and propagation were so very different. Yet, the *Concept of Krishna*, being massive, varied and over-powering, has been difficult to ignore. For reasons of one's background or religion, one may not love Krishna; one may even be critical of what He said and did but to ignore him is just not possible. A look at various aspects/stages of Krishna's life and works, some of which are briefly stated below, further magnifies his irresistible personality.

- Krishna as a child, a playful divine, his pranks and mischief.
- as a cowherd, a divine lover of animals and nature.
- as a lover, a darling of gopicas, and almost the whole female world.
- as a dancer, the Natwara of divine excellence.
- as a destroyer of evil Kalia, Kamsa and numerous others.
- as a protector of righteous and virtuous.
- as a musician, a flute player of mesmeric influence.
- as an originator of fashion and festivities.
- as a warrior, matchless and divine.
- as a strategist of incomparable genius.
- as a ruler without direct responsibilities.
- as a pundit of all scriptures and Vedic knowledge.
- as a guru of all gurus.
- as a sage of all sages.
- as a teacher of all teachers.
- as an advisor for invincible situations.
- as a master of all charms and communications.
- as a manager of all forces of creation and destruction.
- as a keeper of commitments.
- as a charioteer of celestial warrior Arjuna.
- as a motivator with non-material technology.
- as a builder of empires.
- as an architect, an employer of Vishvakarma.
- as a wisdom concentrate of unfathomable depths.
- as a liberator of all beings through the Doctrine of Karma and Dharma.
- as an incarnate of mission objectivity.

Lord Krishna has always enjoyed a universal reach. There is hardly any one in India who could escape influence of Krishna, in one or the other form—irrespective of religion or caste that one happens to belong. On the international scale too, Lord Krishna's reach was very wide, even before International Society for Krishna Consciousness (ISKCON) emerged to perform an excellent job of spreading his message of universal love and liberation. His doctrine of Karma and Dharma has universal appeal, validity and following. Innumerable western thinkers, writers and scientists—ancient, medieval and modern, who had direct or indirect exposure to Indian culture or scriptures, could not escape the epidemic influence of Krishna. For those who had direct exposure to Mahabharata and or the Bhagavad Gita, it was an influence for the life time. Several nuclear physicists spotted elements of nuclear science in the renowned Bhagavad Gita, which has been widely translated and reproduced in almost all the major languages of the world. For instance, Dr. J. Robert Oppenheimer, the father of nuclear bomb, was a keen student of Krishna's distilled wisdom contained in the Bhagavad Gita. While witnessing the nuclear explosion in July 1943, He recollected what Krishna had said and could not help himself from exclaiming, "I am become the Death, the Destroyer."

Currently, professors of management education at Harvard, Kellogg, Wharton and other leading centers of management excellence, and also senior executives of large multinationals, are at loss as how to mitigate the adverse impact of growing globalization on performance of the western economies. Their long held concepts and methodologies of manpower motivation and output augmentation have failed them progressively. From Taylor's time and motion to behaviouralists' mind and commotion, from Maslow's hierarchy of needs to the prosperous hierarchy of wants, quest is now moving from matter and ideas to spirit, employing *spirit to enrich ideas and matter*. Executives of large US corporations are learning to put *purpose before self* with the divine help from Bhagavad Gita, Ved Vyasa's immortal gift to mankind. They are discovering that the divine principle of Karma possess some unique powers for perpetual performance. The benefits of selfless action are becoming mysteriously attractive to them.

In fact, I am surprised that they have taken so long to understand and appreciate the divine management utility of the renowned work of the great sage Vyasa; the Bhagavad Gita, a record of a divine dialogue between God and man, in an environ of extreme hostilities on the cruel killing-fields of Kurukshetra, is simultaneously a unique ladder of spiritual enrichment and a practical guide to righteous life. It specifies how effectively integrating body, mind, intellect and the soul, one could make the latter as his or her partner for greater material and non-material performance, and that too without any stress and confusion. The divine vehicle of wisdom, as enshrined in this greatest foundation stone of Indian Philosophy, has the potential to become the ultimate fountain-head of practical management wisdom. We have to wait and see how the future generations of managers benefit from this divine source of light. The present work, being different than the mass of management literature, will strives to

- extract the management wisdom of Lord Krishna lying buried in Mahabharata and Bhagavad Gita, the two great ancient Indian works that record Lord Krishna's life and works, and
- integrate the same with modern management practices, and examine how the same could benefit the modern management fraternity.

Through readings of Bhagavad Gita and the epic of Mahabharata, I could locate answers to the numerous gaps that currently afflict the modern management, greatly limiting efficacy of its practice all over the corporate world. Lord Krishna's divine understanding of the human factor, its key role in management of collective human interactions, commercial or otherwise through collective application of (a) alignment of body-mind-intellect and soul (the Atman), (b) the non-failing doctrine of Karma and Dharma, and (c) his technology of non-material motivation, along with his various principles, practices and tools of management, seem fully capable of filling all the gaps, currently apparent or invisible, in this vital field of human activity.

With hindsight, I see it as a matter of great failure on my part--for not having gone through Lord Krishna's wisdom concentrates much earlier in my life. I am sure I could have avoided a number of deficiencies of omissions and commissions, in long years of my corporate life, if I had timely exposed myself to the management wisdom contained in the ancient Indian treatises related to the divine life and works of Lord Krishna. Corporate life, I am sure, would have been much more smooth and rewarding.

However, one is never too late to attempt actions in support of righteousness and efficiency. Hence, this book is primarily addressed to those who are either attempting to enter the world of professional management or are already in it. Employing some of Lord Krishna's divine management technology, they can more effectively and smoothly deal with the challenges encountered in the day to day operations in this field of active human interaction.

Gaps in Modern Management

I have been through the practice of modern management for almost forty years, in a variety of corporate work environments. Further, I did not refrain from relevant readings on the subject, including works of management gurus; namely

Peter Drucker, Tom Peters, Michael Porter and several others. Nevertheless, I felt deficient in my understanding of the human element, which decidedly seems to be the key to all management concepts, approaches, practices and operations. Various limitations of modern management remaining partly or fully unexplained for a long time, continue to bother a multitude of thinking minds. Some of these limitations include the following.

- Often, the modern management is not modern enough and the same old human weaknesses and limitations continue to mar its practice and performance.
- There is a lot of gap between preaching and practice.
- Often bottlenecks and deficiencies occur at the top.
- Management decisions, in most corporate work environments, are rarely taken on basis of sound principles.
- Personal considerations and other elements of narrowness, rather than consensus, are often the basis for decision making.
- It is not participative in true sense of the word.
- Internal politics and personal agenda often play an important role in corporate governance.
- Human *Prakriti and Gunas* are not adequately employed in understanding and motivating people.
- Negative elements such as greed, anger, intolerance, nepotism, selfishness, and unrighteousness continue to plague the practice of management.
- Interest of the society at large is often ignored.
- Merit, virtue and righteousness are not often treated in a fair manner.
- Good work alone is not enough for fair reward and assignments.
- Credit apportioning often is not fair and impartial.
- Avoidable criticism, rather than cooperation, is more of a rule than exception.
- Being in the right camp, rather than rightly doing one's duty, continues to be the necessity for nearness to boss or the power center.
- Boss, with limited exceptions, continues to be a dreadful animal.
- Insecurity rules the boss, almost at all levels.
- Most bosses respond to unconfirmed rumours rather than factual feedbacks.
- Honesty, often, is not the best policy for trouble free and efficient corporate dealings.
- Merit and skills of a junior are often perceived as threat.
- Righteousness and ethics often go missing in corporate operations.
- Seniority is no security for manifestation of righteousness or efficiency.

- Rules are often bent or interpreted to suit vested interests.
- Experience often tends to teach caution and avoidance instead of correctness and initiative.
- Truth is often unpleasant when told to boss or seniors in an unfiltered manner.
- Requisite communication skills are not often employed, with right objectivity or in right orientation.
- What is taught in management schools and institutes is found of little practicality in actual work environments.
- Black hole of negative and unproductive thought manifestations continue to plague the corporate performance.
- Significance of one's karma or duty is not understood or adhered to, in the right sense.
- Empowerment is more visible in theory than practice.
- Delegation, in practice, often pertains to shifting of what is difficult and inconvenient.
- Employee turnover or job-hopping is becoming an increasingly troublesome phenomenon.
- Work related stress and the ills associated with it, are assuming multilateral dimensions.

The listing of what ails the modern management, or what it has not achieved or is not capable of achieving, can be almost endless. And there are numerous other questions, similar to those presented below, which remain unanswered—and by implication, continue to agitate thinking minds, on one hand and limit the productivity of management operations, on the other:

- Why workers behave the way they do?
- Why professionals do not often behave professionally?
- Why often initiative and cooperation is not actively forthcoming?
- Why do people need supervision while engaged in their simple day to day duties?
- Why does job security breed inefficiency and indiscipline?
- Why people hesitate to own up their mistakes and then improve upon the same?
- Why do many people tend to criticize new ideas and projects even when the same merits support and implementation?
- Why conflict in work environment cannot be fully eliminated?
- Why non-material motivation is not being attempted?

Extending the enumeration of questions left unanswered by the modern management or those generated by its inherent inadequacies, does not seem to serve any divine purpose. Hence, I felt a need to attempt and look elsewhere for answers or explanations. Can science be of any help in understanding or decoding the puzzles and limitations of the modern management? Keeping this in view, Fredrick Taylor's theory of *Scientific Management* [1] which states that management could be practiced scientifically, was examined; it did not turn out to be of much assistance in practical work environments, corporate or otherwise.

Western concepts, thoughts and theories, on which the basic foundations of the modern management were laid, looked grossly inadequate in their abilities, active and/or potential, to throw up solutions or at least explanations, for the various deficiencies and limitations of this vital and expanding field of human endeavour. Thus arose the need to look deep into ancient human history, including Indian mythology, and see if answers to some of these perplexing questions could emerge with some acceptable satisfaction.

Much before the 20th Century, which witnessed the growth and flowering of the modern management, several ancient civilizations [2] had mastered the art of collective and organized works at massive scales. Egyptians (Murlidharan, 2006) constructed the pyramids using management practices of planning, organizing, leading and control of activities associated with the same. Egyptian management practices continued up to 1000 BC, and the Babylonians at that time employed extensive set of laws and policies designed for efficient governance. For managing their well designed cities, Greeks had developed efficient systems 750 BC to 100 BC. Romans were equally developed with their organization and management systems, and communication technologies, for managing spreads of vast empire between 750 BC and 400 BC. During the 1500 BC and 1200 AD, the Chinese were well versed in the art of organizational management involved in the affairs of the state, commerce and arts. Sumerians had well written and documented rules and regulations for governance of their society 3000 BC to 2500 BC. Despite the limitations of the times during which these civilizations developed and prospered, some of these systems of management and governance did marvelously well, probably with less of frustrations, stress, chaos and terror that the mankind faces today, even after having all the benefits of science and technology, on one hand and the modern management, on the other.

In the corresponding period, during the times of Mahabharata [3], India, then known as Bharata, had well developed and prosperous kingdoms of Hastinapura, Kashi, Mathura, Magadha, Indraparastha, Dwaraka and many others, which surely had not developed without the use of some sound management and governance technologies. In the great epic, the Mahabharata, various management principles and practices, such as strategic decision making, conflict management, negotiations and diplomacy, alliances and mergers, federal structure of governance, righteousness in governance, failure management, competition analysis, information collection and analysis, war planning and management, movement of men and materials (logistics), motivational technologies, observance of ethics during war and peace, commitment adherence, and many more, have been detailed with matchless lucidity.

Mahabharata is a great work, in all senses of the term. Its original composition in the Sanskrit language is spread over one hundred thousand stanzas in verse, thus qualifying it to be called as the longest composition in the world: in sheer quantitative terms, eight times longer than *The Iliad* and *The Odyssey* put together. Its thoroughness and coverage of human activities, both of war and peace, is of such magnitude that several commentators of repute have observed that if something is not there in the Mahabharata, then it is not any where in the world. A careful examination of this great epic, especially the Bhagavad Gita, the celestial Song of Wisdom delivered by Lord Krishna to the Pandava warrior Arjuna, who exhibited great reluctance to fight, prior to commencement of the battle of Kurukshetra, confirms with a great degree of certainty that it is capable of explaining most of the unanswered aspects, puzzles, contradictions and deficiencies of the modern management. Answers to the various problems created by men, through deficiencies and inefficiencies of their thoughts and actions, when engaged in activities of business and governance, are to be found therein.

Lord Krishna was the guiding and controlling spirit of Mahabharatha. He was a *Mission Incarnate* [4], the 8th incarnation of Lord Vishnu, who had assumed human body with the specific purpose of getting rid of pernicious ills and evils, which had accumulated in the then systems of governance and management, on account of the unscrupulous and unrighteous operations of the ruling classes, the kings and princes of that time. During his long and eventful life, Lord Krishna secured the total dominance of the cultural, economic, political and diplomatic scene of the landmass of the Bharata, his fame and influence traveled well beyond the barriers of lands and seas. He fought numerous battle, almost one every week during his youth and middle age, in pursuit of his incarnate objectivity of riding the earth free of evil and wickedness. In addition to being a matchless warrior, destroyer of evil and wicked, and protector of the good and virtuous, He was the greatest strategist, diplomat, builder, negotiator and the *Wisdom Concentrate* ever known to the mankind. He planned for and destroyed all the evil and wicked forces which had assembled under the unrighteous yet impressive banner of Duryodhana, on the battle-fields of Kurukshetra, where He participated only as an unarmed charioteer of Arjuna, the celestial Pandava warrior. His massive discourse delivered on the eve of the battle, to secure *non-material motivation* [5] of Arjuna, who was upset on the prospects of having to kill his elders, gurus and relations present, as per force of circumstances, in the opposing side of Kauravas formations. He was refusing to fight and was considerably argumentative and logical against such large-scale bloodshed. It was a long and arduous dialogue covering all vital aspects of (a) life, death and afterlife; (b) body, mind and Atman; (c) killing and being killed; (d) creator, creations and destruction; (e) asuras, devas and God; (f) evil, good and righteous; (g) karma, dharma and jnana yoga; (h) right to fruits and rewards of actions; (i) routes of liberation from the cycle of birth and death; (j) renouncement and renunciation; (k) human prakriti and its impact on human traits and behavior; (l) ethics of war and peace; (m) unity of all beings and things at the micro level; and (n) all that concerns human life and all other beings on this earth and beyond. This concentrate of wisdom delivered by the wise Lord for the benefit of his favored disciple in particular, and the mankind in general, came to be known as the renowned Bhagavad Gita or the Song of Wisdom. When interpreted and applied correctly, it seems capable of solving and clarifying all the riddles and puzzles, and deficiencies and confusions of the modern management, in a concise and convincing manner.

Lord Krishna was the leader of the leaders, manager of the managers, teacher of the wise and learned, and guru of gurus, hence this work attempts a brief interpretation of his celestial concepts and practices of management, and see whether the same could be of help to the modern community of management professionals in better understanding of human nature and behaviour in collective work environments.

Krishna and His Times

Parshurama, Rama and Krishna are the outstanding examples of greatest History Makers, in the ancient Indian history. [6] Of these, the first to arrive on the ancient Indian scene was Parshurama, the great non-kshatriya warrior who is said to have destroyed the unrighteous and arrogant kshatriyas, several times again and again. On arrival of Rama, the great old warrior handed over the job to him. Krishna was the last of the three greats who emerged as the 8th incarnation of Lord Vishnu. All the three of them were Mission Incarnates, i.e. they came to this earth with clear cut objectives.

Parshurama was a great man of action, the destroyer of evil and arrogant and, as such, made a lot of history. But, he neither built an empire nor was a teacher or devotion inspirer. On the other hand, Rama excelled on two counts: firstly, as maker of history through destruction of evils of that time and secondly, as devotion inspirer on account of being most perfect in duty. He was a Purshottama but not a man of action. Krishna is an all sided great, a *purna-avatara* who excelled in all the three directions.

- A destroyer of evil and the wicked which was the main manifesto of his incarnation. He was protector of the righteous and good.
- A builder of great empires, first that of the Yadavas at Dwaraka, and then the Pandavas at Indraparastha too was built only due to his skills and divine strategies.
- A great teacher and devotion inspirer, in fact, the greatest complete teacher that mankind has known and experienced. His Song of Wisdom or the Bhagavad Gita is the most accomplished perpetual teacher of non-aging relevance. The expanse and multitude of his followers is almost endless.

Krishna was indeed the perfect practitioner of multi-tasking. And He commenced his work early as a child, destroying evil which came in varied forms and disguises. Even on the scale of devotion inspiration, Krishna is different. The devotion inspired by Rama is noble, pure, spiritual, straight forward, homely and artless; strong by nature for his love to his parents, family and also the public. The devotion generated by Krishna is much more intense, physical as well super-physical and spiritual, complex and many sided, maddening and transporting, alternating with joy and sorrow, shaking the whole soul to pieces yet always joining the same at end with Love and Life and Light Eternal, like his own life, his loves, his age and his surroundings. He attracts youth--and appeals to it more than any one else, God or non-God.

Towards the end of the Dvapara Yuga and the dawn of the Kali Yuga, Krishna emerged in the cowherd environment of Gokula [7], as the 8th incarnation of Vishnu, on express request of the mother earth who felt tormented by the great accumulation of evil and wicked where the very existence and survival of good and righteous had become almost impossible. At that time, the great nation of Bharata was divided into numerous, small and large, ruling entities, mostly ruthlessly exploiting the masses. Evil and wicked roamed unhindered while the good and virtuous were fast disappearing.

In these times, Bharata was a green and fertile landmass of beautiful woodlands, interspersed with need based clearings for cultivation. Transportation mainly depended upon bullocks and horses. There was no dearth of elephants for work as well as for battles. Weapons of battle mainly consisted of swords, maces, and bows and arrows while some select warriors were in possession of superior astras and sustras. Copper and its alloys were in use while the discovery of iron and its usage in weaponry, by some authorities, has been credited to Krishna and his associates [8].

Whether the man makes the time or the time makes the man has always been a matter of conflicting opinion, among the wise and learned. But in case of Krishna, there exists no such conflict of opinion. He made the time, his own as well a lot more after He retreated to his celestial abode. He continues to guide, motivate and inspire a vast multitude of men and women, young and old, all over India and in many other parts of the world. In the fields of visual as well as performing arts, i.e. painting, music, dance and drama, He indeed is the stream of perpetual inspiration. Without him, beauty and fashion, in the Indian context, had no chance of growth to the present heights. *His divine life and works stress the deciding relevance of man when there is a man of virtue and righteousness!* In management, man is the key or more precisely, quality of human element is of crucial significance as all inputs or factors of production or value addition, are manipulated and catalysed by human element only.

For practitioners of management; in fact, for everyone with a degree of intellect, study of Krishna is important as it transcends one to the realm of karma, dharma, righteousness, Janana, detachment, renouncement, renunciation, oneness of body-mind and atman, life, death and beyond--and all that concerns man and all other living beings. It exposes one to human prakriti and gunas and how to make the most appropriate employment of the human element, blue collar or otherwise.

The *Braham-astra* of management or the *non-material motivation* lies buried deep in works and teachings of the great guru. It needs to be understood and applied in the present context. *Managing the Invincible* [9], only with the weapon of thought and mind [10], lies imbedded in the divine management technology of the supreme motivator and coordinator. The divine *Art of Scaling Up* from cowherd to king, Dwarakadhesh to be precise and finally as the superb manager of Mahabharata, offers a lot to learn from the multifaceted personality of Krishna, especially management of difficult people or situations.

The multilateral superiority of Krishna's personality comes out vividly in the main body of this work, where principle features of his concepts and practices of management are discussed in requisite details. Here, it should suffice to add that among others, Krishna was

- Invincible strategist, both in war and peace.
- Great appreciator of reality.
- Keeper of centrality of objectivity.
- Team builder of total excellence.
- Greatest motivator of mankind.

- Artist of supreme order.
- Musician of divine proportions.
- Greatest among lovers of all times.
- Ruthless destroyer of evil and the wicked.
- Mightiest amongst warriors.
- Pundit of pundits.
- Diplomat for difficult situations.
- Greatest motivator of all times.
- Advisor of celestial proportions.
- A charmer par excellence.
- A reformer of distinction.
- Protector of virtuous and devotees.
- Great commitment respecter.
- Supremely rich with emotions.
- Karama-yogi of highest order.
- Greatest protector and promoter of dharma.
- Greatest dancer of all times.
- Guru of all gurus.
- Greatest teacher known to mankind.
- Manager of difficult situations.
- Practitioner of madhura communication (10)
- Builder of great empires.
- A great reformer.
- A great celebrator of life.
- Maker of time and history.
- A naturalist of highest order.

Like many other men of action, Krishna inspired violent likes and dislikes. There was no dearth of enemies of Krishna, the foremost being Kamsa of Mathura, Jarasandha of Magadha, Shishupala of Chedi, Rukmi of Vidharba, Salva, Dantavaktra etc. The Pandavas were his greatest allies and the greatest accumulation of evil and the wicked under the leadership of Duryodhana, was destroyed with their help. They were the greatest contributors towards fulfillment of his divine Mission Incarnate objectivity.

Bhagavan Das (1990) in his work on Krishna, *A Study in the Theory of Avataras* describes Krishna's greatest contribution as a man of thought, as under; "Beyond and above all Krishna's other great works, stands his work as the teacher of the Gita, wherein he concentrated with the electrical focussing of war conditions, the quintessence of the deepest, the most ancient, and the most practical and real ethics and philosophy, into a few hundred verses, for the enlightenment of the sorely perplexed understanding of Arjuna, and of hundreds of subsequent generations."

For a common man, it is truly difficult to decide whether Krishna's greatest strength is as a man of action or as a man of thought. But when we examine the utility of Krishna's thoughts from the angle of management, the supremacy of thought emerges as a clear winner. This is where a study of life and works of Lord Krishna, offers a true minefield of ideas to the students and practitioners of modern management. The present work, in view of the author, represents only a tiny initiative in this direction.

Lord Krishna: An Appreciation Imbalance

Lord Krishna, his teachings and wisdom, always occupied a central place in the Indian culture, in general and Hinduism, in particular. He was a man of action, creator of empires, destroyer of evil and evoked intense devotion from the multitude of his followers and devotees. He was creator of happiness and well-being through protection and promotion of virtue and righteousness. His divine gift to mankind, in form of the renowned Bhagavad Gita or the Song of Wisdom, continues to render invaluable service to a huge section of humanity, even after passage of five millennia since this great master's presence on face of the earth. He excelled in whatsoever He touched or attempted. Action and initiative was inherent to the personality of Krishna. His ways of governance and development smelt of sophisticated management technologies.

With the passage of over fifty centuries, appreciation and perception of Krishna seems to have suffered certain emphasis deviations, under internal and external stresses that operated in varying severities on the inhabitants of Bharata. The concept of Krishna and his multiple images as butter thief, tormentor of gopicas, friend of gopas, subduer of Kalia, protector of cows, flute player and musician, destroyer of evil, wrestler of repute, initiator of fashion, organizer of dance circles, divine student of scriptures, store-house of knowledge, keeper of friendship, protector of virtue and merit, matchless warrior, strategist of repute, leader of leaders, diplomat par excellence, keeper of commitment, divine architect, lover of beauty, master of alliances, maker of kings, and various others, as an avatara or incarnate had to be, have remained largely intact, with tolerable fluctuations.

However, the concept of Krishna, in relation to science, technology, management and governance got substantially neglected during the medieval period--as there were no large local ruling establishments, which could withstand pressures of repetitive invasions of Islamic forces and also simultaneously promote the techno-economic aspects of Krishna. Consequently, a type of emphasis deviation occurred in relation to Krishna's relevance, denying it an opportunity for future development and manifestation of its management potential, in service of the society.

In modern times, for the purpose of convenience, study of Hinduism is often divided into the following four periods (Arvind Sharma, 2005):

1. Pre-Vedic and Vedic period.
2. Classical period.
3. Medieval period.
4. Modern period.

The first period that had predominance of Vedic values and practices, represented true Hinduism when it had just adequate interactions from the outside world, during which it not only escaped major modifying influence of the outside forces, but it ended up expending its influence outwards. In the neighborhood of Asia and Africa, there were no regimes with matching capabilities and those who came in its contact stood to benefit from it in a peaceful manner.

In the classical period, Buddhism and Jainism germinated in India, out of Hinduism's own deviations. They were results of an internal churning of thoughts and practices prevalent at that time. During this period, concept of Krishna, especially its spiritual and religious components and practices came under some stress as the divergent thoughts were peacefully accommodated. The management, governance, scientific and intellectual components of Krishna's concepts, as evident through Arthashastra of Kautilya, and other political and non-political formations of that period, remained intact and substantially in practice. Major practices and preaching of Krishna continued to enjoy a position of dominance, despite the diversionary pressures created by .the two new concepts of religion and spirituality

In the medieval period, Islam was the major outside interaction with Hinduism and it left substantial influence on the Indian society, on its culture, polity and religion. Highly conflicting and aggressive approach of persistent Islamic invasions, incursions and inflows, pushed the active components of Hinduism into protective inversions, as attempts towards self-preservation. The local governing establishments got weakened and scattered. Their response to the invading forces, physical, political, economic and religious, was largely reactive in nature. They could not anticipate, foresee and plan with any significant efficacy. It was against the concept and practice of Krishna who was never reactive but planned and took timely action. He was pro-active and loved action in support of what was right and virtuous. It partly distorted the image of Krishna; emphasis shifted to cow protection, spirituality and ritualism. Political fragmentation India or Bharata, during this period, did not allow growth or active continuation of managerial, administrative and scientific wisdom of Krishna. Slowly, the technological and economic prowess of India deteriorated.

This imbalance in appreciation of Krishna got further strengthened in a substantial manner, during the next phase of Hinduism when it had to endure active interactions with Christianity, and also had to continue to struggle against the oppressive pressures of declining ruling formations of Islam. In fact, interaction of western forces with India and Hinduism had commenced long before end of the medieval period. Incursions of western forces of commerce and religion started spreading their wings when Islamic ruling establishments commenced experiencing progressive deteriorations. It gave western scholars ample time and exposure to study Hindu scriptures in substantial depth, and copy and translate the same. They appropriated several of the scientific, technical and management ideas and technologies contained therein.

Christian missionary forces had become aware that strengths of Hinduism were enshrined in the wisdom of Krishna, so beautifully encapsulated in the renowned Bhagavad Gita. It was almost impossible to challenge the same. Hence, they concentrated their attacks on Hinduism's avoidable ills of caste discrimination and superstition. They strived to avoid confrontation with the righteous core of Hinduism, the logical and scientific concept of Krishna. His doctrines of Karma and Dharma looked immune to criticism and degradation of any type. Their discrimination against Hinduism and reluctance to confront its core of intellect was reflected in their failure to invite any learned person of Hinduism to participate in the Parliament of Religions held at Chicago in September 1893. The purpose of organizing this parliament was to prove the superiority of Christian religion. Swami Vivekananda, the chief disciple of Shri Ramakrishna, on initiative and persuasion of his friends and colleagues, participated in this international gathering of religious luminaries, on behalf of Hinduism. On afternoon of 11th September, He made a speech to the distinguished gathering expounding the virtue and merits of the Indian culture, especially its Vedantic content. A wave of enthusiasm went through the distinguished gathering and the young Swami received an unprecedented standing ovation. He blunted a lot of unhealthy criticism of Hinduism, which the majority of Christian missionaries often resorted to.

With the advent of industrial revolution in the west coupled with the demands that the First World War, in early 20th century, put on management of factors of production and conflict, several of the insights gained from Hindu scriptures were put to practice.

They were claimed as originated from the west itself. The concept of management further developed more aggressively with the advent of the 2nd World War and its inherent requirements. When J. Robert Oppenheimer, the father of atomic bomb witnessed its test on July 14, 1943 in the desert of Los Alamos, New Mexico, he recollected his study of Bhagavad Gita, and what Krishna said therein. The great scientist exclaimed, "I am become Death, the Destroyer." Not surprisingly, the great scientist did that in Sanskrit or the Devabhasha (the language of celestial beings). It goes to stress how some valuable concepts of Krishna which were got neglected or ignored in India, were eagerly employed and appropriated by the west.

During the two centuries of British occupation, which correspond to the period of modern Hinduism, the latter remained under active pressures from Christianity, on one hand and oppressive elements of governance, on the other. Several of indigenous technologies were ruined, exploited and overwhelmed during this period of imperialistic subjugation. The Hinduism and the versatility of Krishna's vital concepts and their successful survival, despite long and intense incursions of Islam in the past, was a challenge to the aggressive elements of Christianity which were actively supported by the apparatus of governance. Hence, at hands of foreign missionaries as well as certain local elements trained into their thoughts and practices, Krishna rather had a substantially bad press, especially in the 19th century. Raja Ram Mohan Roy actively attacked the concept of Krishna for its licentiousness. They even tried to rubbish his unique "Concept of Karma" by unsuccessfully associating it to defeatism.

It was to the credit of Bankim Chandra Chatterjee (1838-94) that Krishna, in modern Hinduism, possesses a balanced and robust profile. In his Krishnacarita, (Eric J. Sharpe, 1985) this Indian nationalist presented Krishna as the ideal man. Several other subsequent Bengali writers presented Krishna as a hero, a philosopher-statesman, an example for emulation, and above all as a spiritual champion of the people of India, in her times of test and trial. As a consequence of these efforts, in the modern mind, the concept of Krishna is a balanced one along with a romantic association with Radha and gopicas, He is presented as the great manager of Mahabharata, the stirring call of action that He delivers to a despondent Arjuna on the battlefield of Kurukshetra. He is viewed as the fountainhead of wisdom who gifted to mankind the Song of Wisdom or the immortal Bhagavad Gita, to guide all progenies of humanity.

It is truly a matter of great triumph for the concept of Krishna that it survived such strong and diverse opposing forces for such a long time. There must be genuinely divine strengths and merit in what Krishna practiced and preached. It merits substantial celebrations in honour of the divine Wisdom Concentrate, who was leader of leaders and manager of managers, in true sense of the phrase.

Lord Krishna: A Mission Incarnate

Lord Krishna came to the earth with a purpose (11), a *Specific Mission*. Prithvi, the Mother Earth, was suffering for long from depredations of *evil*, in the form of wicked men and women who had forgotten *dharma,* the law of righteousness. Justice and religion were disappearing under the evil forces of persecution and crime. Demon king Kamsa of Mathura was the most dreadful of the evils of that time. He had usurped the throne of Mathura from his father Ugrasena, a righteous ruler. His cruelty had no limits and arrogance no parallel.

Unable to tolerate the evil burden of Kamsa and his likes, Prithvi assumed form of a cow and went to Mount Meru, where all the three most powerful Gods: Indra, Shiva and Brahma had assembled to take stock of the situation on earth, a part of their universe.

Brahma, hearing the tales of woes from Prithvi, approached Lord Vishnu, as he was resting on serpent couch, and begged the benevolent Lord to help Prithvi out of her delicate situation of great sufferings. Ever compassionate, and possibly in good mood, Lord Vishnu plucked two of his hairs, one black and one white. Holding the two hairs He said, "This black hair shall be my incarnate in the eighth child of Devaki and Vasudeva, and shall kill Kamsa, the spring head of evil." And for the white hair, the Lord said, "This white hair shall be born as the seventh child to Devaki. Together, the two shall rid the earth of accumulated evil and wickedness" (Pawan Verma, 1995).

On the eve of marriage of his sister Devaki to Vasudeva, Kamsa became aware of events to come through a celestial voice that proclaimed, "This woman Devaki shall be the cause of your death--her eighth child, a son would kill you Kamsa"

In a flash of anger, Kamsa lifted his sword to kill Devaki but Vasudeva intervened with a plea to spare the life of his wife. He promised that he would hand over all his sons, one by one, as and when they are born. Kamsa relented on having a firm assurance and put both Devaki and Vasudeva in a prison under heavy guard. There Devaki, in time, gave birth to six sons, who were killed by Kamsa, one after the other.

Devaki's seventh child was declared as a miscarriage but in reality, the Lord Vishnu had commanded the goddess Yoganidra, the great illusionary energy of Vishnu himself, to transfer the embryo--formed of portion of Sheshha, the serpent, which was part of Vishnu, to the womb of Rohni, the first wife of Vasudeva, who lived in the nearby Gokula. This child was Balarama, also called Sankarsana, since he was extracted from womb of his mother.

As the eighth conception of Devaki, Lord Vishnu himself became incarnate. Yoganidra herself simultaneously entered the womb of Yashodha, the wife of Nanda, a gentle leader of cowherds in nearby Gokula. While Devaki gave birth to Krishna, Yashodha delivered a baby girl who was none other than the goddess Yoganidra. Vasudeva, as per celestial guidance, picked up the infant Krishna and carried him out of prison unnoticed by any guards who remained fast asleep under influence of Yoganidra. Though it was raining, Shesha, the multi-headed serpent, a part of Vishnu, protected the newly born child and also Vasudeva who carried the Lord unhindered and unnoticed. Yamuna, the great river, was pleased to give way to the Lord and Vasudeva. At Gokula, Vasudeva exchanged infant Krishna for the girl child that was just delivered by cowherd Nanda's wife who did not notice the great exchange, being under the influence of Yoganidra. On the other hand, Kamsa's guards too did know what had transpired in the night.

As soon as the news came of the eighth child born to Devaki, Kamsa came running to the prison and was surprised to find a girl instead of an expected boy. But he did not want to take any chance, and despite pleadings of Devaki, lifted the child and dashed it against a stone, feeling greatly relieved. No sooner the child hit the stone, a terrific sound came piercing the sky and announced, "Kamsa, there is no use of hitting me to the ground, the mighty one amongst the Gods, who was formerly thy destroyer, is born and shall kill you one day. Take care if you can."

Thus, the great Lord commenced his humble childhood in Gokula, among cows and cowherds. For a great mission to be fulfilled, it was indeed a humble beginning.

Divine Imperfect by Design

The most widely accepted concept of Lord Krishna, in the Indian mythology, is that of a Mission Incarnate. He is an idea of a maximally great being—capable of actions and achievements beyond concept and capabilities of mortal beings on this earth.

Lord Krishna, being maximally great, was endowed with multilateral capabilities, much beyond than being a great lover, a matchless dancer, a supreme warrior, a great diplomat, and, above all, a Wisdom Concentrate [12], the true store-house of wisdom and buddhi. Here the term "Wisdom Concentrate, has been employed to define the inexhaustible store of wisdom available on part of Krishna, the maximally great being.

From perspectives of rational theology, the concept of Krishna, always looked coherent and realistic. For over 5,000 years [13], since the largely accepted presence of Lord Krishna on this earth (Mathura, Dwaraka, Kurukshetra etc.) and his management of the epic conflict of Mahabharata, his divinely mesmerizing multilateral concept has densely grown all over India and spilled to several other countries in many parts of the world. He is worshiped, painted, sculptured, crafted, sung and played in countless forms. Some activities, assumed as initiated by him, and the divine event of his birth, have acquired the form of truly massive festivities and celebrations, giving birth to new fashions and businesses.

Lord Krishna, as a Wisdom Concentrate, while delivering this divine capsule of wisdom and advice to Arjuna, his argumentative disciple, was coerced to speak about and reveal his omnipotence, omnipresence, eternity and timelessness (birthless and deathless), as master of the universe. When his verbal arguments and explanations had no decisive impact on his inquisitive and adamant disciple, and when the Lord had no alternate to satisfy the persistent and penetrative argumentativeness of his devote disciple, He granted a brief vision of his cosmic greatness. It left Arjuna totally bewildered and with folded hands, he implored the Lord to assume his mortal human form.

Lord Krishna was a full incarnation, a complete human being, fully capable and equipped for all eventualities but for the purpose of tradition and ambiguity, most of the time (until and unless compelled for or absolutely necessary), He had to act and behave as a normal human-being, with minor deviations here and there. On this earth, irrespective of occurrence, no incarnation can afford to act and behave as God, on account of practical difficulties. Firstly, people will mob him; they would want him to do various crazy things and perform miracles to the extent that the normal balance of the society shall be disturbed. Total chaos and breakdown will occur and eventually, even the God may have to run away. Hence, a God incarnate in human form, for the reasons of practicality, has to remain under a mask or incognito, and essentially be and behave as Imperfect. He can not otherwise function, his action and behaviour cannot, and need not, be fully correct, morally or ethically, otherwise He will become uncommon amongst the commons which will be practically untenable. He has to be imperfect by design. Lord Krishna, hence, was Imperfect by Design. It was a well thought out celestial strategy to meet the mission incarnate responsibilities.

Some of the core attributes assignable to God, amongst others, are maximal goodness, justice and righteousness, and all other perfect virtues (omni-benevolence) as we attempt to understand the notion of divine moral perfection. For a God incarnate, it is not often feasible to uphold the notion of divine moral perfection because he has to act as per prevalent circumstances, norms and practices acceptable at that time, otherwise his divinity runs a terrible risk of uncomfortable exposure. Keeping this in view, Lord Krishna practiced Deliberate Divine Imperfection.

Lord Krishna, at almost all stages of his incarnate life, practiced righteousness, upheld virtue and goodness but He avoided perfection in moral as well functional form. As a child, He did not hesitate to steal curd or butter and often pretended that He did not because, as a child, such activities were normal, except that they left a few eyebrows overstretched. Stealing cloths of girls taking bath and enacting love games with Radha and other girls of the cowherd community, were his other often cited early youth escapades.

Even when He matured into a perfect warrior and diplomat, the manner in which He disposed off Jarasandha, the mighty demonic ruler of Magadha and his along time adversary, with the help of Bhimma, did not meet requirements of moral perfection. Further, when Arjuna refused to fight at Kurukshetra and was almost ready to desert the battlefield, Krishna told him that killing of friends and relatives and all those who were in the opposite line was not wrong for a warrior. He went further to state that all those warriors standing in the field were already dead, they were already killed by him –and that Arjuna would not incur any sin by physically eliminating them.

Besides, during the great battle of Kurukshetra, several invincible warriors in the massive Kaurava line-up, were eliminated only through timely advice and instigation of Lord Krishna, which in assessment of many did not meet the ethics and moral standards of that time. In fact, when a mortally injured Duryodhana attempted to charge Krishna with the morally unsustainable means employed by the Pandavas (under his active guidance) to eliminate, amongst others, Bhishma, Karna, Drona and Jaidharatha, the Lord incarnate responded with the retort that such means were necessary for getting rid of these warriors and that in war, especially when evil is confronted, usage of such means was acceptable.

A few days later, when in company of Pandavas, Krishna visited the humbled Kaurava patriarch Dhritarashtra, Gandhari was very vocal in blaming Krishna for the loss of her numerous sons and the whole Kaurava clan. She said that being omnipotent, Krishna was capable of avoiding this killing of numerous warriors and the consequent mass widowing of women and, out of shear anger, she cursed Krishna that one day his own kinsmen would be destroyed in the same manner. Here again, without any protest, anger or explanation, Lord Krishna accepted the merit of her anger. Vidura, the wise old minister, always accepted and appreciated what the Lord attempted or advised, as he probably understood the reality of the Lord incarnate. Bhishma, the grand warrior of the Kuru dynasty, recognized the divinity of Krishna and, in fact, had become a great devotee of the great Lord.

The concept of Divine Imperfect or moral imperfect seems to have substantial applicability in the present day business management and governance. With the best of intentions, it may not be feasible or easy to be always fully correct or righteous, while taking or implementing corporate decisions. However, attempts should always be made to adhere to or even improve upon the accepted standards of ethics and morality in which-ever field one is operative. Such attempts should not, however, become an end in themselves as the main objectives of operations, business or governance, should not be lost in the process. Perfection need not be the objective at the cost of efficiency and output, near perfection is good enough. Absolute morality or absolute ethics may not always be feasible in the corporate world. Good corporate decisions should meet demands of the situation and should be directed for greater good of the community at large. This, in brief, is the essential core of Lord Krishna's attempts at practicing the approach of Divine Imperfect, and its practice in today's environment may save for a number of professionals loss of speed in decision making and any feeling of deficiency, moral or otherwise, that may be associated with it.

Mahabharatha: A Massive Management Exercise

Ramayana and Mahabharata are the two great epics of ancient India. They offer solid spiritual and religious support to the Indian masses, in a perpetually significant manner. General students of these epics normally do not deviate from the objectivity of religious and spiritual comfort. For students of management, out of the two great epics, the Mahabharata forms a very interesting choice for in-depth study and analysis, to see how, over five millennia ago, a massive exercise in management was undertaken with such precision and efficiency. Its objective of upholding the principle of righteousness against almost invincible forces of evil and wickedness, was immensely bright and impressive, and very few, if ever, would attempt to disagree with justification of the great ancient exercise. The expanse of the conflict, in no manner less than a World War, was so widespread that no kingdom of India, then known as Bharata, and its neighborhood, was left uninvolved. It was a unique battle, designed for protection of virtues of justice and righteousness.

It was a massive gathering of fighting forces, adding up to 18 akshaunis [14] of troops; 11 on the side of evil and the wicked, and 7 with the supporters of good and the righteous, a total of 4-5 million men of arms. The gathering consisted of over 4 lakh chariots, a similar number of elephants, over 13 lakh horsemen, and approximately double of this number as foot-soldiers. Combined with support and supply manpower, the gathering indeed looked massive and menacing. In terms of consequences too, it decidedly exceeded the great wars of the past centaury because (a) the destruction of men and materials was proportionately much greater and (b) the post conflict preservation of peace and righteousness turned out as relatively more durable and long-term.

Planning for this epic conflict must have been, indeed, long-term and systematic. On deeper thought application, it seems to have been an integral part of the specific objectives of Lord Krishna, the 8th incarnation of Vishnu.. The earth had to be cleansed of the massive accumulation of the forces of evil and wickedness, as a large portion of the ruling classes had forgotten their duties and were indulging in intolerable acts of torture and exploitation of weak and virtuous. Some of these forces seemed to have acquired invincibility of various types and hence their arrogance new no bounds. To assist in this massive task, the wise Lord had brought along Balarama, as his elder brother. Almost at the same time, Pandavas, the celestial warriors of matchless capabilities, were caused to be born in the renowned Kuru dynasty of Hasthinapura, where perpetual conflict with their evil cousins, known as Kauravas, laid the basic foundation of the epic fratricidal war. As an essential factor for acceleration of the conflict to its logical conclusion, a celestial female took birth as daughter of the king of Panchala and was named as Draupadi, eventually becoming the joint wife of the five Pandavas. Indecisiveness of Dharitarashtra, the blind king of Hasthinapura and his extreme fondness for follies of his eldest son Duryodhana, fueled and catalyzed the growth of enmity between the two groups of princes. Vyasa, the great thought warrior [15], a sage of repute and an author of celestial capabilities, was already on the scene. He could visualize the sequence of events destined to unfold—and hence advised, fore-warned, and chastised the two warring lines of princes, as and when asked for or deemed necessary. In fact, the two factions of the warring princes at Hastinapura, were his own grand children.

When the basic components of the conflict were in place, process of its destined manifestation and culmination commenced with the collective training of the two lines of princes under the renowned guru Drona. Persistent superiority of Pandavas in learning the art of combat and the great guru's fondness for his gifted disciple Arjuna, pushed the rivalry to unhealthy limits. In view of merits of head and heart, Yudhishtira, the eldest of the five Pandavas, was declared as the crown prince. It ignited the enmity in mind of Duryodhana to the extent that, in connivance with his evil maternal uncle Sakuni, he attempted to burn to death the unsuspecting Pandava brothers and their mother Kunti, in a magnificent palace built with inflammable materials, specifically for this purpose. Pandavas survived the evil episode on account of the secret assistance from the virtuous Vidura, their uncle and an active well wisher. The Pandavas went into disguise, eventually emerging at Panchala, where they won Draupadi, in face of an international competition. Later on, as a consequence of their mother's un intentional comment, she became their collective wife. At the same time, Lord Krishna happened to be present at Panchala and the wise Lord took them under his protection and guidance. Their mother Kunti was sister of Krishna's father Vasudeva. Thus, all the primary elements of the epic conflict fell in place and both the sides now had their combination of thought warriors and action warriors [15]. Now onwards, Lord Krishna actively assumed the role of leading and controlling the conflict. He advised the Pandava brothers to return to Hasthinapura, as invited by their blind uncle, and claim their part of the kingdom.

Lord Krishna contributed massive management inputs, technical assistance and experts from his established empire at Dwaraka, thus enabling the inexperienced Pandavas towards establishment of a magnificent capital city by the name of Indraparastha. They converted the surrounding inhospitable and desolate terrain into fertile lands and soon Indraparastha became famous for its riches and prosperity. On account of the fighting skills of Arjuna and Bhimma, the Pandava kingdom expanded several folds, further fueling the enmity and jealousy in the mind of Duryodhana and his bunch of evil friends.

Under the supreme thought warriorism of Lord Krishna, action energy dominance of Arjuna and Bhimma, and catalyzed by the ever-righteousness of Yudhishtira, the celestial Pandavas successfully celebrated the Rajasuya [16], after eliminating the invincible demonic king Jarasandha of Magadha. It sent an intolerable wave of jealousy in mind and heart of Duryodhana. Thus, all the ingredients of the final conflict of Mahabharatha were systematically assembled under the cosmic guidance of the wise Lord. Final sparks of the decisive conflict emerged when Duryodhana felt insulted in the fabulous environment of the Pandava's Indraparastha.

Through employment a cunning and unethical strategy or negative thought warriorism of uncle Sakuni, Duryodhana cheated the Pandavas of their prosperous empire and its beautiful capital city of Indraparastha, in a manipulated game of dice. He went to the extent of molesting and attempting to disrobe Draupadi in his court, in full view of all the elders and wise assemblage; and except a long distance invisible intervention from Lord Krishna, no one came to her assistance. It was the ultimate evil act of intolerable proportions, decisively leading to the destructive events of Mahabharatha. Draupadi was insulted beyond consolation and Bhimma, the mighty Pandava warrior, took the vow for a fully compensative revenge at the right time.

All through the long exile of thirteen years, overt and covert management actions designed to avenge the injustice and insults inflicted on them, among others, involving the followings were put into action.

- Planning and organizing for all the essentials of the final showdown in the battle-field.
- Development and collection of new weapons.
- Training and specialization of key warriors.
- Strengths and weakness analysis in the rival camp.
- Invincibility of the Kaurava warriors and allies and how to circumvent the same.
- Analysis of potential allies and their resources.
- Strategy for post-exile demand and negotiations.
- Brain-storming on all relevant aspects of the emerging stages of conflict.
- Motivation in order to minimize the impact of forest life.
- Management of the energies of thought and mind.
- Development of the second line of warriors.
- Cost-benefit analysis of the active conflict.
- How and when to redeem the lost honor of Draupadi.

Throughout the period of exile and more actively after its expiry, Lord Krishna played an active management role of a *thought warrior* and advised the apprehensive Pandavas, how and what to negotiate and what to do in the event of failure to redeem their kingdom through persuasion and negotiations. He even acted as their ambassador, in a last ditch effort, to secure some territories for the aggrieved warriors—and when nothing succeeded, and his own safety came under threat, He made an exhibition of his all powerful omnipotent cosmic vision, in order to deter the evil Duryodhana and his bunch of equally wicked friends from their nefarious design to physically seize the great Lord.

Once the finality of intentions of evil Duryodhana became evident, emergency exercise of men and material mobilization commenced, allies and alignments were finalized, logistics were reviewed, supply lines were worked out, command strategies were deliberated upon, and strategies to weaken the invincibility of the key warriors on side of the Kauravas, were put into operation. Finally, during the active combats, frequent situation reviews were conducted and appropriate corrective strategies designed to achieve the final wins and successes.

The greatest non-material motivational management exercise of all times was attempted when a distort and demoralized Arjuna, the key warrior on side of the righteousness, seeing his elders, gurus and relatives on the opposite side, refused to wield weapons and fight. The wise Lord had to employ all his superior communication skills to shake the great warrior out of the state of inaction –and when all attempts of the Lord brought no fruit, He had to let Arjuna know that that the creator of the universe himself was personally wanting him to do his duty as a warrior. And that by killing the people lined up in the battlefield he shall, in reality, not be doing any such act as all those assembled there were already killed by the great Lord himself—he would be only acting as a proxy of the great Lord..

For the two warring sides, supporters, troops, chariots and other war materials came from far and wide and all this involved a massive and efficient management exercise of unimaginable proportions, keeping in view the time and its limitations. Lord Krishna, the master CEO of the theatre of Mahabharatha, had planned and executed all the fine details of the greatest management exercise of all times.

Notes

1. Frederick W. Taylor (1911), in his work "The Principles of Scientific Management," suggested that work could be approached in a scientific manner, i.e., the production techniques could be rationalized to make the same efficient. In 1914, Henry Ford implemented Taylor's ideas and reduced car assembly time consumption from 728 hours to 93 minutes. Through subsequent applications, the techniques of Taylor were not found to be worker friendly.

2. V.S. Murlidharan (2006), "Intelligent Manager," on p-3, para-1 discusses the management practices of ancient civilizations.

3. R.K. Narayan (1978), in his "The Mahabharata," makes an easily understandable rendering of the great epic.

4. "Mission Incarnate," as a term, has its origin from author of the present work. It stresses that the particular characters came with well defined specific objectives.

5. "Non-material Motivation," as an expression, has been employed, for the first time in the present work. It was successfully attempted by Lord Krishna for motivating a depressed, de-motivated and deluded Arjuna, for effectively fighting in the battle of Kurukshetra where he was faced with a great line up of his friends and relatives, and elders and gurus in the opposing side – and finally eliminating all of them as part of his sacred duty as a warrior.

6. Bhagavan Das (1990), "Krishna – A Study in the Theory of Avataras," p-24-32, described the makers of time or the "History Makers", in a very lucid style.

7. Ramesh Menon (1993), in his "Once a Blue God" has beautifully described the origin of the Blue Incarnation.

8. K.M. Munshi (1988), in the "Krishnavatara" and Pawan K. Verma (1995), in the "The Playful Divine" dwelt with the invention of iron and its usage in weaponry.

9. "Managing the Invincible" – this expression, in relation to management, has been initiated by the author of the present work.

10. "Madhura Communication" is a terminology employed by the author of the present work to describe the highly effective and charming methodology of Lord Krishna, visible in his divine dealings with friends as well as adversaries.

11. Pavan K. Varma (1995), in the beginning of his "Krishna–The Playful Divine," beautifully described the great incarnation of Lord Vishnu.

12. "Wisdom Concentrate," is a new terminology employed by the author of the present work, to describe the massive concentration of wisdom in the divine personality of Lord Krishna.

13. There is disagreement amongst Vedic scholars on exact placement or timing of the epic event of Mahabharata; some place it around 900 BC and, as a consequence, Lord Krishna's presence on this earth too gets similarly affected.

14. Akshauni was a fighting unit comprising chariots, elephants, horses, and infantry, totaling men of arms.

15. Thought Warriors and Action Warriors are the terminologies employed to depict the dominant characteristics of the main participants of the epic conflict. Those with greater inclination to use the resources of head and heart – and who could come up with new ideas and approaches were termed as thought warriors. On the reverse, the ones with greater inclination towards action, with little or no component of thought, were classified as action warriors.

Parva in Sanskrit refers to a section/chapter

CAUTION

This work, by design, resorts to repetition of certain terms, views, expressions and events at various places. It has been attempted primarily for the purpose of right emphasis assignment and situation-specific impact correlation.

PARVA I

THE DIVINE SONG OF MANAGEMENT WISDOM

THE DIVINE SONG OF MANAGEMENT WISDOM

Bhagavad Gita is one of the cornerstones of Indian philosophy. This renowned *Song of Wisdom*, the most serene and sublime of the texts, has as its setting the most violent of the places—the war-fields of Kurukshetra, which is also Dharmakshetra, the field of righteousness, where the battle between the forces of good and evil is about to commence. In the divine poem, the dialogue is between Krishna and Arjuna, and reported by Sanjaya to the blind Kaurava king Dhritarashtra. In a large metaphor, it represents flow of words of wisdom between God and man, in a very private manner.

Inspecting the two great armies standing ready to battle, Arjuna comprehends, with horror, the prospects of having to fight and kill his own elders, gurus, friends and colleagues. He feels deeply anguished, desolate and deluded. He drops to the floor of the chariot—totally confused and drained of energy. In a totally uncharacteristic manner, he informs Lord Krishna who has accepted to act as charioteer of the great Pandava warrior that he can not fight. Arjuna elaborates that he has no energy for the purpose; he can't even stand up and hold the Gandiva. Lord Krishna notices the precarious condition of his valued disciple and before He is able to say anything, Arjuna blurts that he sees evil omens; that no good will come out of killing my own kinsmen in the battle. He hastens to add, "I do not want this victory, O Krishna, nor kingdom, nor pleasures, or even life itself?" He elaborates that he does not want to commit this great sin and would not mind even if the sons of Dhritarashtra kill him unarmed and unresisting.

Lord Krishna is confronted with an unexpected situation. His carefully drawn up plans for eliminating the great assembly of evil forces on the battle fields of Kurukshetra, are at a serious risk. He can not allow it to happen. He has vowed not to wield weapon in this war. And without Arjuna, this war can not be won as there is no other warrior on the side of the righteous who can overwhelm the invincibility of Kaurava warriors, namely Bhishma, Karna and Drona. Hence, Arjuna's participation in the war is absolutely essential, for the great Lord, to ensure.

With the objective of motivating a depressed and deluded Arjuna, to stand up and do his duty as a warrior, the wise Lord engages the great Pandava warrior in an intense and arduous dialogue. It ends up becoming a divine exchange of words of wisdom—never uttered earlier in any situation either by man or God. Arjuna is in a nonviolent but highly argumentative mood. He raises a cascade of queries and the wise Lord answers the same patiently. They related, among others, to the followings:

- Futility of war, his inability of killing his own elders and gurus—and likelihood of attracting great sin in so doing.
- Needlessness of victory, kingdom and pleasures.
- Grief, sorrow and sorrowing, and inadvisability of the same.
- Death, birth and rebirth—and beyond death.
- Indestructibility of soul and its migration from old to the new.
- Relationship of soul and Super-Soul.
- Nature of soul: un-manifest, beyond thought and immutable.
- Relation of body, mind, intellect and soul.
- Path of action—the *Karma Yoga*, path of knowledge—the *Janana Yoga*, and path of devotion—the *Bhakti Yoga*.
- The right path—the path of action without worry for results of action.
- Superiority of action over inaction;
- Pleasures, senses, delusion, renunciation and renouncement.
- Anger, ego and their undesirability.
- Attachment and detachment.
- Wisdom, contemplation and peace.
- Control of senses and management of mind.
- Human nature—Sattva, Rajas and Tamas, and their manifestations.
- Desires, the enemies of wise.
- Righteousness and unrighteousness.
- Dharma and adharma—and practice of the former.
- Freedom from fear, passion and anger.
- Sacrifice of material and Janana.
- Service, devotion and illuminated souls.
- Creation and creator.
- Fire of wisdom and purity of the latter.
- True renunciation of work and selfless action.
- Sanyasa and Yoga, and practice of the same.
- Soul as ones friend or enemy.
- Harmonization by Yoga and perpetual peace.
- Unity of all beings—oneness of everything.
- Brahman, the Supreme Indestructible.
- Adhyatma, adhibhuta and adhidaiva.
- Pleasing the Lord—offer by love and faith.

- Devotion, adoration and worship.
- Numerous forms of the Lord and their manifestation.
- Incarnation of the Lord for protection of righteous and virtue.
- Diligence, knowledge, meditation and renunciation—their relative merits.
- Merits and qualities of devotees.
- I, Me and Mine and possessiveness.
- Wisdom, Vedas and Vedanta.
- Memory and Knowledge.
- Purushottama—the Supreme Purusha.
- Presence of God and Abode Eternal.

Lord Krishna answers all these and many other associated queries of Arjuna in a divinely impressive manner. Yet, some residues of confusion linger on in mind of the anguished warrior. The task for which he is being pushed by the great Lord is not easy. Hence, he wants to be doubly sure. Turning around, he asks the Lord to grant him glimpses of His Real Cosmic form. The great Lord has no option but to oblige his divine disciple. With the help of a third eye, Krishna allows his inquisitive pupil to benefit from the omnipotent form of the Master of the Universe. The divine form of the Lord is so magnificent but un-nerving: Arjuna, being totally shaken, requests the Lord, with folded hands, to assume his original mortal form. He incessantly promises to abide by the Lord's dictates i.e. to fight and do his duty as a warrior.

Sanjaya, who was gifted with an ability to view the whole episode, is filled with happiness and reports the same to his blind master. He however does not know whether the blind king is happy or anguished.

This divine dialogue between an eager God and a reluctant man is subsequently immortalized in form of the renowned text of *Bhagavad Gita* by the great sage Vyasa. By virtue of its unique contents, an assemble of 700 priceless slokas, also came to be called as *Song of Wisdom.* It has been published in over two thousand editions in over seventy five languages. Today, it is one of the most widely interpreted and commented upon work of wisdom.

This great work of divine wisdom, in fact, represents a massive exercise in motivation, more precisely in non-material motivation. Further, it rightly honours the time-tested concept of Karma or Action, as nothing gets done in this world without action. As one attempts to burrow deep into the divine slokas, one encounters a never ending field of management jewels, and hence, decides to call it "Song of Management Wisdom." Keeping this in view, an attempt is been made here to study and analyze the management wisdom content (MWC) of some selected slokas.

हृषीकेशं तदा वाक्यमिदमाह महीपते ।
अर्जुन उवाच
सेनयोरुभयोर्मध्ये रथं स्थापय मेऽच्युत ॥
(१।२१)

MWC: When armies of Kauravas and Pandavas are lined up in full battle readiness, Arjuna requests Lord Krishna, who has elected to be the charioteer of the divine warrior, to take his chariot to the centre of the battlefield so that he could have a clear view of the great assembly of the battle ready warriors. It is an exercise in situation assessment and competition analysis, prior to commencement of the action. In business and governance, such final stage assessments are vital for launch of any project or initiative.

सीदन्ति मम गात्राणि मुखं च परिशुष्यति ।
वेपथुश्च शरीरे मे रोमहर्षश्च जायते ॥
(१।२९)

गाण्डीवं स्त्रंसते हस्तात्त्वक्चैव परिदह्यते ।
न च शक्नोम्यवस्थातुं भ्रमतीव च मे मनः ॥
(१।३०)

MWC: On witnessing the great assembly warriors on the battle field of Kurukshetra, which included a number of his own friends, relations, elders and gurus, Arjuna is overtaken by the futility of bloodshed. He is imbalanced by a cascade of unproductive thoughts; his normal logical thinking capabilities desert him. He feels intense weakness of limbs, his mouth is dry, and he is unable to get up and hold his renowned Gandiva. He is depressed and confused; and the evil of delusion threatens to overtake him.

निमित्तानि च पश्यामि विपरीतानि केशव ।
न च श्रेयोऽनुपश्यामि हत्वा स्वजनमाहवे ॥
(१।३१)

न काङ्क्षे विजयं कृष्ण न च राज्यं सुखानि च ।
किं नो राज्येन गोविन्द किं भोगैर्जीवितेन वा ॥
(१।३२)

MWC: Completely disillusioned and confused, Arjuna tells Krishna that he sees great evil omens. He adds that in his view no good is likely to come out of the war. He tells Krishna that he does not want victory, kingdom and pleasures; and even life itself, in return of killing so many nears and dears. In Krishna's divine view, his valued disciple is making a mistake by over-occupying himself with results, instead of concentrating with action.

अहो बत महत्पापं कर्तुं व्यवसिता वयम्।
यद्राज्यसुखलोभेन हन्तुं स्वजनमुद्यताः॥
(१।४५)

यदि मामप्रतीकारमशस्त्रं शस्त्रपाणयः।
धार्तराष्ट्रा रणे हन्युस्तन्मे क्षेमतरं भवेत्॥
(१।४६)

MWC: Arjuna's state of confusion intensifies a great deal. He says that it would be a great sin for him to slay so many of his kinsmen, in pursuance of the greed for a kingdom. He proceeds to say that it would be better if sons of Dharitarashtra kill him without his resisting the same. From the point of view of management wisdom, Arjuna's situation and utterances, in view of the wise Lord, amount to the fact that inadequate understanding of right or wrong—or demand of the situation, can lead to unnecessary confusion of thoughts as well as inaction.

सञ्जय उवाच

एवमुक्त्वार्जुनः सङ्ख्ये रथोपस्थ उपाविशत्।
विसृज्य सशरं चापं शोकसंविग्नमानसः॥
(१।४७)

सञ्जय उवाच

तं तथा कृपयाविष्टमश्रुपूर्णाकुलेक्षणम्।
विषीदन्तमिदं वाक्यमुवाच मधुसूदनः॥
(२।१)

MWC: Sanjay, the personal assistant of the blind king, who was assigned the job of giving a running commentary on the war situation to the benefit of the king, notices the precarious situation of Arjuna and duly informs his master. Madhusudana (Krishna) fully understands the delicate situation into which

Arjuna had landed himself through unnecessary concern for men who are not worthy of the same.

श्रीभगवानुवाच

अशोच्यानन्वशोचस्त्वं प्रज्ञावादांश्च भाषसे।
गतासूनगतासूंश्च नानुशोचन्ति पण्डिताः॥
(२।११)

MWC: The wise Lord responds to Arjuna by saying that, though your words seem learned, there is no justification in your grieving for people who do not merit such a consideration. He adds that wise people do not grieve for either the living or for the dead. In his divine view, to sorrow for such people is not worth the attempt. The wise Lord's exhortation amounts to the fact that repentance and grief have no scope in activities of people involved in process of governance or management. Wisdom provides no basis for unrighteous or wrong decisions.

न जायते म्रियते वा कदाचि-
न्नायं भूत्वा भविता वा न भूयः।
अजो नित्यः शाश्वतोऽयं पुराणो-
न हन्यते हन्यमाने शरीरे॥
(२।२०)

MWC: The wise Lord proceeds to assert that no one kills and no one is killed as the soul is permanent and non-destructible. Similarly, in business and governance, inputs and participants did not matter; what mattered was the primacy of corporate interest or objective. Alteration of product-mix or turnover of the people involved should not change the basic character of the corporate involved.

वासांसि जीर्णानि यथा विहाय
नवानि गृह्णाति नरोऽपराणि ।
तथा शरीराणि विहाय जीर्णा-
न्यन्यानि संयाति नवानि देही ॥
(२।२२)

नैनं छिन्दन्ति शस्त्राणि नैनं दहति पावकः ।
न चैनं क्लेदयन्त्यापो न शोषयति मारुतः ॥
(२।२३)

MWC: Here, the Lord explains to Arjuna that migration of soul from one body to another i.e. from death to rebirth is similar to discarding of old clothes for new ones. Soul casts off old body to manifest itself anew. He re-stresses the non-destructibility of soul; its immunity to be affected in any manner by any sharp weapon, fire, water, wind or any other destructive force. From this vital utterance of the Lord, it is feasible to conclude that lack of correct understanding of a process or situation can lead to needless concern or attention diversion. Over-analysis can lead to paralysis. In the wise Lord's view, there is need for a correct understanding of vital matters, including those related to life, death, birth, rebirth and the permanent nature of the soul.

अच्छेद्योऽयमदाह्योऽयमक्लेद्योऽशोष्य एव च ।
नित्यः सर्वगतः स्थाणुरचलोऽयं सनातनः ॥
(२।२४)

जातस्य हि ध्रुवो मृत्युर्ध्रुवं जन्म मृतस्य च ।
तस्मादपरिहार्येऽर्थे न त्वं शोचितुमर्हसि ॥
(२।२७)

MWC: In the above slokas, the Lord stresses the un-manifest nature of the soul—it being beyond thought and immutable. He tells Arjuna that knowing all this, there is no need to sorrow for any one. He emphasizes that death is unavoidable for all beings that take birth, in view of the need for life's renewal; rebirth of all those who die is normal part of the divine system. And that there is no need to worry about something that is unavoidable. From angle of management and governance, non-permanence of all goods, products and people must be accepted, in order to permit more rational decision-making.

कर्मण्येवाधिकारस्ते मा फलेषु कदाचन।
मा कर्मफलहेतुर्भूर्मा ते सङ्गोऽस्त्वकर्मणि॥
(२।४७)

योगस्थः कुरु कर्माणि सङ्गं त्यक्त्वा धनञ्जय।
सिद्ध्यसिद्ध्योः समो भूत्वा समत्वं योग उच्यते॥
(२।४८)

MWC: This sloka contains one of the most important assertion of the wise Lord in context of work and its results or fruits. Here, He clarifies to Arjuna that one has right only to work or action—but never to its fruits. The wise Lord adds that let not the rewards of action be your motive or concern; work is not to be done for rewards but for the work's sake. Don't be attached to rewards in any manner, yet inaction is not permitted

The above sloka has tremendous implication for corporate workers or those engaged in activities of governance. There exists an intense engagement with results, fruits of work or targets. It vitiates a workers attention or work energy apportioning. And in most cases, the sole concern of bosses is result or reward of any action undertaken or planned. It ends up, in the final analysis, in the doer's attention diversion—and eventually leads to minimal initiative and limited co-operation, leaving absolutely no room for innovation. Result should be left to the superior to assess and examine—or bother for. The doer should be made free from this avoidable stress. Application of the wise Lord's advice in corporate work environment can greatly reduce resistance to work, suggestion, co-operation, and initiative. It can make the doer a self sustaining and productive force.

In view of the above, Lord Krishna advises the great Pandava warrior to be steadfast in yoga i.e. his own work or duty, by totally renouncing attachment (results) and be balanced in success as well as failure. Failure should not depress one and success should not go to the doer's head. Such evenness of mind is called "Yoga or Karma-yoga." What a valuable learning for superior management!

दूरेण ह्यवरं कर्म बुद्धियोगाद्धनञ्जय।
बुद्धौ शरणमन्विच्छ कृपणाः फलहेतवः॥
(२।४९)

बुद्धियुक्तो जहातीह उभे सुकृतदुष्कृते।
तस्माद्योगाय युज्यस्व योगः कर्मसु कौशलम्॥
(२।५०)

कर्मजं बुद्धियुक्ता हि फलं त्यक्त्वा मनीषिणः।
जन्मबन्धविनिर्मुक्ताः पदं गच्छन्त्यनामयम्॥
(२।५१)

MWC: In the above slokas, Lord Krishna further attempts to clear the action related cobwebs in mind of Arjuna. He asserts that selfish action (where there is active concern for results or fruits of actions) was inferior as per wisdom of the Karma-yoga. Hence, He exhorts the great Pandava warrior to seek the shelter of wisdom. He goes on to add that the doers, whose motive is primarily reward, are truly wretched—they persistently suffer the pain of expectation, leading to work stress accumulation and unease. Hence, disassociation of reward expectation from work, even in a partial manner will make working life much more pleasant.

In the next sloka, the wise Lord informs that the wise workers cast off the shackles of both good and evil deeds in this very life by renouncing their concern for rewards. In light of this He proceeds to advise Arjuna to seek the equanimity of Yoga: Yoga being the skill in action.

The wise workers, who possess the knowledge of righteousness or Yoga; who are able to renounce fruits of their actions, are freed from the bondage of birth and rebirth, and go to the abode of salvation.

यदा ते मोहकलिलं बुद्धिर्व्यतितरिष्यति।
तदा गन्तासि निर्वेदं श्रोतव्यस्य श्रुतस्य च॥
(२।५२)

MWC: Here, the wise One stresses the clarity of mind and thought: when mind is free from delusion, then it is feasible to understand what has been said and even go beyond. For corporate workers, it is necessary to be free themselves from delusion (false belief or false opinion)--as only one who possesses such freedom will be able to cast off the highly damaging concern for rewards of action, planned or undertaken.

क्रोधाद्भवति सम्मोहः सम्मोहात्स्मृतिविभ्रमः ।
स्मृतिभ्रंशाद् बुद्धिनाशो बुद्धिनाशात्प्रणश्यति ॥
(२।६३)

नास्ति बुद्धिरयुक्तस्य न चायुक्तस्य भावना ।
न चाभावयतः शान्तिरशान्तस्य कुतः सुखम् ॥
(२।६६)

MWC: The above two slokas pertain to the wise Lord's advice in regard to *anger management*. In his divine views anger and passion are the root cause of delusion. From delusion sprouts the lack of righteous judgment and also loss of memory. From here grows the loss of intelligence—resulting into lack of discrimination. Finally, such a doer perishes due to wrong actions and his perpetual concern for rewards.

In the next sloka, Lord Krishna explains the wisdom of being steady and controlled, because without, these there is no retention of wisdom on part of the doer. And without wisdom the constructive process of contemplation will not give company to the doer. One can achieve no peace without righteous contemplation. And without peace how can one have joy? What is said here is of considerable relevance in day to day corporate work. Steadfastness and, consequently, a capacity to persist is one of the essentialities for success in collective work environment. Peace of mind and joy of work are the two vital essentialities for being a successful and productive corporate worker. The key for it lies in the wise Lord's advice rendered as above.

इन्द्रियाणां हि चरतां यन्मनोऽनुविधीयते ।
तदस्य हरति प्रज्ञां वायुर्नावमिवाम्भसि ॥
(२।६७)

तस्माद्यस्य महाबाहो निगृहीतानि सर्वशः ।
इन्द्रियाणीन्द्रियार्थेभ्यस्तस्य प्रज्ञा प्रतिष्ठिता ॥
(२।६८)

MWC: The above slokas concern with proper control and management of mind. The wise Lord looks at the major part of Arjuna's problems as consequence of his wandering mind—as the mind that follows the wandering senses, loses its wisdom on account of non-concentration. This destructive action is like a boat in water being carried away by the wind. Therefore, the stability of the thought process is vital for constructive thought energy to transcend into constructive work energy.

Hence, to the mighty warrior, the wise Lord advises to withdraw from an excessive interplay of senses and be steady in wisdom.

Similarly, corporate workers have to take precaution of avoiding excessive interplay of senses or sense gratification, to stay wise, focused and productive.

अर्जुन उवाच ।

ज्यायसी चेत्कर्मणस्ते मता बुद्धिर्जनार्दन ।

तत्किं कर्मणि घोरे मां नियोजयसि केशव ॥ ३-१ ॥

व्यामिश्रेणेव वाक्येन बुद्धिं मोहयसीव मे ।

तदेकं वद निश्चित्य येन श्रेयोऽहमाप्नुयाम् ॥ ३-२ ॥

MWC: Arjuna is in an argumentative mood, and hence retorts that when knowledge is better than action, then why you insist me to engage into the terrible act of war. Your confusing advice is bewildering in nature. Please tell me clearly which path is truly better—the path of highest good?

Management value of these two slokas lies in the need for clarity of advice rendered by a senior and its proper grasping by the recipient. No productive action is feasible when recipient is in a state of confusion. And ensuring clear understanding is the job of the senior or the boss.

श्रीभगवानुवाच ।

लोकेऽस्मिन् द्विविधा निष्ठा पुरा प्रोक्ता मयानघ ।

ज्ञानयोगेन साङ्ख्यानां कर्मयोगेन योगिनाम् ॥ ३-३ ॥

न कर्मणामनारम्भान्नैष्कर्म्यं पुरुषोऽश्नुते ।

न च संन्यसनादेव सिद्धिं समधिगच्छति ॥ ३-४ ॥

MWC: In order to satisfy Arjuna's need for clarity the wise Lord explains that there are two paths of spiritual discipline—*Janana-yoga*, the path of knowledge (wisdom) which is a function of intellect; and Karma-yoga, the path of action, primarily a function of body. In terms of management wisdom, it boils down to the fact that one has the choice of becoming a knowledge worker (a specialist or technocrat) or a general worker, engaging in line-function where often the major job involves action for implementation of planned works.

The wise Lord proceeds to emphasize the essentiality of action and states that refraining from action does not mean freedom from action. Mere renunciation too assures no perfection. Perfection, in fact, sprouts from practice which is another name for regular action.

न हि कश्चित्क्षणमपि जातु तिष्ठत्यकर्मकृत् ।
कार्यते ह्यवशः कर्म सर्वः प्रकृतिजैर्गुणैः ॥ ३-५ ॥
कर्मेन्द्रियाणि संयम्य य आस्ते मनसा स्मरन् ।
इन्द्रियार्थान्विमूढात्मा मिथ्याचारः स उच्यते ॥ ३-६ ॥

MWC: Here, Krishna further stresses the significance of action—as not even for a moment man can be without action. Human nature, by its irresistible force, drives one into action. Those who attempt to refrain from action but inwardly dwell on objects of sense, are confused souls and false in conduct.

The management significance of the wise Lord's assertion lies in the fact nothing gets done, commercial or otherwise, in absence of action. Since action is a vital component of human nature, any attempt to avoid it is bound to bring in undesirable results. Dissatisfaction, confusion and finally frustration are bound to prevail in absence or inadequacy of action.

यस्त्विन्द्रियाणि मनसा नियम्यारभतेऽर्जुन ।
कर्मेन्द्रियैः कर्मयोगमसक्तः स विशिष्यते ॥ ३-७ ॥
नियतं कुरु कर्म त्वं कर्म ज्यायो ह्यकर्मणः ।
शरीरयात्रापि च ते न प्रसिद्ध्येदकर्मणः ॥ ३-८ ॥
यज्ञार्थात्कर्मणोऽन्यत्र लोकोऽयं कर्मबन्धनः ।
तदर्थं कर्म कौन्तेय मुक्तसङ्गः समाचर ॥ ३-९ ॥

MWC: The above three slokas are in appreciation of action. He advises Arjuna in regard to the fact that one who is master of his senses and free from attachment, is likely to engage himself in the Yoga of action or the Karma-yoga. The wise Lord in the next sloka proceeds to make a very important assertion:
Action is better than inaction!

Therefore, do your assigned work; without work the very life in one's body can't be sustained. He proceeds to elaborate that the whole world is held together only through the forces of action. "O son of Kunti, perform your actions without any attachment and consecrate the same as sacrifice," He exhorts.

In these utterances lies the *management philosophy of Lord Krishna*, the world's most efficient manager.

कर्मणैव हि संसिद्धिमास्थिता जनकादयः।

लोकसंग्रहमेवापि सम्पश्यन्कर्तुमर्हसि ॥ ३-२० ॥

यद्यदाचरति श्रेष्ठस्तत्तदेवेतरो जनः।

स यत्प्रमाणं कुरुते लोकस्तदनुवर्तते ॥ ३-२१ ॥

MWC: In this connection, the wise Lord cites the example of the great king Janaka, who acted entirely in public interest without any attachment to fruits of action. He exhorts Arjuna to act for greater good i.e. for destruction of the evil and the wicked, a majority of whom were assembled on the battlefields of Kurukshetra.

"The actions of a great man are an inspiration to others; whatever he does becomes a standard for others to follow." This utterance of the Lord has a very bright management advice. Righteousness of conduct on part of senior management, or the seniors in general, serves as the guiding force for junior staff in work as well as in observance of ethics of work.

सक्ताः कर्मण्यविद्वांसो यथा कुर्वन्ति भारत।

कुर्याद्विद्वांस्तथासक्तश्चिकीर्षुर्लोकसंग्रहम् ॥ ३-२५ ॥

न बुद्धिभेदं जनयेदज्ञानां कर्मसङ्गिनाम्।

जोषयेत्सर्वकर्माणि विद्वान्युक्तः समाचरन् ॥ ३-२६ ॥

MWC: Wise and learned should act without attachment, for good of the world despite the fact that ignorant remain attached to their actions. The wise man should not disturb the mind of unwise: he should rather concentrate on setting example for others to follow with righteous actions free of any attachment.

मयि सर्वाणि कर्माणि संन्यस्याध्यात्मचेतसा।

निराशीर्निर्ममो भूत्वा युध्यस्व विगतज्वरः ॥ ३-३० ॥

MWC: Keeping in view progress of the dialogue, the Lord urges the great Pandava warrior to integrate his mind and soul and offer his selfless actions to the Lord. The master of the universe counsels his worthy disciple to discard his vain hopes, selfishness and delusion. "Fight your war", the Lord enjoins Arjuna in a very direct manner.

From angle of management significance, the great Lord's strong advice goes to stress the directness and clarity on part of senior or boss, in dealing with a reluctant and non-performing junior. There is no point in beating around the bush.

श्रेयान्स्वधर्मो विगुणः परधर्मात्स्वनुष्ठितात् ।
स्वधर्मे निधनं श्रेयः परधर्मो भयावहः ॥ ३-३५ ॥

MWC: Since the Lord finds further need to push Arjuna into action, He proceeds to add that, howsoever humble, it is better to do one's own duty instead of attempting to do another's work, irrespective of its greatness. One should concentrate on his own work or duty instead of attention or effort dilution on account of others' work.

Even to die in performance of one's duty or assigned work has tremendous blessings. Engaging in work of another person, when it is not your own duty is in deed perilous. In corporate work environment, adherence to this divine direction has potential to greatly boost productivity.

अर्जुन उवाच ।

अथ केन प्रयुक्तोऽयं पापं चरति पूरुषः ।

अनिच्छन्नपि वार्ष्णेय बलादिव नियोजितः ॥ ३-३६ ॥

श्रीभगवानुवाच ।

काम एष क्रोध एष रजोगुणसमुद्भवः ।

महाशनो महापाप्मा विद्ध्येनमिह वैरिणम् ॥ ३-३७ ॥

MWC: Hearing the wise Lord's long and arduous advice, Arjuna wants to know why men engage in wrong-doing, sometimes even against their own will, as if some invisible force were compelling them.

The wise Lord is eager to cleanse Arjuna's mind and explains that often it is the greed and anger born out of the nature of passion (the rajas), all consuming and sinful. They are your dangerous enemies.

From management standpoint, these two negative human traits (namely greed and anger) are responsible for most of the corporate ills in the modern times.

धूमेनाव्रियते वह्निर्यथादर्शो मलेन च ।
यथोल्बेनावृतो गर्भस्तथा तेनेदमावृतम् ॥ ३-३८ ॥
आवृतं ज्ञानमेतेन ज्ञानिनो नित्यवैरिणा ।
कामरूपेण कौन्तेय दुष्पूरेणानलेन च ॥ ३-३९ ॥
इन्द्रियाणि मनो बुद्धिरस्याधिष्ठानमुच्यते ।
एतैर्विमोहयत्येष ज्ञानमावृत्य देहिनम् ॥ ३-४० ॥

MWC: Like smoke clouds a fire, as dust covers a mirror and as a womb envelopes an embryo, negative components of passion are capable of clouding or dimming human wisdom. When a person is overtaken by greed and/ or anger, his faculties of logical thinking are rendered ineffective or non-functional.

The Lord continues to elaborate the undesirable impacts of passion. In his divine opinion, the fire of desire is insatiable—a constant enemy of the wise and virtuous. It is capable of inactivating the forces of wisdom and knowledge.

The evil of passion is coiled in the senses, the mind and the intellect: through these it blinds man by veiling the wisdom.

तस्मात्त्वमिन्द्रियाण्यादौ नियम्य भरतर्षभ ।
पाप्मानं प्रजहि ह्येनं ज्ञानविज्ञाननाशनम् ॥ ३-४१ ॥
इन्द्रियाणि पराण्याहुरिन्द्रियेभ्यः परं मनः
मनसस्तु परा बुद्धिर्यो बुद्धेः परतस्तु सः ॥ ३-४२ ॥
एवं बुद्धेः परं बुद्ध्वा संस्तभ्यात्मानमात्मना ।
जहि शत्रुं महाबाहो कामरूपं दुरासदम् ॥ ३-४३ ॥

MWC: Therefore, O Bharata, first of all take control of your senses as it is the only way of destroying this sinful foe of wisdom and discrimination.

Senses are greater than the flesh (the body), greater than the senses is the mind, greater than mind is the intellect, and greater than intellect is the soul. Thus the great Lord explained the relationship of body, mind intellect and soul—which, at occasions, even wise are found confused about.

Through the knowledge of the above relationship, the wise Lord wants Arjuna to smite the forces of desire, his true enemy.

यदा यदा हि धर्मस्य ग्लानिर्भवति भारत।
अभ्युत्थानमधर्मस्य तदात्मानं सृजाम्यहम् ॥ ४-७ ॥
परित्राणाय साधूनां विनाशाय च दुष्कृताम्।
धर्मसंस्थापनार्थाय सम्भवामि युगे युगे ॥ ४-८ ॥
जन्म कर्म च मे दिव्यमेवं यो वेत्ति तत्त्वतः।
त्यक्त्वा देहं पुनर्जन्म नैति मामेति सोऽर्जुन ॥ ४-९ ॥

MWC: In saloka-4.7, Lord Krishna explains to Arjuna his divine system of incarnation on earth. The wise Lord states that whenever righteousness declines and evil and wicked assume sway, He manifests himself in human form. In management terminology, He is the CEO of the universe and occupier of the earth—and as per his responsibility to maintain righteousness and virtue, for organized and peaceful running of the system, He manifests as per needs, to correct and rebalance the same. Here, responsibility of CEO is clearly explained and hence in the corporate work environment, whenever significant deviations from the right path are noticed, the CEO of the corporate concerned should take corrective and restorative actions.

To protect the good, to subdue the evil, and to firmly establish "Dharma" or rule of law, is the responsibility of each and every CEO.

Lord Krishna further explains that the activities related to his birth are divine and he who knows about and recognizes the same, is freed from the from the shackles of birth; he comes into the Lord and rests with him. From angle of management it implies that truly committed and performing workers should be properly taken care of by the respective bosses. It is necessary for keeping plans and performance on track.

वीतरागभयक्रोधा मन्मया मामुपाश्रिताः।
बहवो ज्ञानतपसा पूता मद्भावमागताः ॥ ४-१० ॥
ये यथा मां प्रपद्यन्ते तांस्तथैव भजाम्यहम्।
मम वर्त्मानुवर्तन्ते मनुष्याः पार्थ सर्वशः ॥ ४-११ ॥

MWC: The Lord explains here that many wise ones have come to him in this manner after freeing themselves from fear, passion, and anger--becoming one with him they are purified by the penance of wisdom in the past. In whichever way men seek me--through any of the paths of action, janana and devotion, they are able to find me—because that is my path. From corporate wisdom angle, it signifies that all high performing and righteous workers should enjoy the protection of the boss.

श्रेयान्द्रव्यमयाद्यज्ञाज्ज्ञानयज्ञः परन्तप ।
सर्वं कर्माखिलं पार्थ ज्ञाने परिसमाप्यते ॥ ४-३३ ॥

तद्विद्धि प्रणिपातेन परिप्रश्नेन सेवया ।
उपदेक्ष्यन्ति ते ज्ञानं ज्ञानिनस्तत्त्वदर्शिनः ॥ ४-३४ ॥

MWC: Here, the wise Lord dwells on purity of wisdom. In his divine view, the sacrifice born of knowledge is greater than any material sacrifice, for the purpose of culmination of all work into wisdom. He establishes the significance of knowledge in human work environment.

In the next sloka, the erudite Lord emphasizes the need for reverence, service, and devotion to great men of knowledge (the sages) as such illuminated souls are of great assistance in teaching and guiding the people who are interested in attainment of this virtue. For the present day corporate work environment, it signifies the importance of knowledge workers.

यज्ज्ञात्वा न पुनर्मोहमेवं यास्यसि पाण्डव ।
येन भूतान्यशेषाणि द्रक्ष्यस्यात्मन्यथो मयि ॥ ४-३५ ॥

MWC: When truth thus enlightens you, there remains no scope for confusion. You will see the unity of creation—all beings of creation within you and consequently within me. Here, the wise Lord emphasizes oneness of all beings and all things. It bears direct relevance to his divine unified concept of management.

अपि चेदसि पापेभ्यः सर्वेभ्यः पापकृत्तमः ।
सर्वं ज्ञानप्लवेनैव वृजिनं सन्तरिष्यसि ॥ ४-३६ ॥

MWC: The Lord emphasizes value of such knowledge and says that even great sinners, with the help of this knowledge, will be carried through on the path of salvation like a boat is carried across the waters.

In view of Lord's assertion, despite deficiencies, knowledge workers' contribution should be respected.

यथैधांसि समिद्धोऽग्निर्भस्मसात्कुरुतेऽर्जुन।
ज्ञानाग्निः सर्वकर्माणि भस्मसात्कुरुते तथा ॥ ४-३७ ॥

न हि ज्ञानेन सदृशं पवित्रमिह विद्यते।

तत्स्वयं योगसंसिद्धः कालेनात्मनि विन्दति ॥ ४-३८ ॥

MWC: The wise Lord continues to emphasize the value of wisdom and says that the fire of wisdom has the capacity to burn all works and actions into ashes. On this earth there is nothing as pure as wisdom. He who perfects himself through yoga realizes it within himself in course of time.

He who subdues his senses and posses faith, gains wisdom and thus attains the peace supreme.

श्रीभगवानुवाच।

संन्यासः कर्मयोगश्च निःश्रेयसकरावुभौ।
तयोस्तु कर्मसंन्यासात्कर्मयोगो विशिष्यते ॥ ५-२ ॥

MWC: In this chapter are enshrined the wise Lord's explanation in regard to renunciation and selfless work. In his divine view, renunciation of works and the performance of selfless actions—both lead to the highest bliss. But out of the two, the Yoga of selfless action is superior.

Since work leads to production or service, adding to the Lord's creation, it merits greater attention and appreciation.

साङ्ख्ययोगौ पृथग्बालाः प्रवदन्ति न पण्डिताः।
एकमप्यास्थितः सम्यगुभयोर्विन्दते फलम् ॥ ५-४ ॥

MWC: In view of the Lord, on deeper analysis, knowledge and Yoga (of action) are one or the same thing; they can't be differentiated truly distinct. One, who is truly set in either one, finally obtains the fruit of both.

From point of view of its management implication, it would be right to view contribution of a knowledge worker and that of a generalist, engaged in line function of implementing plans and projects approved by the management, with equal emphasis.

संन्यासस्तु महाबाहो दुःखमाप्तुमयोगतः।
योगयुक्तो मुनिर्ब्रह्म नचिरेणाधिगच्छति ॥ ५-६ ॥
योगयुक्तो विशुद्धात्मा विजितात्मा जितेन्द्रियः।
सर्वभूतात्मभूतात्मा कुर्वन्नपि न लिप्यते ॥ ५-७ ॥
श्रीभगवानुवाच।
अनाश्रितः कर्मफलं कार्यं कर्म करोति यः।
स संन्यासी च योगी च न निरग्निर्न चाक्रियः ॥ ६-१ ॥
यं संन्यासमिति प्राहुर्योगं तं विद्धि पाण्डव।
न ह्यसंन्यस्तसङ्कल्पो योगी भवति कश्चन ॥ ६-२ ॥

MWC: The fifth chapter of this divine song of the Lord deals with one's relationship with his soul: *it describes how one can make his soul a partner in works of one's life*. The Lord goes on to explain that he who does his duty without expecting its reward or fruits, is both a Sanyasi and a Yogi. There is no difference between the two as both involve renouncement of fruits of action or effort. No one becomes a Sanyasi by merely renouncing the sacred fire—or a Yogi by just giving up action.

From the point of management relevance, the supremacy of action is important to note. While undertaking performance evaluation of workers it is important to examine whether the planned actions were taken in right intensity and with adequate commitment. The evaluator should not engage himself with results alone.

उद्धरेदात्मनात्मानं नात्मानमवसादयेत्।
आत्मैव ह्यात्मनो बन्धुरात्मैव रिपुरात्मनः ॥ ६-५ ॥

MWC: Here, the wise Lord speaks of one engaging into the process of self-help—as one's soul can be his friend: it can be his enemy too if there is no integration of a being with his soul. From angle of management, the Lord here implies that soul can be made a co-worker, and when such a linkage is effected, performance output is bound to surge irrespective of the kind of activity the doer is engaged in.

बन्धुरात्मात्मनस्तस्य येनात्मैवात्मना जितः ।
अनात्मनस्तु शत्रुत्वे वर्तेतात्मैव शत्रुवत् ॥ ६-६ ॥

MWC: The great Lord here attempts to instruct Arjuna to conquer his own-self (by subduing the forces of senses) and then his soul will become his friend—a co-worker in attaining aims of divine life. He elaborates that when one does not control his own-self, the soul is likely to turn as enemy. *Its management significance lies in need for integrating the body-mind-intellect and soul relationship for superior productivity*.

युञ्जन्नेवं सदात्मानं योगी विगतकल्मषः ।
सुखेन ब्रह्मसंस्पर्शमत्यन्तं सुखमश्नुते ॥ ६-२८ ॥
सर्वभूतस्थमात्मानं सर्वभूतानि चात्मनि ।
ईक्षते योगयुक्तात्मा सर्वत्र समदर्शनः ॥ ६-२९ ॥

MWC: A true Yogi, fully harmonized within himself, free from blemishes of sin, is capable of experiencing the infinite bliss of union with the divine. And fully harmonized by Yoga, a Yogi sees the self in all beings—and all of them within himself; everywhere he sees the same. It signifies the unity of everything or oneness of everything.

आत्मौपम्येन सर्वत्र समं पश्यति योऽर्जुन ।
सुखं वा यदि वा दुःखं स योगी परमो मतः ॥ ६-३२ ॥

MWC: In this sloka, the wise Lord explains to Arjuna qualification of the most superior Yogi—the one who looks on all as on his own self, experiencing the delights and sufferings of others as his own. The management utility of this teaching of the wise Lord lies in the fact that if and when corporate workers celebrate success or performance of others with unbiased happiness, the forces of positive energy so generated would, without doubt, amplify performance of the entire corporate body beyond expectation.

चञ्चलं हि मनः कृष्ण प्रमाथि बलवद् दृढम् ।
तस्याहं निग्रहं मन्ये वायोरिव सुदुष्करम् ॥ ६-३४ ॥

श्रीभगवानुवाच ।
असंशयं महाबाहो मनो दुर्निग्रहं चलम् ।
अभ्यासेन तु कौन्तेय वैराग्येण च गृह्यते ॥ ६-३५ ॥

MWC: Arjuna here interjects to the fact that mind's turbulence, restlessness and obstinacy is difficult to master: in fact as difficult as to control mighty winds. The wise Lord agrees with the fact that mind control is difficult. He proceeds to explain that the restlessness of mind, though tough to curb, can be restrained by constant practice and by dispassion. Mind management i.e. directing it's massive thought energy in constructive direction, is of considerable significance in management of human resources.

असंयतात्मना योगो दुष्प्राप इति मे मतिः ।
वश्यात्मना तु यतता शक्योऽवाप्तुमुपायतः ॥ ६-३६ ॥

MWC: As final opinion and advise in this regard, the wise Lord tells Arjuna that one who is master of oneself can, through ceaseless striving and practice, achieve control of mind—*the Yoga of Action and Thought*.

श्रीभगवानुवाच ।
अक्षरं ब्रह्म परमं स्वभावोऽध्यात्ममुच्यते ।
भूतभावोद्भवकरो विसर्गः कर्मसंज्ञितः ॥ ८-३ ॥

MWC: Sensing that his divine disciple is not fully free from doubts, the wise Lord explains to Arjuna the relationship between himself, the Super-Soul and soul of a human beings. Brahman (or the Super-Soul) is the Supreme Indestructible; His light within one's own self is called Adhyatma; and Karma is the creative force that brings all beings into existence.

The relationship of the great Lord with his all beings is ideal for a corporate CEO to visualize and manifest between him and his employees and workers—seeing a part of himself in each and every one of them--and all of them collectively being within him. It can lead to a totally tension free model of management.

तस्मात्सर्वेषु कालेषु मामनुस्मर युध्य च ।

मय्यर्पितमनोबुद्धिमार्मैवैष्यस्यसंशयः ॥ ८-७ ॥ or संशयम्

MWC: Here, Lord Krishna advises Arjuna to remember him all the times while fighting his battles. The great Lord assures his disciple that with your mind and reason fixed on Me, you shall definitely come to Me. This special rapport between Arjuna and the Lord is unique in all respect. Such a support and assurance no corporate CEO can give to his performing workers but if some variation of it is devised, then the doer would have no difficulty in achieving desired result even in most difficult work situations.

पत्रं पुष्पं फलं तोयं यो मे भक्त्या प्रयच्छति ।

तदहं भक्त्युपहृतमश्नामि प्रयतात्मनः ॥ ९-२६ ॥

MWC: It is one of the most important slokas of the renowned renderings of the wise Lord, where He goes to explain how easy the Lord is to be pleased. With faith and love whosoever offers him a leaf, a fruit, a flower or even a little water—all these offerings from beings of pure heart are readily accepted by the Almighty. In deed, the Lord has a beautiful relationship with his beings. Corporate CEOs, if they desire to be truly effective, should work out somewhat similar, a truly simple, relationship with his subordinates and workers.

यत्करोषि यदश्नासि यज्जुहोषि ददासि यत् ।

यत्तपस्यासि कौन्तेय तत्कुरुष्व मदर्पणम् ॥ ९-२७ ॥

MWC: Here, the benevolent Lord advises Arjuna that all his actions should be offered into him with love and faith; He will accept them all.

Similarly, all actions of subordinates, good or bad—productive and unproductive, finally end up with the boss. And when the same are performed in good faith and with due dedication, the responsibility and accountability moves up to the boss.

शुभाशुभफलैरेवं मोक्ष्यसे कर्मबन्धनैः ।

संन्यासयोगयुक्तात्मा विमुक्तो मामुपैष्यसि ॥ ९-२८ ॥

MWC: The wise Lord proceeds to further assure Atjuna that acting as advised i.e. fighting his battle without bothering for results, and with his mind steadfast in renunciation, he would be freed from the bonds of Karma and its fruits of good and bad; then he shall definitely come into the Lord.

What a beautiful assurance! It can do wonders in corporate environment.

श्रीभगवानुवाच ।
पश्य मे पार्थ रूपाणि शतशोऽथ सहस्रशः ।
नानाविधानि दिव्यानि नानावर्णाकृतीनि च ॥ ११-५ ॥

MWC: The dialogue between the Lord and Arjuna was long and arduous. Arjuna, to be sure of what he heard the Lord say, wanted to see the Lord's true celestial form. Krishna could not refuse the request of his great disciple--as without his co-operation the Lord's ultimate objective of eliminating the great assembly of evil forces on the battlefield of Kurukshetra could not be fulfilled. So, the benevolent Lord gave Arjuna the benefit of a celestial eye so as to enable him to view the Lord's true cosmic form.

Arjuna was imbalanced by the magnificent view of the Lord's omnipotent form; wave of bewilderment overtook him and he lost no time in requesting the Master of the Universe , with folded hands, to assume his original mortal form.

The management significance of Lord's exhibition of his true form underlines the fact your star performer, whom you are asking to undertake a truly difficult and risky maneuver, needs to be fully convinced about you as well as about the validity of the objective.

सञ्जय उवाच ।
एवमुक्त्वा ततो राजन्महायोगेश्वरो हरिः ।
दर्शयामास पार्थाय परमं रूपमैश्वरम् ॥ ११-९ ॥

MWC: Sanjay, the gifted personal assistant of the blind king of Hastinapura, was giving a live commentary for the benefit of his master. He glimpsed the cosmic form of Lord Krishna and duly informed the blind king, who already had a lingering doubt about the all mighty Lord's presence in favour of the Pandavas. He was now certain of the eventual destruction of his evil progeny.

त्वमस्य विश्वस्य परं निधानम् ।
त्वमव्ययः शाश्वतधर्मगोप्ता
सनातनस्त्वं पुरुषो मतो मे ॥ ११-१८ ॥

MWC: Arjuna views the splendour of the Master of the Universe and is considerably unsettled. He sings in praise of the mighty Lord and is ready to do his bidding—do his duty as a warrior without worrying about results or consequences. Through this act of ultimate affirmation, Lord Krishna transports his valuable disciple beyond the apparent reality.

मय्येव मन आधत्स्व मयि बुद्धिं निवेशय ।
निवसिष्यसि मय्येव अत ऊर्ध्वं न संशयः ॥ १२-८ ॥
अथ चित्तं समाधातुं न शक्नोषि मयि स्थिरम् ।
अभ्यासयोगेन ततो मामिच्छाप्तुं धनञ्जय ॥ १२-९ ॥

MWC: In this chapter, the wise Lord unfolds his *Wisdom Concentrate* character—He being the ultimate source of wisdom. First, He advises his disciple to concentrate his attention and understanding on the Supreme divine, where he could dwell for ever.

In event of Arjuna's inability to so concentrate, he is offered an alternative i.e. to reach the Lord through the practice of Yoga concentration.

Significance of Yoga, the selfless action, and concentration in whatsoever one attempts is re-stressed here.

अभ्यासेऽप्यसमर्थोऽसि मत्कर्मपरमो भव ।
मदर्थमपि कर्माणि कुर्वन्सिद्धिमवाप्स्यसि ॥ १२-१० ॥

MWC: The wise Lord continues to advise and says that in case you can't do any of the above two things, then just do your assigned work in my name. Even in my service you shall attain perfection. Here, it worth noticing the degree of concentration that the wise Lord applies in making sure that his disciple acts as desired. *Hence, concentration and persistence have great practical utility in the field of management.*

श्रेयो हि ज्ञानमभ्यासाज्ज्ञानाद्ध्यानं विशिष्यते ।
ध्यानात्कर्मफलत्यागस्त्यागाच्छान्तिरनन्तरम् ॥ १२-१२ ॥

MWC: While sustaining the dialogue of wisdom, the wise Lord proceeds to shower some *gems of wisdom*, for the benefit of his divine disciple. He says:

Better than diligence is knowledge;
Better than knowledge is meditation;
And better than meditation is renunciation of the fruits
of action, for peace springs from such renunciation.

As the wise Lord does not lose sight of action adorned with renunciation of it's fruits, a wise corporate CEO or a senior professional too should be very particular of action, without overdue concern for it's fruits.

अद्वेष्टा सर्वभूतानां मैत्रः करुण एव च ।
निर्ममो निरहङ्कारः समदुःखसुखः क्षमी ॥ १२-१३ ॥
सन्तुष्टः सततं योगी यतात्मा दृढनिश्चयः ।
मय्यर्पितमनोबुद्धिर्यो मद्भक्तः स मे प्रियः ॥ १२-१४ ॥

MWC: Now, the wise Lord shifts his attention to tell Arjuna the kind of disciples or devotees He likes. He who hates no one, is friendly and compassionate to all, free from thought of I, me and mine, equal alike in joy and sorrow, and ever forgiving, is dear to the Supreme Lord. One who is self-controlled and strong of resolve, and surrenders his mind and heart to the Lord, is dear to him.

The liking of the Lord is totally based on purity of heart and clarity of mind: His choice is crystal clear. Similarly, if a professional manager ever exhibits any preference, then it should always have a very clear and perceptible basis.

यस्मान्नोद्विजते लोको लोकान्नोद्विजते च यः ।
हर्षामर्षभयोद्वेगैर्मुक्तो यः स च मे प्रियः ॥ १२-१५ ॥
अनपेक्षः शुचिर्दक्ष उदासीनो गतव्यथः ।
सर्वारम्भपरित्यागी यो मद्भक्तः स मे प्रियः ॥ १२-१६ ॥

MWC: The wise Lord continues to elaborate his attachment for virtue and merit. One who does not troubles the world, nor gets troubled by it and remains unfettered from the evils of passion, agitation and fear, is again very dear to him.

Freedom from vanity of expectation, purity of heart, wisdom and impartiality, and above all selfless action, are the other qualities that the great Lord eagerly looks for in his devotees.

यो न हृष्यति न द्वेष्टि न शोचति न काङ्क्षति ।
शुभाशुभपरित्यागी भक्तिमान्यः स मे प्रियः ॥ १२-१७ ॥
समः शत्रौ च मित्रे च तथा मानापमानयोः ।
शीतोष्णसुखदुःखेषु समः सङ्गविवर्जितः ॥ १२-१८ ॥

MWC: Lord is, indeed, an intense seeker when it comes to qualities of his disciples He prefers them neither to rejoice nor hate: not to grieve but abandon desires, and above all, renounce both good and evil. It is in deed a tough demand. Similarly, a CEO or senior professional should have tough standards for any one to qualify for his preference or an out of the way attention.

A good devotee of the wise Lord needs to be alike to friend and foe, unmoved alike by honour or disgrace, beyond perception of pain or pleasure, unaffected by heat and cold, and also free from all types of attachments.

तुल्यनिन्दास्तुतिर्मौनी सन्तुष्टो येन केनचित्।
अनिकेतः स्थिरमतिर्भक्तिमान्मे प्रियो नरः ॥ १२-१९॥
ये तु धर्म्यामृतमिदं यथोक्तं पर्युपासते।
श्रद्दधाना मत्परमा भक्तास्तेऽतीव मे प्रियाः ॥ १२-२० ॥

MWC: The wise Lord strives here to explain some more of his preferred qualities that He looks for in his devotees. They are:

Equal mindedness in praise or blame;
Contentment with what is available;
Silence of spirit;
Without possessiveness of ownership;
And firmness of mind.

Finally, the demanding Lord is able to specify what He loves most in his preferred devotees. Most dear to me are those who, with faith and love, heed his words of divine wisdom.

सत्त्वं रजस्तम इति गुणाः प्रकृतिसम्भवाः।
निबध्नन्ति महाबाहो देहे देहिनमव्ययम् ॥ १४-५ ॥

MWC: The wise Lord does not want to leave anything unexplained to Arjuna, as He does not often land into a situation of intense discourse. He proceeds to explain the basic nature of human beings, various virtues and deficiencies that it assigns to the beings falling in it's major groupings. As per the wise Lord, there are three Gunas (qualities) born of nature that tie down the perishable soul to body. They are:

Sattva—the purity, Rajas—the passion, and Tamas—the inertia.

Of these, Sattva is pure and immaculate; it gives the light and health to life. It exhibits attachment to happiness and joy.

रजो रागात्मकं विद्धि तृष्णासङ्गसमुद्भवम्।
तन्निबध्नाति कौन्तेय कर्मसङ्गेन देहिनम् ॥ १४-७ ॥

Rajas is of the nature of passion—the basic source of thirst and attachment. It quickly binds the soul to selfish actions and their fruits.

तमस्त्वज्ञानजं विद्धि मोहनं सर्वदेहिनाम् ।

प्रमादालस्यनिद्राभिस्तन्निबध्नाति भारत ॥ १४-८ ॥

Tamas, the third one, is born of ignorance and deludes all beings coming under its influence. It has a very fast binding capability through heedlessness, indolence and sleep.

सत्त्वं सुखे सञ्जयति रजः कर्माणि भारत ।

ज्ञानमावृत्य तु तमः प्रमादे सञ्जयत्युत ॥ १४-९ ॥

Sattva binds to happiness, Rajas to action and Tamas clouds wisdom, leading to negligence and indolence.

रजस्तमश्चाभिभूय सत्त्वं भवति भारत ।

रजः सत्त्वं तमश्चैव तमः सत्त्वं रजस्तथा ॥ १४-१० ॥

Sattva prevails when Rajas and Tamas are overcome by prevailing environment. At certain times, Rajas prevails over Sattva and Tamas. And it is also not uncommon when Tamas is dominant.

कर्मणः सुकृतस्याहुः सात्त्विकं निर्मलं फलम् ।

रजसस्तु फलं दुःखमज्ञानं तमसः फलम् ॥ १४-१६ ॥

सत्त्वात्सञ्जायते ज्ञानं रजसो लोभ एव च ।

प्रमादमोहौ तमसो भवतोऽज्ञानमेव च ॥ १४-१७ ॥

ऊर्ध्वं गच्छन्ति सत्त्वस्था मध्ये तिष्ठन्ति राजसाः ।

जघन्यगुणवृत्तिस्था अधो गच्छन्ति तामसाः ॥ १४-१८ ॥

The fruits of righteous actions are said to be Sattvik, without any blemish. Rajas, on the other hand, produces sorrow and pain, and Tamas tends to generate ignorance.

Sattava gives birth to wisdom; from Rajas sprouts greed and carelessness; and Tamas gives birth to delusion and ignorance.

Consequently, those who are rooted in Sattva tend to rise upwards, those who are Rajasik remain on middle ground, and those engulfed by Tamas sink ever lower.

These qualities of human nature, so impressively described by the wise Lord, are of substantial importance in human engagements of business and governance. People with Sattvik tendencies excel in activities of head and heart—often being good with information, logic and learning. They can master technologies and be good teachers, planners, advisors, and head office support functionaries. They are likely to be relatively just and impartial.

Persons of Rajasik quality dominance can be good managers and may excel in line functions. They are good in assuming authority, giving orders and implementing plans and projects.

People with Tamsik nature are good as base level workers and soldiers; they can follow orders when there is perceptible threat of punishment in the event of non-compliance. They lack initiative and positive perception.

Human nature, as described by the wise Lord to the great Pandava warrior, can be a very strong and effective tool of management, particularly for work assignment, location and placement, and for selecting effective means of motivation. It can be a true minefield of management effectiveness if nature of people involved is diligently and impartially analyzed and worked upon.

सर्वस्य चाहं हृदि सन्निविष्टो
मत्तः स्मृतिर्ज्ञानमपोहनञ्च ।
वेदैश्च सर्वैरहमेव वेद्यो
वेदान्तकृद्वेदविदेव चाहम् ॥ १५-१५ ॥
द्वाविमौ पुरुषौ लोके क्षरश्चाक्षर एव च ।
क्षरः सर्वाणि भूतानि कूटस्थोऽक्षर उच्यते ॥ १५-१६ ॥

MWC: In this chapter, the wise Lord enlightens his favourite pupil on relationship of soul and Super-Soul. He proceeds to state that He abides in heart of all; and that He is the memory and knowledge or lack of the same. He is known through the Vedas as well as the knower of the Vedas. He is the ordainer of Vedanta.

He explains that there are two types of spirits in this universe—the perishable and the imperishable. Perishables are these existences that you see, the creatures of creation. Immutable and imperishable is the Soul Eternal.

उत्तमः पुरुषस्त्वन्यः परमात्मेत्युधाहृतः ।
यो लोकत्रयमाविश्य बिभर्त्यव्यय ईश्वरः ॥ १५-१७ ॥
यस्मात्क्षरमतीतोऽहमक्षरादपि चोत्तमः ।
अतोऽस्मि लोके वेदेच प्रथितः पुरुषोत्तमः ॥ १५-१८ ॥

The Highest Spirit is yet separate, the Supreme Soul, the Deathless Lord, He who pervades and sustains whole the universe.

The Lord informs Arjuna that because He is beyond the perishable and transcends the imperishable, He is known as Purushottama—the Supreme Purusha, in this world and in the Vedas.

यो मामेवमसम्मूढो जानाति पुरुषोत्तमम् ।
स सर्वविद्भजति मां सर्वभावेन भारत ॥ १५-१९ ॥
इति गुह्यतमं शास्त्रमिदमुक्तं मयानघ ।
एतद्बुद्ध्वा बुद्धिमान्स्यात्कृतकृत्यश्च भारत ॥ १५-२० ॥

He who knows Me and sees Me with a clear vision, as Purushottama, knows all and worships Me with whole of his being.

He further informs Arjuna that you, being a sinless one, are being blessed with the most secret doctrine of wisdom directly by Me. In knowing this lies the wisdom and accomplishment of duty.

ईश्वरः सर्वभूतानां हृद्देशेऽर्जुन तिष्ठति ।
भ्रामयन्सर्वभूतानि यन्त्रारूढानि मायया ॥ १८-६१ ॥

MWC: Here, the wise Lord tells Arjuna that God dwells in heart of all beings. But being unaware of the same they turn and spin through the wonder of His illusive power.

Similar to this situation, corporate management should free workers at all levels from un-necessary prevalence of illusion about corporate policies, objectives and mission in order to enable them contribute their best

तमेव शरणं गच्छ सर्वभावेन भारत ।
तत्प्रसादात्परां शान्तिं स्थानं प्राप्स्यसि शाश्वतम् ॥ १८-६२ ।
इति ते ज्ञानमाख्यातं गुह्याद्गुह्यतरं मया ।
विमृश्यैतदशेषेण यथेच्छसि तथा कुरु ॥ १८-६३ ॥

MWC: The great Lord here assures Arjuna for his ultimate salvation, for his place in the Abode Eternal. In a similar manner a corporate boss should clearly assure a good and judicious worker for his eventual welfare.

The Lord reaffirms to Arjuna that he is the special one to know these secret directly from him. He advises the great Pandava to ponder over them well—and then do his will.

मामेवैष्यसि सत्यं ते प्रतिजाने प्रियोऽसि मे ॥ १८-६५ ॥

सर्वधर्मान्परित्यज्य मामेकं शरणं व्रज ।

अहं त्वां सर्वपापेभ्यो मोक्षयिष्यामि मा शुचः ॥ १८-६६ ॥

MWC: Here, it is visible that the wise Lord wants his complete hold over the Pandava warrior: He does not want to leave any scope for deviation—as it is a crucial moment in the Lord's presence on this earth. He tells Arjuna to fix his heart on him, love him and worship him and so you shall come into Me, as you are dear to Me. The management significance of this effort is self-evident.

राजन्संस्मृत्य संस्मृत्य संवादमिममद्भुतम् ।

केशवार्जुनयोः पुण्यं हृष्यामि च मुहुर्मुहुः ॥ १८-७६ ॥

MWC: Sanjay, the personal assistant of the blind king, who was watching the divine dialogue between the Lord and the Pandava warrior, is influenced by the wondrous words of the wise Lord, and he rejoices again and again.

It is not clear whether Sanjay's reaction was liked by his master; but one thing is sure as a conclusion that words of wisdom when uttered in a non-offending manner do influence even those who are not your allies or supporter.

यत्र योगेश्वरः कृष्णो यत्र पार्थो धनुर्धरः ।

तत्र श्रीर्विजयो भूतिर्ध्रुवा नीतिर्मतिर्मम ॥ १८-७८ ॥

MWC: The above sloka says that wherever there is Krishna, the Lord of Yoga; and Arjuna, the wielder of the bow, there victory and prosperity are sure to prevail, leading to joy and righteousness.

The vital management essence of the above is that in presence of superior wisdom and equally immaculate action, success is bound to be there. And other essential manifestations of the situation shall follow unrestricted.

PARVA II

LORD KRISHNA AS A DIVINE MANAGER

A Professional with a Manifesto

Lord Krishna was a divine incarnate with a well specified manifesto—his aims and objectives, in human life, were very clear to him. Such clarity, when available to leaders and professionals, renders the job of leading people or businesses much easier and significantly efficient. Hence, a superior professional should always strive for and assist his disciples or subordinates in acquiring a capability to draw for themselves a clear manifesto for efficient and measurable performance in subsequent times.

Lord Krishna's **Celestial Manifesto** was, in fact, drawn well before his incarnation. Right at the time of marriage of his parents, a celestial voice had proclaimed that the 8th child of Devaki will kill Kamsa, the demonic ruler of Mathura. This prophesy, on the one hand, condemned the demon ruler to sleepless nights for several years, and torments and hardships of prison life to the Lord's parents, on the other. During these intervening years, paranormal acts and antics of the child *Gopala* and predictions by numerous astrologers on impact of the Lord's birth in human form, had imparted certain visibility to the young Lord's unwritten manifesto which appeared to contain;

- The first and the foremost part of the Lord's manifesto was to rid the earth free of evil and wickedness that was manifesting in numerous forms—suffocating virtue and righteousness beyond tolerance. In addition to killing Putana, the female demon sent by Kamsa to harm the child Lord, the little Krishna eliminated numerous demons and asuras who came or were sent, in form of animals and reptiles, with the purpose of hurting him and or his kinsmen. Kicking and overturning a loaded cart by the blue child, had astonished one and all. Uprooting of arjuna trees and thus freeing the two gandharvas—Nalakuvara and Manigriva, from curse of their previous birth, by the touch of the little Lord, were vividly witnessed by people of Gokula. These and many other incidents made the little Lord's manifesto very clear to the whole cowherd community of Gokula and its neighborhoods.
- Spreading love and happiness was another important component of Krishna's manifesto. His activities as butter thief, tormenting gopis, subduing of Kalia—the evil serpent king, enchanting play of flute, and enacting dance circles were part of his love and happiness generation manifesto. The waves of happiness, love and celebrations initiated by the young Lord, are still going strong in the Indian society.

- Promoting superior knowledge of righteousness in governance and social interactions, was another important part of the wise Lord's manifesto. Hence, just after eliminating the demonic ruler Kamsa of Mathura and restoring the job of governance to an elderly and virtuous Ugrasena ,the young Lord proceeded to the ashram of guru Sandipani [1] and, in a fast track learning operation, acquired all the available knowledge of sixty-four subjects of sciences and arts, available at that time, in as many days. It was, in fact, the first step in the Lord's scheme of things to spread knowledge in an organized manner.
- The brightest effort by the Lord in the field of knowledge genesis and dissemination was his divine discourse to Arjuna, in the battle-fields of Kurukshetra, which subsequently came to be known as the **Song of Wisdom or Bhagavada Gita,** an in-exhaustible store-house of wisdom and knowledge—with non-fading relevance for all the times to come. Lord Krishna's unmatched knowledge of scriptures coupled with his astounding skills of delivery left all people, friends and foes alike, so spellbound that few dared to argue with the wise one. It sharpened his diplomatic skills to an un-imaginable level and the same, often employed with the tool of **madhura,** made him truly invincible in verbal duals as well as in delicate persuasions. He became a great negotiator, diplomat, teacher and guru, through employment of his divine skills of knowledge and expression.
- Krishna, based on his skills of logic and valour, won the confidence and friendship of Pandavas, the celestial warriors, through whom the wise Lord implemented the final phase of en-mass killing of evil forces in the battle of Kurukshetra, which almost cleaned the earth of the undesirable elements.
- The final point in the great Lord's divine manifesto was to establish the rule of just and righteous--and the same was beautifully achieved by him through the great Pandavas who, under guidance of the wise Lord, survived, almost intact, from the devastating conflict of Mahabharatha.

Thus, utility of a well defined manifesto, towards success and productivity of a leader or a professional, was clearly underlined in vivid practicality by Lord Krishna and hence, a study of his methods of intensely focused management can prove of immense guidance to the present day professional managers—irrespective of the type of activities they are engaged in. His teachings—as enshrined in the Bhagavad Gita and briefly summarized in this work—from the express point of their applicability in modern management, enjoy an ever-green multilateral utility as ever effective problem solving tools.

Work Performance as a Play

Those who enjoy their assigned work are destined to perform better. Your own resistance to work, or your dislike for the person who assigns work to you or one who is expected to supervise or assess the same, diminishes output and quality both. Work is best done when it is taken as a play. Lord Krishna was the most efficient practitioner of the **work-play concept.**

As a child, Lord Krishna was full of play and frolic. With his every act as a child, He manufactured happiness, bliss and amazement—whether stealing butter or breaking water-pots of gopis. Even in trying conditions, He had no trace of anger, agony or arrogance while enacting pranks or subduing demonic forces that came or were sent to harm him. In early infancy, he killed a female demon called **Putana,** who was sent by her evil boss Kamsa of Mathura, to harm the celestial baby Krishna. Suckling on her poisoned breasts with abandon, without any adverse effect on himself, He sucked life out of this terrible evil that fell to the ground and lost her beautiful deception, revealing her monstrous form. The size of this female evil was said to be so huge that, in her struggle to escape grasp of the Lord, a number of trees were uprooted, and subsequently, cowherds faced considerable difficulty in disposing off her dead body. For the baby Lord it was just a play.

Years later as a small cowherd, Krishna subdued the evil serpent king Kalia by ceaselessly dancing on his multi-hooded head, with total joy and abandon. Now, no play or ballet on life of child Krishna is complete without enactment of this dramatic act. Frustrated with the little Krishna's pranks, mother Yashodha once tied him to a heavy wooden mortar, and soon, as He strained at it and the mortar got entangled between two huge trees—uprooting them with a thud and dragging them to a distance. While every one was dazed, the little Lord had only a miner smile on his moon like face.

Lifting hill Goverdhana on his little finger and keeping it up there in protection of all his fellow cowherds, their cows and all other living beings, till Indra felt defeated and accepted the blue Lord's supremacy, who just smiled all through the ordeal. Several years later, killing of demonic Kamsa at Mathura, along with several of his famed wrestlers and elephants, was just a sort of game for the young Krishna and brother Balarama. They exhibited a lot of joy in clean-up of the evil elements and freeing innocent people from numerous prisons of the evil king..

Even in grave situations, Krishna never lost his usual smile and charm. When evil Duryodhana attempted to seize the great Lord in court of Hastinapura, where He had gone as a representative of Pandavas for a last ditch settlement, and the great Lord had to escape by exhibiting his all powerful multilateral cosmic form with divine revelations. He kept smiling all through the great celestial exhibition that dazed all those who witnessed it. Here too a difficult task was performed with great ease—without any agony or arrogance.

No work was too small for him to hesitate or dislike its handling by this great worshiper of action. When the war between Kauravas and Pandavas became inevitable, the Lord gladly accepted to act as the charioteer of Arjuna. He himself performed the job of feeding ,watering and grooming the horses despite the fact that his various devotees, disciples and attendants viewed the same as avoidable for him. Whatsoever He preached, He applied the same first on himself—so as to leave no corner of doubt in mind of his followers about the validity of what He said and did. He worked with perpetual and infectious joy on his face.

Only one example comes to light, in his long carrier as a cowherd, warrior and diplomat, when the great Lord seemed to lose his normal composure of charm and smile. It happened in the heat of the battle of Kurukshetra where the great Lord was participating as an unarmed charioteer of Arjuna. On finding his great disciple Arjuna unable or unwilling to effectively tackle the old warrior Bhishma, who was inflicting huge losses on the Pandava forces, Krishna jumped from the chariot that He was handling, picked up a broken wheel and ran towards Bhishma, but Arjuna intervened in time and promised to make greater attempt for effective handling of the old invincible warrior.

In essence, these and many other incidents from the event intense life of the great Lord, proceed to stress that all acts of work or karma, whatsoever difficult, should be performed with a smile on face of the performer. It improves work environment and enhances impact on those who witness the action; it creates wider acceptance and appreciation—reducing work tensions and negativity. This practical aspect of Lord Krishna's personality and works, offers a great opportunity to modern professional managers for stress free performance acceleration on continuous basis.

Dignity of Work

Work is the most important aspect of human-life. In this **Sansara** [2] work is as vital to all humans as food and entertainment. It is equally important to a king and a commoner. The type of work may differ but its vitality remains the same. Irrespective to one's origin or place in social order, he or she has to engage in some productive work, to earn or otherwise. It is necessary to maintain balance of body, brain and also the living environment.

In Bhagavad Gita, the compendium of highest philosophy, there lies a store – house of practical guidelines for daily life, to the common man caught in the mire of "Sansara" and plagued by doubts, fear and restlessness. The matter of fact advice of Lord Krishna to common man, is the path of **Karma Yoga;** simple and unambiguous. He stressed practice of selfless [free from greed and expectation] action, i.e. doing honestly and diligently whatsoever one is engaged into, as a means of fulfillment and salvation. Daily routine which involves performance of various acts, small or big, is very important. The spirit that should guide the various actions of an individual is the essence of Karma Yoga. The Lord explained it at great length to Arjuna when he was overtaken by doubts and confusion about his role and participation in the battle of Kurukshetra.

The Lord said, "You have the right to work , but to work's sake only. Let not the fruit of action be your object or motive in working. Neither should you yield to inaction." The value of Lord's advice lies in both the performance of action and in the right attitude and spirit behind the action. Total commitment to action and need to relinquish any desire for fruit of action are the key watchwords. Extent of involvement and degree of commitment to whatsoever the nature of work—whether mundane or spiritual, is the key of Karma Yoga. Conscious avoidance of action or half-hearted involvement is not permitted.

The most important task is to train oneself (to condition the mind) to fully align with whatsoever one does. It is an internal command that enables work without craving for fruit or reward. Thus, the right mental work mode is the most vital part of Karma Yoga. The disciplined activity is the essence of renuntiation. It requires effort and training to reach such a state of coordination of body, mind and the intellect.

Lord Krishna himself was a **Karma Yogi** of superior order. He incarnated to human form for a specific purpose of freeing the world of evil and wickedness. He observed the centrality of this objective whole his life. He completed the job of substantial elimination of the forces of evil and tyranny, in massive exercises of destruction at Kurukshetra and Parabhasa, without any partiality or preference.

Being part of a nomadic cowherd community in his early life, he enjoyed his work as a cowherd boy, tending cows and bulls and enjoying butter and curd with full abandon. Dignity of Work, irrespective of nature of work that came his way, was the Lord's basic approach as a human incarnate. He loved whatsoever he did and ,in return, he was greatly loved by his gopas, gopies, cows, bulls and the whole Yadava community.

In latter times at Dwarka, he acted as a prince and built an impressive kingdom which had no parallel, in the whole world, in respect of beauty and prosperity. He was not an armchair prince or guru. Whatsoever he preached , he did himself with happiness and dignity.

While in active consultation with Pandavas on how should they reclaim their kingdom from Duryodhana, he did not merely advise and preach, but went to

Hastinapura as their ambassador with the explicit purpose of pleading their case The climax of Lord Krishna's devotion to duty was most evident during the great battle of Kurukshetra, when he acted as charioteer of Arjuna .He meticulously watered and groomed the horses and maintained the chariot in battle fit condition. This is the most inspiring example of Devotion to Duty or Karma-Yoga. He had, in fact, no need to do all that; and could have well acted as an armchair advisor from comforts of royal tents. It was his total sense of commitment and dedication to work or duty that propelled him to do what He did and created the best known example for respect for duty or work assignment. He discharged his duty to fullest perfection. In Lord's opinion, there is no work that is too low or unworthy of attention. The thought of work—as low or high lies in the one's brain only since nature has not made any such discrimination. Normally, it is the negative energy thought that classifies a work as low, which by itself be avoided. From a review of life and works of Lord Krishna, there is no evidence of activity or event which He viewed as low or not worth attention if the same was to be done in a given situation. He did all that came his way, with full energy, commitment and pleasure.

The Lord washed feet of his long lost friend Sudama with his own hands when he had an army of servants and attendants. The Lord created an example for posterity (in respect to the dignity of work) and honoured his childhood friend.

Commitment Appreciation as a Management Tool

Value of commitment or to honour what is said, orally or otherwise, has great significance in human relations. In corporate world commitment adherence is as valuable as in the field of religion and spirituality. It determines the long-term dependability of a leader, on one hand, and ability of followers to abide by what is said or commanded, on the other. Value of commitment rises further when it comes from a senior person in an organization.

Lord Krishna exhibited a very high value to commitments made by him at various stages of his life. Some interesting instances from his life fully underscore the **principle of commitment appreciation.** Shishupala, an evil manifestation of great magnitude, was related to Krishna through an aunt who was Vasudeva's sister. She had given birth to a monstrously deformed child with four hands and three eyes. A celestial voice had proclaimed that the child would become normal when placed on lap of a person who would years later kill him. One day when Shishupala's mother out of anxiety, put the child on Krishna's legs, the child's extra arms and eye disappeared. She immediately was certain that her son would be killed by Krishna but thought that Krishna was not aware of it. But being a mother she could not contain her anxiety and asked Krishna for a favour i.e. to be gentle with her child and forgive him for mistakes or pranks if committed by him. Krishna understood his aunt's anxiety and grief, and out of generosity promised that he would condone even a hundred insults or pranks that the child may hurl at him, at any stage of his life. Krishna's aunt was very happy to have such a promise but the wicked Shishupala, when he grew up, gave a lot of problems to Krishna. By force of promise Krishna had to bear the same, with persistent smile and charm..

It is stated in Mahabharata that after the grand ceremony at Indraparastha for celebration of Rajasuya by Yudhishtira, Krishna, as per tradition, was requested by Pandavas to stay back as a special guest of honour. Accordingly, Krishna was ritually worshiped by Pandavas and in conformity to custom, to show respect, Yudhishtira and his brothers washed his feet. It is mentioned in Mahabharata that heavens rained flowers at this auspicious occasion.

Shishupala of Chedi kingdom, out of jealousy was very unhappy at turn of this event. He had a long-standing feud with Krishna as per his evil prakriti, and as per promise given to his aunt, Krishna had always ignored insults hurled at him by this fellow. Their enmity dated back to when Krishna had run away with Rukmani whom Shishupala was expected to marry. Shishupala's tirade of insults, as per onlookers, grew unbearable and at one point Krishna took out his Sudarshana and cut off Shishupala's head as the latter had crossed a hundred marks in his events of insults to the Lord. There was no evidence of any hatred or remorse on Krishna's face. The Lord knew that the job had to be done to fulfill the prophecy.

When Pandavas were condemned to a forest life after losing in the game of dice at Hastinapura, through cunning of Sakuni and Duryodhana, Krishna came to visit them in the forest. He spoke with Yudhishtira "I had to be away on another mission, otherwise I would have come to Hastinapura and stopped the game that brought you to this pass. I would have persuaded Kauravas to give up their sinful ways or I would have destroyed them all on the spot." Draupadi was moved by the Lord's sympathy and narrated her humiliation at hands of Kauravas in the full view of all the elders and her five warrior husbands. She was bitter and inconsolable. She said, "Nowhere in the universe has any woman been so humiliated. Karna, Dussasana and others leered at me and asked me to take a new husband as if I were a harlot." "Five warriors—were my husbands who could not lift a finger to help me, except Bhimma who was held back. You alone came to my rescue—You heard my call—You are my saviour. Arjuna's Gandiva and someone else's mace or sword—of what avail were they when I was dragged before assembly of monsters." To console her Krishna had to appease her and said "I promise you—Duryodhna, his brothers, Karna and the evil genius behind them all, Sakuni—all of them will be punished .Their blood will stain the dust.

Krishna while attempting to convince the Yadavas to vacate Mathura, in face of the intractable threat from the demonic Jarasandha and his allies, had made a solemn commitment that they would have a great future at Dwaraka. He had further committed to punish the then invincible Jarasandha at a later date. Lord Krishna kept an active track of commitments that he made, by design or otherwise, at any stage of his life, including those to the followings;

- to his fellow cowherds of Gokula and Vrindavana,
- to his Yadava kinsmen,
- to the Pandava brothers and Draupadi,
- to his aunts and relations
- to mother earth prior to deciding to incarnate in human form,
- or to any friend or colleague.

Lord Krishna meticulously fulfilled all commitments—irrespective of the cost or efforts involved. For him commitments had a divine value: they were, in fact, one of the most important tools of management available to him—to manage people and events both. Commitment adherence was his divine way of attracting and aligning the forces of righteousness with his own apparatus of fighting the evil and wickedness. Commitment appreciation or adherence also has immense utility as a modern management tool and the present day professionals should attempt to find ways and means for maximum use of it in improving all-round productivity and quality of performance.

Effective Situation and Competition Analysis

Superior practitioners of management develop and acquire dependable techniques of strength and weakness analysis of competition—opponents and adversaries, in situations encountered and/or likely to be encountered. Success of projects and campaigns, military or corporate, depends considerably on such capabilities and expertise—and, more precisely, on exercises attempted employing the same.

In present times, with the immense benefits of EDP [3] technology, professional managers usually undertake SWOT [4] analysis prior to launch of a project or product. Over 5000 years ago, Lord Krishna had no recourse to these modern tools of EDP and e-governance, yet He painstakingly undertook precise analysis of strengths and weaknesses of all of his key adversaries—evils in form of humans and animals. Background analysis of how some of them came to acquire such uncommon strengths and invincibility, was also developed-- and ways and means of circumventing the same were worked out with target specific precision.

Demonic Kamsa's capabilities of cruelty and torture became easily known to the Lord in early youth, due to immediate vicinity of Gokula and Vrindavana to Mathura, and the special circumstances of his incarnation in the demon's prison.

Persistent attacks by Jarasandha, after the death of Kamsa, brought to light the uncommon strengths and invisibility of this king of evils. A search of circumstances of this great evil's origin revealed that he was born in two pieces, as a consequence of a boon from a sage, and a smart midwife had joined the two parts to form a demonic child. The only way that any one could kill him, was to tear the evil skillfully into two parts while ensuring that the same did not come near to each other. Lord Krishna did not want to confront this unique devil, as a boon from Lord Shiva had ensured that no Yadava could kill him. And it looked for the Lord too much and too early, to abandon human form for eliminating the evil Jarasandha. Further analysis of alternatives prompted Lord Krishna to abandon Mathura and move out, with all of his willing kinsmen, to the relative safety of Dwaraka, in order to afford time and resources for planned battles against troublesome evils at more convenient times.

In relentless pursuit of his major objective, Lord Krishna kept himself free from rigours of direct governance at Mathura as well as Dwaraka, so as to apportion greater attention for planning and resources collection and alliance workouts. Also, He had to continuously monitor and update groupings and regroupings of evil forces, and it was essentially for this reason that the wise Lord took special interest in affairs of the warring cousins at Hastinapura.

He kept an eagle eye on developments during the thirteen years of exile of Pandavas, and as and when necessary, gave them suitable guidance to acquire strengths and weapons for meeting future contingencies.

Lord Krishna built an enviable network of intelligence collection, in all friendly and unfriendly kingdoms. Royal ladies, especially unmarried princesses, who had special leanings for the Lord's charms, were a valuable source of dependable information.

At Hastinapura, the Kaurava forces had warriors of repute, and the combination of Bhishma, Drona, Karna, Aswathama and Duryodhana looked invincible--and yet, all of them had to be subdued if righteous forces had any chance of a final victory. Through rigorous efforts, the wise Lord found secrets of invincibility of each and every one of them--and how to circumvent the same. Details of who will fight and kill each one of these and many other warriors siding with the evil forces were worked out in requisite details. As a master strategist, He was aware that when action starts, there would be no time for any exercise of information collection and analysis. Hence, an advance effort was deemed necessary.

A summary view of Lord Krishna's long-term intensive efforts in direction of organized analysis and study of strengths and weaknesses of major evil and demonic forces, troubling the earth at that time, and also of the righteous forces pitched against the formers, sets an interesting example for practitioners of the modern management, to be systematic and thorough in advance analysis and assessment of negative and positive factors, and their magnitudes, prior to launch of a project, product or service of significance, if the desired quantum of success is to be ensured.

Respect for Reality

Assessment of reality of a situation, or facts that prevail, is an important management function. Whether it is necessary to proceed in a pre-set direction or stop, reassess and alter the course of action, to avoid failure or to succeed fully or partially, is decidedly of critical significance. Great leaders—CEOs or commanders have a unique capacity for quick and correct assessment of reality, and assume corrective or most appropriate line of action. They assume full responsibility for uncommon decisions taken under challenging situations

In reference to this unique capacity, there seems to be no parallel to Lord Krishna who encountered an uncommonly difficult and challenging situation in his early life as a ruler. After eliminating the demon king Kamsa of Mathura, He ruled the newly liberated kingdom through virtuous Ugersena and Balarama, but Mathura saw no peace. Jarasandha, the mighty king of Magadha, whose two daughters—Asti and Prapti, were widowed on death of Kamsa, had vowed to avenge their widowing by Krishna and Balarama. True to his wraith, he attacked Mathura as many as seventeen times—each attack being more intense and vicious than earlier one. Though Krishna and Balrama stoutly defended the city of Mathura, but they never saw peace. While Jarasandha was never conclusively defeated, the perpetual conflict left no time and energy with the two celestial brothers for any developmental activities.

Soon, Jarasandha was joined, in his campaigns against Mathura, by an asura named Kalayavana, who had a huge army of *malechchas.* [5] He was also favoured by a boon that he could not be killed by any Yadava. Assessing the situation on merit, Lord Krishna, in consultation with brother Balarama and senior members of his clan, decided that the reality of the situation demanded an uncommon solution. The young Lord took recourse to **Lateral Thinking.** He decided that discretion was the better part of valour. Instead of getting defeated at hands of evil forces, to destroy which He had incarnated on this earth, it would be better to fight these presently invincible enemies at a later date, with better preparation and strategy. Although kshatriya code of honour, which valued sacrifice and death over retreat, did not permit it, He withdrew his forces and all willing members of his clan, from its traditional areas of Mathura and its neighborhood, to distant and desolate location of Dwaraka. This strategic decision of Krishna must have had its active critics, in his own camp as well as outside, yet He took this uncommon decision, in appreciation of the situation of reality—adhered to it and made a grand success of it. Soon, Dwaraka was turned into a prosperous and powerful kingdom as large territories of Gujarat and Maharashtra were added to it and the great Yadava clan flourished here a great deal. Their influence extended beyond the southern tip of India, then called Bharata. There are references to Yadavas' influence extending even beyond the Arabian waters.

Despite the grand success of Lord Krishna's strategy, this unique decision of his lateral thinking, was never fully accepted by his clan and as a symbol of dissent, He was given a somewhat derisive epithet of Ranchchor [6], which despite lapse of over 5,000 years, still continues to be attached to his bright name. In Dwaraka , in at least one temple, He is still worshiped by this name.

Despite overwhelming appeal of his myth, this uncommon act of withdrawal by the Lord in face of powerful opposition, has never been fully explained. Why the all-powerful Lord did not destroy his evil enemies—namely Jarasandha and Kalayavana, right in the beginning? Probably, it would have been premature for him to exhibit his superhuman or godly powers without which their elimination was not feasible. He did not probably want to handle this job himself or He desired his right disciples to emerge to undertake this job. He was the great follower of right **Time or Samaya** which, in his divine opinion, was not ripe or appropriate to eliminate the collective evil of Jarasandha and Kalayavana. Both of these enemies of Lord Krishna were protected by unique boons of invincibility—and, hence right time and right resources were of critical significance in this regard. The wise Lord was not the one to stick to any false prestige—He greatly respected reality of a situation.

To the Lord, the statecraft of this strategic decision was very clear. It was probably very safe for him to clarify it to Ugersena, Balarama and other seniors of the Yadava clan. It suited, quite possibly, the larger scheme of things of the Lord as when the right time came, He destroyed Jarasandha with the help of Bhimma, the mighty Pandava warrior. In Bhagwata Purana, it is mentioned at several places that Lord Krishna had allowed Jarasandha to escape at several occasions from battlefield at Mathura. The whole issue continues to be debatable and, as such, there is no way to have a decisive view in this matter. Irrespective of the truth behind this great decision of the Lord, its significance from the point of management decision process continues to be of truly great significance.

In brief, it proceeds to instruct modern managers that if an unpalatable decision becomes necessary under challenging situations, it must be taken promptly without fear of criticism. Long-range validity of a decision is more important than its immediate perception by people. False prestige should not be allowed to stand in the way and reality of situation should be respected in most appropriate manner.

Strategic Intervention as a Management Tool

Professional managers are expected to delegate part of their responsibilities. They have to keep track of various projects and developments and decide when to intervene or render help to a subordinate or a coworker-- if there are signs of unexpected deviations. Intervention at the right time, often termed as **strategic intervention,** is necessary if inconvenient results are to be avoided. Lord Krishna was an expert at **strategic intervention**. He often delegated critical jobs but knew exactly when to intervene if the involved coworker was faltering or if the assigned job was beyond his capacity. His timings and extent of intervention were well measured—in right quantum and just in time.

When Draupadi was being insulted and disrobed by Duryodhana and his group of evils, and all the elders (including her five warrior husbands) failed to come to her rescue, with folded hands and closed eyes-- she implored Krishna to come to her help. He responded to her **call of distress,** making her body clothing endlessly long—without himself being physically present on the scene. It was the best example of **just in time intervention** by the wise Lord. To make himself physically present at this critical moment would not have achieved better results in- terms of unnerving her tormenters.

When Bhimma was unable to make headway towards killing Jarasandha, in the one to one wrestling combat lasting several days, as each time the Pandava warrior tore his opponent into two—the separated halves rejoined miraculously, and noticing the criticality of the situation Krishna, the wise onlooker, picked up a leaf blade, tore it into two and threw the same into two different corners of the hall. Bhimma took the signal and repeated his action of splitting his opponent and threw the two halves in different directions—which lead to the end of the dreaded fighter, the greatest demonic ruler of that time—and a self declared enemy of Lord Krishna.

Lord Krishna's role as charioteer of Arjuna in the epic battle of Kurukshetra, afforded him another unique opportunity for strategic intervention, when the Pandava warrior faced an angry and unstoppable Karna, after the latter was installed as the Commander-in-Chief of the Kaurava forces. Karna fired his choicest weapon *the serpent* which, spitting fire was searching out for Arjuna's head-- but at the crucial moment, Krishna with his celestial powers, pressed the chariot and sunk it five fingers deep into ground.

The arrow missed Arjuna's head and the Lord's key disciple escaped a sure death—and the Lord himself avoided a non-explainable embracement.

Krishna was aware of Karna's possession of a magic spear, a gift to him from Lord Indra, and it could be sent on a specific errand only once and was sure to finish a specified enemy. In order to inactivate this unique weapon threat to Arjuna, He convinced the Pandava camp to send for warrior Ghatotkacha to attack the Kaurava forces. This asura warrior's campaign was so horrific that the heavily battered Kauravas requested Karna to do away with this unstoppable peril. In the ensuing fight even Karna was badly bruised and battered and, in apparent need for self-protection, Karna forgot the final planned use of this magic spear and launched it on Ghatotkacha. Though, it ended the brilliant fighting career of this unique warrior, the threat to Arjuna's life was averted.

Anther strategic intervention by the all powerful Lord was attempted when Arjuna failed to kill Jayadratha, as per the vow that he had taken and planned to self immolate at day end. Kauravas had kept the targeted warrior well hidden behind chariots and elephants all through the day and Arjuna failed to reach him till the fighting stopped at day end. Krishna had understood the situation well in advance and employing his celestial powers clouded the sun much earlier creating an illusion of actual sun set. A few moments later, the cover of clouds parted and Arjuna, as prompted by his wise charioteer, gained his composure to eliminate Jayadratha with a singe arrow.

There were numerous instances in Lord Krishna's long life as (a) an illiterate cowherd, (b) a warrior against evil and wicked, (c) a righteous ruler, (d) a splendid builder, (e) a diplomat par excellence, and (f) a great advisor and wisdom concentrate, where He had to attempt strategic intervention to ensure needful support to his disciples, supporters and co-workers, for meeting his basic commitment as a mission incarnate. He was, in deed, the most successful manager known to mankind and the numerous superior management techniques evolved and employed by him so decisively and fruitfully, continue to hold validity even in today's work environment. His ancient wisdom is available to all—to learn, copy and benefit.

An Efficient Facilitation Agent

Most of the collective activities—whether managed through project teams or task forces, tend to run into unexpected roadblocks. In many such situations, analytical or discrimination energies of the managing team may not be adequate or suitably oriented to automatically throw up a solution, adopt the same and arrive at the assigned target. Multiplicity of opinion within the team and consequent lack of direction often precipitates a situation of indecision. Normally, a team leader should be capable or well trained to undertake a correction course—but in practice such a normality is often invisible. The role of problem solving, de-bottlenecking or the task of facilitation is an important one—and hence, should not be underestimated in reference to outcome relevance.

The task of facilitation, especially in a difficult situation, is a very demanding one. An efficient facilitator should ideally possess long experience, relevant superior skills and charisma laced with faculties of communication and diplomacy. One has to be not only capable of providing the right corrective inputs but the manner of such provision should generate wide and enthusiastic acceptance. The catalytic interaction so generated should precipitate a forceful group action. There have been numerous leaders—corporate, political or religious, with efficient facilitation skills—who successfully stirred difficult situations in desired directions—earning significant appreciation from those involved either in the action process or who were affected directly and indirectly. In this area of outcome management or performance facilitation, nothing seems to come near to Lord Krishna's skills as an **ever-efficient and successful facilitator**, even after scanning of relevant literature and scriptures. A few of the incidents from life and works of this celestial manager of people, will suffice to illustrate this formation beyond doubt:

- At Panchala, when Pandavas won Draupadi as their bride—and Vidura came there with invitation of their uncle Dhritarashtra, for them to return to Hastinapura, Krishna who happened to be present there by pure chance or intelligent design, facilitated their decision to return—despite significant reluctance on their part, in light of their unpleasant experience of the past. Further, He persuaded them to accept the offer of the fifty percent of the kingdom of Hastinapura, without any discontent or murmur of displeasure, despite the fact that the part of kingdom allotted to them was substantially inferior and unproductive.
- Further, Lord Krishna acted as a powerful facilitator to the Pandava brothers - ,in converting the barren desolate waste-land of Khandavaparastha into a highly productive kingdom; in fact, a virtual paradise—the fame of which quickly spread far and wide. Indraparastha, the Pandava's capital, soon emerged as a city to rival the best in the world. According to the legend of Mahabharata, Lord Krishna had summoned Vishvakarma, the celestial

architect, to plan and build the splendor of the capital city of the Pandavas.

- Having made his kingdom secure and prosperous, Yudhishtra wanted to perform *Rajasuya* to proclaim his pre-imminence amongst all other states and kingdoms. Krishna knew the strategic roadblock likely to be encountered in this endeavour. As an astute military genius, He assessed the political situation and in a calm and composed manner told the Pandava brothers that with the line up of Duryodhana and his friends on one hand, and presence of Jarasandha and his demonic allies such as Shishupala, Dantavakra, Ruckmi, and Paundraka, on the other, they had no chance of such a celebration. Jarasandha, an old enemy of Krishna, had captured hundreds of kings and princes and wanted to make a grand sacrifice of royal heads to Sankara. As such, he was the biggest impediment in implementation of Yudhishtra's plans to claim greatness. If we manage to eliminate Jarasandha, said Krishna in a matter of the fact manner, then other kings and princes shall have no courage to stand in way of this project. After through brain storming, Krishna explained the circumstances of Jarasandha's birth and how he could be killed. As a great facilitator, He got the job done through a long-drawn wrestling bout with Bhimma, under his direct supervision, i.e. by signaling what to do at the most appropriate moment.
- The great epic of Mahabharata is full of instances where Lord Krishna effected numerous acts of facilitation in order to enable the righteous Pandavas eliminate the most impressive line-up of invincible and near invincible warriors on side of Duryodhana. It is also visible from Lord Krishna's great acts of timely and efficient facilitation in favour of Pandavas, the celestial front of righteousness, that the assistance of facilitation can either be requested by the performer in need or sensing the situation, the same could be volunteered by the senior or the supervisor. In team work, the responsibility for performance is never one sided.

The concepts and practices of success facilitation as employed by Lord Krishna, the Supper Celestial Manager, are of great practical utility to the present day corporate professionals—and if the same are practiced in right earnest, the performance of business teams shall improve a great deal and the vital senior-junior work relationship will become highly productive and totally stress free.

As a Re-engineering Expert

Re-engineering is a modern management buzzword or fad that almost all practitioners of modern management encounter at one or the other stage of their professional exposure. Many have opportunity of teaching or being taught how to employ it—while only a small minority ever makes any practical and productive use of it. In most cases, it rarely travels beyond class rooms or conference halls—as often theory overshadows the practical aspects of this useful tool.

It is true that re-engineering, when undertaken correctly, can be a powerful tool for implementing positive change, depending upon its objectivity orientation. For example, it can be an effective instrument for pushing responsibility and accountability down to the level where it genuinely belongs—or where empowerment can effectively take place. But when implemented erroneously, it becomes a game of desk shuffling and failure discredit apportioning.

Evidence of intense interest of managers in the concept of re-engineering flashes out of the fact that over two million copies of Re-engineering the Corporation [7] were sold in the last decade of the 20th century and it was translated into over a dozen languages.

The re-engineering journey, on most of corporate paths where it was attempted, often ran into trouble in approximately seven out of ten cases. In case of Hallmark Cards, Federal Express and Bell Atlantic, a productive use of this concept was made—while in number of other instances it was more or less a fizzle.

Re-engineering, as such, is not entirely a concept of modern origin, except that its repackaging and presentation in the recent past made a substantive impression. Lord Krishna, over five millennia earlier, employed this useful concept with great finesse and efficacy. Early in life, as a practicing cowherd, He moved his entire cattle rearing clan from Gokula to Vrindavana, in order to benefit from better availability of fodder and forest resources, on one hand and for reasons of greater security, on the other. Even as a very young and inexperienced member of the nomadic rural community, based upon his superior communication and logic, He was able to convince his whole clan to his point of view.

A few years later, after the dramatic elimination of the great demonic ruler Kamsa of Mathura, Lord Krishna presented the human history's most impressive feat of re-engineering, by moving the whole of the mighty Yadava clan of Mathura to a distant locale of Dwaraka, on the western sea coast of the country. For a common Yadava, it was a massive migration from a productive, prosperous and well established locale of Mathura and its surroundings, to a distant and desolate desert at the far end of the country. While for Krishna it was part of a grand strategy for safety and prosperity—an opportunity to establish a truly grand empire of celestial proportions, many of his clan members did not see the same with such a perception.

Jarasandha, the father-in-law of the slain demon Kamsa, on having his two daughters widowed as a consequence of the latter's death, had vowed to avenge the same. Being true to his word and vow, he attacked Mathura seventeen times—each campaign being more intense and savage. Though, the celestial combine of Krishna and Balarama was able to safeguard the town of Mathura against the demonic attacks of this persistent enemy, they were unable to decisively defeat him. On the occasion of the 18th attack, the invading forces were so overwhelming that Krishna decided to implement his plan of vacating Mathura in preference to an almost certain defeat at hands of the evil forces. It was one of the most difficult decisions of the eventful and arduous life of Krishna and there were dissensions and disagreements amongst the senior members of the Yadava community—yet almost every one had to comply with it—as they had little or no choice. In Mathura, the ruling Yadavas were always under tension and uncertainty—and it did not allow them any time or opportunity for any constructive work or development. Even otherwise, at their ancestral location, there was little or no scope for expansion of their kingdom as it was bordered with such regimes which could not be easily subdued.

Lord Krishna was aware of the circumstances of Jarasandha's birth, his military resources and also the boon that he could not be eliminated by any Yadava. While confining this secret of Jarasandha's invincibility only to himself and a few senior Yadava warriors, He planned and implemented the massive re-engineering effort to vacate Mathura and migrate en-mass to a more appropriate locale at the right time afforded by the 18th invasion of Jarasandha. It was executed with the minimum loss of men and materials—except earning for Lord Krishna an almost derogatory epitaph of Ranchoor—lasting even beyond his life time.

In the relative security of distant Dwaraka, the industrious Yadavas created a highly prosperous and extensive empire, within a short span of time under the celestial guidance of Krishna. Highly specialized earth related skills of Balarama came very handy in this unique endeavour of massive re-engineering. Soon, the fame of riches and splendour of Dwaraka spread far and wide—even across the Arabian sea. The Yadava clan, under the wise guidance of Krishna, flourished here even beyond their own expectations.

Several years later, when Pandavas were allotted the barren expanse of Khandavaparastha, as their part of the kingdom by their uncle Dharitarashtra, Lord Krishna again got a chance to implement a re-engineering plan of massive proportions that enabled Pandavas to create Indraparastha, a capital city that excelled even Dwaraka in certain aspects of splendour and grandeur. For the purpose, it is said that Lord Krishna had commanded the celestial architect

Vishvakarma to execute the job of planning and erection of the most impressive capital for the righteous Pandavas.

As evident from Lord Krishna's truly illustrious works in the field of re-engineering—it becomes an exercise of significant long range consequences for a corporate or government that elects to implement the same. It involves significant investments in terms of men, materials, money and time—and determines, in a significant way, the very future of the executive organization. Hence, re-engineering should be implemented with a lot of thought and care—as fallback or mid-course corrective measures, in this case, are often highly painful and expensive.

Multi-tasking Expert

Some corporate experts consider **multi-tasking** as a **management mantra**—while many others doubt its efficacy. In fact, only managers gifted with extra-ordinary capabilities and superior time management can practice this technique with an acceptable level of success. When practiced correctly, it can help improve output several folds. A successful multi-tasker should possess multilateral capabilities so that, at all moments, there are a lot of important matters to attend to. There are two basic essentials for multitasking—one, an inbuilt capacity in the worker to handle multiple tasks—and two, availability of significant works to serve as raw material for this task to be operative.

Lord Krishna was an undisputed expert in all forms of sciences and arts known at that time. It is stated that at the Sandipani ashram, the young Lord mastered all the available sixty-four fields of sciences and arts, in as many days—creating a truly magnificent record in speed of learning. Hence, He possessed the divine capability to handle multiple tasks at any given time. Further, the task that Lord Krishna had at hand, as a **Mission Incarnate**, was truly huge and onerous. Fighting evil was never easy and removing it as a clean sweep, from face of the earth must have been very difficult. In view of demands of the job, the great Lord had to resort to multi-tasking—without loss of quality or results in any manner. He did many things at a time and did them all well. For him multi-tasking was a **normal action process**—neither a myth nor an exhibition.

As a young and illiterate cowherd, He herded and cared for animals—found new pastures and water- holes. From him originated the basic care for cow as an animal of economic values With his vibrant young workmates, gopas and gopis, He played flute, invented music and dance forms. He started a fashion trend by dressing in bright yellow. As a boy of charms and physical prowess, He promoted rural games and martial arts. As and when challenges arose, the Young Lord destroyed demons and asuras who came or were sent to harm the emerging incarnate. He protected the cowherd community from natural disasters, on one hand, and altered their systems of worship, on the other.

In his youth and middle age, as an erudite warrior, the great Lord, among others, performed the following multi-tasking components, with ease of a celestial dancer;

- Destroyed demons and asuras.
- Acquired all knowledge of science and arts.
- Rebuilt a kingdom of righteousness at Mathura.
- Organized the great migration of Yadavas.
- Built a huge empire at Dwaraka.
- Undertook strengths- weakness analysis of all evil forces.
- Created an unrivaled intelligence collection network.
- Built strong alliances with righteous rulers.
- Conducted military campaigns at regular pace.
- Married a number of beauties of his times.
- Acquired trusted and capable disciples.
- Promoted knowledge, wisdom and dharma.
- Worked as an advisor and diplomat of repute.
- Was a matchless architect and built cities of splendour.
- Worked as a super-ruler.
- Protected devotees friends and disciples.
- Acted as a mediator for dispute resolution.
- Planned and guided the great battle of Kurukshetra.
- Secured elimination all major evil forces.
- Undertook numerous other tasks difficult to recount here.

In the post Kurukshetra period, the greatly relieved Lord paid prime attention to (a) strengthening the surviving righteous forces, (b) rebuilding infrastructure of dharma, (c) helping the surviving Pandavas in righteous governance, and (d) finding ways and means to prevent re-emergence of evil and wickedness. Towards end of his stay on this earth, He planned and executed destruction of his own mighty Yadava clan that, in his absence, had the potential to turn into an invincible and destructive force. He had to leave the earth with opportunities of continued righteousness.

All through his life of high event intensity, Lord Krishna displayed a superior game of multi-tasking—where every thing attempted was performed with utmost perfection. Multi-tasking, thus, is not a myth—it can

be a high performance reality, provided requisite expertise and efforts are invested in a right mix.

Lord Krishna as Outsourcing Expert

Outsourcing is an integral part the **globalization**—the less hindered and ever-expending march of the international trade. [8] In principle, it means acquiring goods and services—primarily produced or generated as per specifications and requirements of the client, production of which at home or in house will be more costly, cumbersome and inefficient than securing the same from a dependable predetermined source. It is, in fact, a contract operation—having an outsourcer who either provides its own specifications or approves those adopted by the source, and among others may include

- contract research and development.
- original equipment manufacture and supply.
- contract designing and manufacturing.
- management and medical services.
- contract packaging, storage and transport.
- marketing, advertising and customer services.
- contract construction and labour works.
- contract cultivation, and any other product or service that is mutually convenient.

Outsourcing is a term of growing opportunities and today, even extortion, fighting and killing are falling under its sphere of contract operations. With the effect of distances becoming insignificant under influence of growingly efficient communication, outsourcing seems positioned to assume many new, even unexpected, forms in the near future. The basic principle that either produce the best or outsource the best, will assume ever increasing applicability.

Out sourcing, in fact, is not new. It has only assumed a more visible form in the recent times. Human societies always benefited from it, whenever and wherever opportunities arose. Centuries old and time tested barter system operated efficiently before emergence of currencies that facilitated a more efficient exchange of goods. Throughout human history, kings and emperors—locals and invaders, successfully employed the technique of outsourcing to subdue non-cooperative regimes, on one hand and to administer newly acquired territories, on the other. In the not so distant past, Britishers in India employed this technique with astonishing success to expand territories under their control, with very small combat manpower of their own. Revenue collection was fully outsourced to local strongmen with matchless success and efficacy.

Much before any one else, Lord Krishna practiced efficient operation of outsourcing for organized governance and also for fighting evil and wicked forces. His first outsourcing attempt was to organize governance of the kingdom of Mathura through Ugrasena and his clansmen, after killing of the demonic Kamsa. Instead of involving himself in the intricate and time consuming works of the state, He wisely thought it better to get this job done through those who were experienced in the field of governance and had deep stakes in the same. At that moment, it was more important for him to equip himself with superior knowledge of available sciences, scriptures and arts than getting marred with the day to day affairs of a state that had suffered, for long, tyrannies of the worst kind. Hence, it was a very wise step on the part of the divine operator. He along with brother Balarama, joined the renowned Sandipani ashram for a fast track course that could equip and prepare them for the great task they had incarnated for. Whether a corporate or an individual, as a matter of principle—one should, at a given time, engage oneself in activities which are most essential or most beneficial in light of larger objectives. The young Lord highlighted this principle at a early stage of his life. It was a beautiful example of **wise outsourcing.**

Under the wise guidance of Lord Krishna, the mighty Yadava warriors created a vast empire at Dwaraka by wining territories in west, central and south of the country—and some even beyond the Arabian seas. As a matter of strategy, most of these newly acquired territories were ruled through a defused federal system that assured the wise Lord, effective controls and vital revenues on one hand and trained manpower contributions for his continued campaigns against evil regimes, on the other. It was a highly successful practice of outsourcing and beautifully met the wise Lord's objective of waging an all out war against evil and wicked ruling entities.

Lord Krishna's Yadava warriors, for certain reasons, were not capable of eliminating Jarasandha, the leader of all evil operators of that time. Due to persistent attacks from this demonic ruler of Magadha, Krishna with his whole Yadava clan, had vacated Mathura and migrated en-mass to Dwaraka—but this failure continuously pricked him for a long time. He was in constant lookout for some capable party or group that could be trusted with outsourcing of the great job of eliminating Jarasandha—the most demonic evil of that time. He studied the great Pandavas for their invincible capabilities and at the right time employed them to eliminate the demonic Jarasandha, thus creating another magnificent example of outsourcing.

The greatest work of outsourcing—ever performed in the history of mankind, ancient or modern—written or otherwise, was most magnificently executed by the wise Lord at the time of Mahabharata, by enabling and motivating

Pandavas—the invincible celestial warriors, to slaughter en-mass most of the organized evil forces which had elected to support Duryodhana, the great Kaurava evil, a sworn enemy of righteousness. In the great battle of Kurukshetra, lasting eighteen days, evil forces were totally and brutally eliminated under the valuable guidance of Lord Krishna who participated as an unarmed charioteer of Arjuna. He completed the major part of the job of freeing the earth from the accumulated forces, evil and wickedness—for which the great Lord had taken the trouble of adorning a human form. He achieved it so beautifully and efficiently through the vital process of outsourcing. Some students of Bhagavad Gita conclude that it was not Arjuna or Bhimma who had destroyed the armies of Kauravas and their allies—they were simply instruments in hands of Krishna, as effective out-sources of the wise Lord who let them have the credit for the job.

Outsourcing, thus, is a celestially approved management practice. It has potential to benefit the parties involved—outsourcer and the outsource both. Here, the most efficient—in terms of cost and output, gets a chance to perform in a perpetually competitive manner and benefits of works so performed are distributed far and wide—in a sweep of greater economic good.

Intense Rapport as a Management Tool

In public work environments, corporate or otherwise, a leader or manager encounters a variety of people, each one with a different prakriti and orientation. They attempt to connect to him in a variety of ways and with varied intensities. To be truly successful in public dealings, a good leader or manager should be able to put each one of such persons in **comfort zone,** allowing him or her to feel that a special rapport has emerged between the visitor and the visited. Such a development of **intense rapport** between a manager and his coworkers/ subordinates, a leader and his followers, a teacher and his students, a guru and his disciples—and in any other situation of similarity, will tend to promote an environment of positivism and cooperation, finally leading to smoother movement towards achievement of objectives being pursued.

Intense rapport (IR) is defined [9] as a situation of intensive interaction, independent of limitations of time and space, where junior participant of the association, does not hesitate to connect or request for help and the divine process of bonding ensures that;

- no undue difficulty is encountered in securing the connection,
- mutual pleasure is felt in serving or being served,
- none of the participant hesitates in demanding/expecting compliance, and

- no active obligation is created from any side.

In fact, a good manager or leader should be like Lord Krishna, who had special capacity for intense rapport with whosoever approached him in good faith or even otherwise—to let everyone feel existence of a special bond between his divine persona and the being attempting to come near to the Lord.

Despite the great magnitude of the **mission incarnate** responsibilities that Lord Krishna was burdened with, He made himself easily accessible to all of his friends, colleagues, disciples and devotees—at times, even to enemies. As the omnipotent Lord of the entire creation, his gracious nature was fully manifest during his human incarnation too. During childhood, He endeared himself to all the beings—humans, animals and otherwise. In Gokula and Vrindavana, every one—children or grown-ups, males or females, gopas or gopicas, calves or cows, loved him and wanted to relate to him, at the slightest opportunity. They all responded to his calls on flute, joining in dance circles and other activities, rarely raising any point of dissent. Further, they followed him to Vrindavana, abandoning Gokula without a whisper of disaffection. Each person, rather each being, experienced him as per his or her capacity and desire to relate to the divine magnetism. To the cowherd boys—He was their dear companion who frolicked with them whole day. To the gopicas (cowherd maidens), He was their sweet despair—always outwitting them with his pranks, yet making each one of them feel and believe that she was the most privileged one. For elders of the community, his respects always matched their adulations. To the high priests who performed sacrifices, He was the Lord who always accepted their offerings. No one was disappointed in want of nearness or rapport to the charismatic Lord—as he, sometimes, even multiplied himself to be with those who intensely so desired.

He endeared himself to Kabuja, the deformed oil girl of Mathura—and responded to her intense feelings—first pulling her out of deformity and subsequently fulfilling her desire to love and serve the young Lord, at her own house and in her own special manner.

At the ashram of the great guru Sandipani", He earned endearment from one and all—studying hard, on one hand, and performing well all other tasks assigned to or expected of him, on the other. He did not disappoint his guru, even when the respected one made an almost impossible demand for locating his long lost son from depths of the Arabian sea. Intensity of Lord Krishna's rapport with his friends, devotees and disciples was immune to the normal adverse impact of time and space on such relationships. This fact, amongst others, was evidenced by the great Lord's deeply sensitive and responsive interactions in the following two cases;

- With gap of decades, when school friend Sudama, very hesitantly, came to see the Lord of Dwaraka, He was so amazed to experience the love and care from his old friend that he forgot the very purpose of coming and meeting the great Lord. Trials and tribulations of his long poverty and also its deprivations, totally escaped his mind. On the other hand, Rukmani, the chief consort of the Lord, felt jealous of the attention that the kind Lord showered on his old friend. And when Sudama returned, in the Lord's own royal chariot, to his village and failed to locate his old hut as the same was converted, through celestial courtesy, into a magnificent palace, his bewilderment lost all bounds. The meaning of friendship was truly redefined for the posterity to talk about and appreciate. The validity of intensity of rapport was established for all times to come.
- Draupadi, an intense devotee, too was not abandoned or ignored in her hour of inhuman torment and humiliation in the court of Duryodhana, despite the limitation of long distances that separated her from the caring Lord. Her clothing was being shamelessly pulled by Dussasana, the younger brother of evil Duryodhana. It was endlessly lengthened in such a manner that her tormentors were amazed and ashamed beyond expression. He attempted to smoothen her hurt and, hence, regularly visited her during the torturous exile of long years in inhospitable forests. It continued to remind the Pandava warriors about the need to decisively fight the evil and the wicked.

Lord Krishna always valued and respected merit and virtue, irrespective of its place of location and occurrence. Presence of the virtuous Vidura and the ardent commitment adherent Bhishma, in the camp of evil Duryodhana, did not deter the great Lord from an intense rapport and interaction with them. The grand warrior Bhishma recognized the presence of the **Master of the Universe** in Lord Krishna and hence had become his intense devotee. Vidura's erudition and virtuosity had always attracted the wise Lord's attention and appreciation.

Lord Krishna's intense rapport with the great Pandava warrior Arjuna is too well known to be dwelt upon in detail in the present context. He was Arjuna's guru as well as benefactor—He volunteered even to act as his charioteer during the epic battle of Kurukshetra. And it was only their intense rapport and interaction that gave birth to what is today known as the Bhagavad Gita or the Song of Wisdom.

Thus, the value of intense rapport between two participants of an association, irrespective of differences of seniority, erudition, authority or sex, cannot be over-emphasized. The bondage of intense rapport always ensures;

- **fulfillment of expectations from both the sides,**
- **instant cooperation and eventual performance excellence, and**
- **total fulfillment of objectivity of a given situation—without creation of any feelings of obligation or indebtedness.**

It would, therefore, be always beneficial to actively employ the tool of intense rapport, so effectively wielded by Lord Krishna, in all fields of human interactions, including the modern corporate management.

Internal Conflict Management

All human organizations—corporate, political or otherwise, possess some elements of internal conflict, an essential requisite for their existence and vibrancy. Within a molecule, constituent elements constantly exert intra-molecular forces of attraction and repulsion, for it to stay in form and be active. Similarly, intra-organizational conflict is an innate character of association. It is human nature or parkriti to conflict and criticise—only its manifestation and degree differs, as per participants involved and intensity of their interactions. Such conflicts, if not managed effectively and well in time, can inflict considerable damage, sometimes even negating the very purpose of association. In corporate environment, efficient conflict management plays a very vital role and senior corporate professionals can benefit a great deal through skilful employment of Lord Krishna's **inner-conflict management technology.**

Lord Krishna's brief for incarnating on the earth was to eliminate accumulated evil forces, which in the guise of human forms of kings and princes –intoxicated with power and effluence, had become machines of torture and exploitation. His job was not just to manage them, but to finish the same as efficiently as possible. Keeping the prime objective in view, after disposing of the demonic king Kamsa of Mathura, the undisputed chief of demonic forces at that time, Krishna restored the throne to Ugrasena, its original claimant. He did not, as a wise thought, burden himself with the day to day engagements of governance. He had to be free to plan and organize the major job for which He had taken the trouble of adorning a human form. Even after shifting to Dwaraka and establishment of a splendid capital and a huge empire, the Lord continued to operate without the formal charge of ruling the kingdom, though he was often called as Dwarkadheesh.

This intelligent arrangement afforded the Lord time and energy to operate on a wider scale as a warrior, politician and diplomat, for the vital purpose of consolidating righteous forces against the accumulated load of evil and wickedness. The mighty Yadava clan consisted of several sub-groups and it had a number of warriors of repute, young and old—always ready for greater action and newer opportunities to expand their vast empire. Whenever they were free from fighting their opponents or were free from campaigns for expansion of the empire, strains of internal conflict emerged in varying intensities. Some of their second and third level of leaders criticized each other, and at times, they did not even spare the great Lord. While for some the old fox Ugrasena, who ruled with the support and approval from Krishna, was the center of criticism, many others felt restricted for operating their personal agenda. There were comments and taunts—direct and indirect. Some youngsters acted without express permission of elders and often landed into sticky situations.

How did the Lord manage the huge Yadava clan, without the direct authority of a ruler, is a very fascinating subject for students as well practitioners of modern management, and an insight into the same can be of immense practical utility to the present corporate world. From an in-depth study of the eventful life of the Lord and his acts of wisdom and velour, it becomes apparent that He employed his hugely impressive and charming personality—his divine aura and charisma, to control and manage unavoidable internal conflicts in the vast and mighty Yadava clan. Lord Krishna was a man of celestial wisdom and He employed a divine technology to manifest the same. He acted as a magician of **smile, expression, charm, speech, etiquette, diplomacy and madhura**. His words were dipped in honey and the efficient Lord could easily disarm angry and agitated, just with a smile and a splash of charm. Most of the Yadavas who were not very skilled in the art of words, were easily handled while some others proved difficult, but the Lord's unique method of **madhura** always seemed to work, despite irritation and ennui. **Madhura** technology, the wise Lord practiced in combination with some of his other tested and tried techniques of manpower management, the chief components of which were

- leading by example.
- active appreciation of virtue and merit
- non-material motivation.
- supervised delegation.
- management of mind as means of superior control..

No disciple, friend or foe, could resist falling in line to the celestial charms of Lord's communication expertise.

Although, He succeeded in keeping the mighty and quarrelsome Yadavas as a united and invincible force, the divine Lord, some-times, was not happy doing the trouble shooting within his own organization. The Lord once expressed the feelings of discontent in this regard while conversing with the sage Narada [10], who often visited the Lord uninvited. The latter commented that the Lord had made a mistake in not assuming role of a direct ruler, after killing the demon Kamsa at Matura, right early in life. The wise Lord, however, did not seem to agree with the errant sage's opinion. In his divine opinion, directly assuming the role of a ruler would have created various limitations for the wise Lord, making the job of meeting the basic agenda of his incarnation much more difficult and cumbersome.

Without further elaboration in regard to the Lord's unique methodology of intra-organizational human resources management, in brief the "Madhura", it can safely be concluded that his wise and hugely successful approach could have wide utility in modern corporate situations of internal conflicts. Madhura, when suitably combined with his other renowned management practices, can yield far superior dividends, for free of cost promotion of cooperation and enhanced productivity.

Anger Management: A Necessity

Anger display is not uncommon in work environments. In senior-junior relationships, it is often the senior who experiences the need for anger expression—whether it is boss-subordinate, teacher-pupil, parent-child or any other combination. Possibly, it is the ingrained sense of authority in a position of seniority that prompts emotions to lose track and manifest as anger. Some seniors do so as an expression of right, on slight flash of challenge to their authority—while others may express the same, sensing a delay in not being automatically understood and or obeyed. Bosses, normally, are the most frequent vehicle of anger manifestation—and often, they fail to see or appreciate the junior's point of view. Some times, they may perceive the junior either not measuring up to expectation; willingly or otherwise, unable to see or appreciate their point of view. In case of anger outbursts, the offender or the boss—more often than not, fails to make the right impact. An imbalanced junior, often fails to pick up the intended point or in reactive response, avoids to do the needful. While the boss may mistake his anger expression as tool of persuasion or correction, the victim normally perceives it as unfair treatment. Juniors too experience the need for anger display but more often than not, they prefer to suppress the same out of considerations of (a) respect for authority, (b) lack of alternatives, and (c) the consequences that such expressions might result into.

More often than not, anger ends up deepening misunderstandings, perceived and or real. It is not good for creating rapport—or for enhancing productive work efficiency. In fact, anger is neither good management nor efficient communication. Since it does not motivate—it can not be categorized as a tool for performance up-gradation—though, in certain situations, it serves as tool of management—particularly when chastisement or discouragement, from an undesirable path or practice, is the objective.

Anger is a form of energy expression—more precisely that of negative emotional energy. Often, it has a misconceived utility for its expresser. While positive usages of anger are few and far between, its negative implications and consequences seem virtually endless. Despite its destructive nature, anger seems to be an essential evil or unavoidable part of human interactions—and hence, it has to be managed, in a manner that its productive potential is fully exploited and the negative impact is minimized. The best way seems to be to treat it with the **time lapse pill,** i.e. let the passage of time cool it. Besides, anger burst into words need to be avoided—as silent anger is more effective and much safer than its active verbal variety. Reply or even attempt to reply, is often misunderstood by the active party. Impression of defiance, active or passive, is always destructive. The faculty of memory, on part of human beings, complicates consequences of anger. Here, we can draw a leaf from animals—which do get angry but cool down or normalize very fast. Often, they tend not to linger it-- no longer than necessary.

Anger manifestation occurs with the escape of bottled up negative energy. Why this negative energy can not be put to productive usage? Theoretically, it seems possible to put anger energy to productive applications—but most people lack technology and training for the same. In fact, some worker unions have attempted to register their protest or anger by doing some extra work. Mahatma Gandhi successfully attempted to convert anger and provocation into passive resistance of satayagraha [11] and non-violence with most impressive results. He met anger with an effective anger antidote—turning it into an invincible weapon of human struggle management.

Beneath several manifestations of anger lies failure--often on part of the active partner. Failure in making the other party see your point of view—or appreciate it adequately or in right time, often gives rise first to frustration (i.e. loss of judgment how to handle the situation) and than to anger. Mahatma Gandhi, in his early life, failed in making the perpetrators of apartheid in South Africa, see his righteous point of view and it angered him so much that a meek and mild personality, turned into an effective fighter against injustice and discrimination. Much earlier, Lord Krishna was angered when Draupadi was disrobed and humiliated for no fault of her's. He constructively channeled his own anger into letting the Pandavas see and appreciate his point of view that the evil maker Duryodhana and his bunch of friends were to be suitably punished.

Negative aspects of anger manifestation mostly emerge from the fact that under influence of anger one loses the capacity of logical thinking and discrimination—resulting into imbalance of expressions as well as decision making. One becomes devoid of the powers of concentration in the right direction. Bhagavad Gita, the treatise of wisdom, dwells as under on this vital aspect of human behavior:

"From anger comes delusion, and from delusion loss of memory. From loss of memory comes the ruin of discriminative power, and from ruin of discrimination, the person perishes."

Lord Krishna calls absence of anger as daivi sampat or moral quality. He tells Arjuna, "The gateway to hell, destructive of the self, is of three kinds, namely lust, anger and greed. Therefore, one should forsake these three."

At the same time, He tells Arjuna to fight for his rights—irrespective of the fact that the opposing side had a lot of his relatives, seniors, gurus and friends. He stressed practice of **constructive anger**, what in other words is termed as the **Righteous Indignation.**

In normal life, anger can not be totally done away with—but, as to safeguard oneself from its destructive influence, it should be used in a controlled and righteous manner. It is a natural energy and when employed constructively, it can have immense utility in a variety of situations. In intelligently designed applications, anger can serve as a highly useful tool of management.

In corporate work environment, anger manifestations—more often from seniors than the rest, cause a lot of performance disturbance. Indiscriminate spills of negative energy by bosses, often damages conducive work environments. Its subtle impact is more injurious and persistent than the direct and the immediate one—generating silent resistance to suggestion, cooperation, initiative and innovation. Hence, as suggested by Lord Krishna, there should be only constructive and measured expressions of anger, better termed as righteous indignation, in support of what is correct or in opposition of what is incorrect, evil or wicked—and the initiative for the same should come from seniors. Seniors should not delude themselves by uncontrolled or non-constructive display of anger—and preferably, they should exploit the creative energies of anger, for superior motivation of the work force involved.

Participative Management

An effective manager is supposed to get work done, through and with people—whether subordinates or otherwise. Nothing much can be accomplished if he attempts to do every thing himself. Corporate managers are often hesitant to assign important work to their subordinates, even when the latter have necessary skills and expertise to perform the job. Sometimes, when little delegation is effected, requisite guidance is not volunteered, as the objective often remains to find faults in the event of failure.

In case of Lord Krishna, even a miner glance on his life and works, renders it brightly visible that the wise Lord made an effective use of the **Principle of Effective Delegation** or performance enhancement through motivation.

- Why did He not take up arms in support of Pandavas?
- Why did He not destroy Duryodhana and his group of evil makers—when an attempt was made to arrest him in the court of Hastinapura?
- Why did He not himself eliminate the super demon Jarasandha?

These and many other questions from the Lord's life are best explained with the fact that He was a superior manager, and that He got various jobs performed effectively through his wisely chosen disciples and subordinates who were endowed with basic strengths for the same. He could have undertaken all these tasks himself—but **management wisdom**, even in those ancient times, suggested otherwise. Perhaps, He did not want a blatant exposure of his divinity or celestial form, or He wanted his disciples and followers to attain adequate confidence and motivation. He was, in fact, a **perfect team manager.** The Lord desired all those involved in the fight against evil, to develop strong faith in righteousness and the need to protect the same. Perhaps, the Lord's purpose was to demonstrate that his mere presence was enough for his disciples to achieve results for which he had incarnated. He wanted **Karma** or action to unfold—as no rewards without efforts, He wanted to flow to people whatsoever close or dear to him. To the extent possible, He wanted to participate at the transcendental level. He had to be involved yet detached—not to be directly credited for. It is an important lesion for efficient corporate managers of today. The Lord's approach to delegation was in fact unique—He did not want his disciples to fail and hence, on the spot guidance when necessary, was provided to avoid unpleasant failures. For instance, He gave active signals of guidance to Bhimma while killing the demonic Jarasandha and Duryodhana—the two great leaders of organized evil

By his decision not to wield any weapon in the great war of Kurukshetra, the great Lord totally delegated the task of decimating the great warriors such as Bhishma, Drona and Karna,, who were invincible but had sided with evil forces of Duryodhna, to Pandavas and their allies. Yet He ensured his active presence at the site of action by becoming charioteer of Arjuna. And He rendered vital advice and guidance, without which the course of the struggle could have been totally different.

Lord Krishna, right early in youth, established the bright example of delegation, when He restored the kingdom of Mathura to Ugrasena, after killing Kamsa—the main evil force of that time. The young Lord was, however, always available to protect the newly liberated kingdom from outside attacks. Years later, when He persuaded the Yadavas to move to Dwaraka where they built a magnificent capital and extended their rule far and wide, He left the function of direct governance in hands of other competent Yadavas.

There exists no superior example of effective delegation, in entire history of war or management, modern or ancient, where crucial jobs were delegated so intelligently and credit apportioned so righteously. Practitioners of modern management can draw vital lessons of long term and universal applicability, from life and works of the wise Lord.

Talent Recognition and Management

In general terms, talent is defined as a person's ability—his or her intrinsic skills of thought, logic and performance, to have and employ information in suitable combination of aptitude, experience and character. It also includes one's ability to learn new skills and grow to higher levels of performance. A great guru or corporate professional should be able to quickly spot talent in a subordinate or disciple—and then enable to grow the same to superior levels, as per needs of a situation. Some people have a nose for it; they can smell talent on first exposure of a person. In the modern management, especially in realms of HRD and head-hunting, such skills are of great value. In corporate work environment, one is required to understand and determine the specific talent profiles needed for meeting its business objectives. However, it is not easy either to define an organization's talent requirement profile—or fulfill the same. And finding suitable people to cover such requirements is much more difficult—because despite a blurry hallo around the concept, talent is a seductive term—one which people seem to implicitly understand, in most cases, without adequate clarity of its essentials, behaviour and employment.

The word *talent* itself dates back to antiquity. For ancient Greeks, Romans and Hebrews, talent was a unit of weight, and it developed into a unit of money through exchange of precious metals of that weight. In time, the meaning and understanding of talent has grown in abstraction—from a unit of weight to—a unit of money—to a person's innate ability for superior action and output.

Professor Wee (2001) in his work on **Inspirations of Tao Zhu-gong, [12]** while discussing relevance of over 2500 years old practices of an oriental business wizard, stressed a great deal on talent spotting and its exploitation for superior business management—emphasis primarily relating to

- **Recognition of Talent**: There is need to recognize talent before it could be deployed or exploited in any manner. Recognition of talent primarily means the ability of management to spot and pick out the gifted and more capable people from the ordinary. People rich with talent and desire to use the same do not come by easily.

- **Bringing Talent on Board**; Recognition of talent is only the first step—as one should recruit them, or in other words, bring them on board—and it is a crucial operation—as priorities of the spotted talent may not coincide with that of yours.
- **Deploying Talent**: Right deployment of talent in view of its capabilities and willingness, is crucial for it to successfully perform an assigned task.
- **Relying on Talent**: It has always been a great challenge for CEOs and senior management to rely on talent and use the same towards furtherance of objectives of the organization involved. Just hiring and dumping them in some obscure corner is not enough. Talented people are often ego-rich and hence need very skillful handling.
- **Valuing Talent:** Talent must be valued and treasured-- for it to be productive in relevance to organizational goals. If ignored or neglected, it can either destroy itself or be substantially harmful to the organization. Talent is rarely neutral or lethargic.
- **Trusting Talent**: If a CEO or a professional is unable to fully trust the talent available at his disposal, then results turn to be negative to both the parties involved. When bosses are able to allow independence of action to their talented juniors or experts, results are superior and long-term.
- **Respecting Talent**: More than anything else a talented employee or associate requires respect from his seniors or employers—which, in essence, amounts to respecting his suggestions and judgments. In today's knowledge based work environment, it becomes still more important to assign requisite respect to talent.
- **Promoting Talent**: In addition to trusting, treasuring and respecting talented people, they need to be cultivated and groomed suitably through retraining or reassignment so that their skills continue to be relevant.
- **Retaining Talent**: Retaining talents and keeping them in good performing form is not easy—it needs superior skills of man-management and motivation.
- **Synergizing Talent**: Effective deployment of available talents in an organization and to make them cooperatively perform for common good is a highly skillful task, and CEOs and senior managers must perform the same if productive use of talent is to be achieved in good measure.

- **Managing Talent**: In fact, all that Professor Wee said in so many words, is adequately covered by the expression **managing talent** as management in its extent and spread encompasses all that is said under the various elaborations made by the learned professor.

In fact, and without doubt, Lord Krishna was the **greatest professor of management**—and also its greatest practitioner—in the whole written and non-written history of man-management. He possessed great ability for spotting and deploying talent, and over a time nurtured and employed the same—on one hand, for the benefit of its holder and on the other, for fulfillment of the larger objective of fighting and eliminating evil forces. At a very early stage, He spotted talent of his elder brother Balarama and employed the same to

- destroy the evil kingdom of Kamsa at Mathura.
- repulse for a long time attacks from the demonic king Jarasandha of Magadha.
- help persuade the mighty Yadava clan to migrate to Dwaraka from their traditional kingdom at Mathura.
- win large territories around Dwaraka, to build an un-enviable empire there.

Balarama always carried a plow which he employed as a weapon with devastating effect. He was very close to soil, forests and all other aspects of the nature, and the wise Lord exercised his superior persuasive skills to take best out of the industrious Balarama. His great skills related to plants and soil, were used to create a uniquely prosperous empire and an equivalently beautiful capital at Dwaraka, out of a desolate wasteland. Splendour and wealth of Dwaraka had no known parallel. These are just only a few of the uses that the wise Lord made of his elder sibling's celestial talents. Similarly, He made wise use of talents of other prominent members of the Yadava clan—including Akrura, Ugrasena, Sattaki, Daruka, Udhava, Samba and many others, for running the vast federal empire from Dwarka as its capital.

The greatest reservoir of talents that Lord Krishna spotted pertained to the Pandavas—his cousins through Kunti who was sister of his father Vasudeva, and was married to Pandu, a promising prince of the Kuru clan at Hastinapura. He had watched them discretely at the time of ceremonies of marriage of Draupadi to Pandavas, in king Drupada's capital. Through his uncommon skills, the wise Lord recognized them despite the fact that they had disguised themselves as Brahmins. He took initiative to go and talk to the Pandava warriors and took them in his protective circle of advice and guidance. The wise Lord advised them to accept their uncle Dharitarashtra's invitation to return to Hastinapura. Vidura, their uncle and a well-wisher, had brought personally the invitation from the blind king. Pandava brothers' reluctance to return to their parental kingdom was smoothly neutralized by the wise counsel of Krishna. Further, He accompanied them to Hastinapura, where He was instrumental in Pandavas' acceptance of a desert and desolate Khandavaparatha as their share of the kingdom. Through the wise advice, guidance and assistance from a benevolent Krishna, it was converted into a fertile and prosperous kingdom. Its capital Indraparastha, came to be known even more beautiful and vibrant than the Lord's own Dwarka.

Lord Krishna took special interest in the intrinsic capabilities of Arjuna who became the Lord's most capable and trusted disciple—in fact, the most potent agent in the hands of the all powerful Lord—in his campaign to substantially reduce the load of evils on the mother earth. Lord Krishna had also recognized massive strengths of Bhimma who came handy for wiping off the major part of the Kaurava forces in the battlefields of Kurukshetra. Special talents of Bhimma's son Ghatotkachha, Arjuna's son Abhimanyu, and Draupadi's brother Dharritadhumyna did not escape the wise Lord's notice, and He employed these young warriors with devastating impacts.

On the opposite side, Krishna spotted and accurately assessed destructive talents of his enemies such as Jarasandha, Kalayavana, Sishupala and many others and took necessary measures to first minimize their impact and finally eliminate them at appropriate times. In the Kaurava camp, invincibility of warriors such as Bhishma, Drona, Karna and Aswathamma was spotted and assessed in time--and strategies to eliminate or neutralize the same were worked out well in time.

In brief, Lord Krishna's campaign against evil forces was successful simply because of the great Lord's ability to recognize and assemble a great combination of talents in one camp—deploy, motivate and manage them into a truly invincible force. He was truly a master in talent management—and kept all components of his assemble of talent well motivated, trained, deployed, counseled, managed and provided for—without any trace of dissatisfaction or dissension—despite the highly trying conditions. He employed his uniquely efficacious technology of talent management enriched with non-materials motivation and madhura—to keep the every tool of useful or potentially useful talent, well sharpened and ready for employment as and when opportunities arose. Practitioners of modern management, corporate or otherwise, will do well if they could read through the wise Lord's life and works and pick up even a few invaluable pearls of management wisdom in regard to talent management and beyond. Corporate success will accelerate to a surprising pace when even a little of Lord Krishna's celestial management wisdom is imbibed and practiced.

Superior Team Management

Assembly and management of a good team is an essential requirement for a leader to perform—whether the field of activity for the concerned entity is sports, business or religion. Every leader, in fact, wants a **dream team**—like a cricket captain would like to have likes of Sachin Tendulkar, Gary Sobers and Don Bradman, in his team. In business, politics and religion too, without exception, great leaders attempt to assemble and maintain a dream team of their choice. Some succeed more equally than others, in consequence to intensity of efforts invested in that direction.

Performance energies of thought and action become available through a team only. Lord Krishna was fully aware of this fact--and He employed it to the maximum limits of its feasibility. Despite limitations of the ancient times, He attempted to assemble a **dream team** of virtuous and brave, in view of his specific objective of removal of accumulated evil and wickedness from face of the earth, for which He had incarnated. He succeeded a great deal in his efforts for acquiring the desired team, through innovative employment of **Superior Team Management Technology (STMT),** consisting of the following seven components.

- Active identification and assembly of team.
- Strengths specific deployment.
- Training for specific strengths.
- Non-material motivation of constituents.
- Superior delegation & guidance or active mentoring.
- Right credit apportioning for performance.
- Protection and development of team constituents.

For the purpose of right team assembly, the Lord launched his efforts fairly early. He brought Balarama along for company in childhood and also for assistance in early youth for effectively dealing with the great evil forces that had to be eliminated without delay. After eliminating the demon king Kamsa of Mathura, He enrolled the prominent Yadavas—namely Akrura, Sattaki, Ugrasena etc, in his camp. After a few years, when it became nearly impossible to withstand persistent attacks of the demonic Jarasandha and his evil allies, He persuaded the whole Yadava clan to move with him to Dwaraka, for establishing a more peaceful and prosperous kingdom.

Soon after, in the court of king Dhrupada of Panchala, on the occasion of swayumvera of Draupadi, He watched with keen interest, emergence of Pandavas who were missing after the fire episode at Varnavata. Since they were related to him—their mother Kunti being sister of Vasudeva, He promptly took them under his wings of protective guidance. As a consequence of the bond of marriage between Pandavas and the kingdom of Panchala, Dhrupada and his warrior son Dharisthadyumna became an active component of Krishna's camp.

Lord Krishna was aware of the background of the key characters of his time--the righteous as well as the evil and the wicked. He had information on circumstances of their birth and their consequent strengths and weaknesses. The wise Lord employed such secret information for desired results. He knew Bhimma's great physical strengths and his wrestling skills. Lord's long sworn enemy, the mighty demon Jaradsandha too was a wrestling enthusiast. Hence, prior to celebrations of the Rajasuya yajna of Yudhishtira, He took Bhimma and Arjuna, disguised as Brahmanas, to Magadha, knowing fully well that if challenged, his demonic opponent will elect to fight only with Bhimma, in preference to any one else in the group of three. The Lord knew that only Bhimma could kill the demon, for which the mighty Pandava was given right guidance at end of the long drawn fight.

Similarly, during the great battle of Kurukshetra, all members of the Pandava's camp were deployed as per their specific strengths. Yudhishtira was persuaded to visit Bhishma, one evening during the conflict and extricate secret of his death from the old but invincible warrior. Further, during the growing darkness of the evening, he was also employed to announce to the highly destructive and virtually unstoppable Drona that Ashwathamma was dead, which led the great warrior to drop his weapons. Yudhishtra's utterances were highly valued by one and all, for their maximal content of facts and truth. In an equally effective manner, Ghtotkacha—the Bhimma's son with demonic powers, was deployed to harass and injure warrior Karna who, out of frustration and helplessness, fired a celestial weapon that he had reserved for Arjuna. In an equally intelligent move, Draupadi's brother Dharishtadyumna, who was destined to kill the great warrior and guru Drona, was appointed as commander-in-chief of the Pandava forces.

Arjuna was the key player in the battle of Kurukshetra for killing Bhishma and Karna, the two invincible warriors in the Kaurava forces, and hence during Pandava's exile of thirteen years, he was sent to seek celestial weapons from Indra and other devas. It was part of the wise Lord's unique enabling or capability enhancement process for components of his team.

Motivation is the most vital requisite for keeping a team active and effective on long-term basis, especially when competition is severe and odds very high. After expiry of Pandavas' exile, when Duryodhana refused to restore their kingdom to the celestial brothers, Krishna had to remind them that as kshatriyas, they must fight for their rights. He had to refresh Bhimma about his vow to avenge the insults that Dussasana and Duryodhana had hurled at Draupadi.

The greatest act of motivation was, however, performed by the Lord when a depressed and nervous Arjuna refused to fight, as he saw no justification in killing many seniors and gurus in the opposing forces of Kauravas. The great Lord had to employ all his skills of **mind management** and brain-wash his reluctant disciple about (a) his dharma as a kshatriya, (b) indestructibility of soul, (c) the destiny of all the evil forces and their supporters to die, and (d) last but not the least, the Lord's own omnipotence as creator and master of the universe. It was indeed a tough job, and the long and arduous dialogue between the Lord and his inquisitive and argumentatively persistent disciple turned into a Song of Wisdom, widely known as Bhagavada Gita.

Lord Krishna employed the principle of delegation in uniquely effective manner. While He arranged Bhimma to destroy the mighty Jarasandha, the principal leader of evil forces pitched against righteousness, He was present and alert to give the right and vital signal without which it would not have been possible for the Pandava warrior to kill the invincible and arrogant demon. The Lord's right mentoring and timely guidance was most vital. It was a case of well-supervised delegation. The credit of the good job done went to the Pandava warrior, while the accountability all through stayed with the Lord.

Lord Krishna was always very careful and judicious in apportioning credit for a good job done, whether the performer was Arjuna, Bhimma, Abhimanyu, Dharisthadyumna and or any other warrior.. He practiced the same just and encouraging approach at Dwaraka with his Yadava warriors. This kept every vital participant of his camp active and proudly performing.

Lord Krishna took pains to provide protection to and look after well being of all of his disciples and followers. When Draupadi ran into problem at hands of Duryodhana and his brothers, the Lord in his own invisible but effective way protected her modesty and surprised her tormenters. In thick of the battle of Kurukshetra, when an infuriated Karna sent a sure weapon on Arjuna, the divine charioteer, sensing the danger in nick of time, pushed the chariot five fingers into the ground, thus saving the Pandava warrior's head.

Ashwathamma, a long time friend of Duryodhana, was greatly annoyed at the brutal demise of the last Kaurava, and to avenge the same, in darkness of the night, he attacked residential camp of the Pandavas when all the five sons of Draupadi were killed while asleep. Uttarai who was carrying Abhimanyu's son in her womb too was grievously hurt. The kind Lord saw to it that the child in her womb survived and was delivered safely. He was named Parikshat. He grew into a charming and righteous prince and continued the renowned Pandava legacy for a long time.

To the extent possible, Lord Krishna kept active track of righteousness people and in pursuance of the same, took the Pandava brothers to the old and wise warrior Bhishma who lay wounded in the battlefield and waited for the right time to depart from this world. The whole post Mahabharatha generation benefited from the wise counsel rendered by the departing warrior in relation to the methodology of good governance. After completion of the mandatory period of mourning and relevant rituals, Krishna helped Yudhishtira ascend to the thrown of Hastinapura. The work of governance was wisely distributed among the Pandava brothers, as per their capabilities and interest

To conclude, one can safely state that Lord Krishna employed a very judicious and rewarding methodology of capable dream team assembly and its productive management, for a long period full of challenges and uncertainties, in face of formidable competition. Practitioners of modern management can greatly benefit from some his methods that seem extremely practical even after lapse of over five thousand years.

Superior Management of Uncertainties

Uncertainties in any work environment, especially business and governance, can present a situation of nemesis, even to the most experienced professionals. Some executives decide to hedge their bets through diversification of resources deployment—while for others, wait and watch becomes a more preferred option. This traditional approach often leads executives to view uncertainties as a bifocal phenomenon—that the world is either certain or uncertain i.e. predictable or unpredictable. On deeper analysis, it seems to be a defective approach in the sense that in absence of a factual assessment, uncertainties tend to remain underestimated from the point of their damage genesis potential. It may lead one into a position of defenselessness against emerging threats. Loss of unnoticed opportunities is another likelihood in such a situation—as planning to benefit from the same is not resorted to, under such an eventuality.

Entirely unpredictable or very difficult to predict situations can lead managers to abandon the analytical choice of the traditional planning process altogether and base their strategic decisions primarily on the **gut instinct.** On the other hand, risk-averse managers who do not trust their gut instincts may suffer from decision paralysis—which, in most situations, can be substantially damaging. Normally, the managers who are either basically deficient in **energy of thought and mind** or suffer from job related skills deficiencies, respond in this manner. Persons with excessively negative tendencies too may land corporate bodies into such sticky situations.

Lord Krishna, in various phases of his life and works, encountered situations of intense uncertainties. With his superior skills of situation analysis, He was able to employ the **intensity of uncertainty** as tool for effective determination of options and alternates—for each demanding situation. Several incidents from the divine life and works of this great manager and decision maker, illustrate this fact very clearly.

- When faced with an urgent need for shifting his cowherd community out of Gokula, possibly on account of depletion of resources of food and fodder, with his very young but fast acting skills of analysis and instinct, He took a quick decision regarding the opportunities offered by the virgin pastures and forests of Vrindavana. The young leader—almost a child at that time, must have summoned all his skills of superior communication and logic to convince elders of the community to share and appreciate his point of view..
- The catch 22-situation in which the whole Yadava community had landed itself on elimination of Kamsa, the demonic ruler of Mathura, by the young Krishna, presented itself as an immense uncertainty. Widowing of two daughters of Jarasandha on death of Kamsa, had made the aggrieved father take a vow for avenging the same. He was a powerful demonic ruler of Magadha—and had great boons, resources and allies. He repeatedly attacked Mathura, almost with predictable frequency—and each time with greater vigour and resources of destruction. Although, the warrior pair of Balarama and Krishna was able to safeguard Mathura, but they never really succeeded in decisively defeating the persistent evil. It never left the mighty Yadavas in peace or with energy and resources to develop and grow into a big empire.
- Several other evil forces, joining hands with the mighty Jarasandha, had made him almost invincible. Further, the Pandava brothers had not yet emerged on the scene to extend a helping hand or to be instrumental in tackling this formidable evil. On occasion of the eighteenth attack from this evil enemy of Lord Krishna, in logical assessment of prowess of the invader, the Yadavas faced the likelihood of a sure defeat. Krishna, at such an early stage of his life, did not desire to exhibit his Godliness. Quite possibly, He did not see the right opportunities for the large and mighty Yadava clan to grow and develop into an empire of celestial proportions at Mathura. It was surrounded with such empires or kingdoms which could not be subdued easily. Hence, in face of situations of immense uncertainties, the young Lord decided that it was better and safer to vacate Mathura and migrate en-mass to Dwaraka, located on the western sea coast of the country. He convinced the proud Yadaya clan to bear the taunts and humiliations associated with the situation, in hope of a better and more prosperous future.

- In the post Panchala phase when Pandava brothers returned to Hastinapura after winning Draupdi as their bride, they were allotted the desolate desert expanse of Khandavaparastha, as their part of the kingdom by their uncle Dharistarashtra. The harsh reality of the situation presented a totally uncertain future—and they were in two minds whether or not to accept the offer. Krishna who was present on the occasion, in a moment assessed the enormity of the uncertainty encountered by the Pandavas, and in view of his first hand experience with a similar situation encountered at Dwaraka, advised them to accept the offer. Through hard work coupled with scientific approach—and under expert guidance of Krishna, it was transformed into a highly productive land of plenty and unmatched riches. Their capital city Indraparastha became known for its beauty, splendour and wealth—sending waves of jealousy in hearts of Duryodhana and his evil friends at nearby Hastinapura, as many prosperous traders shifted from there for greater opportunity offered by the new capital.
- When Pandavas had established an impressive empire at Indraparastha—and many kings and princes of nearby kingdoms had accepted their supremacy, Yudhishtra wanted to celebrate **Rajasuya** but the presence of the invincible demonic ruler Jarasandha of Magadha on the scene, presented a situation of immense uncertainty—as his joining hands with the other anti-Pandava forces could have derailed the whole plan. Lord Krishna through his massive **thought warriorism** evolved a way to destroy this old enemy of Yadavas, employing the unparallel action warriorism of the mighty Bhimma. Udhava, a bright disciple and devotee of Krishna had suggested a noble plan.
- Whether Arjuna will fight or abandon his duty as a warrior, in face of the challenge that he faced, i.e. the inevitable need to kill his elders and relations present in the opposing line-up of forces in the battlefields of Kurukshetra, presented a situation of total uncertainty for Lord Krishna. His whole long-term design of things for massive elimination of evil forces was at risk of failure.

Through superb display of thought warriorism, in intense and arduous argumentation with Arjuna, and finally through the need based display of his omnipotent multilateral cosmic form, He subdued the adamancy of his depressed and disoriented disciple. Finally, Arjuna did as desired by the great Lord. The post Kurukshetra situation brought on those who survived the battle, even a greater challenge of uncertainty, to rebuild the ruined empire and heal wounds and scars of the disaster. Here, the wise Lord's **Song of Wisdom** that He had delivered to his disciple Arjuna, came very handy in ameliorating the desperate situation.

Perusal of the life and works of Lord Krishna, thus reveals that situations of uncertainties, whatsoever great they might seem to be, need not fox true professionals into imbalance or desperation. Energies of thought and action when employed in right combination, are bound to subdue all such adversities into favorable developments. These wisdom distillates from the Great Guru and Master of Management should serve well our present and future armies of professional managers and corporate functionaries.

Time Management

While delivering the renowned Song of Wisdom to Arjuna, Lord Krishna deliberated in detail on *time* and its importance, in respect to individuals, organizations, kingdoms, regimes and all that falls under umbrella of the universe. He stressed the omnipotence of time—its all pervading influence on all happenings and occurrences. He elaborated that the wheel of time always moves—it is never static and that time is most powerful--as it encompasses all changes into itself. Time does not grow old, stale or unproductive. With time always comes change, in every living being—small or big. New buds, leaves, flowers and fruits come with time. Seeds germinate and grow—and seasons change in regular sequence. Time makes the *Circle of Life* and it remains and keeps every thing in perpetual motion. Time governs response of man to various situations—dharma and adharma, right and wrong, action and inaction—and everything else—living or non-living. It is the *Celestial Tool* that manages everything and every occurrence in the whole universe.

The very fact of its omnipotence lies behind the importance that every student and practitioner of modern management today assigns to **Time Management**—and mostly without much success. Being a celestial resource, time is beyond human control; we can only use and or misuse it as per an individual's wisdom, efforts and capacity.

Time and timing, both are important for any human venture—commercial or non-commercial. It is crucial for war, as well as, for peace and business. For launch of any project and or product, importance of time and timing can not be overemphasized as competition and opportunity both are time related. And despite practice and efforts of generations, we still do not get it right for obvious reasons. The right way to use and or manage the vital element of time still eludes us.

Lord Krishna was **Master of Time Management**. He was very astute and selective in relation to time and timing of all of his activities—whether related to love, governance, diplomacy or war. He selected the timing of the epic battle of

Kurukshetra in right relation to season, soil conditions, and availability of food and fodder—for the huge multitude of men and animals that were to assemble there. All of his interventions on behalf on Pandavas or other forces of righteousness, represented masterly selection of time and timings.

Lord Krishna very rightly timed his interaction with the Pandava brothers at Panchala-- at the time of their marriage to Draupadi. They had escaped from the furry of fire at Varnavata and as their disguise had come off; they needed advise and guidance for future course of action. Whether or not to accept the invitation of their uncle—the blind king Dhritarashtra, to return to Hastinapura, was a question of crucial importance. For the wise Lord, it was the most appropriate time to take them under his celestial protection and guidance. Any earlier attempt, in this direction, would have been counter productive.

Krishna superbly timed his long distance celestial assistance to protect Draupadi from the evil attempts of Duryodhana and his friends, to disrobe her in Hastinapura court, in full view of all the respectable assemblage. When Pandavas lost the game of dice and were banished to harsh forest life, the wise Lord critically timed his visits to share their problems and pains, on one hand, and influence their thought process for future actions, on the other. He played with the psyche of the banished warriors, especially Draupadi and Bhimma--whose feel of hurt and agony had to be kept alive in interests of the destined events that were to unfold after completion of their exile. Additionally, He had to cement his bond of trust with them—and to give them hope for a bright future that awaited them.

In course of the epic battle of Kurukshetra, Lord Krishna as an unarmed advisor to the Pandava camp, superbly timed his assistance to the forces of righteousness. At a very critical moment, in dead heat of the battle, when an enraged Karna fired a deadly weapon targeting Arjuna's head, the celestial charioteer—in nick of time, dipped the chariot a few inches into the ground--thus saving the Pandava warrior from certain doom. Clouding the sun and creating an illusion of sun-set, a few minutes before the due time, He saved Arjuna from self immolation on his failure to keep his pledge to kill Jaidharatha, to avenge the latter's decisive role in killing of Abhimanayu, in contravention of the code of ethics of war prevalent at that time. There were numerous other instances of rightly timed interventions by the wise Lord in bringing the epic battle to the desired conclusion. Elimination of the most impressive line up of invincible warriors on side of Kauravas, namely Bhishma, Drona, Karna, Jaidharatha and Duryodhana, became possible only through the timely advice and assistance from the unarmed Lord.

Much before the massive evil elimination exercise of Kurukshetra, Lord

Krishna perfectly timed the killing of his sworn and invincible enemy Jarasandha—through rightly timing it with the celebration of Rajasuya yajana by Yudhishtra, for the success of which the Pandava warrior Bhimma was skillfully employed by the wise Lord. An in depth study of the life and works of the divine Lord, only one instance comes to view where the great Lord acted as per time and timing selected by someone else. It pertained to the elimination of the evil king Kamsa of Mathura, who himself—as per-provisions of destiny, had invited young Krishna and Balarama, with a plan to kill them under pretext of participation in certain festivities.

Just after freeing Mathura from the evil rule of Kamsa and handing over the job of governance to his maternal grandfather Ugrasena, the young Lord along with elder brother Balarama, proceeded to the ashram of renowned guru Dandipani, a long distance away in center of the country, to acquire formal education necessary for the upcoming princes of the Yadava kingdom. There, the young Krishna created a unique record in **most efficient time management** by working hard and completing a several years course just in sixty four days—mastering the available disciplines of scriptures, logic, astrology, astronomy and technologies of war and governance at the astonishing rate of one per day. Such a bright exercise in time management has never been repeated.

Further, the wise Lord's decision never to visit Gokula and Vrindavana, after He left the place at the invitation of the evil king Kamsa, was also only a part of effective time management—as any physical link with these places would have amounted to drain on his precious time—and an agony to his numerous lovers and devotees for inadequacy of time spent with them. Hence, a physical disconnection was the best and the least painful solution to this massive problem of broken hearts. There is an endless list of actions of Lord Krishna in the field of superior time management, detailing which may not serve any further useful purpose from a reader's angle—as what is said above is more than sufficient for a wise mind to grasp the wise Lord's celestial technology of productive time management.

Modern practitioners of management, whether engaged in corporate or governance, are widely dissatisfied with the outcome of their efforts towards efficient time management. No one is able to achieve any where near to his or her desire or plan. Stress and friction within the work environment is such that most of the efforts in direction of superior time management do not bring adequate results. Dissatisfaction is wide and open and experts and gurus seem to be at their wits ends. It is natural and was destined to happen this way—because time is a celestial resource and ordinary approach, in this regard, is bound to bring only ordinary results. To deal with time in a more satisfying and productive manner, one will have to resort to the teachings and technology of Lord Krishna, especially in regard to employment of the principles of karma and dharma—reducing the presently excessive concern for result and augmenting the righteousness content of actions. Once engagement with results is minimized and righteousness of actions is enhanced, stress and friction in work environment will diminish substantially—sprouting cooperation, initiative and innovation. Resultant positivity of thought and action is bound to spring greater productive interaction amongst individuals and work groupings or teams—and with such an occurrence superior performance and output will flow effortlessly—achieving more with less time and efforts, creating greater goodwill and well-being. And that is what superior time management is aimed at, in terms of its objectives.

Sanctity of Objective

Lord Krishna was a **Mission Incarnate** who was born in human form with the specific purpose of ridding the earth of accumulated evil and wicked forces which were exploiting and tormenting the masses, particularly the righteous and virtuous. Highly undisciplined and selfish ruling classes, at that time, had assumed demonic behaviour of intolerable proportions. He had specific, rather divine, terms of reference—which had to be fulfilled within the specified time. Objective always needs to be central in business or war. In incarnate context, it turns sanctimonious—because deviation of any degree or extent is not expected or provided for. With a little loss of track or laxity, the whole exercise can be lost—one can be overtaken or taken over. In corporate plans, short and long term objectivity is always defined—and resources are accordingly assigned or collected. And situation is not any different in case of war as well, irrespective of scale and whether the adversary is an evil force or otherwise. Even for five year plans which are primarily aimed at the economic and social development of the country, due care is taken to set detailed sector and activity-wise objectives or targets. Again, assessment of progress or evaluation of works completed, is based on its primary objectivity—defined right in its beginning or as revised periodically. Objective specification serves as a beacon or direction finder for executives and workers to stay on course and achieve the specified goals within limits of time and resources.

Lord Krishna respected the centrality of objective of his mission, all through his activities as child, youth, warrior, ruler, diplomat and saviour. What was righteous and virtuous had to be supported against all odds. Right in childhood, He had to subdue the demonic naga king Kalia who had created a nuisance by poisoning the waters of Yamuna and terrorized all those who came his way, animals or humans, to quench their thrust or take bath. Unmindful of his own safety, the little Krishna jumped on to the multihooded head of the dreadful serpent monster—and danced on the same with such ferocity and abandon that the evil serpent had to ask for forgiveness—offering to immediately vacate the waters that were so very vital for the cowherd community and their animals. This unique act of little Krishna earned him the title of **Natwara**, the unsurpassable celestial dancer. Here, in mind of the little Lord, the central objective of forcing the great serpent to vacate the said waters was supreme, without concern to the methodology employed. For him the end was more important than the means employed.

Similarly, while attempting to eliminate his arch enemy of long standing—the demonic Jarasandha [13], evil king of Magadha, Lord Krishna did not hesitate to approach him, disguised as Brahmans—along with Bhimma and Arjuna, and when recognized, He tricked the great demon to accept a one to one wrestling dual with Bhimma. During the combat that dragged for several days—and when the Pandava warrior was not able to make any decisive progress, the Lord lifted a little leaf of plantain, split it into two and signaled to Bhimma while throwing the same into two opposing directions. Bhimma took the clue and did the needful by tearing the opponent into two –and throwing the same in such a manner that the two halves had to chance of coming together.

Krishna did not physically participate as an active warrior in the battle of Kurukshetra. As per the choice offered, Duryodhana preferred to take the mighty Yadava army on his side—and Krishna, without wielding any weapon, became the charioteer of Arjuna. Yet, Krishna's role in the war was not free from controversies. For him the objective of victory of the righteous Pandavas was more important than the likelihood of some disagreement on appropriateness of the means employed for achieving the same. In views of some critical commentators, during the epic battle of Kurukshetra, the forces of righteousness operating under indirect guidance of Lord Krishna, exceeded the **righteousness of means** employed, in getting rid of several of the great warriors namely Bhishma, Drona, Jaidharatha and Karna, who were present in the opposing camp of Kauravas.

Even the final acts of war, namely elimination of Duryodhana at hands of Bhimma, needed Krishna's skills to remind the Pandava warrior that there was the need for him to fulfill his own vow of breaking the thighs of his most dreaded opponent. While the Pandavas camp had no warriors(except Arjuna) comparable to Bhishma, Drona and Karna (which had made Duryodhana intensely arrogant and unwisely adamant), the Kauravas had no strategist of Lord Krishna's calibre. Further, they suffered from the total absence of sustainable objectives.

In fact, sustainability of objectives of any action or campaign gives rise to

the *Centrality of Objective* which in final turn causes the *Sanctity of Objective* to emerge—with which the operating group develops alignment or commitment for its achievement. Resources deployed or means required have to be in proportion to the challenges poised by such objectivity of an operation. Practitioners of the modern management can draw highly useful clues from the Lord Krishna's assignment of sanctity to the objectives that happened to fall upon him in reference to his mission incarnate activities.

Superior Failure Management

Encounters with failure are often unavoidable in every one's life. They get significantly amplified in case of leaders—whether political, corporate, religious or otherwise. Despite best intentions, efforts may fall short of creating stresses necessary for genesis of target results—or the combination of opposing forces may be too strong for a desired orientation to develop. Failures can take a variety of forms often unexpected ones. They could relate to men, materials, plans, strategies or a combination of various causatives. In all the situations, they need to be tackled and managed, the first priority being damage control. Corrective measures or alternatives, immediate or as delayed response, are the basic follow-up requirements. While the first requires a quick decision which may or may not be the best one, the second or the delayed response comes from active thinking. This phase represents a sort of transformation, i.e. to dump the old approach and to come up and try a new one may be a totally different or radical one. And such alternatives, in some instances, can turn out to be very bitter and unpalatable to the people involved. In principle, such transformations should be smooth and systematic; simultaneous on various fronts which may or may not alter the basic rhythm, character and objective of existence of an organization. It is like change of a caterpillar into a butterfly. This biological process called **metamorphosis** apparently looks simple and painless but when it happens or made to happen in human organizations, corporate or otherwise, can be terribly painful and inconvenient. On completion, it can be truly rewarding too like a butterfly; impressive to look at, admire and appreciate.

To lead an organization through radical change or through difficult times, especially as an attempt of failure management, needs a truly uncommon leadership that can take tough and unpleasant decisions, face criticism and outbursts, and still keep the organizational ship on right course—in direction of its specific objectives. It requires men of intellect, courage and commitment, equipped with nerves of steel. Failures, if not remedied or managed well in time, tend to develop into fully blown crisis situations, leading eventually to unpleasant results and disappointments.

Lord Krishna, despite being a mission incarnate and a **wisdom concentrate,** could not, at several occasions, avoid running into situations of failure, during his long and arduous campaigns of freeing the earth of accumulated evil and wicked forces. His life as a cowherd, a warrior, a ruler, a diplomat and/or a charioteer, was not always a bed of roses. He faced numerous challenges—some truly difficult ones. With his uncommonly superior capabilities, while most of these challenges were settled with positive outcomes, a few turned out to be so gigantic that his true greatness and even Godliness faced toughest possible tests of wisdom, valour and diplomacy.

The first great failure that He encountered was the persistence of attacks on Mathura by the asura king Jarasandha of Magadha—seventeen attacks to be precise, each more savage than the previous one. Although, through all of these attacks, Krishna and Balarama were able to defend the kingdom of Mathura but Jarasandha, the persistent irritant, was not eliminated. This demonic irritant was father-in-law of Kamsa, the cruel ruler of Mathura who was killed by Krishna, to free His parents from long captivity and also as relief to the long suffering people of the kingdom. Some experts on life and times of Lord Krishna, felt that the persistent demonic attacker was left off the hook by the Lord for some unexplained design or reason. Probably, destiny willed it that way.

Further, Jarasandha had acquired a friend called Kalayavana who had a vast army of malechas and he himself flouted a unique boon to the effect that he could not be killed by any warrior of Yadava origin. Hence, a time came when against the combined strengths of Jarasandha and Kalayavana, the Yadavas faced a certain defeat. And so early in career of the young Lord, a defeat at hands of demonic forces would have been truly disastrous for His divine mission of eliminating the evil forces from face of the earth. Sensing this insurmountable challenge, Lord Krishna employed His divine skills of communication to let the brave Yadavas see the writing on the wall and convinced them, with the hope of a successful fight at a later date, to abandon their well established and prosperous kingdom and migrate to a distant and desolate Dwaraka, on the western sea front of the country. It was a radical decision—a totally uncommon solution to a situation of failure or rather a crisis of Himalayan magnitude. Moving out with all of His followers and devotees to a situation of total uncertainties, must not have been an easy task from any point of view. The young Lord must have debated this move in all possible details, with elder brother Balarama, the wise old Ugrasena and various other key warriors and commanders of the vast Yadava clan. There must have emerged serious differences of opinion and perceptions—creating immense frustrations, bitterness and discontent.

To subdue such dissensions and disagreements, the young Lord employed

His celestial charm and skills of **madhura communication**. There is, however, no reference to any rebellion in the Yadava clan to this inconvenient—and, to an extent, an apparently dishonorable move on part of the Lord. Evidence of the great Lord having employed His cosmic manifestation for subduing the proud Yadavas into acceptance of this uncommon move is also not visible. This unique challenge encountered by Lord Krishna was, from any standards, more serious and demanding than, in the present day corporate context--either having to change a product line or to shift a plant location. In fact, a comparative contemporary situation or a situation of comparative magnitude seems wholly impossible to find. But the wise Lord took this--apparently unwise decision and implemented it with supreme professional efficiency, creating a vast and prosperous Yadava empire on the western coast of India. Within a short period, wealth and splendour of Dwaraka became famous world over—and in due course, the glorious Yadava empire became truly powerful to implement the wise Lord's larger design of eventually eliminating evil and wickedness from face of the earth. For this uncommon act of failure management or a deliberate mask of failure, Lord Krishna acquired the derogatory epithet of **Ranchood**. He, however, did not seem to mind it—and finally His decision turned out to be uniquely successful. At Mathura, it was not possible to create a large and powerful empire as it was encircled by well established and strong kingdoms such as Hastinapura, Panchala and Magadha, just to name a few. Thus, through His unique decision making and management skills, Lord Krishna was able to convert

- a serious failure into a great opportunity.
- a crisis of vast magnitude into a massive blessing.
- a disgrace and humiliation into perpetual admiration.
- a weakness into a massive strategic strength.

Finally when opportune time came, Lord Krishna successfully eliminated Jarasandha, employing the mighty Bhimma as the right tool. Hundreds of kings and princes whom the demonic Jarasandha had kept imprisoned for sacrifice and celebration, were released in one go, creating a wave of appreciation and gratitude in favor of the Pandavas and their mentor—the divine Lord. This was the final act of the **classic failure management** implemented with superb planning and patience.

The second case of substantial failure, the great Lord encountered at the court of Kauravas, where He had volunteered to go—as an emissary of Pandavas and make a last ditch attempt for obtaining a minimum reasonable settlement for them. He presented the righteous Pandavas' case with the utmost force of reason and logic, facts woven in a divine web of diplomacy and reality. As a divine solicitor of righteousness and fairness, He stressed costs of conflict and benefits of cooperation. The whole assemblage of learned and wise men benefited from His celestial presentation that could not be faulted from any angle or account. But an adamant and arrogant Duryodhana refused to be convinced. He even refused to heed the wise Lord's plea for granting just five villages to the five Pandavas, as a last resort to avert the fratricidal conflict that seemed inevitable in the event of failure of this celestial mission of conflict resolution. Not only all the divine logic and arguments of Lord Krishna fell on deaf ears, Duryodhana—the great leader of the evil forces, attempted to seize and confine the mighty Lord, as a foolish attempt to force the Pandavas to desist from demanding any part of their kingdom. This unwise attempt aborted in face of Duryodhana and his evil cooperators--as the great Lord displayed his **omnipotent cosmic form** that dazzled whole the court assemblage out of balance and a duly chastised Duryodhana beat a hasty retreat.

The great Lord left empty handed—it was a mission failure of great magnitude. He did not attempt to destroy all the assembled Kauravas in one quick sweep—(a) to avoid a charge of total partiality, and (b) this job was destined to be subsequently completed by the Pandavas, under the mask of righteous justification. As per the Lord's scheme of things, this failure was to be converted into success—or rather a great success. On one hand, He motivated the dejected Pandavas to prepare for a fight for the finish, and on the other, engaged himself to find ways and means of eliminating the massive line-up of invincible warriors on side of the opponent Kauravas. Soon after, the job was done with the considerable speed and efficiency, on the battle-fields of Kurukshetra, where the epic battle lasted eighteen days—and in the process, the great master of the universe delivered the immortal **Song of Wisdom,** the renowned **Bhagavad Gita** for the benefit of the posterity.

Prior to the commencement of the great battle of Kurukshetra, Lord Krishna again faced an uncommon and unexpected challenge, when Arjuna—his trusted disciple and most valuable warrior, noticing a line-up of his numerous elders and relatives in the opposing Kaurava forces, refused to fight. He logically and forcefully argued that it was not of any worth for him to kill so many people for the mere purpose of regaining the kingdom and that he would not mind even if he had to beg and survive—or even if the sons of Dharitarashtra killed him for their pleasure and satisfaction. His duty as a warrior did not mean anything and that he was prepared to try and explore the other ways of salvation i.e. janana or bhakti. No argument of the Lord cut any ice with the adamant and argumentative warrior. Lord Krishna almost sensed a defeat but He did not want the work of his whole life-time to turn into total waste. He did not want the evil forces to have the last laugh.

So, as a last resort, in order to push a demoralized, dejected and depressed Arjuna into action, the great Lord was not left with any option but to suitably coerce the non-cooperative warrior. As a last resort, He assumed his omnipotent cosmic form adorned with all the celestial beings and devas. He told an astonished Arjuna that the master of the universe desired him to act and do the job as a warrior--and in doing so he shall not collect any discredit because the warriors about whom he was so worried, were already dead as per the desire and design of the great master. It made Arjuna tremble with fear and he took no time to request the master of the universe to assume his normal mortal form and assured him that he was prepared to do as desired by the wise Lord. This great dialogue between the mighty Lord and his reluctant disciple lasted a long time – which on account of the celestial camouflage employed by Lord Krishna, was not sensed by any one present, except by the wise-old Bhishma who was also a great admirer and devotee of the Lord. Here again, a failure or near failure was converted into a great success by Lord Krishna as—(a) Arjuna was successfully coaxed into doing the Lord's bidding, and (b) the celestial dialogue formed the basis of what is today known as the Bhagavad Gita, a store house of knowledge and code of conduct for a civil society.

In the post-Kurukshetra era, more towards the final phase of his life on the earth, Lord Krishna developed active dissatisfaction with the developments within the mighty Yadava clan. Internal feuds in this mighty grouping of warriors, their growing indiscipline and deviations from righteousness, were causing considerable pain and disquiet for the wise Lord. He even consulted with the wondering sage Narada on this unique problem but no suitable solution seemed to emerge. The wise Lord did not want the deviating Yadavas to assume demonic proportions after his departure from this earth. He was afraid that his good name and works of life time might come to total negation. Something drastically corrective was to be attempted.

Hence, in final appreciation of righteousness, He planned and executed a massive armed internal battle amongst the warrior force of Yadavas, under conditions of drunken celebrations at Parbhasa—a sea front location some distance away from Dwaraka. To impart a clean finish to the job, the righteous Lord himself slew a number of the feuding Yadava warriors. It was the wise Lord's final fight against evil or potentially evil forces—and on its clean completion, He himself departed from this earth under a celestial shower of flowers. This truly great and indeed preventive management of potentially explosive failure, saved the wise Lord from earning the blame of not completing the basic objectives of his incarnation. It also earned him the image of total impartiality in dealing with people—related or unrelated. And by doing so He re-stressed all that was told to Arjuna during his renowned Song of Wisdom on the battle grounds of Kurukshetra. He left no gap between preaching and practice.

The modern management community-students, teachers and its professional practitioners, irrespective of their place and nature of engagement, have a mine-field of fully tested lessons buried in the life and works of Lord Krishna, in regard to tackling and management of situations of failures. The author does not intend to draw a listing of such lessons as it would be more beneficial for readers to attempt and develop the same at their individual levels.

Notes

1. Sandipani ashram was reported to be located at Ujjain in the central Bharata.
2. Sansara or Samsara refers to the mortal world.
3. EDP stands for electronic data processing.
4. SWOT is the short form of strengths, weaknesses, opportunities and threats analysis.
5. Refers to warriors from outside Bharata.
6. One who runs away from battlefield.
7. Do Lunch or Be Lunch by H. N. Stevension, Harvard Business Press, Boston, Missachusetts, p. 8.
8. It may soon develop self-limiting characteristics.
9. By the author.
10. Sage Narada, son of Lord Brahma, was a devotee of Krishna and had immense capacity to create trouble for friends as well as foes.
11. It stresses insistence on truth in a passive way.
12. Wee Chow Hou (2001),"The Inspirations of Tao Zhu-gong" published by Prentice Hall, Pearson Education Asia Pte Ltd, 317 Alexandra Road, Singapore 159965.
13. Jarasandha, as per circumstances of his birth, could instantly rejuvenate even when split into two. Further, he had a boon that he could not be killed by any Yadava warrior.

PARVA III

LORD KRISHNA AS A UNIQUE LEADER: A MAN OF ACTION

LORD KRISHNA AS A UNIQUE LEADER: A MAN OF ACTION

Extraordinary Leadership: By Example

What makes a good leader? Are great leaders born or can they be created through education and training? These questions have never been answered with any degree of agreed finality. Modern management practitioners have not been able to arrive at a commonly agreed definition of a leader or leadership, despite long efforts in class rooms and conference halls of leading management schools and business corporations. All these thought warriors have missed the right place while looking for answers to this complex question. If they have a look at the personality of Lord Krishna, his life and works, then answer to this perplexing question will quickly fall into their lap. He was an extraordinary leader, a leader of leaders—a complete leader, in every sense of the word.

In human history, there are numerous examples of **born leaders**, while the leaders who emerged or were activated as consequence of some specific circumstances, are also not uncommon. Mahatma Gandhi exhibited no leadership qualities in his childhood or early youth, but soon something within him pushed to stand up to injustice and discrimination, as a young lawyer in South Africa. Churchill's leadership came to fore only after the events of Dunkirk. Mayor Rudolf Giuliani of New York was catapulted to limelight after his handling of the 9/11 event. Only some truly great leaders were recognized early in life. Indira Gandhi showed qualities of superior leadership when, as a small girl, she participated in activities of India's freedom struggle.

Lord Krishna's exemplary leadership commenced flashing right in his early childhood. As a child and a cowherd, He performed numerous miracles—and gopas, gopicas, cows and calves ran to him on a note of flute—words were not often required. His extraordinary leadership potential became crystal clear, when child Krishna unhesitantly jumped into dangerous waters and subdued the demonic naga king Kalia, by ceaselessly dancing on his multi-hooded head, forcing him to vacate Yamuna and its associated waters along with his numerous wives and large progeny, and head for its original abode in the sea.

Attributes of great leadership were so distinctly visible in little Krishna that in his cowherd community, no one was left in any doubt to the effect that, in any eventuality—natural or otherwise, they could always count on him. He persuaded them to migrate from Gokula to Vrindavana, for better prospects of fodder and pastures. Soon after, He convinced them to abandon long observed practices of ritualistic sacrifices and worships in favor of better care and love for their cows and bulls. Lord Krishna had great capacity to exhibit love, empathy, courage and strength. Unique charisma and aura of greatness glowed from his whole physical being, all through his different phases of life.

Normally, a leader should excel in one or two aspects of his life or work related activities—but Lord Krishna excelled with any thing or every thing that He touched or attempted. Through his charismatic communications, He transcended people beyond the clouds of certainties—far into the world of karma, dharma, jnana, bhakti, righteousness, renunciation, renouncement, and the path of atman or even life after death. He could capture mind and soul of anyone He wanted to—and reorient him the way a potter works with the clay. Even when it appeared that He failed, it sure was as per his intelligent design only.

A good leader should direct and lead organizational change through the use of his superior character, inter-personal skills, situation specific motivation, and being fully focused on target objectivity. He effected the best known organizational changes through replacement of demonic regimes at Mathura and Magadha, and finally at Hastinapura, after the total ruin of the last great accumulation of the forces of evil and wickedness.

His focus on removal of evil from face of the earth was matchless. His foresight and anticipation was so great that the warriors, demons and evils that were virtually undefeatable, were subdued through exploitation of their carefully observed and researched weaknesses. Action style and personality of Lord Krishna was so uniquely different that it attracted capable followers and disciples and prompted them to perform beyond expectations.

In today's world of business and governance, teachers, seniors and leaders do not teach or lead by example—they leave an unhealthy gap between their preaching and practice, consequently failing to create the necessary stress for meaningful acceptance. In this regard, Lord Krishna set numerous examples during the pre and post Kurukshetra phase of his worldly presence. One bright example pertained to utility and employment of knowledge and expertise acquired through proper schooling and education. He wanted people to follow righteous path of life which is not possible without exposure to scriptures and other available sources of knowledge.

Having incarnated in a non-Brahmin family, He had no benefit of learning scriptures in a family environment. He was part of a cowherd family (Nanda and Yashoda) and spent most of his time in fields, pastures and forests—and all that was wild and natural. On the other hand, being a Godhead, He could have claimed to posses—and, in fact, posses and display knowledge of all scriptures without really reading them. But that would have been too much for his followers to stomach—or even for him to convince them to study and learn scriptures and other sources of knowledge, without himself doing the same. He had to emphasize that only the knowledge acquired from a guru shall be fruitful. Hence, after getting rid of the demonic Kamsa, his pre-adulthood project, He went to the hermitage of guru Sandipini. His elder brother Balarama accompanied him.

As diligent and obedient students, they willingly and actively submitted to the rigor and discipline of the ashram life. Guru Sandipani was known to be a hard task master, yet he was amazed to see the speedy grasp and retention of what was taught, by the celestial brothers. Not only they worked hard and learned well—they served the guru well. There was no need ever for the great guru to repeat any instruction and the learned guru understood that they were not ordinary pupils. In sixty four days, they mastered all the 64 branches of knowledge available at that time i.e. at the rate of one discipline a day.

As was the tradition, on completion of their studies, the Yadava princes expressed desire to offer some *recompense* to their guru. Knowing that they were not ordinary beings, he put them to a near impossible task, namely to go and locate his son Prabhasa who had drowned in the sea while taking a bath and his body was not recovered at that time. This assignment was difficult, rather preposterous, in light of the infeasibility of bringing back a person who was long dead and lost. But in the great guru's assessment, they were the right people to attempt it. When both the brothers reached the sea and challenge it, the deity of the sea immediately appeared and explained the situation. Asura Panchajanan, in the form of a conch had claimed the boy and lived at the bottom of the sea. Krishna immediately dived into the sea, killed the asura and retained the conch and named it Panchajanya. The brothers proceeded to the abode of Yama, reclaimed the soul of the lost boy. Krishna restored the original form and features of the boy and handed him over to his guru with perfect humility and respect. The guru was very happy to get back his son. This incident highlighted the prowess of the two brothers far and wide. When the Lord blew this conch, the devas regained the power of righteous—and strength of evil and wicked declined.

Throughout his long and arduous life from Gokula to Parbhasa, Lord Krishna relentlessly exhibited Extraordinary Leadership. Among others, He persistently led through

- Instrument of example.
- Protection of righteous.
- Thought and action balance.
- Management of mind.
- Instruments of Karma and Dharma.
- Power of Jnana or Knowledge.

- Total impartiality.
- Right credit apportioning.
- Commitment appreciation.
- Non-material motivation.
- Madhura communication.
- Centrality of objectivity.

To re-stress the *leading by example* aspect of Lord Krishna's management it would suffice to say that today's professionals can benefit a great deal by remembering that

- knowledge and expertise is necessary for any good worker,
- preaching without practice is not advisable,
- an example set by a senior or the boss has multilateral utilities and
- humility, despite knowledge and prowess, is essential for good following.

Corporate managers and also those involved in activities of governance, can benefit a lot from the golden rule of *leading by example*, as followed by the wise Lord—the principle being that one should first sharpen/ improve one's own knowledge/expertise before advising others to follow. Be grateful to those who help or guide you in such learning. It will help a lot in smooth running of the corporate train.

Two Faces of Leadership

Right from early youth, in line with his mission requirements, Lord Krishna had to interact with lot of kings and princes. All of them, small or big, had to be assessed and evaluated, as per their Prakriti—and decide whether they had, in their nature, predominance of evil or goodness and to what extent? Those who could be relied upon in his divine fight against the forces of evil had to be identified, assessed and categorized away from the ones who could not be depended upon for this purpose. And what capacity each one had or could grow to –as the fight against the forces of evil was going to be long and arduous, had to be determined. Since it was not an ordinary job, all possible precautions were to be observed in assessing utility and strengths of each and every ally or potential ally. In terms of his long term objectives, all this assessment and evaluation had to be undertaken by the young Lord, either first hand or through his trusted disciples and devotees. Impulsive action, or action in vacuum, was not advisable. Further, the Lord had to maintain the human mask that He had adorned, as per his own choice, by incarnating in human form. All of his actions, thus, had to manifest as coming from a normal human being. In his divine exercise of assessment, as expected as per rules of prakriti, the wise Lord made two categories of rulers of that time, as described below.

Category I: contained kings and prices with high content of positive energy, having dominance of sattavic prakriti, displaying preference for goodness and righteousness, active observers of dharma, interested in welfare of people—and, as such, could be assets for the future.

Category II: included persons of high negative energy, rich with tamsic prakriti, displaying tendencies for evil and wickedness, engaged in actions of adharma, exploited the public, and, in brief, could not be depended upon.

To enumerate the known few, the category-1 included Bhishma, Vidura, Yudhishtra, Arjuna, Ugersena etc. while the second category had a larger number—including Kamsa, Jarasandha, Kalayavana, Salva, Sishupala, Rukmi, Duryodhana etc. Some great characters who should have qualified for the first group, such as Karna, Drona, Kripa etc. per force of circumstances, supported the evil forces headed by Duryodhana. Thus, in times of Lord Krishna, leadership, particularly that related to governance, manifested like two sides of a coin, right and evil, good and bad, and dharmic and adharmic.

Even in the modern times of IT superhighways and globalization, two sides of leadership continue to emerge at every stage of the process of management and governance. Leaders with greater concentration of negative tendencies (thought and action) continue to amass wealth through political, bureaucratic and corporate corruption and mismanagement, smuggling, extortion and many other nefarious activities. All these activities, in essence, are anti-social—and against the concept of greater good or righteousness. They are all manifestations of the tamsic Prakriti concentrations.

On the other hand, leaders with positive energy of thought and action, too continue to emerge but one—their number exhibit a decreasing trend, and two—they seem to command less visibility and impact. The balance seems to be tilting in favor of the forces of negative thought and action. In phases of history such deviations, however, do occur but the forces of righteousness, at one or the other point, are always able to rebound and reassert to overwhelm such negative or evil resurgences.

The fight between good and evil exhibit characteristics of perpetual reoccurrence. Supremacy of one over the other is never final or permanent. It is a continuous struggle.

Negative leadership manifestations in the corporate world are more prevalent than commonly admitted—and its impact on output and efficiency—and finally on bottom line and competitiveness, is considerably higher than normally visible or appreciated. Among others, the following symptoms of negative energy manifestations are always visible, in varying intensities, almost in all corporate work environments.

- Nepotism/favoritism in selection and placement.
- Discrimination on account of caste, creed or religion.
- Gender based discriminations & exploitations.
- Senior-subordinate conflict and non-cooperation.
- Peer non-cooperation and conflict.
- Non-cooperation with new recruits.
- Reluctance to offer /share information.
- Unproductive/ non-constructive criticism.
- Opposition to new ideas/ proposals.
- Resistance to change/ improvements.
- Unjustified transfers and harassment.
- Biased appraisals-improper credit apportioning.
- Unfair work allotment.
- Raising unnecessary/avoidable objections
- Overt and covert corruption, and innumerous other types.

For minimising negative energy/action manifestations, senior management should promote positive energy flow in the work environment. The policy of righteousness, correct credit apportioning, capability based work assignment, performance based rewarding, training for merit refinement, and emphasis for non-material motivation, as practiced by Lord Krishna, are highly productive in promoting greater flow of positive energy in an organization or work environment. His divine technology of manpower management, thus, can be highly useful in improving corporate performances in the present competitive work environments.

Leadership through Purushottama

As per the Hindu mythology, the world was created as an Extension of the Almighty's Leela or the Divine Play, the effortless unfolding of his boundless energy. The supreme Lord, when incarnate in human form, merely continues to expend that divine play. This leela may not follow conventional morality; not because it is its essential character. It is beyond such categorization or simplification, because it comes right from the supreme Lord, in form of Goodness Incarnate, selecting to present itself for a specific purpose. Thus, the butter thief, the chitchoor, natwara and many more, are nothing but expressions of his limitless energy and skills. Here, the God played the human role with a gusto.

Lord Vishnu, in his earlier avatara, Rama—the hero of epic Ramayana, He was known as the Maryada Purushottam or rectitude personified. As Krishna, He incarnated as Purna-Avatara or the complete incarnation—and, a complete God had to be a unique child, a unique youth (dancer, lover, wrestler etc.) and later on, a complete warrior, diplomat and guru. In this incarnation, He was a Leela Purushottama exhibiting his unique/ uncommon skills and energies at different stages of his life.

As a warrior and a ruler, He presented numerous instances of his Purushottama expressions. As winner of various battles against enemies of virtue and goodness, destruction of whom was the main objective of his incarnation, He never annexed kingdoms of vanquished evils, their wealth or their harems. Allowing wives and relations of the demon ruler Kamsa of Mathura, after his slaying, to go to the safety of their father's kingdom of Magadha, was a unique act of Purushottama, despite the fact that the kind Lord's own parents were imprisoned and tortured for long by this epitome of evil and wickedness.

The magnificent treatment that the poor and hesitant Brahmin Sudama got from the Lord of Dwaraka, was so unique, so humane and indeed touching, greatly enforced the fact that such an action could emerge only from a Purushottama. The way in which the wise Lord took care of the basic purpose of his long lost friend's visit, even without any overt or covert indication, spoke volumes of his Purushottama manifestations.

While in divine discourse with his warrior disciple Arjuna, on the battlefield of Kurukshetra, Lord Krishna tried all his celestial skills and knowledge of scriptures, to shake him out of inaction resulting from confusion and depression, that had overtaken the great warrior on finding himself face to face with the massive opposing armies which had several invincible warriors of repute—and most of whom were his seniors, gurus and relations. Lord's divine arguments failed to alter the mental state into which Arjuna had fallen, with strong desire not to fight—and equally strong arguments in support of his position of inaction. His queries were very forceful and penetrative, to the extent that at several points, the wise Lord ran the risk of losing the tussle of judicious argumentation. Lord Krishna, per force or more appropriately--for not allowing the golden opportunity of eliminating a large concentration of evil forces, to slip away so easily, had to reveal his true omnipotent form by bestowing Arjuna with the benefit of a view of his Vishvaroopa. He had to tell Arjuna in a very certain and crisp manner that, as master of the universe, creator and destroyer of all beings, He had ordained all these warriors to be eliminated. He went further to state that all those warriors standing in the opposing formations were already dead; He had already killed them himself—and all that Arjuna had to do, was to just play the role of physically slaying them. His pupil could take the credit for it without being scared of attracting any sin for doing so.

In flow of the celestial dialogues and in the process of divine exhibition of his cosmic form, the Lord also elaborated that He was Purushottama, the Supreme Purusha in this world and in the Vedas, and that He was beyond the perishable and transcends the imperishable. He who sees me as Purushottama with clear vision—sees all and knows all", spoke the Lord. Hence, the knowledge that the Lord imparted to the mankind through his Song of Wisdom, courtesy the in depth and ceaseless questioning by Arjuna, could come only from the ultimate guru i.e. the Purushottama Guru.

Purushottma, in fact, is the manifestation of positive energies--its basic elements being goodness, justice and empathy, application of which in any human endeavor, business, governance or otherwise, invariably leads to better work environment and enhanced productivity. Its positive energies annihilate the anti-work elements, at the levels of thought as well as action, liberating the positive forces of initiative and cooperation. Senior management professionals can definitely benefit by actively incorporating the basic elements of Purushottama in their daily work schedule—and bring immense dividends to all concerned i.e. the employer, employees and also the general public.

Excellent Judge of People

For any collective activity, corporate or otherwise, people constitute as the most important component or input. Success of all efforts, in collective work environment, depends upon (a) the quality of people selected and (b) the way they are managed. People management is, thus, the most important aspect of collective human action play—irrespective of work relevance or type of activity.

A good practitioner of management or a management guru should perform this crucial function better than his or her competitors or adversaries, not just to qualify for the title but also to continuously hold on to the same.

Lord Krishna was actively aware of this vital principle of management, right from early stage of his life. In fact, as a precaution, He arranged elder brother Balarama to come ahead of himself so that an effective team was available right from the beginning of the great Lord's long and arduous fight against evil and wicked forces.

In early youth, Krishna had to eliminate demon king Kamsa and his bunch of evil supporters, and Balarama was very useful for this first great fight of significance. Soon afterward, the wise Lord commenced his rigorous efforts to locate and recruit supporters and allies—beginning with some virtuous and brave

Yadavas who, in absence of a right leader, were unable to face the cunning and cruel Kamsa.

Soon after completion of training under the great guru Drona, young Pandava brothers were asked by their guru to attack the kingdom of Panchala, and arrest and bring its warrior king Dhrupada, as their *gurudakchna*. The newly trained Pandava princes did an excellent job and pleased their guru. This act of Pandava's first battle success against a well known warrior, impressed Krishna a great deal—as Dhrupada was Drona's colleagues at the ashram of the latter's father. The wise young Lord decided to take them under his protective wings at a right moment. The fact that they were related to the wise Lord through their mother, who was a Yadava by birth, made the job much easier.

Lord's conviction about Pandava brothers' great potential to be useful for his continuous fight against the well-entrenched forces of evil, was further strengthened when He witnessed Arjuna win the Panchala princess Draupadi, at the time of her sawayamvara, against stiff competition from a large gathering of warrior princes and kings from the extended territories of Bharata. He took active interest in their progress and well being.

Balarama' worth, as a great asset, was well settled in the Lord's mind but the righteous elder could not be pushed beyond a level and hence, the blue one's search for allies and supporters extended far and wide—even beyond shores of the Arabian Sea. Elimination of Jarasandha, the mighty leader of demonic forces, through expert employment of Bhimma, afforded a unique chance for large scale attraction of allies and followers, as hundreds of kings and princes imprisoned by the mighty evil, were released in one go-- a superbly mastered move in diplomacy and alliance building.

About the Kaurava camp, the Lord had an in-depth assessment of worth of mighty warriors such as Bhishma, Karna, Drona, Kripa, Aswathama and Duryodhana. Virtues of the wise Vidura and indecisiveness of Dharitarashtra were also well known to Krishna. He had prepared a detailed strengths and weaknesses analysis of each one of them. Their combined strength, often, worried him as they supported the evil Duryodhana and He had to find ways and means to surmount the elements of invincibility in this camp of the evil. All those who did not join the Lord, in one way or the other, in his divine efforts to subdue the evil forces, but were virtuous and mighty, had to be weakened or discouraged in some effective manner. A lot of intensive intelligence work went into this exercise. Even warrior Sikandi, an incarnate of Amba and destined slayer of the invincible Bhishma, did not escape the keen attention of a wholly committed Krishna.

The wise Lord also actively scanned the second generation of warriors—

foremost among whom were Draupadi's brother Dharisthadyumna, Arjuna's son Abhimanyu, and Bhimma's son Ghatotkachcha. Not only a wise and committed Lord Krishna identified people of virtue, strength and valour, He attracted them through his unique gravity of righteousness and He did not hesitate to decide where and how to use each one of them, with greatest stunning effect.

Lord Krishna, the great master in judging people and an expert of man management, has left a rich scroll of examples—all practical and effective, which the present day senior corporate managers can benefit from, in their ever frustrating engagement to move people do what is desired of them. His method of sharp observation, decisive analysis, productive engagement, right credit apportioning, active mentoring, madhura technique of communication and non-material motivation, just to recount a few, are particularly of current relevance.

Superior Crisis Management

Crisis is an abnormal situation that unfolds unexpectedly—without adequate warning, and may affect a large number of people. Loss of life, material goods or profits, is inherent in crisis situations where decision making, on part of those who are expected to remedy the situation, is either inadequate or inefficient.

Lord Krishna's incarnation on this earth had the backdrop of a grim crisis where dharma and righteousness were suffering a great deal at hands of organized evil and wickedness. It was a crisis situation of immense proportions where pious and the good were being treated with torture and humiliation by demonic rulers such as Kamsa of Mathura and Jarasandha of Magadha, just to name the major ones.

Right from childhood, the Lord incarnate faced a series of crisis situations—one of the early ones that unfolded at the community level, pertained to the unbearable nuisance created by Kalia, the naga serpent king who had colonized and poisoned a large number of water bodies along the river Yamuna, making life miserable for the young Lord's cowherd community. In a totally unexpected manner, the young Lord subdued the arrogant evil by dancing nonstop on its head, forcing it to withdraw, along with whole of its poisonous clan, to the distant seas, its original abode.

Soon afterwards, another major crisis developed when an angry Lord Indra threatened residents of Vrindavana with incessant cloud bursts, leaving no space for protection of cows and cowherds. Lord Indra had felt insulted by the cowherd community's sudden and unprovoked stoppage of ritualistic obeisance to the rain God, as per advice of Krishna who had argued successfully to convince the community, based on the fact that they were neither farmers nor traders—and being nomadic cowherds who sojourned in forests, they should instead worship and decorate their cows which had multifarious utility for them. In order to successfully ameliorate the crisis, the young Lord lifted the mount Goverdhana—rendering protection to the threatened community—on witnessing which the envious rain God presented himself and asked for the young Lord's forgiveness. Since then, the hill named Goverdhana is held in perpetual reverence to Krishna's crisis management approach.

The demonic ruler Kamsa of Mathura had come to know that he would soon be killed at hands of Krishna, through the mischievous disclosure of events to come, by the wandering sage Narada. He decided to take initiative to neutralize the threat at time and place of his own choice and in a clever move, invited young Krishna and brother Balarama, with the intention of finishing them off at the time of some festive celebrations. For long, the evil king had prepared his wrestlers and elephants for this purpose in a clandestine manner. The two celestial lads came to Mathura as per the king's invitation and finished the demonic ruler's warriors and elephants, in a quick move and also broke his sacrificial bow.

As a normal looking mortal, without exhibiting any supernatural powers, Krishna swiftly killed Kamsa in one to one combat. People roared with joy while Kamsa's two wives (Jarasandha's daughters) screamed in grief. Vasudeva and Devaki, along with numerous other prisoners, were freed from jails of the great evil. Krishna reinstated his maternal grandfather Ugersena to the throne of Mathura, which rightfully belonged to him.

The most serious crisis of the great Lord's life unfolded soon after the elimination of the demonic ruler of Mathura—as Jarasandha, the great evil king of Magadha was incensed at widowing of his two daughters at hands of a cowherd. He had vowed to take revenge on the Yadavas and assembled resources and allies for the purpose. He attacked Mathura seventeen times—and each campaign was more serious and savage than the earlier. Yadavas were fed up of these attacks and for some obscure reason, they were not able to eliminate this immense and persistent evil. On the next campaign, Jarasandha's massive forces were joined by Kalayavana who had superhuman powers and Krishna, for some unexplained reasons, was not yet ready to eliminate him. As a unique crisis management step, he decided that discretion was better part of valour. It was better to retreat and fight another day than face a certain defeat at hands of the evils. He defused the great crisis by persuading the great Yadava forces to retreat, in an organized manner, to distant Dwaraka where He got requisite time and resources to establish a great empire--adorned with a splendorous capital, the fame of which spread far and wide.

Subsequently, at Hastinapura in the court of Kauravas, after Yudhistira's utter loss in the game of dice, Draupadi who was a devotee of Krishna, was being publicly humiliated by Duryodhana and his evil friends. Dussasana was attempting to disrobe her by tugging at her sari and none of the elders and wise assembled there, was in a position or willing to help her out of this merciless violation of her modesty. No one lifted a finger for her protection and finally a terrified and molested Panchali, out of utter helplessness, closed her eyes and with folded hands prayed to Krishna. At distance of thousands of miles, a devotee's cries of anguish came to the Lord loud and clear. A crisis of immeasurable magnitude had developed and He could not let down a devotee. Physical intervention by the Lord was not possible—and yet a solution had to be found—there was no time to lose. Hence, He endlessly extended his devotee's sari to the extent that Dussasana, as an exhausted tormenter, helplessly fell to the ground. The whole court of evil Kauravas was dumfounded and was at total loss of wits. Honour of a woman devotee was saved, without the great Lord having to physically manifest himself. A grave crisis was managed so magnificently.

Lord Krishna, in his eventful life, was never free of crisis of one or the other type, for any long interval of time. The greatest and most serious—and probably a totally unexpected crisis , the great Lord faced when a totally depressed and demoralized, weak and shivering—and confused and incoherent Arjuna, in the battle fields of Kurukshetra—his chariot standing between the two great assemblage of opposing warriors, including gurus, seniors and relatives, refused to fight. With all the respect and humility to Krishna, who was acting as his chosen charioteer, Arjuna with folded hands said that it was not worth for him to have this fight; that the cause was not big enough to warrant killing so many of his respected relations and gurus. The likely blood-bath seemed unnecessary and avoidable to him. He was prepared to go and live like a hermit in a forest and bear all indignities of a warrior deviating from his chosen path of duty. Lord Krishna tried to brush aside his disciple's doubts and worries but no argument or words of logic seemed to work, His invaluable disciple was argumentative, inquisitive and also adamant and nothing seemed to matter to him. Lord's immense knowledge of scriptures and theories of karma and dharma were proving inadequate in pushing the celestial warrior out of the mode of doubts and inaction.

The crisis encountered was immense—all his plans to finally rid the earth of the accumulated evil were at a risk. What will He tell Draupadi? What will happen to the vow of Bhimsena—to tear open the chest of Dussasana and breaking thigh of Duryodhana, as revenge to the insults meted out to Draupadi? Sensing the ominous signs of humiliating failure, the great Lord mustered all his motivational skills and technology to convince his great disciple—but no act of verbal or nonverbal communication seemed to work. The great dialogue that ensued between the Lord and his great disciple, became immortally known as Bhagavad Gita where all the penetrating queries of Arjuna about birth and death, karma and dharma, action and rewards, duties and responsibilities, of all categories of people in all circumstances, were explained in all relevant details. Even non-human life forms were not left out of this exhausting series of sermons.

Frustrated and out of wits—the almighty Lord revealed his multidimensional and omnipotent celestial vision—as creator and destroyer of the whole universe—and openly told Arjuna that He was the supreme Lord of the universe and that he had no choice but to do as advised and fulfill his duty as a kshtaryia warrior. He told Arjuna that you are only an instrument and all the killing was already done by the Lord that all those warriors that he saw standing in the battle field were already dead. Finally, Arjuna accepted the advice and direction of the great Lord and was ready to do his assigned job as a warrior.

During the ensuing battle of Kurukshetra—at its various stages, several other crisis situations emerged out of invincibility of warriors present on the opposing side of Kauravas. Through celestial skills and vast information pool available on part of the great Lord, all these challenges were successfully met, though in some of the cases, the methodology employed was not beyond apparent violation of the code of conduct prevalent at that time. Finally, the evil forces were subdued and dominance of the righteousness, in form of Pandavas prevailed.

At the fag end of the epic battle, after the death of Duryodhana, another crisis unfolded in form of acts of Ashwathama, who destroyed the whole second generation of Pandavas, as a revenge to the treatment meted out to his friend Duryodhana. Even Uttarai's unborn child in her womb was mortally hurt by his savage attack and the very continuation of the Pandava clan was at total risk. Here again the great Lord had to act and employ his celestial powers to re-infuse life into this child of Uttarai and Abhimanayu.

There exists no example of such magnificent achievements in the field of crisis management in the whole written or oral history of mankind that could come somewhere rear to the Lord Krishna's performance in this critical field of management. His supremacy in crisis management remains unchallenged and, as such, it should be a matter of great pride for Indian management professionals to learn something from their such a bright heritage in their field of specialties. These highly inspirational examples of crisis management from the life and works of the wise Lord should serve as most appropriate case studies for management training institutes to rely upon, in furthering excellence in this field.

Art of Managing through Chaos

Chaotic situations are often encountered in business, politics and war—always offering dual opportunities to those who command the situation at that moment. To the wise and energetic, there comes an opportunity to take leadership initiative and manipulate the mass of chaos to his own advantage—and to the incompetent and lethargic, a safer chance to flow with the chaotic mass. Lord Krishna landed on this earth as a Mission Incarnate, when it presented a totally chaotic scene. A number of small kingdoms ruled by asuras, demons and selfish kings and princes had conspired to perpetrate a reign of terror and exploitation. Evil ruled supreme and righteousness suffered a great deal at every step and every moment.

Chaos, in fact, is the right stage for a wise and energetic leader to stand up and establish rule of law or at least initiate steps in that direction—because public, the reactant part of the chaotic mass, is in ripe mood to be led into acts directed at remedying the situation.

Not far away from Gokula and Vrindavana, where the Lord spent his childhood and early youth, people of Mathura were suffering immense exploitation at hands of the demonic king Kamsa. Situation at Magadha was equally grave under the demonic rule Jarasandtha—who, blessed with invincibility, on one hand, and ties of marriage of two of his daughters to Kamsa, presented a situation with no hopes of redress. Nearby Panchala and Hastinapura too were in a situation of turmoil. Numerous other small and large kingdoms and principalities too presented a hopeless situation of oppression and terror.

As a mission incarnate, right in his early youth, Krishna took initiative, worthy of a great leader, to swiftly eliminate Kamsa and his bunch of oppressors, and, as a wise strategy of effective governance, handed the reigns of the kingdom to Ugersena. The divine process of mending the chaotic mass generated by the evil and the wickeds thus commenced through the divine grace of the young Lord. Soon after, the sparks of emerging divine leadership were revealed at the ashram of guru Sandipani, where the young Lord and his elder brother Balarama broke all the records in speed-learning by mastering all the available subjects of sciences, arts, humanities, warfare, management and diplomacy, just in sixty-four days, at the rate of one subject per day. The two celestial princes—on one hand, gained a perfect view of the prevailing grim situation and how it was to be ameliorated—and on the other, sent warning signals to all who occupied the canvass of terror and wickedness at that time.

The young Lord moved with a well thought-out strategy to deal with the evil's admixture of chaos—and some of the approaches employed with great efficacy were as under.

- He kept himself free from the direct responsibility of governance—by delegating it to Ugersena. It afforded him a lot time and opportunity to think and plan for the future.
- As an intriguing strategy, He vacated the kingdom of Mathura and moved the whole Yadava clan, with bags and baggages, cows and bulls to distant Dwaraka. Though the real logic of the wise Lord behind this historic exercise of migration has never been fully understood, the fact that it afforded the divine Lord an opportunity to establish a magnificent empire, on one hand and afford time to gather resources for a great fight against evil forces, on the other, have often been assigned as the likely explanations. An invincible army of Yadava warriors was raised and the unique prosperity of Dwaraka became known far and wide.
- Simultaneously, He developed an active partnership with the Pandava princes who were destined to play the most decisive role in the great Lord's massive fight against the organized evil. First, He fueled the Pandava-Kaurava animosity through active display of empathy towards the aggrieved Pandavas and then assisted them in establishing an un-enviable empire with Indraparastha as its capital.
- A chain of relations, supporters and sympathetic rulers/ kingdoms were established keeping in view the long-term objectives.
- The wise Lord kept his focus totally undiluted. He studied and located weaknesses in armors of the invincible warriors, evils and demons of that time and worked out foolproof strategies to tackle each one of them, singly or collectively. He identified right person/ warrior on his side to take on the each evil target—and implemented the strategy, even if its elements sometimes did not match the accepted morality or ethics prevalent at that time. For him the objective was always more important, in fact, sacrosanct.
- He paced himself—did not unnecessary hurry. He allowed situations, alliances and opportunities to present themselves. His center of attention and action was Arjuna, the celestial Pandava warrior who was to finally become the greatest instrument in hands of the wise Lord to subdue and destroy evil. He kept Arjuna under his intense influence and tutelage to the extent that He allowed his own sister Subhadra to elope with him.
- In a micro-sense, his campaign for elimination of evil became an Active Partnership between the key actors of his team—namely Yudhishtira, Bhimma, Arjuna, Draupadi, Dharitarashtra, Bhishma, Karna etc. He successfully converted his mission into other's necessity for justice or revenge.

- He maximized his knowledge assets at distinguished gatherings and occasions with telling effects. His supernatural powers-physical as well as intellectual, were accepted and admired by one and all.

Lord Krishna successfully ploughed through complex situations of chaos—and succeeded magnificently in meeting the objectives of his incarnation. For today's corporate managers, the wise Lord has left vital management lessons to the effect that situations of chaos are in fact opportunities of great magnitude for leaders of strong minds and hearts—who can keep their cool and employ time, efforts and resources towards their declared goals. Altering strategies, allies and product mixes should all be directed in one selected direction—and when chaos finally gives way to success, there remains no dearth of either allies or appreciations.

Master of Change Management

Change is the only reality of permanence in this world, perpetually re-occurring without any gap or pause. All living and non-living entities suffer change, some visible and some invisible. Normally, living beings tend to resist change because uncertainties, as inherent in change, are always uncomfortable. Present (time) is often viewed as hard and uncomfortable, because survival and growth take efforts. To complicate the situation, competition and conflict creep in uninvited. Most of the people are uncomfortable with the thought of future, because unforeseen and unexpected invariably cause apprehension and anxiety. It generates fear of unknown, severely undermining one's ability to face and manage the phenomenon of change. But, change must always be faced as it arrives uninvited, there is no escape, neither for man nor any other living being. Hence, it is always better if one faces the inevitability of change with understanding and resolve and still better, if it is done with some enthusiasm.

In the business of management and governance, change is not only a constant challenge but also a factual necessity for continuity as well as growth. However, only few professionals in these fields are adequately equipped to suitably anticipate change—and a further minority looks forward enthusiastically for the same. Among modern management professionals, only a very small fraction rides smoothly the inevitable waves of change; majority are noticed resisting the same uncomfortably and unsuccessfully despite the fact that a lot of literature, guidelines and methodologies are available to help them in this matter.

Lord Krishna, in times when nothing was available in terms of statistics, EDP, telecom and IT etc, and when word of mouth or physical observations were the only available means of analysis and assessment to serve as basis for decision making, did an excellent job of Change Management. His anticipation and forecasting of events was totally matchless and planning and implementation of approaches and strategies for achieving planned goals far superior than any and all of his contemporaries, friends or foes. He was a Mission Incarnate and He efficiently employed inherent capabilities to turn himself into the mankind's best known Change Management Expert. Some of the events and happenings from his life and times, are cited below to illustrate this fact of significance:

- The earliest example of Lord Krishna's superior change management capabilities pertained to his and brother Balarama's quick and complete transformation from cowherds to magnificent princes, after efficient elimination of Kamsa and his evil friends and supporters, when they were just young teenagers.
- When need arose to be literate and knowledgeable, during a short tutelage in ashram of guru Sandipani, He became an unbeatable pundit in all available fields of scriptures, sciences, astronomy, diplomacy, logic, and in art and technology of war along with all that was available to learn and master. In view of the fact that He had no benefit of princely childhood, it was a masterly example of change management.
- When harassment and challenge to the Yadava clan, from dead Kamsa's deeply aggrieved father-in-law, the mighty king Jarasandha of Magadha, became truly insurmountable, Krishna effected a planned retreat of his forces and followers from Mathura to distant Dwaraka. Huge doubts must have been raised about the righteousness of the decision—and also about the future awaiting the new settlement. He, however, surprised every one by creating a vast and highly prosperous empire on the western sea coast of the country. Dwaraka, the capital city of Yadavas became famous for its unmatched riches and splendour. It was the most vivid example of **efficient change management**.
- Few years later, He assisted and guided the Pandavas, his celestial cousins, in converting the waste lands of Khandavaparastha, into such a prosperous and productive kingdom that numerous merchants migrated from Hastinapura and other well established capitals, to the renowned Pandava capital that came to be known as Indraparastha. This unique example of magnificent change management was enacted under the direct celestial supervision of Lord Krishna. In fact, it was Lord Krishna who had persuaded the reluctant Pandavas, to accept their uncle Dharitarashtra's offer of this waste-land as their part of the kingdom.

In the post Kurukshetra era, for thirty-six years that the Pandavas ruled the combined kingdoms of Hastinapura and Indraparastha, and the Yadava clan flourished at Dwaraka, Lord Krishna successfully managed a number of change management challenges, in a manner that the legend of Krishna exists and grows stoutly even after the lapse of over 5,000 years. Lord Krishna did not resist change—He did not restrict himself to one place, one role, one expertise, one position or one objective (within his express mission objectivity)—exhibiting a magnificent flow with the wave of time, need and opportunity.

Practitioners of modern management, irrespective of their area of specialization, can draw immense benefits from Lord Krishna's concepts and practices of change management, the most important teaching in this regard being—that it is often futile to resist change and in fact, to the extent possible, one should welcome and invite change. Once it is accepted enthusiastically, it always works for the benefit of people involved.

Out-of-Box Approach of Management

Most of the modern day managers look for normal procedure, guidelines or precedence, when faced with difficult situations for decision making. Some push the matter upwards to seek guidance or downwards, in order to escape the responsibility. However, a truly competent and professional manager, does not normally hesitate to deviate from preset procedure and take unconventional decision, if situation so demands. Lord Krishna was faced with several inconvenient situations in his life, and in each case, He acted in an unconventional manner, offering unexpected Out of Box solutions to a variety of challenges. He loved to be different, to surprise and still be on the right course.

As a young boy, He was different as a lover. Radha, the center of his adolescent love, was not married to him—further she was elder to him in years. Yet, she followed him as his shadow—she could not resist the call of his flute. He held Radha and all other gopis (the young girls of the tribe) in Rasaleela or dance circles, whole night—and night after night. He was the ultimate Rashik [1] and Natwara. [2] Despite his divine activities of love, dance and music, He was the most valuable star of his nomadic community; He created no resentment or conflict—except love and more love. He changed the fabric of his community for all times to come.

When He liberated Mathura from the cruel rule of the demonic Kamsa, it was totally unconventional for him not to assume the role of the king, as being the killer of Kamsa it was his natural right to ascend to the throne of Mathura. He amazed every one by not doing so and by restoring the elderly Ugrasena as the king of the liberated kingdom. It was truly an out of the box approach. Even learned sages like celestial Narada deemed to doubt the logic and intelligence behind the wise Lord's decision. Despite overt and covert criticism from various quarters, it turned out to be a very wise and practical solution. He had all the powers of a king or more correctly of a king maker—with no headache for day to day management of the kingdom. Further, it afforded him a lot of time and flexibility to engage into activities that He deemed necessary for being on a right track, in view of his Mission Incarnate responsibilities.

It was also totally unusual for a young warrior to kill the demon Kamsa and not to harm or imprison any of his immediate family members despite the fact that his own parents were imprisoned by the demonic ruler for a long time.. The two wives of Kamsa, daughters of Jarasandha, the mighty demonic ruler of Magadha, were allowed to return safely to their father who, in turn, to avenge the widowing of his daughters, made several repetitive attacks on Mathura, rendering the life of Yadavas totally miserable and uncertain. Although, Krishna and Balarama were able to defend Mathura from frequent and massive attacks of the mighty demon Jarasandha, they were not able either to decisively defeat or capture him. He looked truly invincible as, on one hand, he was favoured by a boon that he could not be killed by any Yadava and, on the other, he had assembled a massive combination of allies and supporters, in his crusade against the *kingdom of cowherds*, as he mockingly called Mathura.

Unwilling to disclose his Godliness so early in life and faced with inability of all other Yadava warriors to handle the formidable Jarasandha, Lord Krishna proposed and implemented a unique *out of box strategy* of vacating Mathura and migrating to the distant Dwaraka, with whole of his willing clan of Yadava warriors, not even being discouraged from earning of a disgraceful title of *Ranchood* in this strategic move of celestial significance. In the whole history of mankind, written or otherwise, there exists no better example of out of box thinking (or practice) and most probably, He was the first great practitioner of the concept of *Out of Box Thinking,* raising it to the level of an unfailing management tool.

With the passage of time, Dwaraka established its predominance as a celestial kingdom of unmatched effluence and power—and through these long years, the perpetual conflict between Kauravas and Pandavas consistently refused to be settled in any peaceful manner. When the process towards active war efforts warmed up, for soliciting support, both Arjuna and Duryodhana visited Krishna at the same time, and the wise Lord again came out with an entirely unique *out of box solution,* saying that one of them could have the entire mighty Yadava army and the other him alone(and that He would not wield any weapon). He could have, if He so desired, denied any help to Duryodhana because (a) he was at fault for denying to yield any part of their kingdom to the Pandavas, and (b) he had attempted to seize and arrest the Lord when He attempted to solve the conflict, for the last time. Despite that, the wise Lord gave Duryodhana a choice that was truly an *out of the box* one.

Further, during the active battle of Kurukshetra, while working as charioteer of Arjuna, Lord Krishna suggested totally unconventional or out-of-box solutions to tackle the invincibility of the Kaurava warriors, particularly Bhishma, Drona, Karna, Jayadratha and Duryodhana, who in the normal manner were not to be easily defeated or killed. In each case, He devised such strategy that the opponents had no escape route of any type despite having benefit of unique boons and weapons. Elimination of each of these unique warriors represented a truly out of box solution

Even prior to commencement of the battle of Kurukshetra, when Arjuna refused to wield weapon saying that he did not want to kill so many of his friends, relatives and elders present in the opposing forces—and that he was not interested in regaining of the kingdom at such a high cost, the great guru-mantra advice that Lord Krishna gave to Arjuna, that later came to be known as the Song of Wisdom or the Bhagavad Gita ,was also a totally and truly out-of-box solution or methodology for the non-material motivation of the persons involved. Any lesser person or God, in that situation, would not have taken the trouble of reciting so many Verses of Wisdom and so persistently washing Arjuna clean of his all doubts and confusion. He professed entirely new concepts/approaches towards karma, dharma, janana, duty, action, rewards, results, renouncement, renunciation, prakariti, varnas, gunas, doshas, and all other vital aspects of life—and after life. All what the wise Lord said continues to be perfectly valid despite the lapse of several millennia.

And finally the electric shock that He administered to Arjuna, in order to break his argumentativeness, by allowing him to have a view of his *Vishvaroopa,* too was an entirely out of the box approach to the vexing problem. It gave Arjuna an entirely new view of the life and he was again up and ready to wield his Gandiva to eliminate all those who perpetuated evil or assisted the evil makers in an active manner.

Normally, an out of box or unconventional approach is not easily appreciated. There is no dearth of those who either resist such an approach or forecast failure of the same. There is always a tendency to travel the beaten path or prefer the certainty of known over the uncertainties of an unconventional approach. But difficult or abnormal situations demand unconventional or out of box solutions—which only truly efficient managers are able to attempt and implement. Such professionals of caliber can draw a lot of support and guidance from life and works of Lord Krishna who never hesitated from taking the out-of-box approach to problem solving.

Art of Managing Difficult People

In every work environment, one can always encounter some difficult to handle people. By default, such people turn out to be difficult to work with as well. They represent, in a way, a concentration of negative intentions and attitudes, primarily non-conducive for smooth working, in collective work environment. Most managers find it distressing and distasteful to manage people of such uncooperative nature. Their own mindset or perceived distaste for dealing with such persons often discourages them to take initiative or find ways and means of successfully managing such deviants and non-cooperators. The troublesome or non-cooperative people, work or behave in a peculiar manner on account of operation of certain mix of negative and positive factors, the sum total of which tends to impel them in a particular direction of expression and behavior. Sometimes, they perceive receipt of some tangible or intangible gains from their deviant disposition. It needs to be ascertained with substantial accuracy so that the same could be factored while attempting to find a way to effectively deal with them.

Managing them successfully is an art as it demands a set of superior skills, (a) for managers to come up with a methodology to either adequately motivate them into cooperative action, or (b) to stress them in a manner that dividends from their behavior are turned totally negative and unacceptable to them and or their supporters, if any.

Lord Krishna, in light of the objectivity of his incarnation, encountered a number of *difficult to deal with people,* at all the stages of his life—as in view of the huge accumulation of evils and perpetrators of evil on face of the earth, the very nature of his engagement mandated such encounters, at a certain unavoidable regularity. He continued to face them right up to the end of his sojourn in this world. Through divine anticipation and exposure, Lord Krishna developed a successful strategy and methodology for dealing with such deviants and trouble makers. He could recognize them from a distance, irrespective of the camouflage adopted and circumstances of their emergence. In dealing with them, the wise Lord followed *The Principle of Stress Balance* [3] which mandates an analysis of various negative and positive stressors operative on a person—as all responses are consequences of such stress balances only. No action of any type emerges without operation of the process of stress balance. With a quick look—and that too from considerable distance, Lord Krishna could read the mind and body of such deviants and come to a precise analysis of

- the set of negative and or positive stressors operative on the subject deviant,
- the magnitude of such stressors and the degree and direction of balance of the

same,

- and factors or stressors that were likely to work upon him either to make him cooperate or force him to abandon his negative behavior.

His analysis and assessment of deviant elements was always accurate and effective and hence, he was always able to either mould the deviants in direction of his own requirements or neutralize them well in time, before any damage could be effected. In the event of persistence or obstinacy, he employed swift and terminational stressors to neutralize the trouble maker. Manny of such deviants and non-cooperators, eventually turned into the Lord's disciples and devotees as they could not resist his celestial charms and charisma.

As leader of young cowherds, one afternoon young Krishna found, most of his colleagues and also a number of cows and bulls, dead or unconscious near to a deep pool in the river Yamuna, which was known to be the abode of the naga king Kalia who had become a terrible nuisance to all those who visited the pool for one or the other purposes. Unable to further tolerate the troublesome Kalia, the young Lord decided to face the challenge heads-on. On being challenged by the mischievous and arrogant Kalia, the little Krishna jumped into the pool, climbed on to the hood of the threatening devil and danced ceaselessly on it till the miscreant was fully pulverized and repeatedly asked to be forgiven. He offered to move out of the pool and the river Yamuna, with his whole family and followers and then only the gracious young Lord let him go free. Marks of the little Lord's divine footwork are still visible on head of naga serpents.

After the slaying of demonic Kamsa by Krishna, Jarasandha—the victim's father-in-law, along with his supporters and collaborators, repeatedly attacked Mathura to extract revenge and, in course of time, turned fully invincible for the Yadavas. Sensing a certain defeat at hands of the king of evils, Krishna decided to employ wisdom instead of force and moved out of Mathura to the distant Dwaraka, along with Yadava forces and whole of their clan. In this case, the wise Lord demonstrated that in certain circumstances, selection of an effective measure might be determined entirely by specificities of the situation. Hence, suitability of a stressor, in terms of its nature and magnitude, to the challenge posed by the difficult to handle person or opponent, is most important in determining the outcome. A unique challenge has to be met in a unique manner. One can not and should not, as per the example set by Lord Krishna, stand with a weak or a false shield, when faced with a truly serious threat.

In certain situations, when a persistent troublemaker can not be removed or done away with, non-reactant tolerance becomes the only way out. Lord Krishna exemplified it by consistently tolerating insults and pranks from Sishupala, who could not be eliminated because the Lord had himself restricted his scope of action by promising to the mother of this demonic fellow that He would pardon up to a hundred of insults and pranks from the persistent trouble maker.

Some times, in difficult to handle situations, superiority of information is employed as a decisive tool, as was evidenced by Lord Krishna, in finding ways and means of eliminating Bhishma, Drona and Karna, the almost invincible warriors of the epic conflict of Mahabharata. An in-depth analysis of inherent weaknesses of the warriors had led to solutions of their individual invincibility. Superior information on part of Krishna, as to how the invincible Jarasandha could be eliminated, was employed with decisive efficacy when Bhimma was placed in direct one to one wrestling duel with him. He had erected an efficient system of intelligent gathering and analysis in regard to all evils and potential evils, about their capacity and intentions to create obstructions in the job of elimination of evil load from this earth.

Normally, each difficult to handle person has his or her signature response to certain stressors or provocations and therefore, the same can be employed to imbalance the subject opponent. Lord Krishna successfully employed this technique to overwhelm or subdue a number of his adversaries. Some of his disciples too learned this technique from the wise Lord and employed the same with superior results.

That timeliness of a move or right timing of an stressor is always of decisive significance was a very dear principle of operation to Lord Krishna. He often employed it so as to avoid substantive damage in future events. Intercepting Duryodhana, while going totally necked to see his mother as per her advice, and persuading him to cover at least his manhood, saved Bhimma's life when the two were in mortal combat at end of the battle of Kurukshetra.

From the above narration of Lord Krishna's highly effective approach towards handling of difficult to deal with people, one can safely conclude that the most effective way of the same is to employ the right type of stressors, in right quantum and at the right time, so as to persuade or force a trouble maker, active or potential, to deviate from his intended erroneous course. Today's management professionals, irrespective of the field of their engagement, can chose to significantly benefit from the wise Lord's experiences and practices in this vital field of human nature management.

A Celestial Blend of Leadership and Management

Leadership and management skills are always in demand in the spheres of business and governance. Modern management teachers and writers, often go crazy in their attempts to specify the qualities and characteristics that high performance leaders and managers should possess. And despite sustained efforts, no consensus seems to emerge in this respect. What qualities of a leader distinguish him from a manager? Can a good leader be a good manager—and vice versa? These simple questions do not seem to settle, despite immense efforts and debate. And it seems certain that this gap of perception shall never be fully bridged. It seems, possibly, beyond the modern human capabilities. As per standards and expectations of modern management, only a celestial being shall be capable of possessing and perpetuating all the desired qualities and capabilities to be a really good leader and a good manager at the same time a perfect two-in-one.

In view of some analysts, Jawaharlal Nehru was an excellent leader of people, he inspired them for superior action. Many of his critiques often proceed to assert that he failed or partly failed as the nation's chief executive. Similarly, there is no dearth of people who rate Sardar Patel as a better manager and organizer of affairs of the state. In my view, Indira Gandhi was a good leader as well as a good manager; she led the nation well in times of challenge and difficulties. She was also able to effectively handle the deviant elements in her ruling party. Yet, on several counts, she seemed to fail. She was gunned down by the very persons she trusted so deeply. On a larger horizon, Mahatma Gandhi succeeded as a leader as well as a manager as he was able to inspire a vast multitude of Indians, from diverse backgrounds and with varied means and perceptions, into a fairly cohesive struggle for independence. And as a good manager, he delivered the targeted results, with limited means and resources, in a hugely challenging situation. Yet, there is no dearth of critiques of the Mahatma, primarily because different people had different expectations, and their perceptions, patience and persistence manifested equally differently. He too had no celestial virtues and capabilities to fully satisfy requirements of a truly great leader as well as a great manager at the same time, in eyes of one and all.

While casting the net of analysis and assessment much wider, in terms of time and space, one may find even such great personalities of human race as Jesus Christ, Gautam Buddha, Ashoka, Akbar and Einstein (just to name a few) deficient in one or the other essentiality for qualifying as a good leader and a good manager, in one go. Jesus Christ and Gautam Buddha were, in deed, great leaders of people; they initiated two truly great religious faiths and paths of spirituality. But were they great managers? Here, nothing much can be said with requisite certainty. Emperor Ashoka and Akbar were definitely in category of great leaders—they inspired people a great deal. They were also able to deliver an efficient, stable and progressive governance. They could work through and with people in a very efficient manner and hence, are rated as good managers too. On the other hand, Einstein was a pure scientist and a thinker. He exhibited no inclination or interest in the field of management or leadership.

Several millennia ago, a true blend of leadership and managerial skills occurred in form of Lord Krishna. He was a real Two-in-One, right in his childhood and youth and by the mid-life, turned himself into a Three-in-One as in addition to being a good leader and a good manager, He became an excellent advisor too. He took the great Pandava warriors into his protective guidance in order to safeguard them against the nefarious designs of Duryodhana and the bunch of his evil friends as He had to subsequently employ them as the most effective tools in his fight against the vast accumulation of evil and wicked forces, for destruction of which He had incarnated in human form.

Lord Krishna, right in his childhood, exhibited qualities of great leadership. Whenever his nomadic cowherd community was faced with any challenge or difficulty, the little Krishna came forward to see it out of the same. As a child, He freed the community from the persistent mortal nuisance of the evil serpent king Kalia who had colonized the waters of Yamuna and adjoining water bodies frequented by the cowherds and their animals, by dancing ceaselessly on the devil's multi-hooded head till it begged to be pardoned and offered to immediately move out to his original abode in the sea, collectively with its extended family of numerous wives and a multitude of offspring. Further, the little Krishna persuaded the cowherd community to move en-mass out of Gokula to the better endowed grasslands and pastures of Vrindavana. A centuries old pernicious practice of the cowherd community of offering ritual sacrifices was replaced with love and care for cow and its progeny--which had a significant long-term economic value for the community. And when angry Indira lashed out at the community with ceaseless cloud bursts--and its very existence was at risk, the young Krishna lifted the mount Goverdhana, to provide protection to his cowherd community and its cattle wealth.

As a young lad, he organized the boys and girls of his community into multifarious activities related to music, dance, drama, games, competitions, celebrations and festivities which attracted intense appreciative attention of neighborhoods as well as authorities engaged with functions of governance. Soon after, Krishna freed the suffering people of Mathura from the demonic ruler Kamsa and his evil associates. After restoring the function of governance to the elderly Ugrasena, He inspired the long suffering people of the kingdom into speedy rejuvenation of prosperity, happiness and celebrations.

Soon, the newly liberated kingdom of Mathura had to face repeated attacks from the mighty demonic ruler Jarasandha of Magadha, whose two daughters were untimely widowed due to Krishna's killing of their demonic husband Kamsa. He had vowed to avenge the widowing of his daughters and hence, made seventeen repeated attacks on Mathura, each one more savage and intense than the earlier. Though, Krishna and Balarama were able to safeguard Mathura from each of these repetitive invasions, but the same left them with no energy and time to undertake development of any type—and the lives of the inhabitants of the kingdom had become miserable under frequent spells fighting, encirclement and uncertainty.

On the eve of the 18th attack, Jarasandha was joined by the massive forces of his allies and supporters, and Krishna sensing a certain defeat at hands of the evil forces, advised the proud Yadava community to vacate Mathura and march out to a distant and desolate Dwaraka. Krishna's superior skills as a manager came to the fore at this delicate occasion.

First, He employed his immense communication skills to convince the proud Yadavas for this strategic retreat, and then He made sure that the migration was safe and orderly. Further, He fully met his managerial responsibilities to see that all those who accompanied the Yadava forces, were suitably settled and provided for. It is also said that He employed his celestial skills to quickly create an impressively productive and prosperous empire at Dwaraka and its capital was rated as the best and most splendorous in the world. The fame, riches and prowess of Dwarka had no match in the whole world. In the process, the great Lord had amassed all the requisite resources, tools, weapons, allies and expertise to effectively deal with the accumulated evil forces spearheaded by Jarasandha of Magadha, Duryodhana of Hastinapura, and their numerous allies and supporters.

Under Krishna's celestial guidance, the Pandava brothers had grown into a mighty force at Indraparastha. Having delegated, in a truly managerial fashion, the responsibilities of day to day governance and management of affairs at Dwaraka, to the wise and mighty senior Yadavas, Krishna now took his advisory role at Indraparastha very seriously. He assisted Yudhisthra and the other Pandavas to celebrate the Rajasuya and in the process, with help of Bhimma, destroyed the almost invincible Jarasandha, the most formidable and troublesome enemy of Krishna.

Lord Krishna's role as an advisor, became truly intense during the thirteen years long exile and banishment of the Pandavas. He had to, in a discreet way, keep the fighting spirits and capabilities of Pandavas active and alive during this long and arduous period of their life. Additionally, Draupadi's anger and frustrations had to be managed in a tactful manner. He successfully fulfilled this delicate role in an impressive manner. And finally, when the numerically inferior forces of righteousness were faced with the massive line-up of Kauravas, fortified with the presence of invincible warriors such as Bhishma, Karna, and Drona on their side, Krishna assumed the truly challenging job of guiding and advising the Pandavas, on the battle grounds of Kurukshetra. He became the non-arms wielding charioteer of Arjuna and performed the job in a gloriously impressive manner.

Through his illustrious life and works, Lord Krishna generated unchallengeable evidence to the effect that He was the humanity's best known and undisputed three-in-one blend of managerial, leadership and advisory skills. All his concepts and practices of men, materials and situations management were so practical and superbly effective that with each passing day they tend to become more relevant and rewarding. There is, however, a need to intensively study and assimilate the same in light of today corporate management and governance challenges--and actively benefit from their celestial efficacy.

Long March as a Management Tool

In the past century, two great leaders namely Mao Tse-tung and Mahatma Gandhi employed Long March as a superior management tool with brilliant political gains in each individual situation. Much before October 1934, when the Central Red Army moved on the now renowned Long March, it had come under compelling pressures from the Nationalist forces of Chiang Kai-shek. At that time, Mao was neither commander of the communist forces nor political head of the Chinese Communist Party (CCP): he was simply a member of the Politburo (J. Chang and J. Halliday, 2005). Po Ku was Party No.1, while Chou En-lai had charge of the army as chief of military affairs: actual command of the 80,000 strong retreating forces was with Lin Biao and Peng De-huai. During its ruinous march extending a full year (October 1934—October 1935), while it lost over ninety percent of its soldiers and support workers, its leadership was fully secure and in good form. Through his cunning and intellect, and fully unmindful of sufferings of the people involved, Mao managed to rise to a position of senior leadership in the party. And Po Ku, Lo Fu and Chou En-lai seemed to support him. He was able to sidetrack Kao-tao, who commanded a strong and intact Northern Red Army, and also established useful contacts with the Soviet Union, which at that time was spearheading the international communist movement.

In brief, Mao utilized the difficult time of the Long March to (a) side-track rest of the leadership and attain the position of a Supremo, and (b) work out a distilled strategy for a long and stable future for himself and his supporters. From an isolated location on the Yellow Earth Plateau and with active support from Soviet leadership, in terms of armaments and other war supplies, he finally captured the whole of China. The Nationalist forces of Chiang Kai-shek had to retreat to an island known as Formosa. He came to be Known as Chairman Mao, and an international political cult figure.

A few years earlier, Mahatma Gandhi had employed Long March as an effective tool against the unrighteous ways of the British imperialism. And his achievements were even better than those of Mao. Through the unique weapon of a Long March, he laid the ground for humbling the world's mightiest empire in a short period. He came to be known as Father of the Nation. Except for a walking stick, he used no physical weapon of any type. It was, in deed, a miracle of an uncommon variety.

On the morning of 12th March 1930 (J.B. Kripalani, 2004), with a carefully selected group of seventy-nine satyagrahis [4], he left on foot in the direction of seacoast. Strong non-violent credentials of each marcher were the basic criteria for his or her inclusion in the group. Many volunteers eager for the march were left out, as too large a group was considered unmanageable in view of the great leader's declared objectives and the strict code of conduct that was specified for the participants. They were totally unarmed and fully determined to stay so against all possible provocations and punishments from the British administration. The only arms that they carried were the walking stick of their leader.

High government circles in Delhi viewed the Mahatma's Salt Satyagraha with derision and ridicule as a crank's fantasy, and even Congress leaders doubted whether the campaign would succeed in any significant manner. But, the Mahatma's army of seventy-nine unarmed soldiers marched to defy the world's mightiest empire, without concern for results. Here, the great leader was following the Doctrine of Karma, so brilliantly detailed by Lord Krishna in the Bhagavad Gita. As the disciplined and totally peaceful column moved through villages, it swelled to an unexpected strength. The marchers received rousing welcome in all the villages that they passed through; often whole population, including children and women, came out to welcome and support. Food, water and arrangements for marchers' rest and stay were all organized by villagers without any charge or grumble. It was a march for pilgrimage—target being the village of Dandi on Gujarat seacoast.

In every welcome meeting, which occurred in almost each village touched by the march, Gandhiji asked people to engage themselves in constructive socio-economic activities and to be ready to break the salt law after he had picked up a handful of it at Dandi. As a substitute of martial music, the marchers sang in praise of God and His glories, the local instrument Ekatara serving as their marching band. Gandhiji and his unarmed soldiers reached the village of Dandi on 5th April, covering a distance of 250 miles in 24 days. By this time the tempo of the march and enthusiasm of people all over India had risen so much that the imperialistic government was on verge of losing its cool and composure. There were signs of an uncontrollable movement of civil disobedience all over the country.

When Gandhiji and his companions picked up fistful of salt at Dandi, there was no active interference from the Government. Some of the marchers camped at the sea shore and spent time to manufacture salt from saline water. In the meantime, Gandhiji was ready with a plan to march to a nearby government salt works at Dharasana, and his coworkers enthusiastically followed the same. In this case, they were not lucky enough as the totally unnerved administration proceeded to arrest Gandhiji and spirit him away to Yeravda jail at Pune on the night of 4th May itself. The arrest was made under a century old regulation of 1827. For the restless people of India, Gandhiji's arrest was signal for a countrywide agitation, comprising demonstrations meetings, marches, hartals and strikes in various parts of the country.

In Bombay, Pune and several other places, industrial workers went on strike. In Sholapur, to control the striking workers and the situation arising out of it, martial law was declared; firing was resorted to, killing and injuring several agitators. The agitation spread to villages and at some places rural population migrated instead of putting up with the inhuman methods of the government. The agitation took such a turn that in June, the Indian National Congress was declared as an unlawful organization. Jawaharlal Nehru, his father Motilal Nehru and scores of other leaders were put behind bars.

After Gandhiji's arrest, his co-marchers continued to carryout the programme as designed earlier by their leader. The second rung of leadership took the job of running the campaign with renewed vigour. Under Sarojini Naidu's guidance over two thousand satyagrahis marched towards government salt works, which was surrounded by barbed wire fence, and a water filled moat. In addition, over four hundred men of native police under command of half a dozen British officers had surrounded the works. When the first column of peaceful volunteers approached the salt depot, the police with iron-rimed lathis mercilessly assaulted it. An American journalist, Webb Miller, in the following words, vividly described what followed: "Suddenly, at a word of command, scores of native police rushed upon the advancing marchers, and rained blows on their heads with steel-shod lathis. Not one of marchers even raised arms to fend off the blows. They went down like ninepins. From where I stood, I heard sickening whacks of the club on unprotected skulls. The waiting crowd of watchers groaned and sucked in their breaths in sympathetic pain at every blow. Those struck down fell sprawling, unconscious or writhing in pain with fractured skulls or broken shoulders. In two or three minutes the ground was quilted with bodies. Great patches of blood widened on their white clothes. The survivors without breaking ranks, silently and doggedly, marched on until struck down." [5]

The American journalist, as per his own admission, had never seen or expected such a happening: a totally disciplined, dedicated and fearless encounter of volunteers with grievous hurt and possibly death. The second batch moved in the same manner. There were no fights, no commotion, and no outcries, only groans after they fell. Such a resistance to official terror was encountered never before.

Miller went to the temporary hospital and counted over three hundred injured, many still unconscious due to serious head injuries. He wrote that he had never seen any thing similar to what happened at Dharasana, in his long career of over twenty years during which he had witnessed numerous agitations and civil disobedience marches in several countries.

The pattern of agitation was repeated at several places all over India for months at stretch. Particularly, Gujarat, Bombay, Orissa, Madras, Bihar, Sind, Bengal and North West Frontier Province took active part in the long drawn struggle. All the leaders, big and small, were pushed into jail, often without trials. It galvanized the whole nation into a massive movement. Even the moderate leaders of the movement who in the past had seen and advocated scope of some accommodation with the British occupants, lost all hopes of reconciliation.

The Government of India and also the British Government in London got totally unnerved from severity of the non-violent agitation. In January 1931, Lord Irwin, the then Viceroy of India, realized that solution to India's problem could be found through negotiations with Gandhi. All prisoners were released without any condition so as to prepare atmosphere for negotiations.

Thus Mahatma Gandhi's Long March and its immense fallout made the world's mightiest empire to tremble. It could never recover from this jolt and after a decade of fumbling and mismatched measures, decided to vacate its long occupation of India.

Mahatma Gandhi, as per considered opinion of the author, was a disciple of Lord Krishna. He had located the great weapon of non-violence, skillfully hidden in the Bhagavad-Gita, the wise Lord's Song of Wisdom, which was rendered for the benefit of Arjuna, on battlefield of Kurukshetra. In fact, it was Arjuna who had vehemently argued with Lord Krishna in favour of alternative for violence; he seriously thought that there was an alternate. But Lord Krishna, who had a specific agenda for elimination of all possible forces of evil and wickedness, could not permit his warrior disciple the luxury of an alternate to killing the evil forces and their supporters assembled at Kurukshetra.

In fact, much before Gandhi and Mao, Lord Krishna had successfully employed the tool of Long March. After killing of the evil king Kamsa and his equally terrible supporters by young Krishna and elder brother Balarama, the kingdom of Mathura had run into long years of turbulence. On account of Kamas's death at hands of Krishna, two daughters of the great demonic king Jarasandha of Magadha were widowed. Krishna, for considerations of compassion or righteousness, had allowed them to return to their father's kingdom. On seeing their misery, the great demonic king had vowed to take appropriate revenge on the Yadavas of Mathura.

To be true to his vow, Jarasandha gathered huge forces, and made great alliances with an eye on eliminating the mighty and arrogant Yadavas. He went to the extent of seeking and obtained special boons that he could not be killed by any avatara or incarnates. He never bothered about normal mortals since he thought, and possibly was, stronger than all of them. Being well-equipped with tools of war and effective boons to safeguard himself, he started attacking Mathura in an intense and repetitive manner. Almost every year, he came to attack Mathura with increased vigour and ferocity. In all, he made seventeen attacks: and each time

Krishna and Balarama were able to safeguard Mathura. But the intensity of evil campaigns did not leave any energy and time with the Yadavas for development and/ or growth. They could not peacefully enjoy their status as rulers. Once, the two avataras even had to rush back from the ashram of guru Sandipni where they had enrolled themselves for obtaining formal education and training suited to princes of a mighty clan. They could not afford the luxury of normal learning process and consequently, had to resort to high-speed learning.

Krishna and Balarama intensely discussed ways and means to deal with the demonic troublemaker. They knew their limitations in view of Jarasandha's protection through celestial boons. There was no other great Yadava who could match up to the might of Jarasandha. They also looked at possible alternatives.

So early in life, Krishna did not want to fully reveal his Godliness as it could have long-term repercussions adverse to his mission incarnate objectives. In the great Yadava clan of warriors, there were substantial differences of opinion on how to deal with this persistent evil threat.

Soon, Jarasandha reappeared on border of Mathura, the 18th time—and with a massive fighting force that included large contingents of foreign fighters called malechhas, under the command of Kalayavana. Krishna saw a confluence of evil omens and told the senior Yadava warriors that it was preferable to live another day and have an opportunity to fight at time and place of one's choice rather than facing a sure defeat—and possibly death. He employed his divine charisma and communication technology to convince them to vacate their beloved Mathura and migrate to Dwaraka, a distant location on the western sea coast. It was a very difficult proposition for the proud Yadavas to accept against the then prevalent code of kshatriya behaviour.Krishna gave them a preview of what kind of future awaited them at Dwaraka. Consequences of confronting a far superior and better prepared enemy too were elaborated with graphic details. After intense and protracted discussions, Krishna's arguments prevailed—and the whole Yadava clan left on a Long March of over a thousand miles to the unknown wilderness of Dwaraka. Massive columns of carts, chariots, horses and elephants passed through several kingdoms, mostly friendly as the route was selected with considerable deliberations. No dependable information is available to ascertain what problems the great migration of a warrior clan faced on way to its new destination. What is known with certainty is that the great Yadava clan earned the non-flattering epitaph of Ranchood. It continued to stick to Lord Krishna with uncommon tenacity, becoming one his numerous names.

On the new location of Dwaraka, the uprooted Yadavas worked hard with renewed vigour and tenacity, under the divine guidance of Krishna and Balarama. A large and prosperous empire was created in the western, central and southern Bharata, and its influence extended even beyond the Arabian Sea. Magnificence and beauty of Dwaraka was unmatched and its fame spread all over the world. It became celestial capital of a divine and invincible regime. Lord Krishna fully delivered on the promise of prosperity that He had extended to convince the adamant Yadavas to desert Mathura and migrate westwards. Further, He achieved the following objectives by implementing the first organized Long March by a proud warrior clan:

- Broke the arrogance of the Yadava clan.
- Rendered them more cooperative and dynamic as a consequence of uprooting.
- Provided the Yadavas substantial growth opportunities at the new location.
- Converted the Yadava warriors into an invincible fighting force.
- Employed them to eliminate numerous evil rulers and princes.
- Tested his principle of non-material motivation and the madhura technology of communication.
- Confused the evil Jarasandha by providing him with feeling of temporary victory.

From the examples employment of Long March as a management tool, one can proceed to conclude that no adversity should be viewed as totally hopeless or too large from angle of possible improvement and /or reversal of fortunes. Situation specific management tools can always be located and employed for desired results.

Practitioner of the Game Theory

For the past four to five decades, *Game Theory* [6] has been a popular preoccupation of economists, all over the world. In 2005, the two main advocates of this theory, namely Robert J. Aumann of Hebrew University of Jerusalem, and Thomas C. Schelling of the University of Maryland, shared the Nobel Prize, for having enhanced our understanding of conflict and cooperation, through game theory analysis. The game theorists have attempted to explain strategic behavior of individuals, groups, corporations and nations, in different situations of conflict and uncertainty. In the recent past, the economics Nobel has been awarded to several others who attempted to focus on understanding decision making at the micro level. In 2003, Daniel Kahnemann of Princeton University, shared the Nobel, for employment of psychological inputs to explain decision making in situations of uncertainty. Again in 2001, Joseph Stigitiz shared the prize with George A. Akerlof and others, for work on decision making in situations where competitors in market have varied levels of information.

John N. Nash, the father of the modern game theory, got his Nobel only in 1994 while his work in this field became evident much earlier. Thomas C, Shelling, through his book **The Strategy of Conflict** published as early as 1960, originated the concept of *mutually assured destruction or MAD* as a deterrent against use of the nuclear weapons. It became a very popular concept in the years of the cold war, for avoiding activation of disaster.

In fact, the game theory is not new to the mankind--as its subtle applications have been visible since time immemorial. Lord Krishna, over 5000 years ago, practiced the concept of the game theory, with considerable clarity and success. The first instance in his divine practice of this concept pertained to vacation of Mathura by the proud and mighty Yadava clan, in face of persistent attacks from the invincible Jarasandha of Magadha, who was incensed by Krishna's killing of his son-in-law, the demonic Kamsa of Mathura. Jarasandha had vowed to avenge this misadventure of the Yadavas by teaching them a suitably punitive lesson. He attacked Mathura seventeen time, each attack being more severe and savage than the earlier—which introduced an active interplay of the elements of the game theory between the two strong and opposing sides.

Jarasandha acquired hugely superior military resources through active cooperation of friends and allies—and, in the process, even attained a celestial boon--promising that no Yadava could kill him. Though Krishna and Balarama were able to protect Mathura each time the invaders attacked, but Jarasandha was neither eliminated nor defeated decisively. As a move of celestial wisdom, on the eve of the eighteenth attack and in face of sure defeat at the hugely strengthened hands of the evil, Krishna advised the Yadavas to retreat to the distant

Dwaraka—and preserve themselves for a decisive fight, at a more opportune time in the future. Here, the major benefit of the power game played between Krishna and Jarasandha, in the short-run, went to the later. But in the long run, Yadavas were the real winners, because (a) they were able to establish a truly mighty and prosperous empire at Dwaraka, and (b) at the right time, they eliminated Jarasandha with the help of Bhimma, the mighty Pandava warrior.

Through divine providence, Lord Krishna got actively involved in attempts to resolve the long drawn fratricidal conflict between the Kauravas and Pandavas of Hastinapura. On behalf of the Pandavas, He went on a diplomatic mission to the court of Duryodhana, and made a truly grand effort for Kauravas see reason. He detailed, on one hand, the righteousness of the Pandavas claim for their part of the kingdom—and on the other, highlighted the horrible consequences which the two sides were to suffer in case of war—employing his celestial skills logic and communication. He painted a grim picture of the *mutually assured destruction* in case the war was not averted. But the wise Lord's pleadings, logic, persuasion and even warnings, fell on deaf ears. Despite elders of the Kaurava camp being in favor of a compromise, the evil adamancy of Duryodhana led to failure of the Krishna's divine mission. Lord Krishna had even applied the *Chicken Approach* of the game theory by suggesting that in order to avoid the horrible consequences of a war, let Pandavas be given only five villages, to afford them the minimum opportunity to keep their body and soul together. Even this chicken game approach or the last ditch attempt, could not make the evil Duryodhana see reason and respond in a reconciliatory manner. The total irrationality of Duryodhana's approach did not allow the wise Lord's diplomacy to succeed. The famous *matrix of chicken* failed to yield any visible or direct result, on account of the absolute adamancy of one of the negotiating parties. Indirectly, the wise Lord's play of the game theory generated two very vital results;

- One, it created widespread sympathy in favor of the righteous camp.
- Two, it cleared the way for the great Lord to implement his bigger design for en-mass elimination of the forces of evil and wickedness.

While returning from the failed diplomatic mission to secure some minimal ground for the Pandavas, Lord Krishna invited Karna to join him in his chariot. He explained to Karna his origin and background—and stressing that on account of being the eldest son of Kunti, he was the eldest amongst the Pandavas, and invited him to come and join camp of the righteous. Krishna assured him that Yudhishtra would gladly abdicate in his favor—and that he could rule the Pandava kingdom, as soon as the same was regained. Karna thanked the Lord and said that he could not abandon his friend Duryodhana in the critical hour. Here , the bold play of the game theory succeeded only in part—it considerably softened Karna's attitude of active enmity towards the Pandava brothers. It proved very rewarding in the war that followed.

The most impressive play of the game theory enacted by the Lord was with Arjuna, when just before commencement of the battle of Kurukshetra, the Pandava warrior refused to fight, threw his weapons and dropped, depressed and in tears, to the floor of his chariot which was piloted by the Lord himself. The Lord offered him all the inducements of grandeur and fame as victor of the conflict. He assured his reluctant disciple that he would not attract the sin of killing so many of his elders, gurus and friends—as the soul never dies. No argument of karma or dharma seemed to work against the intellectual adamancy of Arjuna. Finally, the Lord had to exhibit his real omnipotent form, as master of the universe—its sole creator, destroyer and manager—and in the end Arjuna's doubts were removed, queries were answered and his nerves were calmed. He got up to do his duty as a warrior. Here, the great Lord was successful but the whole benefit of the game play went to Arjuna. He forced Krishna to reveal his real form and had the benefit of viewing the magnificence of the Lord. The Lord too was not a loser, because in Arjuna He strengthened the greatest agent of righteousness to finally destroy the forces of evil.

Narrated above are just a few of the instances of Lord Krishna's direct exposures to the interplay of the game theory—which the common people with limited knowledge about his long and illustrious life, can easily understand and relate to. In fact, at every moment of his life, even as a small child, He intensively played the elements of the game theory—primarily to win friends and followers, subdue opponents and enemies, and finally create conditions for completing his mission incarnate objectivity.

A review of the mankind's greatest manager's intense play and practice of the game theory, in a variety of challenging situations that He encountered in his long and arduous life, suggests that modern professional managers, some of whom are already fairly apt at the intricacies of this area of expertise, can productively employ the elements of this theory, in practical situations to accelerate and perpetuate superior efficiency and productivity with requisite fairness and righteousness, in day to day corporate affairs.

Magnificent Shaping of Future

Future is nothing but extension of the present—it never comes except that the present gets extended in relation to time or movement of celestial bodies. In other words, there exists no tomorrow—it never arrives or can not arrive—because it is not there! Only today takes its form and remains today! Re-appearance of the bright phase of the day, after the dark one(what we call night) is erroneously termed as tomorrow and for the shake of convenience, its likely repetitive occurrence is called Future. Hence, future is nothing but expansion or continuation of the present. So, it is today or the present that is important—but, without exception, all the human beings, are excessively concerned, preoccupied and apprehensive about future that, in fact, is just an illusion.

Despite the truth of the matter being as above—and its realization, at least by a part of the populace, our over-occupation with the future or tomorrow continues to be overwhelmingly strong. Since human beings suffer from persistent anxiety for the future, all great leaders and gurus, are expected to define it and preferably give it a definite shape and direction for our convenience. Most of the leaders and gurus fall into a trap—and as per people's expectation, attempt to give future a shape by inspiring and directing their people or followers to act in a particular way or manner. Since shaping or re-shaping of future is beyond capabilities and control of human beings—only collective and persistent action of people or a section their of, can consequence into bettering of their present and through it their future.

Great leaders and gurus, realizing their limitations, attempt only to alter or remedy the present of their people or correct whatsoever they find in it not suiting their thinking or requirements. Gautam Buddha, Mahavira, Jesus Christ and many others attempted it with varied degree of success. Emperor Ashoka and Akbar too made certain appreciable attempts in this direction. More recently, Mahatma Gandhi made valiant efforts to shape the future of India—and he succeeded significantly by directing its people to attain independence from foreign occupation. Further, he left a good bunch of disciples in form of Jawaharlal Nehru, Sardar Patel, Lalbahadur Shashtri and several others, to carry forward the good work of social emancipation and economic development. In many other countries, leaders of stature arose to give shape to aspirations and requirements of their people. In most cases, impact of these leaders and their contributions lasted only for short periods--one or two generations of people. Any long –term impact was not feasible—because requirements, expectations and appreciations of people continue to change with the passage of time. There is, in fact, no permanency for such impacts and influences—until and unless, a great leader succeeds in altering the very thought process and value system of the people involved—and leaves behind a guideline, frame-work or yardstick that could be employed during the ensuing times.

The really great leader and guru who succeeded in magnificently shaping or reshaping the future of people, was Lord Krishna. He had incarnated in human form as a Mission Incarnate with the specific agenda for freeing them from the excessive load of terror and exploitation that the organized and powerful forces of evil and wickedness had imposed upon them. First, He freed his own people i.e. the cowherds and Yadavas of Mathura, Gokula and Vrindavana, from the inhumanly cruel and exploitative regime of demonic Kamsa and his equally terrible associates. Subsequently, He moved the vast clan of Yadavas from Mathura and its adjoining areas, to a distant but potentially more rewarding and safe location of Dwaraka, on the western coast of the country where He inspired his industrious and valiant people to create a highly prosperous and successful empire, widely rated as the best in the world at that time.

Soon after, He took the mighty Pandava brothers under his protective guidance and tutelage—thus developing a strong front for the forces supportive of righteousness. With their assistance, He eliminated the biggest evil perpetrator of that time—the mighty demonic ruler Jarasandha of Magadha, liberating his vast empire from his evil and pernicious rule—and freeing hundreds of princes and kings whom he had seized and imprisoned for a sacrificial celebration. Without any loss of time, He took initiative and persuaded the celestial Pandava warriors to undertake the massive elimination of evil and wicked forces which had accumulated under the protection and guidance of Duryodhana of Hastinapura. Despite the massive numerical superiority of Kauravas and their supporters—and the presence of several invincible warriors on their side, this large assembly of evil forces and their supporters were decisively destroyed on the battlefields of Kurukshetra--in a high intensity battle lasting for eighteen days.

The epic battle of Kurukshetra that Lord Krishna supervised as charioteer of Arjuna, not only eliminated the major part of the massive load of the evil and wicked—substantially cleaning up the environment of governance, it led to emergence of the massive stream of wisdom and a valuable code of ethics in form of the Song of Wisdom or Bhagavad Gita when Lord Krishna was forced to clarify to Arjuna the essentiality of conflict and numerous issues of ethics which had clustered and clouded the mind of the key Pandava warrior. Through this immortal discourse of Lord Krishna, the mankind was gifted priceless pearls of wisdom and knowledge along with a depth of insight into issues of life, birth, death, karma, dharma, body-mind-soul alliance and relationship of men amongst themselves and with rest of the numerous life forms—and all other relevancies of spirituality.

Thus, through the intelligent design of Kurukshetra, along with his illustrious works of long and arduous life, Lord Krishna valiantly succeeded in giving a definite shape to the future of his people by (a) massive elimination of evil and wickedness, (b) spread and perpetuation of righteousness, (c) stimulating learning and development, and (d) gifting a permanently correct code of ethics and righteous behavior, for all its future generations to profit from in a ceaseless manner.

Lord Krishna's life and works are full of illustrations and insights into all intricacies of human interactions and behavior—in spheres of corporate, governance and numerous other areas of human engagements. His concepts, philosophies and preaching when related and applied to corporate management, are capable of successfully pulling any one out of a difficult situation. They are even capable of achieving revolutionary or totally positive metamorphosis in efficiencies and productivity of organizations. He is, indeed, the real leader and guru of potent celestial capabilities, equipped to positively shape and reshape future of communities and organizations—irrespective of their composition and objectivities.

Unique Professional Detachment

An outstanding manager or a guru, for considerations of functional necessity, can not afford to be too liberal with emotions—even with best disciples or nears and dears, as a heavy load of the same tends to act as a drag on quality performance. Lord Krishna was a master tactician in employment of emotions in a need dependent manner, a right mix of positive and negative came to him as a natural disposition.

In early life, as a child and as a young cowherd, the emerging Lord displayed a high voltage of emotions with members of the cowherd community, as the fact of his incarnation had to dawn in a defused manner. Here, it was a necessity. Evil neighborhood of Mathutra had to pick up signals of the Lord's emergence, for future events to unfold. Lord Krishna, as a young lad, left Gokula and Vrindavana—his cows and cowherds, gopis and gopas, in response to greater calls of duty. The high gravity of emotions exhibited in early life, continued to torment the Lord for a long time, and while enduring the sufferings, He vowed to practice strict *professional detachment* for all events of significance in the future.

Several years down the line, Lord Krishna had to vacate Mathura, as He was faced with a certainty of defeat at hands of the combined might of Jarasandha and his demonic friends who were immune to Yadavas' might, as per some favourable boons granted to them by Lord Shiva. The young but wise Krishna did not allow his high emotional attachment to the ancestral kingdom, to become cause of early destruction and mission failure. With detachment of a professional manager, He vacated a green and prosperous Mathura, for the unknown desolation of Dwaraka, over a thousand miles away—across the great desert of Thar. For him, survival of his clan for future action was more important than his love for lands, forests, palaces and riches of Mathura.

Lord Krishna's management of the kingdoms of Mathura and Dwaraka too exhibited an intense degree of professional detachment as the same were ruled indirectly through the elderly and virtuous Ugrasena. Except for matters of larger concern and those related to neighboring kingdoms, Balarama, Ugrasena and other senior Yadavas, handled all the affairs of governance.

Highest level of professional detachment, on part of the Lord was visible during the great battle of Kurukshetra, when he advised Arjuna to fight and do his sacred duty as a kshatriya, irrespective of the fact that the latter's senior relations and gurus were lined with the opposing forces. Here, the Lord utilized his higher capabilities of play of emotions to create walls of professional detachment. He succeeded in bringing around a nervous, confused and dejected warrior anew with greater vigour, determination and clear vision, in terms of his duty and dharma. The wise Lord having gained valuable exposure to it while dealing with his own clan, rising to the occasion as a responsible guru, created a divine rock of professional detachment in Arjuna in respect to consequences of war.

When the young warrior Abhimanyu, Lord's own sister's son from Arjuna, met an untimely end at hands of scheming Kauravas, He employed his practiced detachment and consoled Arjuna and other grieving Pandavas, stressing that the loss of the young warrior was great to him too and that He did not know himself how to face his sister.

Another bright example of the Lord's practiced detachment was visible when He persuaded Yudhishtra to visit the wounded old warrior Bhishma-- who waited for the right time to depart from this world. Lord Krishna thought it necessary for the future king to benefit from wealth of rich thoughts of the wise warrior's accumulated wisdom. Bhishma was happy to see the charming Lord come to him and gave a rich discourse to Pandavas, on righteous ways of governance.

After the conflict ended with the destined end of Duryodhana, victorious Pandavas had to visit their grieving uncle and aunt who had lost all of their one hundred sons. Though it was not necessary for Lord Krishna to go with them but the delicacy of the situation and etiquette demanded that the great Lord should ensure his divine presence at that time. The wise Lord not only went with them but, on one hand, saved Bhimma from deadly embrace of Dharitarashtra, and on the other, absorbed the venomous blast of an angry Gandhari

Genuine detachment emanates from a karma centered thought process where the prime task at hand or in plan-fold, is viewed as most vital, totally ignoring likely negatives of the situation and or consequences likely to emerge.

Lord Krishna's entire life was full of events where He had to increasingly

practice an uncommonly high degree of detachment. The supreme example of detachment, the great Lord presented, when prior to his own departure from this earth, He destroyed his own rowdy and quarrelsome clan. He did not want remnants of his own clan to become a bottle- neck in achievement of the objective for which He had incarnated. Centrality of the objective was very dear to him. Senior corporate professionals, hence, can draw substantial guidance and incentives from the illustrious life and works of the divine incarnate and use, at least in part, his unique methodology of perfect detachment, to further centrality of their corporate objectives—even in difficult situations.

Notes

1. Rashik, in general sense, refers to an incorrigible lover.
2. Natwara means a dancer par excellence.
3. It emanates from the fact that any action is feasible only when the pro and opposing forces are not fully balanced, allowing force balance to flow in a direction.
4. Such terms are explained under Notes & Elaborations (24-28).
5. D.G. Tendulkar, Mahatma, Vol. III, P-40.
6. Game theory, broadly speaking, analyzes the interactions between agents and formulates hypotheses about their behaviour and the final outcomes in games and also in intricate negotiations. Even international environmental problems have been treated to the formulations of this theory.

PARVA IV

LORD KRISHNA AS AN INTENSE THOUGHT WARRIOR

LORD KRISHNA AS AN INTENSE THOUGHT WARRIOR

A Power Thinker

Lord Krishna's early life was spent in a nomadic cowherd environment of Gokula. Despite lack of formal education in early youth, He had developed characteristics of a *Power Thinker* or a born leader. He exhibited significant symptoms of such a personality very early in life. His divine personality of an active power thinker was further sharpened when years later, along with brother Balarama, He attended the ashram of guru Sandipani. In a fast track learning marathon, the young Lord imbibed the complete knowledge of all the available sixty-four subjects of arts, sciences, astrology, astronomy, scriptures, warfare and all that was available at that time, in as many days. His renowned guru was truly astonished at the young Lord's learning, retention and rendition capacity.

As per Mangieri and Block [1], a power thinker should have superior strengths in three basic domains—namely reasoning, insight and self-knowledge. For the purpose of clear understanding, they are elaborated as under:

- Reasoning pertains to an individual's capacity to logically think through, without bias, and arrive at best solution of a problem, depending upon situation limitation and resources available. It is a capability of taking thoughts, facts and analysis based actions.
- Insight is an individual's ability to know, in a spur of moment, and act without giving prior conscious thought to an issue.
- Self-knowledge encompasses one's attitude, beliefs and cognitive assessment capacity.

In all the three departments, Lord Krishna was endowed with unmatched strengths and capabilities. His power of reasoning was laced with uncommonly superior knowledge of scriptures and all the available sciences of that time. Coupled with the celestially smooth communication skills of the Lord, the same emerged as the best known diplomatic skills of all times. The wise Lord gave an immense display of the same when He convinced the whole Yadava clan to abandon an established kingdom of Mathura and migrate en-mass to an unknown location of Dwaraka which offered, at least in the beginning, only a promise of uncertainties.

Later on, much superior manifestations of Krishna's skills of power reasoning or power presentation were visible in the following instances;

- When the great Lord presented, as a last ditch effort, the Pandavas' case for return of their kingdom, in Kauravas' court at Hastinapura, and the intensity and flow of logic of his arguments, justifications and pleadings left every one present fully convinced and impressed, except the evil Duryodhana who, as destined, refused to listen to anything that was right.

- Even a superior and more intense exercise in logical reasoning and persuasive argumentation was attempted by the great Lord when he attempted to convince a disheartened and demoralized Arjuna on the battle fields of Kurukshetra--where finding his elders, relations and gurus in the opposing Kaurava forces, the great Pandava warrior refused to fight and do the assigned karma of a born kshatriya. That most intense exercise in reasoning known to mankind came to be respectfully referred as the Song of Wisdom or Bhagavad-Gita for the benefit of the whole human race.

Lord Krishna's divine personality was rich with merits of *insight* [2] as well as "Foresight", and numerous instances in his eventful life demonstrated the same. His intuition was exemplary as He could see evil coming, irrespective of the camouflage attempted. Even as a small child, He took timely action to destroy or subdue the evils that came or were sent to harm him. The brightest instance of the wise Lord's unique faculty of incisive insight was his assessment of the invincibility of Jarasandha, the mighty evil ruler of Magadha, at hands of the Yadavas. And the wise Lord, despite the risk of being branded as a coward, decided that it was better to deal with the great evil a few years later when right resources were to become available for this purpose. For him, a strategic retreat was better than sure defeat at hands of a leader of evils, elimination of which was the main aim of his having incarnated on this earth. The other glorious instances of insight and foresight were

- Identification of Pandavas, as a great resource and useful tool, for fighting evil forces, at an early stage and cultivation of a mutually supportive relationship with them, was a great instance of active foresight.
- He did not hesitate to remind the three elder Pandavas of their origin and greatness and the actions that they were destined to perform. He was conscious of the greatness of Arjuna's capabilities and actively helped him to sharpen the same, for an eventually destined role.
- Elimination of several invincible warriors, such as Bhishma, Drona, Karna etc. who happened to be present on side of Kauravas by force of unavoidable circumstances, became feasible only through the unique insight and foresight on part of the great Lord. Without his guidance and support the epic destruction of mighty Kauravas could not have taken place.

Lord Krishna's knowledge of his own celestial capabilities became amply evident at numerous occasions in his childhood and youth, and afterwards, his friends and foes contributed ample publicity for him in this regard. At some occasions, the great Lord, out of compulsive demands of the circumstances, had to exhibit his superhuman capabilities.

To summarize, there is no hesitancy of any type in re-stressing that Lord Krishna not only possessed the capabilities of a "Super Power Thinker", but was able to employ the same to alter course of thoughts and actions of great personalities of his time and assign a unique course to key events, through the unique power of logic and play of words. Neither friends nor foes could escape the magic of his personality and communication. He employed elements of *madhura* with decisive efficacy. Corporate leaders, management teachers and gurus can learn a great deal by imbibing and employing the great Lord's techniques of influencing people and events, to further their corporate as well as personal agendas.

Principle of Thinking Ahead

Thinking ahead, or long term planning, is an essential attribute of any effective management activity. Its significance in regard to corporate management is of fundamental nature as any negligence or inadequacy of thought or action may lead to loss of market and or revenues. With the current availability of numerous tools for information collection and processing, resulting from growth spurts in the information technology, long-term planning today is not too difficult to manage. Availability of trained manpower and efficient computerization makes the job all the more efficient and rewarding. But despite all the modern facilities and consequent feasibilities of efficient data processing and conclusion emergence, numerous organizations fail to notice changes emerging in their respective business environments and consequently run into problems. In most organizations, planning department is an integral part of corporate office but often resources are not assigned intelligently or in proportion to the challenges encountered, or likely to be encountered. Consequently, failures in the corporate world to foresee or forecast challenges likely to be encountered, is not uncommon. It occurs, primarily, due to overriding—and, some times, a blinding emphasis on current operations. Singularly preoccupied with today, most managers tend to lose track of tomorrow.

A perusal of life and works of Lord Krishna brings to light numerous instances which confirm that Lord Krishna actively observed the principle of long term planning. The work agenda that He had drawn for himself, and the challenges that He encountered, were truly massive--and successful attention to the same necessitated an intelligently planned action sequence. The process of thinking ahead, on part of Lord Krishna, commenced even before He assumed human incarnation, in light of the fact that the task that He took on his head i.e. freeing the earth from accumulated forces of evil and wickedness, was extremely difficult and hazardous. Hence, He caused Balarama to precede him and be of assistance, in times of difficulties. Further, goddess Mahamaya's assistance was ensured to create suitable environment/illusion for Krishna's birth and his transfer to the safety of Nanda's home in Gokula, without creating any suspicion amongst the intelligence network placed on full alert by the demonic Kamsa, for guarding the imprisoned Devaki and Vasudeva.

Lord Krishna had beautifully planned ahead for the post Kamsa phase of actions needed to progress in direction of his pre-set larger objective, namely the massive elimination of the forces that were perpetuating evil governance, with utmost terror and exploitation. After the death of Kamsa at hands of the young Krishna, survival and progress of the ruling Yadava clan at Mathura became very difficult and uncertain, on account of persistent and repetitive attacks from Jarasandha, the mighty demonic ruler of Magadha, whose two daughters married to Kamsa, were widowed due to Krishna's action. An incensed Jarasandha had vowed to teach the Yadavas a suitable lesson.

After repulsing seventeen repetitive and persistent attacks from the evil combine of Jarasandha and his associates and ascertaining that it was not the right time to eliminate this persistent evil, the great Yadava migration to distant Dwaraka was organised by Lord Krishna, as per a well thought out plan and the following pre-determined objectives.

- To escape from the persistent nuisance of Jarasandha.
- To conserve time and energy, and afford resources for an effective fight against the well established and strong forces of evil and wickedness.
- To provide the Yadava clan an opportunity and matching physical expanse to grow into an invincible empire—as at Mathura, there was no scope for such an expansion.
- To effectively disconnect from the Gokula-Vrindavana phase of life for more focused attention to the larger objectives at hand.

Creation of a large, prosperous and invincible empire at Dwaraka was implemented as per Lord Krishna's well thought out plans. It gave the needed status and confidence to the Yadava warriors, and all of them were meaningfully engaged in an intelligently crafted scheme of federal governance. Lord Krishna thus acquired the requisite status, image, and resources to play his greater divine role as a diplomat and advisor of matchless capabilities.

The perpetual conflict between the evil Kauravas and righteous Pandavas afforded him a celestial opportunity to implement his long rang design of massive and single stroke elimination of majority of evil forces. It was enacted at Kurukshetra in a masterly efficient manner. Lord Krishna's participation in the epic battle, as an unarmed charioteer of Arjuna, was a consequence of thinking ahead. In continuation of the same effort, He actively assisted the Pandavas in finding ways and means to eliminate several invincible warriors present in the Kaurava forces—Bhishma, Karna, Drona and Duryodhana being the prominent ones.

Arjuna's argumentative reluctance to fight, as required from a warrior or his status and caliber, offered Lord Krishna a golden opportunity to intensely dialogue with him and, in the process, leave for the posterity a righteous code of conduct, for people of all walks of life—to work and progress harmoniously. It was later on compiled into what is now called as the Bhagavad Gita or the Song of Wisdom.

His cosmic plan further contained a provision i.e. not to leave behind any large force, with potential for evil manifestations, at the time of completion of his human incarnate period—and in pursuance of the same, He enacted at Parbhasa, a total destruction of the great Yadava clan—and then left for his original abode.

In view of Lord Krishna's rigorous practice of thinking ahead, practitioners of modern management should apportion greater emphasis to *Long Range Planning* in all vital departments of a business enterprise and review and update the same at regular intervals for (a) sustained growth and (b) to avoid negative surprises in business progression.

Non-material Motivation

I prefer to define motivation as a process of positive thought acceleration, resulting into action or readiness for action. It starts from thought genesis and culminates into action. If the process remains incomplete, stopping at thought itself, then we shall end up becoming *Thought Warriors* only. For any action, active thought should first convert into active desire and then into need, for action to emerge. A good motivator, in addition to being a thought warrior, should also be a superior *Action Warrior,* only then he will be able to initiate and direct a positive thought process in the target beings i.e. subordinates or coworkers, to a desired and conclusive extent.

In the present corporate environment, motivation has become an area of significant challenge. Professionals are attempting to understand and implement it only in material context, while in real sense it should bear a very limited relevance to money and material. The basic process of motivation is primarily related to the state of mind, i.e. to the interplay of energies of thought and intellect. On account of inadequate understanding, motivation is being viewed in terms of salary raises, enhanced perks and on account facilities, preferred placements, flashy designations, paid holidays, stock options, and numerous other inputs of similar nature. They do only a temporary job; dissatisfaction, more expectations and fresh demands do not take much time to re-emerge. A number of corporate today are at their wits ends as how;

- to retain their high performers,
- to keep mediocre workers happy, and
- to get rid of the non-performers.

In the western concept of management, which presently enjoys the dominant advocacy and application, failures on various fronts, particularly long-term motivation and productive association of employees with corporate bodies, are openly accepted. Intense studies of Japanese and other eastern systems of management have been attempted in last 2-3 decades of the past centaury, with a view to locate some lasting solution to this perpetual challenge. The problems of present day HR-professionals, in relation to their inadequate efficacy on front of motivation, primarily seem to arise from their failure to understand man-work-reward relationship. In view of the author, work is an expression of thought and action relationship. In other words, mind is the centre of thought genesis. The latter (action) controls conversion of thought energies into work desire, work need and work output.

There is thus an intense body-mind and Atman relationship. Satisfaction or lack of it is governed by mind, intellect and spirit (Atman) interaction. So, if with every Karma or action one remains pre-occupied with results or fruits, which are governed by a lot of other factors, in addition to action, disaffection is bound to emerge. Excessive expectation or inadequate fulfillment of the same, negatively binds positive work energy, consequently limiting further action or intensity of it on part of the workers. It results into output drop and the concerned worker is rated in need of further motivation. The process goes on repeating itself; with every cycle it complicates the issue. Lack of job satisfaction is a consequence of excessive concern for fruits of action. It inhibits further initiative on part of the corporate worker as fear of results sets in, and in such a situation no new ideas or innovation tend to emerge. Quality of association between worker, work and the corporate deteriorates which leads to unhealthy expectations and responses.

Understanding the positive concept of the art of living and the art of working can reduce genesis and flow of negative energies in work environment, freeing more constructive energy for work output. When concern for fruits of action or work is kept out of active view, as under the doctrine of Karma, dissatisfaction does not germinate, and cooperation and innovation tend to bloom in a perpetually rewarding manner for everyone involved in the collective processes. It is the concentrate of Lord Krishna's divine concept of Karma, the selfless work. It is the *work positive orientation (WPO)* that offers freedom from all worries and challenges of manpower motivation, in a long term and mutually rewarding manner.

The responsibility for results should always rest with the higher authority. In case of Arjuna, on the battlefield of Kurukshetra, the wise Lord freed his divine disciple, the operative warrior, from the concern for results or output; He took it upon himself, leaving the Pandava warrior only with the responsibility of action. In a similar manner, if and when a boss or senior assumes responsibility for results in corporate work environment, a lot of positive work energies will get liberated for intense and well-targeted actions.

Association of Dharma with the concept of Karma or selfless action is always more useful as in any complicated situation, it reminds a worker (and also his coworkers) of his righteous duty. It allows corrective measures to be automatically initiated, without delay that might occur if one were to be excessively concerned with consequences. In the concept of *non-material motivation,* apart from the divine doctrine of Karma and Dharma, the following play a vital role in making it fully operational and rewarding:

- Righteous use of human prakriti.
- Right talent spotting and its exploitation.
- Respect for virtue and merit.
- Respect for reality.
- Impartial credit apportioning.
- Dignity of work.
- Commitment appreciation.
- Ethicality of operation.
- Balance of thought and action warriorism.
- Madhura communication.
- Active equation of body-mind and Atman.

Human prakriti is a very important component of worker motivation and performance process. It refers to his or her technical as well non-technical background. The environment in which one is brought up or is exposed to, determines one's response to work as well as attitude towards its fruits or results. An individual's value system is the key component of his or her prakriti. Hence, work assignment and employment of various motivation stressors should be selected in accordance to specificities of the performer's prakriti.

What is the scope for application of the non-material motivation in the present corporate environment? While attempting to answer this question, most professionals are likely to commence with a negative expression. Such a reaction will be natural, as by training and experience, they are not exposed to such a proposition. Here, it is important to remember that the body-mind-Atman interaction has not ceased to operate. It has been always operative, only our perception of it has dimmed under conditions of non-use and the over active clouds of materialism. There is a need to activate it—to render it jagarat [3] so that its benefits could be extended to the working community.

One should begin, in this direction, with study of our scriptures. Each reading is bound to strengthen the depth of understanding and perception of the reader. In fact, one does not have to go beyond a working exposure to the divine Bhagavad-Gita. Dr. S. Radhakrishna's works on Hinduism and associated matters (1927, 1953 and 1960) are a good beginning in right direction. One should take the precaution to the effect that one reading is not likely to be sufficient. First, the seniors, teachers and trainers should gain understanding of the body-mind-Atman combination and when convinced of its relevance, then attempt to employ the same as a tool of motivation. Other components of the divine non-material motivation will be much easier to understand once the basic of relevance body–mind-Atman linkage is comprehended. The second stage of its implementation shall not be difficult as all elements of virtue and righteousness tend to flow from top downwards. Institutions engaged in imparting management training need to follow the same route. Students would love to be exposed to the alternate path, which is destined to be decisively more effective, once a beginning is made in right earnest.

Under active practice of non-material motivation, negative arguments employing terms such as impossible and infeasible, are likely to disappear from communications, and consequently positive thought content will attain significant domination. Lord Krishna was an active practitioner of non-material motivation. His toughest exercise in this field was motivating a totally de-motivated, depressed and deluded Arjuna who refused to fight after seeing a number of his seniors, gurus and relations standing with the opposing Kaurava forces on the battlefield of Kurukshetra. He gave very strong and convincing arguments in favour of his stand but the wise Lord was able to locate indefensible holes in the same. Arjuna had no valid reason for running way from his Karma as a kshatriya warrior, as per his basic prakriti. The alternates to the path of action i.e., the paths of Jnana and Bhakti did not suite Arjuna's prakriti. Further, Lord Krishna freed him from results or fruits of action as He told the Pandava warrior that, in fact, he was not the killer; that all the killing was already done by the master of the universe and that Arjuna was to just act as performing the job and appropriate the credit. The wise Lord also explained that soul (Atman) does not ever get killed—it simply shifts from one body to another. He assured Arjuna that there was no question of him being burdened with the sin of killing so many people. The intense dialogue between Lord Krishna and his argumentative disciple was very long and arduous. The doctrine of Karma and Dharma was revalidated there. Finally, Arjuna did as willed by his divine charioteer and the latter's words of wisdom were subsequently immortalized by sage Vyasa, in form of what we now know as the "Bhagavad Gita".

Employing the same tools, Lord Krishna converted another impossible into possible. He persuaded Yudhishtira, a Dharmaraja—the greatest practitioner of truth, to utter a lie in order to facilitate killing of guru Drona who was proving truly invincible in the battle of Kurukshetra. Without elimination of Drona, the war against forces that were supporting evil could not have progressed any further. Earlier, on several occasions, Lord Krishna employed the technology of non-material motivation with decisive results.

Of these, the most significant occasion pertained to convincing the mighty Yadava clan, which had ruled Mathura for centauries, to vacate its ancient empire and migrate to a distant and inhospitable locale of Dwaraka. It went against the basic prakriti and Dharma of the illustrious warrior clan--as running away from a battle was worst than death for any kshatriya, as per the code of honour prevalent at that time. But for the wise Lord, the objective of his incarnation was sacrosanct; means employed for achieving the same were important but they were never assigned the seal of inviolability. So, the arrogant and mighty Yadavas were told not to be too sensitive about the non-flattering title of "Ranchood" that they attracted on account of running away from Mathura. They were also told about the benefit of living for another day and have a fight on their own terms and quite possibly win it. They were briefed about the great opportunities of development and prosperity that awaited them at the new location.

What needs to be appreciated here is that a near impossible was achieved through the righteous employment of the divine tool of non-material motivation. Defeat and death at hands of the demonic forces of Jarasandha of Magadha, even for a kshatriya clan of distinguished Yadava lineage, was not acceptable to the wise Lord. He did not want to abandon his mission incarnate objectivity. Also, He was not ready to unmask his Godliness so early in life. And the force that was destined to kill the almost invincible Jarasandha, was not yet on the active horizon. Hence, the best feasible alternative in those circumstances was adopted, but preparing the arrogant and mighty Yadavas for such an action needed the wise Lord's management tool of non-material motivation, assisted and enabled by his equally divine communication technology of madhura.

The current technology of working manpower motivation suffers from obvious deficiencies. It is entirely based upon material or monetary benefits--ignoring the fact that man does not live by money or material alone. It is just a small part of his existence, even a smaller one of his satisfaction and happiness matrix. The basic process of work generation is also being ignored. Further, the Human prakriti is not allowed to play any part. The ever-decisive linkage of body-mind and Atman does not seem to have been factored in the present game of motivation. All these gaps in the present methodology of motivation are correctable through progressive adoption of Lord Krishna's well tested divine technology of non-material motivation.

Doctrine of Karma as a Management Tool

"Business is Karma—and consequence of karma. [4]

Karmic balance determines the degree and direction of success"

Standing between the two mighty armies on the battlefield of Kurukshetra, Arjuna experienced serious pangs of conscience. He saw a number of his elders, gurus, relations and friends standing in the opposing Kaurava forces. His energies of thought overwhelmed those reserved for action. Tormented and confused, he cried, "Ah Krishna! Look, my hands shake, my mouth is dry, all my body trembles, and my hair stands on end." He added, "I can't hold my bow straight! My skin crawls and burns as if it were on fire! My mind reels." He saw evil in the sky and elaborated that no good would come from killing of so many people. On further impulse, the great Pandava warrior blurted out, "I will not fight!" and fell silent and sombre.

Krishna, who had accepted to work as Arjuna's unarmed charioteer, was suddenly foxed out of balance. His well thought out celestial scheme for the massive elimination of evil forces, was in danger of being lost unceremoniously. How could the Lord of the Universe allow this to happen? In fraction of moment, He summoned his superior thought energies and launched himself into a long and arduous dialogue to convince Arjuna that he had to fight. That he had no option! During this divine discourse, the wise Lord put substantial emphasis, among others, on what came to be known as the *Doctrine of Karma,* the major formations of which are as under:

- That there was no trace of justification in Arjuna's sorrowing for people who were not to be grieved for; the killing of all those people was not a big deal; they were all destined to die; He had, in fact, already killed them; He was the creator and destroyer of all beings—a real Two-in-One.
- That soul, the basic element of a being or the life force, is never killed—it

simply migrates from one body to another, from old to new, and the cycle of birth-death and rebirth continues in an effortlessly smooth manner. Why grieve for the inevitable? You do not determine, even for yourself, when and where to be born. How can you hope to decide when or not one is to die?

- That being a kshatriya, to battle was Arjuna's sacred dharma, the greatest good fortune.
- That by refusing to fight Arjuna was to lose a golden chance to prove that he was a true warrior. He would sin by not fighting and he would earn a bad name. People would say that Arjuna was scared of the great occasion and that they would mock at him.
- That Karma is the sure path of liberation or salvation; Jnana (knowledge) and Bhakti (devotion) are the two alternatives.
- That the preferred path for one to adopt is that of Karma—one should act as per one's prakriti [5] or nature. On Arjuna's questioning, the wise Lord explained that though the way of mind (refers to the path of Jnana) was finer than the way of action, the latter was superior to rest of the two paths.
- That the dual path always existed, the way of knowledge for men of contemplation; but for men of action, the way of deed is always preferable
- That one does not become free or liberated by doing nothing; he who does nothing but sits dreaming his desires is no sage.
- That one should do the work one is born to or that one has accepted or is assigned to.
- That one should not delude oneself by feeling, *I am the doer*; everything gets done by the essence, the gunas, of nature, in an eternal interplay.
- That the way of Karma or action is not easy; even wise get perplexed about action and inaction. Only the realized ones can detach from the lust of fruits of actions. A realized soul is satisfied with whatever comes as fruit of action; he is untouched by success or failure.
- That one should act and not be bound by his actions or their results.
- That all selfless work is sacrifice, a ritual of worship. An enlightened heart beats as one with Brahman, the Holy Spirit.
- That no individual becomes a yogi or yogin without renouncing selfishness; selfless Karma is the essence.
- That work is the way of the Rishi who wants to attain to yoga, to yoke himself to eternal. Once one attains to yoga, which is union, then serenity is attained.
- That for a man of self-control, his will becomes his soul's friend, but the self-indulgent man's will is his soul or Atman's enemy.

- That Karma is the force of creation; nothing happens without action.

Swami Vivekananda while commenting on *The Ideal of Karma* as per the settings of Vedanta(Sawananda, 1990), stated that one could reach the same goal by different paths; and these paths he generalized into four, viz. those of work, love, psychology and knowledge. He added that the division among them was not very sharp and that one could merge into another. In fact, all methods of work and worship are aimed at freedom or liberation.

When the line of action or work is proper—we call it good—and when the line of action taken is not a proper one, then we call it evil. As per the learned Swami, Karma Yoga is the attaining of the freedom or liberation through selfless work. Every selfish action tends to reduce the chances of achieving the goal. He tied to link the selfless or selfish work to morality or immorality.

In his learned view, Karma yoga is a system of righteous work, a system of ethics and religion. A true Karma Yogi does not need to believe in any doctrine, not even in God; may not even ask what his soul is. He has his own special way of conquering selfishness and thus attain to the Brahman.

Through righteous Karma one can add to happiness of the working or living environment, the quality and intensity of Karma creates inequality amongst the competitive beings. True equality is never feasible on earth as per the learned Swami, as Karma differentiation always remains the decisive factor. Karma-Yoga is the way of work to reach any goal.

According to the glorious Swami, Lord Buddha carried the teachings of Karma Yoga into true practice. He is the only prophet who said, "I do not care to know your various theories about God. What is the use of discussing all the subtle doctrines about soul? Do good work and be good. And this would take you to freedom and to whatever truth there is." He was, in conduct of his life, absolutely free from personal motives. He was, as per the Swami, the ideal Karma-Yogi, acting entirely without motive.

He who works without motive, works the best; neither for money, nor for fame or reward and when a man can do that then he becomes Buddha. That is the essence of lord Krishna's non-material motivation or motive for work or more work.

In the medieval period of Hinduism, when under the oppressive stresses of invading forces concepts and teachings of Krishna got dislocated, Karma was erroneously equated to fatalism or defeatism. What was happening to one in the present was deemed as being associated to the karma in his or her previous life. Belief in fate or excessive dependence on the same was an unfortunate consequence of inadequate communication or erroneous interpretation of the principle of Karma. It led to emergence of several ills in the socio-economic system of the people; prompting them to lose initiative and competitiveness.

The dislocation of emphasis on Karma among the people of India, in view of the author, resulted into avoidable extension of subjugation of the masses at hands of foreign forces, which were intensely hostile of Hinduism, a tolerant and accommodative faith. The nation of Bharata, unjustly suffered due the continued weakness of its own thought warriors who failed to keep the main stream faith process, i.e. Krishna's concepts of Karma and dharma, in right interaction with people.

Karma in Corporate Work Environment

Corporate environment represents work; and progressively growing productive work. The divine doctrine of Karma, when applied judiciously, can play a very constructive and rewarding role in improving corporate work performance. The necessity of action, as stressed by Lord Krishna, has vital implications in the corporate environment; everyone has to do his or her assigned work as per individuals prakriti or the nature of job. Here, the alternative path as described under the doctrine of karma, has only limited applicability. One is supposed to have or acquire knowledge of the job one is assigned to do, but knowledge by itself or the plea to acquire more of it, as an alternative, is not feasible. Yes, one can acquire superior knowledge of an area and become an expert or specialist. Bhakti or devotion as an alternative route, too is not available. It limits its application to the extent that one should be devoted to one's work or duty. It is not enough by itself. The following bits from the divine formations of Karma, can be very fruitfully applied in the corporate work environment:

- One should do the work one is born (job acceptance) to do.
- Action(or work) is sacrifice (or worship).
- Act and not be bound by its results/ fruits—selfless or detached work.
- Selfless work is the essence.
- Selfless work leads to serenity.
- Karma is the force of creation.
- No liberation or freedom without work.

All the above components of Karma have immense potential to make corporate work (a) more rewarding, (b) totally stress free, and (c) immensely enjoyable. Emphasis on selfless work, making workers rightly aware of it, can rid the corporate work environment of the various ills or deficiencies of modern management listed earlier. A little effort towards making work little selfless at the doer end, can substantially reduce negative energy, boosting cooperation, leading to immense initiative and innovation. And in such an environment output is bound to flourish. Any reduction in concern or attachment to results or fruits of work will free a lot of productive positive energy in individual doer. Many corporate workers do not do their best for a particular job under the uncertainty of results and the fear for consequent criticism. They prefer to take the route of limited action or action as directed by the boss. The scope for initiative and innovation is thus unnecessarily blocked. People often refrain from giving constructive suggestions or offering alternatives as they are scared that they might be asked to do the job. In reality, their concern for results intimidates them in advance of the results. Thus, excessive concern with the fruits of work or anticipated work becomes a major hindrance in progress.

Selfless work will induct serenity in the work force. It will free a lot of creative energy that often remains unnecessarily bound and inactive due to over concern for fruits of action. Serenity is a catalytic force for new ideas: to posses it will be so very useful for senior management and professionals.

Karma is also good for competition. Its quality and intensity creates output differentiation. The degree of unselfishness association with work or action, will allow different workers to possess differing quantities of productive positive energies. It will make a real and rewarding difference. Swami Vivekananda argued that differentiation or inequality was a natural essentiality. It is not an undesirable occurrence and, as such, should be respected. In non-corporate environment Karma is often misunderstood; people attempt to drag it in fatalistic direction. Karma pertains primarily to what we do than to what happens to us. However, most of the time it is invoked to explain what happens to us and in this context, it is then argued that what happened was the inescapable consequence of our own past deeds. By the same token, the doctrine also implies that when we set out to achieve some thing our success is inevitable too if we keep at it! Thus, if some one insists to attach fatalism to the concept of karma then he or she should also express triumphalism when it is seen on the positive edge.

Karma is also seen to possess the characteristics of (a) karmic interaction,(b) karmic accumulation, and (c) karmic balance. All these features have active relevance to the applicability of the doctrine of Karma in the field of corporate work environment.

In non-corporate environment people are often seem to employ the terms of good karma and bad karma. Here, the scale of discrimination usually is not applied very judiciously. They key to judge must be the degree of unselfishness with which a karma was undertaken. A selfless karma, irrespective of results or consequences, is a good karma. Any attempt of selfishness in any action is likely to turn a karma to a bad one. Working out a balance of karma is not difficult to a trained or discriminating mind. All karmas, good or bad, do possess time relevance in manifestations of their consequences.

Numerous learned persons, at various stages of history, have discussed karma in spiritual context, with varying views and explanations. It was erroneously presumed that spirituality and business did not mix well. The present work attempts, in context of the present situation obtaining in the field of management, to examine the truth in a contrasting manner.

As stated earlier, business is Karma and Karma is business! Good Karma is Good business!! It will be fruitful to understand the interaction of Karma and business and put some of its divine formations to practical use. HR-professionals should attempt to integrate the operational formations of karma into the training capsules for corporate workers and watch its divine impact alter and unfold their horizons of cooperation, initiative and output.

Practice of Karma Yoga

Lord Krishna always led by example! He practiced what He preached! In fact, He practiced an approach before advocating its practice by any one else. He was the ultimate Karma-Yogi! He was a man of action. He never hesitated to initiate it. No work was too small or too big for him.

- He worked hard as a cowherd.
- He did not throw tantrums for lack of facilities.
- At a very tender age, He went to fight and eliminate Kamsa, the greatest evil of that time. He did not complain for absence of an army to help him in this enormous enterprise.
- In interest of Karma, as aligned to his mission incarnate responsibilities, He willingly gave up the pleasures of living with gopis in Vrindavana.
- As a student in the ashram of guru Sandipani, He showed no reluctance in collecting wood and fruits from forest, for his guru's household.
- He worked hard to create an empire at Dwaraka.
- He willingly took the responsibility of advising and protecting the Pandava brothers.
- Despite danger to his own person, He willingly went to the court of Duryodhana to make a last ditch effort towards a minimum acceptable settlement for the Pandavas.
- He eagerly discharged the job of Arjuna's charioteer; watered, feed and groomed the horses.
- He worked hard to find ways and means to overcome the invincibility of Bhishma, Drona, Karna and other Kaurava warriors.

- Even unpleasant works did not deter him; after end of the battle of Kurukshetra, He went to offer condolences to Gandhari, whose all sons, except one, were killed in the fratricidal war. He faced her anger and risked her curse.
- Even at the fag end of his life on earth, He did not hesitate in eliminating the sprouts of potential evil. He crushed his own evil assuming clan in order to keep the earth relatively free of it for a long time.

Enumeration of all of his good karmas is beyond any mortal mind. We will serve him well by following some of his practices in this regard—and the same in turn will serve the humanity well.

Through righteous emphasis on karma, modern management professionals stand to benefit a great deal. It can become a bed- rock for introducing the divine concept of non-material motivation of corporate workers and infuse enhanced dual satisfaction in the process of business genesis and management.

Dharma as a Management Tool

Dharma as a term is understood and interpreted differently by its employers, as per their orientation and objectives. The word dharma originated from the Sanskrit root *dhari*, meaning to support, hold up or bear. Today, in wider understanding, it represents *righteousness* of action undertaken by a doer in a given situation. In Bhagavad Gita, it refers to performance of an act according to one's developmental stage and *varna* (social class). Lord Krishna employed the term dharma a number of times while delivering his renowned discourse the Song of Wisdom or the Song of Motivation to Arjuna who was greatly distressed and depressed on the prospects of having to fight a number of his respected elders and relatives who, as per forces of destiny, had elected to support the evil Duryodhana. He repeatedly reminded Arjuna, with all the force of words and gestures at his divine disposal, that as a born kshatriya, it was his duty to fight against the forces of evil and injustice.

The torrent of arguments and justifications extended by the wise Lord was of an uncommonly intense density, yet the same was having almost no impact on the insistent and deeply argumentative Pandava warrior. But, the wise Lord's commitment to justify and uphold dharma was too great for him to give up and let Arjuna run away from his divine call of the duty. Lord Krishna did not want to fail too otherwise the main objective of his having incarnated on this earth would have remained unfulfilled and the mighty Lord could not afford the same. He had to reactivate the duty related concerns of Arjuna, irrespective of the nature and intensity of efforts it required. Hence, when the verbal and non-verbal elements of his discourse did not cut any ice with the ever insistent and deeply inquisitive warrior, the supreme Lord had to reveal himself in his omnipotent cosmic form and assure a frightened Arjuna that even while killing people in the opposite formations, he would, in fact, not be doing so as all those warriors were already killed by the grace of the almighty Lord. He was further convinced that in any killing, as a matter of fact, no killing takes place as *Atman* is indestructible—it can not be killed by any instrument or weapon. It simply migrates out of a body to a newly assigned one—and in some cases, as per grace of the supreme Lord, is freed from the cycle of birth, death and rebirth, merging finally into the Lord himself.

Exposure to the cosmic immensity of the supreme Lord, administered a violent shock to Arjuna and he was rudely pulled out of his depressive delusion of inaction. He begged the Lord to assume his normal mortal form and pardon him for his unjust insistence. He was ready to do the wise Lord's bidding.

In today's corporate work environment, the *Principle of Dharma,* when suitably explained and communicated, can be a highly effective motivational tool for pushing employees and workers of all type do their assigned jobs with superior results. All corporate workers and also those engaged in activities of governance can be trained to concentrate on *Action or Act* to fullest of individual's capacity, without overdue and in advance emphasis on results or fear of the same. Once right action is initiated, results do come; overemphasis on them—prior to or at the time of action, leads to attention diversion or avoidable wastage of creative energy. Stress is laid on *doing well* whatsoever one is engaged with or is assigned to do. Hence, if you are a student, study your lessons well; if you are a salesman, do your job of selling to the best of your capabilities and energies. Similarly, the logic extends to all other works and workers, managers, non-managers and also CEOs. There is no exception of any type to this cardinal rule.

Many projects, products and corporate entities fail because corporate workers do not undertake actions assigned to them, to the best of their skills and capabilities as their attention remain fixed onto results/fruits. Due to the attention misplacement, action deficiency develops, leading to below par results. In Bhagavad Gita, the wise Lord explains that when mind is controlled, the action at all other levels gets automatically controlled—all thought waves become stable and well directed to the desired focus. Dharma emphasis, in corporate reference, is capable of offering the following uncommon advantages.

- Improvement in an individual's commitment to performance.

- Work focus improvement due to reduced anticipation of results.
- Improvement in ethics and righteousness contents of work.
- Enhanced cooperation, initiative and creativity.
- Reduction in negativity and ego flow in work environment.
- Fair credit and placement distribution.
- Long-term non-monetary motivation.
- Enhanced well-being and feel-good appreciation.
- Reduction in absenteeism and attrition.
- Greater talent attraction for expansion and innovation.
- Reduction in corrupt practices and delays.
- Complaint reduction and superior customer servicing.
- Enhanced competitiveness in globalized economy.
- Unhindered promotion of talent, and amongst others.
- General corporate well-being and rewarding performance.

Thus, senior corporate professionals and CEOs have an immense opportunity to employ *Dharma*, the celestial instrument of man-management and, in fact, a Management Brahamastra to improve the overall corporate performance on continuous basis--and at low cost, creating a problems free work environment. What the wise Lord advocated and employed so successfully several millennia ago, can now be exploited with even better results as available tools of work and communications, in a general sense, have improved a great deal.

Management by Intelligent Design

Modern biologists believe in The Theory of Evolution which was put into its present form by Darwin. His first work *The Origin of Species* in 1859 was enthusiastically accepted by the scientific community. He had put scientific observations in such simple language that even common people with no background of science or biology, could easily appreciate its significance. The first addition of The Origin of Species was sold on the very first day of its printing. As per Darwin, the creation and evolution of living beings was a long drawn and complicated process.

On the other hand, as per Christianity which was the dominant religion at that time, God formed the world in a short period and stocked it with a wealth of clearly distinguishable living beings. From the book of Genesis, Christian theologists extracted several important dogmas and explanations, though always with limited conviction, in regard to various matters related to creation. For them, the matter of creation of living beings on earth and in the sea, was a matter of *intelligent design* by the all powerful creator. In other words, all the creatures—plants and animals, whether on land or in sea, were created by the Supreme Lord, as per his well thought-out plans and designs, as He knew the best. The thought of intelligent design still continues to struggle and its supporters in the western world are fighting a losing battle.

Lord Krishna, in his human incarnate form, was not a creator: He was only a Mission Incarnate. He took birth in human form, with a specific objective or mission in view, namely to rid the earth free of the accumulated evil and wickedness or in other words, to cure and correct the creation that, at least in part, had gone wrong. It had deviated from its assigned course or the designed path of Karma and Dharma, the righteous way of living, working and progressing.

From his celestial perch in *Vaikuntha* [6], He had thought about it for long—and, in due course, had all its basic action elements well defined in the plan of things to be done, corrections to be made and results to be achieved, within the limits of an incarnate life. Also, He was ready with his strategy of plan implementation i.e. the sequence in which the major evils (demonic kings and princes who were exploiting and terrorizing the good and meritorious) were to be eliminated and who was to be handled by whom. A register of his assistants, allies and supporters was also worked out in requisite details. Who was to take birth or emerge when and where, was part of the celestial design. Keeping in view capabilities and strengths of his assistants, coworkers ,supporters and allies, He had decided the key jobs that He had to perform himself--and what could be assigned or delegated to others, in a manner that the limits of incarnation and code of ethics were fully adhered to. Accordingly, capabilities were generated and skills acquired, depending upon the stages of incarnate life at which they were required.

Lord Krishna had come into this world for limited period—a single life span. He had no time for cleansing the earth free of evil and wickedness—following the slow and time consuming process of evolution, by survival of the fittest or the wisest or through genetic deviations to meet the requirements of the desired changes. In fact, the evil and wicked elements were steering the world as per their sweet will and in the normal process of biological evolution, the good and righteous had no chance to overcome or overtake the evil usurpers. It needed outside help—in fact, a supper manager with a supper plan or intelligent design, was need of that hour. The intelligent design had to be backed with equally intelligent and efficient organizing, leading and control, in order to attain the basic objectivity of mission of the celestial incarnation.

The Lord had decided to tackle first the wickedest of the lot, the demonic Kamsa of Mathura. He was the most feared amongst the pack of evil rulers of that time. His exploitation and terrorizing of the masses had no limits—and he was assisted by an equally terrible bunch of supporters and collaborators. Since Kamsa was the first priority and as per term of the incarnation, the young Lord was not to have the benefit of a kingdom and the resources associated with the same, He planned for and brought Balarama with him, to assist in this truly challenging task. Assistance of Mahamaya, who was endowed with great illusionary powers, was also requisitioned in order to successfully misguide and delude Kamsa and his evil prison guards.

Efficient management, especially when competition is well entrenched and truly challenging, is not feasible without intelligent design which, among others, contains well thought out and detailed short term and long term plans. Matching resources mobilization in terms of manpower, funds, tools, technology, training, and information collection and processing network, has to be organized and arranged for well in advance. Since one person, not even an incarnate, is not enough to successfully run campaigns of such magnitude, a team of suitable second level of leaders becomes necessary to manage various key fronts. And contingency plans for unforeseen or unfactored circumstances have also to be built in. Lord Krishna, had provided for all these and much more in his *intelligent design or work plan* for wiping the evil and the wicked away from face of the earth.

After liberating the people of Mathura from the demonic Kamsa, as per plans, He kept himself free from the burden of day to day running of the affairs of the kingdom. The throne was restored to Ugrasena—and again as per plans, the young Krishna went ahead to acquire all requisite knowledge and expertise from guru Sandipani. Subsequently, migration of the mighty Yadava clan to Dwaraka was also organized as part of the larger objectivity, i.e. to establish a truly powerful and prosperous empire so as to (a) have resources required for implementation of the anti-evil master plan, (b) not to take the chance of disturbing potential allies located near Mathura, which expansion there would have definitely necessitated, and (c) for the time being, afford safety from persistent attacks from the invincible Jarasandha of Magadha.

Strategic collaboration with Pandava warriors was planned well in advance. Kunti, the sister of Krishna's father was married to the warrior prince Pandu of Hastinapura. Through celestial blessings, five famous warrior sons called Pandavas were added to the family through his two wives Kunti and Modri. At the right time, Krishna took them under his celestial protection and tutelage. He successfully employed them to eliminate most of the evil and wicked kings and princes of that time. They were Lord Krishna's most potent management tools in meeting the basic components of the grand intelligent design, which He had crafted prior to assuming the responsibilities of his human incarnation mission. Through skillfully planned matrimonial alliances of self and other major warriors of the vast Yadava clan, the wise Lord had created a chain of highly useful allies and supporters. Further his intelligence, bravery, erudition and charisma had created a multitude of admirers, devotees and disciples who were ready to do whatsoever the wise operator of the intelligent design wanted.. Finally, Lord Krishna's intelligent design paid rich dividends as is evident from the following;

- Most of the evil forces, operative at that time, were successfully eliminated.
- Rule of the righteous and virtuous was re-established.
- For the benefit of the posterity, an immortal code of social behavior and ethics was left in form of the Bhagavad Gita, based on the long and stimulating dialogue that occurred between the wise Lord and his equally wise and argumentative disciple Arjuna, on the battle fields of Kurukshetra, prior to commencement of the hostilities.

For the practitioners and operators of the modern management, Lord Krishna's management by intelligent design offers an invaluable lesson that a truly intelligent design, when prepared and implemented with due diligence and care, irrespective of the field of its relevance, is bound to ensure planned results. Hence, one should always pay due attention to it.

High Performance Consulting as a Management Tool

Corporate work environment, as a matter of its innate nature, remains in grip of perpetual change. Continuously spiraling competition speeds up the process of change. In the turbulence of change, organizations attempt for new capabilities of flexibility and responsiveness. Old models/concepts of management that relied on planning, checking and controlling, are being consigned to the dust bin. Also, major shifts in strategies, product lines and service-offerings are taking place. Technology is forcing emergence of new organizational structures. Work and corporate locations are becoming less of an issue. Simply doing more what was done well, looks unlikely to sustain us in the future. That we are better this year than the last, is not good enough—one has to be better than today. Hence, planning parameters have to be set for weeks and months rather than years. Rapid technological changes are prompting for new ideas and approaches for managing and motivating people. Empowerment now seems to encompass acceptance of responsibilities for control and performance of your work. Knowledge management is no more simply a buzzword and what managers traditionally practiced is being questioned. The race is to do right the very first time and it is being interpreted that organizations can no longer afford the large number of managers in controlling or supervisory functions. Many middle management roles are simply avoidable, in order to compete faster and be cost effective.

The concept of bigness is being questioned and big budget and a large number of subordinates is no longer an indicator of competence or contribution—and this approach no longer needs to be rewarded. The old concept of bigness of one's position often germinated internal politicking, game playing and empire building, all indicators of inbuilt inefficiencies. Concentration of decision making power was indeed bad for competitive efficiency. For more innovative and customer responsive organizations, there is always a need to devolve powers to the point of customer contact. Self-directed teams have to rely on their collective motivation, skills and capabilities to come out with the desired performance.

Hence, work environments are experiencing substantial shifts—often causing pains to the laggard and inefficient while rewarding the responsive and efficient, a truly two into one process. The pressure for productivity enhancement and true value addition is relentless. Organizations seem increasingly reluctant to tolerate activities that do not significantly add value. Outsourcing has become a truly global business as more and more organizations are off-loading what can be got done at lover costs and more efficiently, without adding permanent employee bulk.

The speed of work environment changes, as discussed above, have necessitated what is normally called *Consultancy*, internal as well as external. Internal consultancy attempts to produce results through influence (by effecting understanding and acceptance in regard to desired changes) rather than the use of formal executive power mechanism. Such consultants, being aware of the inherent political nature of organizations, can manage to avoid getting entangled in complex and often negative interactions. Specialist technical knowledge is employed to influence skills and in remodeling of organizational change—and thus effect performance up-gradations. They are essentially *Change Agents*, i.e. effecting change with the minimum resistance and controversy. A consultant's work begins when an organization's part of strategy, structures, processes or systems fail to perform and the same is noted with concern by the senior management—and if it has the will to correct the same in a meaningful manner. Consultants are employed to bridge the gap while, sometimes, they begin with identification and quantification of the problem or the non-performing areas with greater clarity. And consultants' assignments can be both short and long-term. A good consultant should operate in a manner that the beneficiary is left with an enhanced capacity to solve future problems, at least of the similar nature, without external intervention. An improved capability should be left behind. But consultants' work is not always free from problems of internal resistance and less than desired cooperation. It is primarily a consequence of engagement of a consultant and handling the same by the senior management without wider deliberations.

External consultants are the *experts* who are called in to solve the problems for which no significant internal capacity or capability exists. They often have highly focused approach, a specific brief, a recognized high level of expertise and, in addition, use all the expertise and resources of the client. They, normally, attempt to upgrade or add to the expertise available with the client, in view of its perceived competitive requirements. Like internal consultants, they too suffer from various difficulties in getting accepted and implemented their recommendations.

To practitioners of the modern management, consultancy seems to be a relatively recent addition, as a means of productivity or performance enhancement. The facts, however, seem to indicate in a different direction. Consultancy, in fact, commenced with the very beginning of collective or organized working by human beings. In one or the other form, it always gave company to the human endeavour to attain dominance, economic or otherwise. There are numerous examples of employment of consultancy in the business of acquiring territorial and or political dominance and superiority.

Lord Krishna seems to be the mankind's *oldest and the most efficient consultant*. He operated as an internal as well as external consultant, at various stages of his life. He neither held any executive powers either in the Yadavas regimes at Mathura and Dwaraka nor with the Pandavas at Indraparastha. No sooner the young Krishna killed the demonic Kamsa of Mathura, old Ugrasena was made the king of the liberated Yadava kingdom and even after their migration to Dwaraka, he continued to rule to the very end of the empire. In case of the Pandavas, Yudhishtra was the sole ruler in pre as well as the post Kurukshetra periods. Through his unique capabilities, some of which are listed below, Lord Krishna was always able to manage decision processes in line of his choice or requirements—and very efficiently fulfilled the demands of his Mission Incarnate responsibilities.

- Possession of unique charisma, an extremely impressive personality.
- Capability to perform in most challenging circumstances.
- Exceptionally superior physical strength and prowess.
- Unique skills of combat and warfare.
- Great skills to devise unique/successful strategies.
- Capacity to find solutions to impossible/ invincible situations.
- Great capacity for correct analysis& foresight—to see and predict the future.

- Divine knowledge of scriptures and capacity to deliver the same with desired impact.
- Unique communication technology—the irresistible madhura.
- Capacity to lead from the front, leading by example.
- Commitment adherence, capacity to deliver as per commitment.
- Unique skills of diplomacy and opponent management.
- Superior management of conflict and crisis.
- To correctly read and judge people, their good or bad intentions.
- Capacity to effect alignments of long-term utilities.
- Superior information collection and analysis.
- Ability to foresee and influence events of significance.
- Immense capacity for empathy, unique emotion quotient.
- Adherence to practical ethicality.
- Upholder of righteousness and protector of the virtuous.
- Right/correct credit apportioning for good work.
- Effective delegation with multiple objectivity.
- Protector of disciples and devotees.
- Supporter of friends, relations and coworkers.
- Active chastiser of evil and the wicked.

Lord Krishna's consultancy operations commenced early in life. When part of the cowherd community, He advised whole of his clan to shift to Vrindavana from Gokula and benefit from better opportunities of fodder and pastures. Further, he convinced them to discontinue the long held practice of untenable sacrifices and rituals—and instead motivated them to take up the care of cow which was in the process of becoming an economic animal of long term significance.

Without being head of the Yadava kingdom, He advised the proud and mighty Yadavas to abandon Mathura and migrate to distant Dwaraka

- to escape the great cost that was being imposed on them by persistent and savage attacks by the great demonic Jarasandha, from the kingdom of Magadha, and
- to benefit from the great potential that the unique location of Dwaraka offered for establishment of a large and prosperous empire.

He consistently advised the migrant Yadavas to convert the inhospitable environment of the new location into a productive and uniquely prosperous empire and also in designing and implementing a truly federal structure of governance. The greatest and the most challenging consultancy assignment of the wise Lord was with the Pandavas; it began at Panchala where He spotted them at the time of Draupadi's marriage to them. Afterwards, at every stage of their eventful life, in exile or otherwise, He was regularly benefiting them with his unique consultancy skills. Some of the memorable divine advices that He rendered to them, when asked or even otherwise, were as follows;

- Advised the five Pandavas, even against the tradition, to accept Draupadi as their joint wife and helped them work out an arrangement to successfully implement the same on a long-term basis.
- He persuaded them to go to Hastinapura as per invitation of their undependable uncle Dharishthrastra.
- Further, it was Lord Krishna who advised them to accept the division of the kingdom of Hastinapura, as made by their uncle and proceed to the Khandavaparastha to reclaim it and develop the same into a productive and prosperous kingdom.
- Lord Krishna not only gave very useful and practical advice to the Pandava brothers in developing their kingdom, He guided Arjuna in taming the divine Agni that offered him unique weaponry.
- Services of his divine architect and construction wizard, Vishvakarma, were made available to the Pandavas—he helped them create a uniquely beautiful city of Indraparastha, giving rise to significant jealousy in the heart of Duryodhana.
- When Yudhishtra wanted to celebrate the Rajasuya yajana and declare himself an emperor, Lord Krishna advised him in regard to its impracticality before getting rid of the mighty demonic king Jarasandha of Magadha. A plan for successful elimination of the demonic challenge was put into play and, through it, the Pandavas got the unique gift of support of hundreds of kings and princes who were freed from the prisons of Jarasandha after he was killed by Bhimma, in a long and difficult combat which was actively supervised by the celestial consultant.
- Pandavas successfully celebrated the Rajasuya as per divine guidance of Lord Krishna.
- After the Pandavas lost their great kingdom through the cunning of Sakuni and Duryodhana and they went on forest sojourns as part of the terms of the exile, Lord Krishna visited them in the forest and advised Arjuna to upgrade his combat skills and weaponry, as the same was to come handy in opinion of the great Lord.
- After the Pandavas completed their period of exile, the wise Lord advised them how to regain their part of the kingdom.

- Finally, He acted as their war consultant, i.e. advised them how to prepare for a final fight and also how to go about for strengthening and renewal of their alliances and relationships.
- In the decisive battle of Kurukshetra, He leads them from the front as the unarmed charioteer of Arjuna.
- During the difficult phases of the epic battle , through his superior knowledge and skills, He found for them, ways and means to break or surmount the invincibility of Bhishma, Drona, Karna and last, but not the least, the mighty evil Duryodhana.
- He advised Yudhishtra to benefit from the immense knowledge reservoir of Bhishma, in regard to righteous governance, before the old and wounded warrior decided to depart from this world.
- And the great Lord's consultancy assignment continued for long years (a) to help the Pandava brothers and Draupadi (who had lost all her sons in the senseless conflict) get over the pain (and also guilt that some of them suffered for the great loss of life) of the ruinous war, and (b) rebuild the damaged infrastructure of governance.

Lord Krishna's great consultancy operations offer lessons of unique significance to the modern management community. He proved beyond any doubts that with merits of skills and righteousness, it is possible to be effective even when one does not have direct executive powers to solve problems. The force of merit and virtue is of great utility in productive management of affairs of governance, whether related to business or war.

Dialogue as a Management Tool

Dialogue is an important aspect of communication. It plays a very substantial role in the process of management where new ideas and inputs have to be conveyed, understood and accepted. A dialogue can occur between any two persons, senior and junior, boss and subordinate, teacher and taught, guru and disciple, equals (peers) and unequals. Amongst others, dialogue is necessary

- to create understanding of a point or position,
- to elaborate, enrich and analyze,
- to remove doubts and objections, and
- to finally create an agreement.

To ensure that a dialogue proceeds in desired direction and at the right pace, is primarily the responsibility of the dialogue initiator or senior one of the persons involved. For proper progression of a dialogue, it is imperative that one is not daunted by depth of queries or contents of the points raised and tone of a dialogue should always be temperate. Inadequacy of dialogue and or its intermission, for any reason, may lead to inadequacy or failure of the management process. Motive, ego and negative reactions are very dangerous for dialogue, and consequently for the very function or process of management.

Lord Krishna was a seasoned Master of Dialogue. He was gifted with a divine capacity for effective employment of words and language, anointed with the right mix of expression and action. As a child, He could steal curd and butter with total impunity and yet, argued effectively in favor of his innocence, when caught. Sometimes, he put his mother Yashoda into emotionally delicate position by mischievously implying that she did not love and care enough for him because she did not give him birth. And his complaints about elder brother Balarama's teasing him in reference to his dark complexion, exhibited his divine dialogue proficiency. In early youth, his intense education and training, at the ashram of Guru Sandipini, transformed him into a truly efficient and, in deed, a divine dialogue master. He had acquired a unique technique of madhura communication that could easily disarm even a very ardent and determined opponent.

Soon, Lord Krishna's capacity of divine dialogue was put to severe test when He realized the Yadavas' incapacity to defend their kingdom of Mathura against repeated and sustained attacks from the mighty Jarasandha, the demonic ruler of Magadha who was rightly angered due to widowing of his two daughters on account of killing of Kamsa by Krishna. As per the force of destiny, Kamsa himself invited Krishna and Balarama, as his long lost nephews, to participate in festivities under pretext of which He thought that He could eliminate them. He had presumed that, being very young and inexperienced, it would be easy to get rid of the potential threat. Since sage Narada had warned him about the threat, Kamsa was spending sleepless nights. Hence, in the given situation, Krishna had no choice but to redeem the long suffering people of Mathura and free his own parents who were imprisoned for long by this most cruel and terrible ruler of that time.

As a consequence of the situation arising out of the insurmountable threat from Jarasandha, Young Krishna had to convince his elder brother Balarama and other senior Yadavas, to vacate Mathura and migrate to distant Dwaraka, against the prevalent kshatriya code of honor i.e. not to run away from a fight or battlefield, at any cost. It was a very difficult and, in fact, a dishonorable proposition for the proud Yadavas. But, as explained by Krishna, with the right mix of reality and madhura, they had no choice as at that stage, Jarasandha was truly invincible. He had a large and well equipped army, a good bunch of allies and supporters and above all, he had acquired a boon that he could not be killed by any Yadava. Krishna explained to the proud Yadava warriors that, in his opinion, it was better to live for another day and give a fight at the right time and redeem the honor. Finally, He succeeded due to his sustained divine dialogue capabilities and the whole Yadava clan migrated to Dwaraka where they prospered in a uniquely impressive manner. It grew into the most powerful and prosperous empire of that period and Krishna, as a *knowledge and action warrior,* emerged as truly invincible force.

The toughest test of Krishna's *divine dialogue capabilities* emerged on the battle- field of Kurukshetra—where mighty armies of Kauravas and Pandavas, along with their respective supporters, had gathered for decisive action, in the long festering fratricidal dispute between the two branches of the Kuru-clan. Surveying the two great armies readying for action, Arjuna, the mighty general of the righteous, developed doubts in regard to the very utility and necessity of the armed action that was threatening to commence any moment. He raised the issue with Krishna, who was acting as his charioteer too, by stating that he did not want to fight. He elaborated by questioning whether it was right to kill so many people, for the purpose of recovering their kingdom and whether one should be concerned only with one's duty to promote a just cause and be indifferent to slaughter and misery that the war would undoubtedly cause. Krishna responded with articulation of his concept of the sanctity of *Karma or Action* based on priority of doing one's assigned duty, a corner stone of the Indian philosophy.

Arjuna insisted on his point, adding that He did not want the kingdom at the cost of such bloodshed and that he would not mind retiring as a hermit into a forest and begging for food etc. On further intensification of the dialogue, Arjuna further added that he would not mind even if the sons of Dharitarashtra killed him in order to benefit from the situation. Arjuna's dejection and depression and growing persistence worried Krishna a great deal, as his disciple raised questions of immense depth and relevance even beyond karma, dharma and one's duty, stretching into realms of birth and death, creatures and creation, janana and bhakti, renunciation and renouncement, salvation and deliverance, body-mind and atman, yoga and cosmic forces and much more. He was intensely argumentative yet genuinely inquisitive to the extent that even Krishna's divine dialogue capacities, at occasions, were seemingly inadequate.

It worried Krishna as He saw his design of life-time on verge of failure. Without the co-operation of Arjuna, the golden opportunity for en-mass elimination of evil forces was bound to fail. There was no other warrior in the camp of the righteous forces who could eliminate all the great warriors accumulated on the side of the evil and wicked. Krishna himself was under a self-inflicted vow--not to wield any weapon in this conflict—and He was not wanting to openly use his cosmic powers. Hence, He recalled mother Yashoda and all the knowledge, skills and powers at his disposal and employing the forces of touch, expressions and madhura attempted to answer and explain all the queries raised by the inquisitive and insistent Pandava. Finally, Krishna employed his cosmic powers and convinced Arjuna to do his duty in light of the fact that it was will of the almighty Lord, the sole creator and destroyer. For all the bloodshed, no blame shall be apportioned to Arjuna, as result or consequence should not be his concern that being the area of Lord's responsibility and concern.

In the entire human history, written or otherwise, dialogue of such intensity, depth and expanse has never occurred. It was so unique in richness of contents and their relevance to mankind, in terms of utility in day to day life and maintenance of the right code of moral behavior that it is often called as the Song of Wisdom. Later on, sage Vyasa and Lord Ganesha compiled the same as the holy Bhagavad Gita.

In summary, the morale of the divine dialogue that took place between lord Krishna and his celestial disciple Arjuna is that;

- even very serious and fundamental issues can be settled through dialogue,
- dialogue is essential to create lasting understanding and acceptance(U/A),
- and when such U/A is achieved-- fully committed action should emerge.

Since U/A is an essential requirement for any collective action, the significance of dialogue as a management tool is automatically established. Hence, the modern management professionals, whether in business or governance, can significantly benefit from the Lord Krishna's example of effective dialogue. They should not shy away from an honest, intelligent and intense dialogue and like the wise Lord, it is always the responsibility of the senior of the dialogue participants to keep it on track in a polite and constructive manner and take it to logical conclusion.

Oneness of Thought and Deed

Prior to commencement of the great battle of Kurukshetra, Arjuna ran into an intense argument with Lord Krishna who was acting as his charioteer, in regard to the very justification and validity of fratricidal war. In midst of the long drawn dialogue, Arjuna asked as to why human beings fall into the net of sin to which the wise Lord clarified that it was important to subdue and control the mind with the help of reason and kill the energy of desire lying within. The Lord added that it was not easy to overcome desire and its associated manifestations such as greed and anger, the force of desire being such that it is never fully eliminated and enjoyment of one set of objects leads to genesis of desire for others.

In order to achieve some success in this field, attainment of *Oneness of*

Thought, Word and Deed or OTWD in brief, is required. When mind is subdued (undesirable thought is curbed with weapon of logic) words and deeds fall in line, i.e. harmful words are not uttered and good deeds are initiated. On attainment of such an integration of thought, word and deed, one's capacity for productive work output is enhanced in a manner that indecision and friction are minimized below harmful levels. Suitable selection of words can avoid genesis of anger, discontent, non-cooperation and de-motivation. Hence, any effort with OTWD tends to become more focused and produces desirable results.

In other words, the wise Lord conveyed that there should be total synthesis of thought and action/deed. There is no scope of any gap between the two and when that happens, the undesirable occurrence of word is automatically taken care of. Neither thought nor deed, alone and individually, is enough or desirable as for smooth working of a being, total synthesis of the two is essential. This well tested approach of Lord Krishna in regard to Oneness of Thought and Deed, can be of uncommon significance for various segments of the modern management, particularly where human interaction is intense and valuable as performance determinant. Some of these, among others, could be

- superior motivation for those engaged in high performance demand areas,
- for enabling training professionals achieve total improvement in performance of trainees,
- for effecting totally unbiased performance assessments, and
- for making meetings, conferences and discussions truly productive.

Through out his intense and arduous life, as evident from Mahabharatha and Bhagavad Gita, Lord Krishna intensely practiced the principle of Oneness of Thought, Word and Deed. One glorious example pertains to his promise to Draupadi wherein He committed that her tormentors, the evil Kauravas shall be suitably punished—and her dishonoring shall be avenged. His words of promise to Draupadi emerged after due integration with his intense thoughts about the matter and He took appropriate actions to create and manage events to the effect that the commitment was fully met.

Lord Krishna's own voluntary commitment not to wield any weapon in the conflict of Mahabharatha, was made after due thought to participate in it only at a transcendental level and He gloriously matched his words with deeds, despite tremendous odds encountered at several occasions.

Towards the massive migration of Yadavas out of Mathura, to a distant and desolate locale of Dwaraka, the wise Lord had given a long and intense thought input. It involved an arduous and exhausting exercise of deliberations and debate with the senior members of the clan, with numerous disagreements and dissensions, and in due course, the great Lord achieved a perfect synthesis of thought, word and deed. A vast, prosperous and glorious empire, befitting the mighty Yadavas, was created in a short time. It even, at least in part, washed away the disgrace that they had earned by running away from the invading forces of the evil Jarasandha and his supporters. And in due course of time, He fulfilled his word of dealing with this evil force in a decisive manner. He motivated Bhimma, the mighty Pandava, to eliminate Jarasandha in a long-drawn one to one unarmed combat.

Most of the present day management professionals and experts, engaged in vital works of corporate or governance, are unable to attain even a fraction of success and sophistication of Lord Krishna, in effective integration of the elements of thought, word and deed—despite the availability of information and communication technologies. Vast scope for improvements to learn from practices of the mankind's greatest management expert does, however, exist in substantially alluring manner.

Management of Intangibles

In almost all management situations, whether related to business, governance or conflict, there always exists a certain mix of tangible and intangible factors or assets and the same tends to act as determinant of direction as well as success of the subject activity. Those engaged with the decision taking process, normally tend to concentrate on the physicals, the visible components, inputs or aspects of the situation. By default, management tends to emphasise the planning and organizing aspects of business which normally involves arranging and providing for capital, work space, equipment and raw materials, the basic inputs of production. These are the tangible aspects of human activities, corporate or otherwise. For instance, it has been reported that during 2003 and 2004, China invested about 50 percent of its GDP in plant and equipment, a rate twice that of India. It is just a case of over-indulgence with the tangibles and by no means it is a solitary instance.

These tangible inputs or the physical assets of business do not work by themselves. It is the thought capital or intellectual capital of the people involved, especially the knowledge workers that releases human potential in form of more efficient products, processes and services. As compared to economists and accountants, stock markets seem more efficient at recognizing future value—which accounts for the apparently high multiples of market value to the book value. The recent spurt in value of financial assets, much beyond the physical assets, signifies the decisive value of *intangibles* in the economic growth. The fact that intangibles often play a more significant role in wealth generation than physical assets, has been empirically established. Accountants and accountancy have, however, often succeeded in overshadowing the intangibles by not quantifying their critical contributions nor reflecting the same in balance sheet in some suitable manner.

Leaders in fields of business and governance, as primary component of their jobs, are responsible for wealth generation and prosperity acceleration and some of them are already using human metrics (for instance education and health) to measure progress. Corporate leaders are getting increasing engaged with tools that can help them measure and monitor the intellectual capital of their organizations and take more efficient decisions in critical areas of resources allocation.

Now board rooms are reported to be increasingly discussing ways and means to better manage (measure and monitor) their intangible assets like human capital, brands, logos, R&D, processes and patents just to enumerate a few. Collectively all these, being results of the positive thought energies of people involved, ensure the maximum value addition.. Management of corporations' intellectual capital now is a growing science and soon more efficient and easy to follow methodologies shall emerge on the corporate efficiency analysis scene. Relative significance of intangibles is bound to grow and their rightful recognition is not far away. Management gurus and training institutions have already commenced to assign these factors their rightful emphasis and significance.

Lord Krishna was a true master in management of intangibles. Right early in childhood, He created long lasting and immensely valuable brands in terms of his divine blue body, yellow robes, poses of stealing butter and curd, flute and ornaments, dance on head of serpent king Kalia, lifting of mount Goverdhana on his little finger, dance circles with gopas and gopicas, and several more. As a young warrior, his battle field accessories such as chariot, Sudarshan Chakara, Panchanjaya conch, Komodaki mace, and Saringa bow became immortal brands of celestial significance. Whatsoever name one called the great Lord by, including the not so honorable "Ranchhod," always became an immortal brand by itself.

His recognition, promotion and employment of intangibles was in deed superb. He could read face and mind of people, whether friends or adversaries, with immense ease and accuracy. He was the matchless judge of virtue and merit wherever it occurred. The wise Lord's support for good and right, knowledge and expertise, in addition to virtue and merit of any type, was legendary.

He recognized the great value of human capital, all through his intense struggle against evil and wickedness. His support for good and righteousness became his most precious brand. Protection and support to his disciples, devotees and lovers became his landmark of commitment. The wise Lord's valuation of human capital was legendry. Pandavas were his most precious human capital which He employed to fullest benefits in his massive struggle against asuras, demons and all that exploited and tortured, the noble, wise and weak. Draupadi, Vidura, Vyasa and Bhishama were his other valuable human capital assets.

In the Yadava camp, Balarama, Ugrasena, Sattaki, Daruka, Pradyumna, Udhava etc. were his invaluable human assets. Each one was put to most profitable use by the wise Lord for completion of his immense mission of incarnation and each one in the process became a valuable brand of perpetual significance.

Lord Krishna's most skillful employment of intangibles unfolded on the battlefields of Kurukshetra, where the wise Lord had elected to act as charioteer of Arjuna. Under his divine guidance, the numerically much inferior Pandava forces humbled the massive collection of fighters in the Kaurava camp, a number of whom were truly invincible. Superior deployment of warriors as per their specific strengths, right information on weaknesses of several great Kaurava warriors, and motivation of higher order were converted into factors of advantage and win-ability. The great intangible of Yudhishtira i.e. the absolute truthfulness, was employed to eliminate the unstoppable warrior Drona. In case of elimination of Bhishma, Karna, Jaidharatha and Duryodhana too, the intangibles were used with decisive impact.

The most spectacular display of usage of intangibles, however, occurred when the great Lord attempted to shake off inaction and adamancy of Arjuna who was refusing to wield weapons and fight as he had noticed in the opposite line-up of forces a number of his own relatives, elders and gurus in killing of whom the Pandava fighter saw no justification. In the arduous process of convincing Arjuna, the wise Lord had to resort to *thought warriorism* of a very high order and in the process created, by design or otherwise, Bhagavad Gita, the brightest brand or intangible of all times. He enunciated the concepts of karma, dharma, jnana and renunciation which continue to guide the social, religious and other vital behavior of a vast multitude of mankind for the past over five millennia.

Senior professionals and CEOs of the corporate world, particularly those possessing capabilities for constructive employment of human/intellectual capital and other available intangibles, should attempt to benefit from the bright record of Lord Krishna's practice of effective deployment and employment of the non-physical inputs, for business and governance. Management training and other human capital improvement institutions should particularly train and equip the emerging army of future managers

and administrators, in efficient use of intangibles factors and inputs. Thought warriorism needs to be encouraged to come up with innovative ways of employing these factors of great significance. Afterwards, the action warriors of the management team should put the same to productive use as in the emerging future only the corporates that can make efficient use of available intangibles, shall be able to compete in the global business environment.

Mind Management as an Effective Tool

While delivering the song of wisdom, Lord Krishna tells Arjuna that one who has a good mind is dear to him. "He who hates no creature, and is friendly and compassionate towards all, who is free from the feelings of 'I and mine,' even-minded in pain and pleasure, forbearing, ever-content, still in meditation, self-controlled, and possessed of firm conviction, with mind and intellect fixed on Me—he who is thus devoted to Me, is dear to Me." The wise Lord explained to his foremost disciple, the vital relationship between *body, mind and soul,* stating that soul or the Absolute is the owner occupier, body like various physical and material assets and facilities of a corporate, viz. factories, depots and branches, and mind as the controlling CEO. In this vital tripod, the first is Me or part of Me—it finally returns unto Me and at my direction. The last two are only mortal manifestations.

Krishna, thus with the above and much more, through his song of eternal wisdom, managed Arjuna's mind, and motivated him to shed his doubts and discharge his obligations as a kshatriya. It was not the first time that the wise Lord employed *mind management technology,* in reference to his disciples, friends and foes. He could read through mind and body of a person who faced him irrespective of distance involved, and worked on him or her from within, if so required. From his long career, numerous instances are known where He effectively employed this ever-effective tool of *mind management*, to either motivate people to cooperate, or scare them away into change or confusion.

- In the backward community of nomadic cowherds, He danced and frolicked with young maidens, without arousing ire of elders as He had taken several measures to push them into confusion regarding presence of an incarnation in their mid.
- The young Lord worked on minds of elders of his community to abandon Gokula and go and settle at Vrindavana. Such change of locations is not normally easy.
- From the isolation of Gokula and Vrindavana, the young Lord worked on

mind of the demonic Kamsa, in a manner that the evil king suffered sleepless nights. The nomadic sage Narada was of immense use towards fulfillment of this objective.

- The young Lord's wise act of installing Ugrasena on the throne of Mathura, after killing the demonic Kamsa and his collaborators, was designed among others, for the purpose of positive influence on minds of leaders of the oppressed Yadavas. It earned the young Lord an instant loyalty of a potentially very strong clan.
- Krishna did not spare even his guru Sandipani in this regard. He persuaded the learned guru, to go fast track in teaching him and brother Balarama, all the available sixty-four types of sciences and arts known at that time, in as many days.
- Persuading Yadavas to vacate Mathura, in face of persistent attacks from Jarasandha, the invincible and demonic king of Magadha, was not a cake walk even for the wise Lord. He had to undertake an elaborate exercise in psychology management of the key figures of the Yadava clan.
- Krishna actively assisted Pandavas in establishing a vibrant kingdom in the wilderness of Kandavaparastha and even loaned his celestial architect Visvakarma to create a wondrous capital city of Indraprastha. It permanently established him as their advisor and well wisher, and that helped the Lord in later years, to get several demonic forces eliminated through the mighty Pandavas.
- In a forest hutment, Krishna assured the grieving Draupadi that the insults inflicted on her in Hastinapura shall be avenged and that Yudhishtra will again be a king and all those who insulted her shall pay for their sins. He advised her to be little patient. It was, in fact, an exercise in deeply influencing the mind of Pandava brothers, for a later day action at Kurukshetra, which only He was sure about.
- After failure of his mission at Hastinapura to persuade evil Duryodhna to return to Pandavas their rightful kingdom of Indraparastha or even yield just five villages, Krishna called Karna to his chariot and talked to him while on his return journey. The Lord disclosed to Karna that he was, in fact, the eldest son of Kunti and, as such, he was the eldest Pandava and that he should return to the their camp instead of being on side of the evil. Karna listened to the Lord patiently and elaborated his own reasons and commitments that prevented him from accepting the Lord's advice. Through this strategic interaction, the wise Lord weakened the invincible warrior's resolve to grievously harm Pandavas.

- Right in middle of the battle of Kurukshetra, when the old warrior Bhishma was inflicting heavy losses on the Pandava formations, Krishna advised Yudhishtra to visit the old fighter one evening and ask him secret of his death, knowing that Bhishma could not disappoint the righteous Pandava. Here too, the Lord's strategy of mind management brought the desired results.

After Lord Krishna, many other wise saints and gurus have stressed the importance of mind and its management for greater welfare of mankind, and enhancing productivity and happiness. Swami Vivekananda said at one place: "He who knows and controls his own mind, knows the secret of every mind and has power over every mind." Lord Krishna fully met the mental strengths described by the learned swami [7], and He made full use of the same during his long and rigorous struggle against evil forces to eliminate which He had incarnated.

Many experienced corporate managers use the technique of mind management, perfected by the wise Lord, such a long time ago. They, however, do not achieve the same efficacy in terms of results because (a) they do not have the gift of the Lord's skills, and (b) do not employ the right communication and motivation technology necessary for visible and reproducible results. Training methodology, to enable senior corporate functionaries to achieve superior results from applications of the wise Lord's methods of mind management, is available and can be transferred for their benefit.

Management of Unproductive Thoughts [8]

Individual worker, blue or white collared, is the basic building block of an organization. In competitive work environment, each one of such workers has his or her objectivity well defined to earn more, shift jobs and rise to the top as fast as possible. In such an individualistic situation, conflict is bound to germinate and it could be inter-worker, inter-team, inter-department, intra worker (within each individual) or any other mutant of the same.

Conflict of Thought: Conflict first emerges at the thought level then grows into conflict of action and behavior, which includes internal politics, non-constructive criticism ,aimless gossip, favoritism, and its numerous other forms-- reducing individual as well as collective or team productivity, giving rise to inefficiency and various associated ills. Visible conflicts or outer conflicts are relatively easy to spot and manage. Conflict of thought can manifest, among others, as anger, hostility, depression, delusion and inaction. This inner conflict primarily emerges as a consequence of contradiction of mind and one's inner – being. Arjuna, the great Pandava warrior, was afflicted with a severe inner conflict prior to commencement of the battle of Kurukshetra, and even Lord Krishna, his celestial charioteer and guru, found it very difficult to free him from the same.

Inner Conflict: Each individual works on two planes, one for the organization or the team, and another for his own-self and conflict tends to arise on both the planes. In the first case, it is relatively easier to spot and identify the conflict and also to come up with remedial measures to minimize or eliminate the same, for ensuring the planned team output. On the individual plane, i.e. within an individual worker where it clashes with the inner self of the person, it is more difficult to be managed, with any substantial degree of success. An individual may get confused on what to do and how much to do, how to cooperate and how much, where to work and how long, when to jump job and for what benefits? What will be the monetary or non-monetary gains? Will the new situation be better than the earlier one and what about the future? These internal conflicts and confusions, the cobwebs of thoughts and non-thoughts, and actions and inactions, continue to bewilder an individual. Clarity of thought and direction continues to desert him.

It is not infrequent when Evil overtakes individuals, pushing them either to act negatively, damaging collective interests or falling into confusion, delusion and inaction. Freeing an individual from strongholds of Evil or wiping off the consequent confusion is necessary, if stability and righteousness of thought and action is to be established. Within each individual, there exists a perpetual tug-of-war between evil and non-evil forces—balance of which decides the direction of action. Oscillations of thoughts and actions occur all the time, activating or preventing right or wrong choices. When Evil overtakes an individual, his or her own output (and by default that of the team too) suffers. Evil can interfere with ones logic of decision making at occasion, putting even righteousness on the wrong path.

When Arjuna stood between two armies in the battle-field of Kurukshetra, Evil took hold of him. Krishna wanted to draw his disciple's attention to war preparations and said gently, *Look Arjuna, The glorious Kuru armies.* And his disciple did not even hear him—he had come under spell of Evil, to a dangerous extent. Arjuna was trembling with fear, biting his lips as anxiety had coiled around him, making him moan softly and shiver visibly. Krishna noted with concern Arjuna's state of confusion and bewilderment and felt as if the same fate awaited him. He was not able to look at his disciple who was in sorry state, beads of sweat falling from his forehead, attempt to wipe which was futile and hiding the same was out of question. Out of agony he cried "Ah Krishna! Look, my hands shake, my mouth is dry, all my body trembles, and my hairs stand on their ends." Unable to stand, like a thin twig in high wind, the great Pandava warrior swayed before the Blue charioteer. He could not hold his bow straight.

With a flash of insight, Arjuna knew why he trembled. He saw no two contending armies, but family relations, fathers, sons, gurus and disciples. A wave of anguish and depression tore its way inside Arjuna. He cried, I don't want to fight and kill. I don't want this victory. Of what use is kingdom if I have to kill my elders, gurus, cousins, and other relations? Krishna, how can I ever dream to be happy killing Dharitarashtra's sons? Arjuna spoke his heart out, his grief, doubts and confusion had pulverized his personality. He was a heap of emotions, totally drained of energy and determination. He doubted that he was a warrior!

Krishna was in a jam. He did not want all the war preparations to go waste. He had to gather strength and skills to combat the Evil that had taken hold of Arjuna and was even threatening to de-activate the great Lord. He collected all his divine strengths and skills, in view of his mission incarnate responsibilities. Through a capsule of unique energies, He attacked the Evil that had overtaken the soul of Arjuna.

From where this coward spirit at such a critical time? It is unknown to noble kshatriyas. It will lead you not to heaven but to disgrace, Arjuna," said Krishna sweetly. Turning back to chariot and with a familiar beautiful smile on his lips and putting a tender hand on his friend's shoulder, Krishna added "Don't give in to this weakness, this womanliness, Partha. It is beneath you, cast it away and rise 'O' Vijaya!"

Evidently, the Evil that had overtaken the Pandava warrior, was not easy to be shaken away. It had a strong grip on body and spirit of Arjuna. He said, "How shall I attack Bhishma and Drona with arrows in battle? When I should worship them instead! I would rather be a beggar in this world than kill my gurus. How could I dream of enjoying a kingdom stained with my masters' blood?" Arjuna again commenced to torment whys and hows, and his inability to fight. Tears fell from his eyes and his royal face was in ruins. He said to Krishna, "I will not fight!" and fell silent and sombre. Krishna sensed that Arjuna was beyond ordinary treatment, he needed divine attention, to push the Evil out of his system. Krishna re-assumed part of his beyond human grandeur and a river of wisdom flowed out of his lips. His stature grew and He donned a unique irresistible charm. As He smiled, a radiant light, from heart of the "Blue One" entered Arjuna. The difficult job of decontamination of the soul of Arjuna had to be done. With an irresistible smile He said, "You sorrow for those who should not be grieved for, Arjuna. Yet you tell me about wisdom. Wise men, Partha, do not sorrow for either the living or the dead."

"You and I, and these kings of men, have always existed, and shall always exist! Just as the Atman passes through childhood, youth and old age in the body, after each human life, the soul assumes another body, another life." He laughed softly and added;

"The wise are not touched by this, because the soul which pervades all the living, the aging and the dying, never dies itself; it was never born or begun! It neither kills, nor is killed! It is eternal, primeval, indestructible!"

He further elaborated that we shed bodies and acquire new ones like we do with worn out clothes. Atman is not touched by fire or weapon, by wind or water. It is permanent, changeless, eternal, and goes on for ever. Hearing Krishna's philosophy, Arjuna frowned, he was unconvinced. But the beam of energy that Krishna had targeted on him started to have some effect. He put counter questions, real deep and difficult ones—about death, birth, life, soul, relations, grief and sorrow, and all that had clouded his mind and heart. Krishna sensed Arjuna's terror receding, he was now arguing, and in argumentation, nobody could really surpass the wise Lord. Krishna said, "You are a kshatriya. For you a battle of dharma is the greatest good fortune. How can you be full of doubts at such a battle? You should rejoice! It is a doorway straight to heaven, this war. But if you do not fight, you will deny your own nature's glory, what you most are. Then you will sin. And for all time men will tell of your dishonour. Surely, You know that for a man like you who knows honour, dishonour is worse than death" Your friends will call you a coward. So rise 'O' Partha! If you die in battle, you will go straight to heaven. If you triumph, you will enjoy the earth before you go to heaven.

Persistent Effort: Under spell of Krishna's voice and his captivating smile, and graced with divine presence, Arjuna began to float on river of the light of wisdom. Lotus now touched the secret mind of the Pandava warrior, and his immortal soul came under the gigantic mesmerism of his God—the charioteer. The Lord breathed strength and rebirth into his disciple, enough for a thousand generations of warriors for Arjuna was a true kshatriya, a warrior born.

Lord Krishna knew the precarious state of his disciple; He knew that Arjuna was not yet out of the woods; the Evil of confusion had not yet been exorcised; he was still in delicate balance. In order to further detoxify the Pandava warrior from the ill-effects of the Evil of confusion, Krishna said; "Arjuna, your mind is confused with what you have read and all that you have heard, your heart is bewildered. But when true insight dawns on you, your intelligence will see clearly beyond these superficial disturbances of bookish, Vedic learning, and your spirit will be unshakable and profound!" Listening to the divine charioteer, Arjuna had become like pulsating bulb of light, ready to argue and ask for much more.

Krishna moved a few steps away from the chariot, and Arjuna floated down from dream of living silence, from the river of light of wisdom created by the Lord. He was not happy by the dream like spell being discontinued. He wanted knowledge! So he said, "Krishna, who is this man who has wisdom, what is he like? How does the man of Brahman speak—how does he sit or walk?" Lord sensed that the Evil of doubts and confusion was about to flee from the sacred body of his valuable disciple. He threw back his beautiful head and smiled aloud. He spoke, "When a man knows the bliss of Atman, all the cravings and torments of his heart vanish, Arjuna—and when his spirit is absorbed in itself, perfectly satisfied, becomes wise, illuminated."

The Lotus felt triumphant and his eyes shined. He continued his push to wash Arjuna's body and soul free of Evil that had possessed him. He continued; "The heaviest sorrow does not perturb him, not does the most pleasurable desire move him. When lust, fear and rage have left him, he is a Brahmrishi. The bonds of his body are broken, he is enlightened." "He who is beyond affection—who does not rejoice or grieve when he is lucky or unlucky, but is imperturbable, he is illuminated."

Lord's discourse on desires, attachment, abstinence, senses, anger, confusion etc. continued. He elaborated that when mind is disciplined, his spirit remains pure, and from purity comes peace, where sorrow ends. Intelligence of a man resides in peace of Atman, his immortal soul.

With Krishna's spiraling song of wisdom, Arjuna floated over the battlefield of Kurukshetra. Waves of Lord's song were the currents of Time. Thoughts of futility of killing and bloodshed that Kurukshetra was to witness had not left Arjuna, despite the pleasure that he felt from the Lord's song of wisdom. From float of time he looked to reality and said, "Krishna, you yourself say that the way of mind is finer than action. Oh, why then do you goad me into this savagery? It is you who are bewildering me now!" He cried, "Ah, I am lost! Show me the one straightforward path by which I can be free!" The Lord again ran into trouble against logic in words of the warrior who was fully confused and roots of clarity had not yet set in.

The Lord felt doubtful of his own capacity to convince his argumentative disciple. He felt the darkness of hopelessness taking over the scene. He experienced the stab of Evil in his back. He needed help to salvage the situation and hence, cried mother Yashodha for help. He did not want the basic purpose of incarnation to remain unattained. Then, in a dream like situation, the great mother came to his help, riding a huge crimson and golden crest, full of tenderness and embarrassed the Lord with love accumulated for so many years of separation. She came from past to contend the present. At once, the spell of hopelessness gave way to a wave of enhanced wisdom—with unstoppable currents of mental energy entering into the Lord. He again took hold of Arjuna and said; "O innocent one, the world has known the dual path taught to it since its beginning—the way of knowledge for men of contemplation, but for men of action, the way of deeds—of battles! You do not become free by doing nothing, by abstaining from action you do not become perfect. He who does nothing, but only sits and broods over his desires, is no sage, he is a hypocrite! Do the work you are born to, for without work you can't sustain even your own body. Let work be your worship, Arjuna!"

Arjuna was now floating in a dream vehicle—the waves of words of wisdom coming from the Lord, ceaseless yet systemic, aimed at washing Arjuna clean of doubts and indecision. The Lord continued; "In the beginning, God made men, each with his nature and duty. By doing this you shall prosper, this work of your nature shall yield you milk of your desires."

There are three types of gunas with which men are born, Sattavic, Rajasic and Tamsic and by doing the guna assigned work, you shall prosper! By your natural duty you worship the Gods and they succor you. You attain to eternal bliss by doing your duty by working unattached. Such karma is sacrifice that maintains the world. Look at me Arjuna! Though I am not bound by any duty in all the worlds, none is anything in them that is not already mine. Yet, I am ever at work.

Only the deluded think, "I am the doer", everything is done by the essence, the gunas i.e. the nature of living, in eternal interplay—and the world goes on. Arjuna, it is always wise to do one's own duty, howsoever imperfectly than the duty of another, done even with immaculate perfection. It is better to die doing one's duty—than either running away from it or trying to do another person's duty, against the law of gunas or nature. And Krishna grew quite and pensive after delivering these words of wisdom. In a flash of thoughts, He felt as if some one else, in guise of Arjuna, was hurling these questions at him. Fearing that evil may strengthen its hold on Arjuna, the Lord continued; "Arjuna, lust veils Atman, like smoke does a fire, like dust does a clear mirror. To pass beyond lust, you must transcend the intellect. For powerful are the senses, greater than they is mind, more potent than the mind is the intellect. But greater than intellect is Atman who sets you free." This is Timeless Yoga.

Arjuna, in his argumentative and intellectual mode did not fully agree with the Lord on the Timeless Yoga, i.e. the relationship between action, karma, and dharma on one hand and senses, mind, intellect and Ataman, on the other. Sensing the same, the Lord pressed further to add; "I taught this timeless yoga to Vivasat once. Vivasat gave it to Manu, Manu taught it to Iksvaku, and so handed down to generations." He added, "O, Arjuna, the blessed one, today you hear it from me directly."

On Arjuna's retort that Vivasat happened long before Krishna was born, the Lord had to explain the sequence of birth and death. He laughed gently and said, "My past lives and yours are many, more than you dream. Only, I remember them all, and you remember none. Yet, I am not born into this world but only seem to be, and I am master of my Prakriti, my immortal nature. Whenever there is tide of evil in the world Arjuna, I send myself forth into it—to protect the good. Who else have they to destroy the evil? Who else will save them? To re-establish righteousness, do I come again and again, from Age to Age."

The man who understands me is never born again after leaving his body he comes into me and is delivered of lust, anger, and fear. Finally, all men come to me, their paths may be different, and I accept them all. I am, however, not bound by karma and neither are those who come into me. So, Arjuna, like ancients –you must also work for your liberation; you must act, do your karma! The way of karma is not easy; even wise get perplexed not able to differentiate what is action and inaction. You are a kshatriya, you should also act, do your karma. Action, work or karma is a sacrifice, a ritual of worship, and this worship is greater than any material sacrifice. All karma end in Brahman. Let the Rishis of wisdom and vision be your masters—learn from them by humble service. Arjuna, cast away the doubt that lurks in your mind, take up the sword of discrimination and fight.

Arjuna's confusion got compounded—and he hurried to ask, "Krishna, first you say renunciation is the way, burning karma with wisdom, then you say the opposite—that karma is the way. tell me the truth?" Both said Krishna, lead to freedom. But your path is of doing of action. You are not greedy for a kingdom or powers that go with it You are not looking for fruits—you will be freed easily. And Arjuna, "Wise do not speak of the ways-wisdom and action as being separate; only the ignorant do!"

You can not renounce action anyway, without knowing what it is. Only he who is engaged in Karma knows its emptiness. Made pure, he knows, the still Brahman, changeless. In detachment, he occupies the senses with the objects of sense. But not himself. Like a lotus leaf is he, resting on water, but not wetted by water. With this body of nine gates, one who masters his nature by giving into it perfectly, without desire, renouncing whatsoever he does even as he does it, only he shall have peace. He knows the Atman does not act, nor is it acted upon, but only nature's gunas. The sins of such a man are cut from him, he reaches the Brahman—from where there is no return, by his sun like wisdom which illuminates the immortal self.

When your soul's light ends your darkness and shines forth from you, the Brahman is revealed, truly splendid like a sun. The enlightened man sees all creation as equal. He finds his endless joy within himself, his light within himself, in his own soul, and he comes to Brahmanirvana, said Krishna, who came to cleanse the world and to make it fair and strong again.

The song of wisdom from the great Lord sent a strong beam of light through Arjuna. It pushed him backwards into the time. He was aware, yet unaware of what the wise Lord was saying. He heard the Lord continuing to add; "He who works serenely, with no desire for the fruits of what he does, success or failure, he is the Yogin, the Sanyasin, not he who lights no lamp on this earth. O Pandava, what men call yoga know that it is Sanyasa, no less. No man becomes a Yogin before he renounces his selfishness." Through his divine explanations, the Lord continued to add; "Work is the way of the Rishi who wants to attain to yoga, to yoke himself to the eternal. Once he attains yoga, which is union, then he is serene."

"The warrior's way is by his own will. The will alone is the soul's dearest friend, and the will alone is the Atman's enemy. For the man of self control, his will is his soul's friend, but the self indulgent man's will is the Atman's enemy."

Arjuna was still battling with the Evil that had overtaken him. He was in a time bubble and oscillated between the conscious and the unconscious. Lord sent his calm to invade Arjuna, He sent his love through his words and embrace. Still holding him tight, as the warrior's shoulders shook with fright and weeping, Krishna said; "When his mind is yoked in Atman, set free from craving, the yogin is united with Brahman." "When you gain the Atman, you know there is nothing left to gain. Then no sorrow will move you; the yogin is disconnected from pain, he is united with Brahman."

Arjuna's tears were falling freely on Krishna's shoulders and the Lotus consolingly said; "He who sees me everywhere, I am ever with him and he is with me, for ever. In the image of his own self does the perfect man see all things, equally."

Arjuna continued to suffer the stresses of confusion and asked; "Krishna, how hard it is to see all things equal. Fickle is the mind, prone to terror, impetuous, strong, obdurate. It is simpler to tame the wind." Krishna replied; "Who said that yoga is easy to come to? Remember, it is the last achievement, beyond it there is no other! Yet it is not impossible, I tell you, you can attain it." Arjuna was still gripped with doubts. Hence, he shouted; "Krishna, where does he go who believes, but can not control himself? Is he destroyed like a torn cloud in the sky, with no support anywhere? Does he fall for ever?" While raising these questions due to division within!

Krishna now spoke like the sun, radiating, wise words flowing endlessly—shafts of light spreading all around. He glowingly added; "Not in this world or next does such a believer perish, Arjuna. A man who seeks Brahman never comes to a sad end."

The Lord sensed, he had to be more direct with his river of wisdom and lights and said; "Hear my song Arjuna, you who do not cavil, it has the secret of wisdom and knowledge, it will set you free. This is the highest knowing, easy and imperishable, and it is known directly. It is my way, the way of the avatara! I pervade all the universe with my un-manifest spirit—everything abides in me but not I in them. This is my mystery. As the tame-less air which moves every where abides in the ether, subtle akasa, so too Arjuna, all existence abides in me."

I am the seed of all creation. When the next creation dawns, I send them forth again, all helpless, all bound in my *Maya.* And I am the Lord of Maya. I send the multitude forth and gather them back into my Being. The Lord continued to elaborate that; The unknowing pass by the human shape of mine, of me they know nothing! The illumined, the great souls who know me, Arjuna, they worship me with an unflikering mind, and with the ritual of wisdom—they know who I am, that I am the source undying!

I am the ritual. I am the sacrifice. I am the world's father.

I am the herb that heals. I am end of knowledge.

I am the holy mantra. I am Aum. I am the melted butter.

I am the world's father, its mother, supporter and its grand-father too.

I am the offering. I am the fire, Arjuna.

I am Rik, Soma, Yajus, whispered Krishna to a spellbound Arjuna.

I am origin and dissolution, the ground, the refuse, and the imperishable seed.

Thunder and lightning crackled the sky silencing the drummers and conch blowers of both the armies. And Krishna said softly to Arjuna; "Worship me! I am the heat of the sun. I with-hold and pour the rains. Deathlessness am I and death manifest I am, and the hidden germ of life!"

Every offering made with love I accept with joy—a leaf, a flower, a fruit, a palmful of water; whatever you eat or sacrifice, whatever you do, offer it to me, O son of Kunti.

I am myself in all creatures. None is hateful to me, none especially beloved. But those who worship me, they are in me surely and I am in them.

Arjuna, know one thing for sure—those who worship me shall never parish! Let them be low born, let them be women, let them be any one—my devotees reach the ultimate goal.

Arjuna startled off his dream of bliss, he hung to every utterance of Krishna, resolution to fight growing stronger within him. His heart was set on battle again.

"Fix your heart to me" sang Krishna, "to me be devoted, love me, and to me you shall come, in life and in death."

Then it rained on Kurukshetra and the rhythms of rain got mixed with those of the Lord's song and Arjuna further heard; "From me came the Sapta Rishi and the four Manus, and from them all these generations of men of the world. I am the origin, and so the wise worship me."

Attempting to reach some understanding Arjuna said; "O Krishna, you are the Brahman, first of Gods, unborn, pervasive. Narada, Asita, Devala, Vyasa, all the sages say as much, and now I hear it from your lips. And I believe it all."

Arjuna further enquired that out of the various forms of the Lord, on which one he should fix his attention. The kind Lord proceeded to recount some of his major forms and added that, in totality, his forms were countless. Arjuna enjoyed the Lord's song, the sacred Bhagavad Gita. It was more interesting than the talk of war. He did not want it to discontinue or conclude. He put many searching questions, either to rid off his persistent doubts or to prolong the period of pleasure.

The depth of Arjuna's queries amazed the Lord but He patiently answered all, one by one with full details. He wanted his great disciple to be fully convinced and satisfied. Dwapara age was coming to an end and yawns of the Kali-yuga were becoming visible. Arjuna wanted a few more clarifications, and hence persisted by asking; "O Krishna, tell me about renunciation and relinquishment and the difference between the two. "To this the Blue Lotus of the Dwapara said; "Renunciation is when you abandon Karma out of desire; relinquishment is when you act but abandon the fruits of karma, O Partha." "Works of sacrifice, tapasya and charity must be done—these are the purifiers of the wise. But the Karma should be done without attachment to its results." "It is not right to abandon one's duty The tamasic renunciation is through ignorance, the rajasic through fear; but if a man does his duty abandoning its fruits to me, his relinquishment is sattvic."

Karma of all types, as per situation, should be done without attachment to results. And this is very difficult. It is not right to abandon your duty! As per Vedanta, there are five participants in any action; the body, the ego, the senses, the motions and providence the fifth.

On Arjuna's probing, the Lord explained that there are three types of conscience and three types of happiness.

- Sattvic- conscience knows right from wrong.
- Rajasic-conscience can not clearly tell wrong from the right.
- Tamsic--conscience is one when man takes wrong for right and vice versa.

Similarly, happiness too has three types. When a man knows his Atman, he experiences pure joy of knowledge; it is the happiness of the Sattvic. The joy of Rajas is of senses—sweet to begin with and then gets bitter. The bestial satisfaction of stupor and sloth is of Tamas. Arjuna, there is no being on earth, none among even the Devas of the heaven, who is free of the Prakirti.

Larger Vision: Krishna felt the war on Evil that had overtaken his most valuable disciple, being won, Arjuna coming out of his clouds of doubts, depression and inaction. Krishna's own cosmic terror and feeling of abandonment, which he had suffered on Arjuna's refusal to fight, and the depth and logic of questions that he raised, was also receding. Now, He felt no compelling situation, where He may have to fight himself to overpower and eliminate the evil, developing and the main objective of his incarnation seemed in sight. The Lord did not want to expose his Godliness by not having Arjuna on his side. Free from the grip of Evil, a transformed, radiant and smiling Arjuna said to the Lord; "You have removed my confusion, I feel my battles already fought and won. I know what you have said is true, but Krishna reveal me your true form—show me your imperishable form."

Krishna smiled and uttered, "You can't see me with your human eye but I will lend you divine sight."

Behold Arjuna, here see my true form—a thousands fold and endless; see Adityas, Vasus, Rudras, the Asvins, the Maruts! See the wonders unseen! See the whole universe—whatever else you care to see! O Arjuna, behold me!

Krishna transformed his human body into splendid Godhood, speaking from many mouths, with numerous hands and eyes, endless visions and marvels, countless ornaments and weapons, clothed in divine garments and garlands, with heavenly perfumes and fragrances, miracles and wonders. If a thousand suns arose in to sky, their collective brightness might not equal the Lord's shine and glow.

Arjuna savored a soulful of the divine sight, all eternity gathered into one, in the body of God of the Gods. He folded his hands in awe, the Pandava fell on his knees, his face in the grass. And the God said in thunder; "Time am I, master of worlds. Fight or stay your hand, no matter-all, all these warriors shall die in me. For that am I come. Therefore take your arms! And win glory by vanquishing your enemies, enjoy a kingdom, O ambidextrous bowman! I have already slain your enemies. You be only the occasion, my instrument, kill Drona, Bhishma, Jayadratha, Karna, and the rest whom I have already doomed. Fear nothing, fight and you will conquer!"

Arjuna prostrated completely on feet of the Lord and uttered—that now he knew why the whole world worshiped the great Lord. And the kind Lord pulled the Pandava warrior from the ground. Arjuna, red faced and not fully certain of himself panted," O Lord, I am quiet again."

Arjuna still shivered but panic seemed to have left his body. Krishna now attempted to allay the terror of a man faced with the pure and absolute Godhead.

He said; " Even the Devas, Arjuna, are ever eager to see me as you did—only by devotion can I be seen like that."

The sun broke from behind the clouds on the fields of Kurukshetra, and once again Arjuna heard the clangour of the two great armies, impatient for a fight. Krishna was now eager to conclude his divine discourse and hence added; "Consecrate all your actions to me , think of me as your dearest loved one, know that I am your only refuge, be united in your heart in me. It is your vanity which says 'I will not fight', you will fight, Arjuna, your own nature will force you to! You yourself create the karma which binds you. And caught helpless in its power, you will even do what you wish to avoid." "God abides in hearts of all creatures. He turns them around on the wheel of Maya. Surrender to him utterly, O Arjuna. By this grace you will find supreme peace, and the place beyond change."

From the new peace infused by Krishna, Arjuna felt totally invigorated and confidently said; "By your grace O Achyuta, my mind is made firm, its doubts are ended. I will do as you say."

Krishna, with his super-normal skills, knew that despite Arjuna's resolve to fight, his actual performance on the battle field had to be watched carefully when he comes face to face with his kin. And at more than one occasions, during the heat of the battle, the great Lord threatened to break his vow of not wielding weapons and through his great strategic approach, He was able to get done, through Arjuna, all that was to be done.

Non-Material Incentives: Workers, blue or white collared, even superior skilled professionals, are today steeped in materialism. Higher wages, salaries and perks –more purchasing power, collection of goods for perceived or actual needs, is the growing trend. All seem to be lost in the forest of materialism for maximum sense gratification. This one-sided emphasis of the economically active human beings is generating immense volumes of miseries for one and all.

Lord Krishna spoke in detail on materialism in his divine discourse known as the Bhagavad Gita, and due to the immense impact of materialism on actions of the conditioned soul, the Lord emphasized the significance of karma or action and not worrying about the results that may accrue from the same because stress on results or fruits takes an individual or conditioned soul deeper into the forest of materialism where it is bound to be lost for sure. Sukadeva Gosvami, the learned son of Rishi Vyasa, while speaking to king Pariksit (who was awaiting death as per a forecast) has further elaborated on ills of excessive materialism. He said that a conditioned soul is led astray on active engagement in sense gratification through greater material/ goods consumption or accumulation. Sense gratification through stealing, gambling, intoxication, over-eating and several such other activities, generates only temporary satisfaction and pleasure but the futility of it all soon becomes visible and often consequences in form of habituation, over-weight and disease can be serious. On this subject of vital importance, Lord Krishna, in the Bhagavad Gita says; "O son of Kunti, all that you eat, all that you offer and give away, as well as the austerities that you may perform, should be done as an offering into me."

One's activities should be aimed at not for sense gratification but for the mission of the Supreme Personality of the Godhead. Towards end of the Bhagavad Gita, the Lord demands Surrender unto Me.

In today's corporate environment, surrender unto the CEO or the boss may not be feasible but working for higher goals such as for common good of the society (or at least not against it) and environment, should definitely be aimed at. Taking benefit of the guidance so clearly provided by the wise Lord in the Bhagavad Gita and subsequently, by the wise men like Ramakrishna, Vivekananda, and Sri-Aurabindo, senior corporate management, particularly HR professionals, should concentrate on educating employees on ills of uncontrolled materialism and workout non-material rewards as tools for superior motivation. It is not difficult to draw a list of such incentives or to use the same, once the matter is properly understood and accepted. Emphasis on non-material incentives or motivators holds great promise for enhancing workers' commitment for greater and more righteous performance, improving output and efficiency on a long term basis. It has potential for significantly reducing negative stresses of work environment. It can liberate the joy of work in form of positive and productive cooperation, with tremendous possibilities for solution of the ills of inefficiency, internal politics, non-cooperation, poor ethics, sabotage, cheating, high employee turnover etc. If attempted honestly and diligently, non-material motivators can serve as strong foundations for superior and tension free corporate performance.

Principle of Thought and Action Balance

Every organization, corporate or otherwise, requires people to work for its stated or unstated objectives. For this purpose, people have to be either hired or motivated to volunteer. Irrespective of the situation, all organizations attempt to recruit *smarts*, i.e. the people with higher I.Q. Hence, it is not surprising to note that human resources professionals and CEOs tend to put excessive reliance on this old fashioned measure, considered as the best predictor of success at the work place. Most of these decision makers fail to appreciate that persons with high I.Q. and bright grades or divisions, in fact, are essentially thought warriors, they can think and argue, and some of them can even present their plans in an impressive manner. In other words, they are good at understanding and analysis, and relatively useless at implementation the most vital precursor of performance.

Unfortunately, there is no dearth of managers who tend to misunderstand *thoughts, arguments and analysis* for output and performance while in reality facts are different.

Undoubtedly, no thought, argument and analysis is of any significance until and unless, it is put to action. Hence, one requires doers or action warriors who can not only do a reasonable job of thinking, discussion and planning—but can put the same into practice, i.e. act and produce results. Normally thought warriors are preoccupied with details and results, and suffer from intense fear of failure. They often tend to congregate around bosses for appreciation and credit without attempting much. They are the "I told you types"—and often succeed in influencing their bosses. On the other hand, "action warriors" are endowed with confidence, will power and resolve to act and possess risk taking ability. They are not scared of inadequate results or failures and despite their superior utility to the organization, they are often inadequately valued by a majority of managers as they probably lack the charm of thought-warriorism.

To those who can not scan through the mask of motives, thought warriors look bright at conferences, meetings and seminars as they come out with impressive terminologies, arguments and presentations. Since demands for actions/results are absent in such situations, they run no risk of being pushed into activities that they tend to escape. They develop excellent skills for escaping responsibilities and often employ their intelligence for negative thoughts and actions. Precedence and beaten path always attract them as they have little or no intention of deviating and no capacity for innovation ever becomes visible at their end.

The writer encountered a number of "thought warriors" in his long corporate career, the mightiest one who went by the name of KNS was totally invincible. He could present and argue for hours without saying anything concrete or substantial, just elaborating alternatives and scenarios, and enumerating merits and demerits of a proposal or a situation. He could answer queries endlessly without giving details and comments of substance. He was always in great spirits if audience consisted only of juniors and if the situation was otherwise, he had to be reminded, often repeatedly, to be brief and to the point. To those who were unfortunate enough to work directly under him, he was an absolute pain in the neck. Finally, he managed himself to be promoted to his level of incompetence and eventually was eased out unceremoniously.

Thought warriors, the intellectual workers with no intention or capability to get into action, to take risks and be responsible for results, are encountered in all types of work environments. The more intelligent ones amongst them, are able to climb the corporate ladder, employing the mask of intellect and erudition until decisively located and isolated by a boss for whom output is more important than mere words. Often, organizations with excellent ideas, products and strategies, are ruined because of an intolerably high concentration of such "thought warriors" at the management level, where decision taking and action are of decisive significance.

Admittedly, one needs to apply intelligence while executing a plan—for example in prioritizing tasks at hand but in the final analysis, initiative and persistence are crucial for getting results. In certain parts of India especially in the eastern zone, an unusually high concentration of thought warriors infects the state bureaucracy as well as the corporate world. As a consequence, nothing much got done, especially in the pre-liberalization period. The active unionism of workers in various sectors of the economy was also, at least in part, a consequence of the high incidence of thought warriorism. For action warriors, one had to look really hard, even to locate just a few and for the crowd effect, even the small number may not be really functional. In total contrast, in one of our western states, the situation was distinctively reverse, it was full of born action warriors. In some other areas, there exists a variable mix of the two types of workers.

In our educational and training institutions, there exists an undesirable brahminical bias in favor of knowledge or intellect that tends to promote a crowd of thought warriors, right at an early stage of work life, creating a big gap between thought and action. Consequences of such practices are unhealthy for the economy because sometimes, especially to the less discerning management, the thought itself ends up looking as action. Many of our corporate and non-corporate leaders who run the world of affairs, suffer from the action deficiency. Profit and non-profit organizations such as schools, colleges, political parties, sports groupings, hospitals etc. lack the same ability to deliver results, while being brilliant in their thought abilities. Millions of our government employees are smart and brilliant, having entered via competitive examinations yet they persistently fail to deliver the targeted or planned results. Right at their training stage, the bias for action and results remains missing while afterwards there is little chance for them to see the need for action against rewards of bureaucratic inaction. They become experts to get promoted without doing much or for employing their skills for pure personal gains through the process of mutual back scratching.

Lord Krishna, the greatest manager ever known to the mankind, was uncommonly rich in skills of thought and action both. He always employed a right mix of thought and action, altering emphasis as per specificities of situations encountered. For instance , as a child He exhibited clear preference for action, suckling demonic Putana dry and dead, uprooting trees, over-turning carts, dancing on multi-hooded head of serpent king Kalia and subduing it to retreat out of the waters of Yamuna, lifting mount Goverdhana, stealing butter and curd, tormenting Gopicas, organizing dance circles, just to enumerate a few. Perhaps, the little Lord found it more effective to express himself through unusual acts and pranks and let his community of cowherds realize that He was not a normal child but an incarnate of divine objectivity. Actions of the blue child established his uniqueness beyond question. The little "action warrior" established his supremacy in his rural cowherd community, with an element of total surprise and amazement.

Krishna's action warriorism was actively visible in elimination of the demonic king Kamsa, his massive wrestlers and menacing elephants, at a tender age. The bright side of the young Lord as a thought warrior emerged at the ashram of guru Sandipini , where He and elder brother Balarama exhibited a record breaking performance in speed learning, mastering all the then available sixty-four fields of knowledge covering science, technology, arts, logic, astronomy and scriptures etc, in just as many days. It left his ashram mates and more particularly his renowned guru, totally astonished and dumfounded. As a consequence, the name and fame of the two incarnates spread far and wide, earning them numerous admirers and enemies at the same time. Despite scaling heights of thought warriorism at an early stage, action emphasis of Lord Krishna continued throughout his youth and middle age, fighting a battle almost every week, against armies of accumulated evil and wickedness.

The first beneficiary of the wise Lord's thought skills was his own Yadava clan which had come under great risk of total defeat and possibly elimination, at hands of the mighty demon king Jarasandha of Magadha, who had attacked the Yadava kingdom seventeen times in order to take revenge for widowing his two daughters on death of Kamsa of Mathura. This great demonic ruler was reported to have somehow acquired immunity against the Yadavas, he was not to be killed by any one of them. And his destined destroyer was not yet active on the scene. Since the wise Lord, a true thought warrior wanted to avoid defeat at hands of a demonic leader, He skillfully employed his mighty powers of thought and logic to convince the proud Yadavas to vacate Mathura, the seat of their well established and prosperous kingdom, and migrate unceremoniously to a distant and desolate Dwaraka. It was a difficult job from all standards. He even succeeded in justifying that his earning the unflattering nick-name of Ranchhod did not really matter as the future was destined to offer an opportunity to neutralize the invincible demonic ruler.

At Dwaraka, Krishna wisely exploited talents of the great action warrior Balarama, to cobble together an impressive empire through addition of vast territories in all the four directions—even beyond the Arabian sea. Desolate landscapes were converted into fertile farms, orchards and pastures and the splendour and riches of Dwaraka had no parallel amongst its contemporary kingdoms. His own thought prowess, the wise Lord employed to weave together a unique federal system of governance for the numerous states that fell under his control, in form of the great Yadava empire which He ruled through an effective remote control.

Lord Krishna's unique relationship with the Pandava brothers who were, in fact, his celestial allies in his long and arduous fight against the evil and wicked, was primarily based on thought warriorism. They needed to be guided and managed in direction of success of righteousness over the forces of evil which were very strong and dominant at that time. As such, there was no one better equipped than the wise Lord himself to undertake this vital job. His important acts of thought warriorism, towards enabling the celestial Pandavas to finally succeed in effectively doing the wise Lord's bidding, in direction of substantial elimination of evil forces in one go, were as under.

- Advising the Pandava brothers to accept Draupadi as their joint spouse—despite the same being against common norms.
- Advising them to accept their uncle Dharitarashtra's invitation to return to Hastinapura, after their presence at Panchala had become known to the outside world.
- At Hastinapura, He persuaded them to accept their uncle's offer of Khandavaparastha—an unproductive desert region, as their share of the kingdom.
- Advising and assisting them to convert the so awarded infertile territories into an impressively productive kingdom and their capital city of Indaraparastha as a matchless splendour.
- Advising Yudhishtra about the danger of evil forces joining hands, against his scheme of celebrating Rajasuya, under the leadership of the great demonic leader Jarasandha of Magadha, if this immense obstacle was not eliminated prior to announcement of such a plan.
- Soothing the hurt of Pandava's on loss of their hard earned kingdom, through the cunning of Sakuni and evil Duriyodhana, and simultaneously assuring Draupadi that the insults and injustice done to her shall be avenged in due course of time.
- Arguing the Pandava's case in Kaurava court, for return of their kingdom, as the judicious means of avoiding a fratricidal conflict of frightening consequences.

- Advising the Pandava warriors for a decisive fight when all possible efforts for an honorable compromise had failed.
- Educating the Pandavas about the presence of a number of invincible warriors on side of the Kaurava line-up and how to neutralize each one of them in the most appropriate manner.
- Becoming an active advisor of Pandavas during the massive battle of Kurukshetra and help turn its scales in favor of the righteousness.
- And finally, after the great battle, taking the victorious Pandavas to the wise old warrior Bhishma who laid wounded, on the bed of arrows, and waited for an auspicious time of his own choice, to cast off his body.

Krishna wanted the post-Kurukshetra governance by the righteous Pandavas, to benefit from the vast reservoir of knowledge of the grand old warrior, a unique thought and action superimo and also a great devotee of Krishna.

During the great engagement of the wise Lord with the destined events of Mahabharatha, the toughest test of his divine thought skills emerged when his most valuable disciple Arjuna refused to fight on seeing the great line-up of the two opposing armies on the battlefield of Kurukshetra where a number of his seniors and gurus had, as per their own choice or as per forces of circumstances, had decided to fight for the opposing side. He saw no justification in killing so many of his nears and dears, just for the sake of ruling a kingdom. He was severely depressed and demoralized and refused to wield weapons and wanted to runaway from his duty as a warrior. Further, Arjuna was highly argumentative and gave a tough time to the wise Lord who was attempting to make him to see reason and do his assigned duty. This dialogue between the wise Lord and his celestial disciple was extremely intense, it encompassed all aspects of life and death, right and wrong, leaving no aspect of life on earth and beyond uncovered—and on account of its thoroughness and depth, it later came to be known as Bhagavad Gita or the celestial Song of Wisdom. For over five millennia, it has continued to guide the social and spiritual behaviour of a great multitude of mankind.

Throughout his long and eventful life, Lord Krishna rigorously attempted to practice a right mix of thought and action warriorism, as per demands of his celestial role as a mission incarnate—and at no point, He allowed any adversity to hinder his righteous mix of work emphasis. He judiciously analyzed all of his kinsmen, colleagues and disciples for their preference in terms of thought and action emphasis(skills, strengths and balance of the same) and utilized each one of them in the most appropriate and rewarding manner. Today's management professionals and CEOs can

learn a great deal from life and works of the wise Lord and improve working of their respective organizations by suitably employing the thought and action warriors in their work force, for most rewarding results.

Magnificent Management Theory

Richness of management thought enables a good professional tackle difficult situations because in a critical situation such a person escapes running into a desert of ideas and way-outs. This is how a strong theoretical base is beneficial for a good performer. Most of the modern management teaching and training institutions lay substantial emphasis on case-studies and theoretical content. Capabilities of their output, however, remains deficient as several of their MBAs, in practical corporate environment, feel perplexed when faced with new and complex situations.

Management primarily pertains to development and employment of skills of people-handling for superior results, because all other inputs or factors of production, whether goods or services, are totally people dependent as

- all machines are operated/worked by people.
- all materials are handled/converted by people.
- all moneys are invested and managed by people.
- all technologies are developed/utilized by people.
- all products are moved and marketed by people.
- no corporate or non-corporate activity ever occurs without people.

In fact, people are the most crucial component of all corporate or non-corporate activities. Lord Krishna understood, in full depth, the significance of human element—for development, governance, war and/or any-thing else. His management thoughts and practices, centered on manipulation and motivation of human element. The key components of the wise Lord's management thoughts and practices, among others, included the following.

- Prakariti or inherent nature assessment of involved individuals.
- Human prakariti based capacity/capability analysis.
- Prakariti/capacity based work/responsibility assignment.
- Prakariti/capability based training and empowerment.
- Centrality of objectives— key emphasis on righteousness.
- Karma and dharma—the two central planks of emphasis.
- Jnanna or gyanna as a useful input.
- Non-material motivation for exceptional results.
- Renunciation and renouncement.
- Effective and well supervised delegation.

- Effective mentoring and, if necessary, timely intervention.
- Intensive use of divine vision.
- Situation specific difficult decision management.
- Madhura communication and diplomacy as productive tools.
- Intensive information collection and analysis.
- Leading by example.
- Right credit apportioning and total impartiality.
- Efficient internal dispute resolution.

Lord Krishna deeply understood the role of human prakariti as the key determinant for an individual's calibre or capacity to assimilate knowledge and interpret and exploit the same. Keeping this principle in view, the wise Lord selected Arjuna to expound the Gita, because the great Pandava warrior was rich with *Rajasic Prakariti or Rajoguna.* And it was for the same reason that Bhishma taught the Vishnu Sahasaranama to Yudhishtra who was sattvic in nature. In view of intense tamas or tamoguna of Dharitarashtra the job of discoursing him was assigned to sage Sanatasujata who had capabilities to handle such people.

Lord Krishna always emphasized that fairness and righteousness was the best hormone for human performance enhancement. It sprouts an environment of positivity, the most fertile ground for initiative and cooperation. Well-being, happiness and prosperity are the by-products of righteousness, and hence it was always the center-point of the wise Lord's emphasis in all of his human interactions. He further stresses that evil has the capacity and potential to suffocate righteousness and reduce output as energies are wasted in infighting and conflict. His primary objective of incarnation was to reduce and, if possible, eliminate evil from face of the earth. In human society, as no such massive objective can be achieved single-handedly, hence creating and managing a large performing group or alliance became indispensable even for the all powerful Lord. It necessitated the great Lord to propound and promote his wise and most effective thoughts and practices of management.

Lord Krishna discouraged over-emphasis on results and, in fact, it was forbidden in many situations as it tends to reduce initiative and innovation. It was, indeed, one of the central points that the wise Lord emphasized in his famous discourse to Arjuna in the battlefields of Kurukshetra, prior to commencement of fighting between the opposing forces of evil and righteousness, which later on was summarized as Bhagavad Gita by the great sage named Vyasa.

The great beauty of the great Lord's management thoughts lies in the fact that there is little or no gap in theory and practice at his end. This narrow or nil gap between the theory and practice of management" by Lord Krishna, also known as the *Zero Gap Approach*, was the main cause for the massive attraction of a large number of supporters and allies who assisted the divine incarnate to achieve the difficult goal of totally subduing the accumulated evil. The wise Lord always followed the principle of *talk after your walk* which means that he never advised what He did not practice. Hence, before giving any suggestion, one should make sure that the same is followed by one's own self. This will enhance the credibility of suggestion giver among members of his team or his followers, motivating them to emulate or even excel.

Lord Krishna's management concepts are, thus, very rich in content. They were very intensely practiced by him and by Pandavas, and also his other disciples and followers for a long time. Many great personalities in human history, saints and rulers alike, imbibed the great Lord's concepts of manpower management and governance, over the past several millennia. Long presence of foreign invaders in India, and their interference in the process of governance, shifted emphasis from the wise Lord's vital teachings. In the past two centuries western management practices had their sway and now that these so called modern management thoughts are exhibiting substantial deficiencies in meeting demands of the time, the great Lord's management concepts and practices shall show the way for multilateral success in the complex situation where human elements shall need a divinely efficient approach for superior motivation and performance. Hence, practitioners and students of modern management will do themselves a lot of good to study and understand the wise Lord's divine ideas and practices of management.

Notes

1. As per the authors, some individuals do acquire qualities of active leadership as a consequences of their "power thinking" capabilities, even when below the age of twelve and without help of any formal education. Krishna was the most brilliant example of such a power thinker.

2. It is an innate capability to see into the true nature of things—or events to unfold (24).

3. Refers to activation of the relevant forces.

4. This thought formation pertains to the author.

5. In context of business management it amounts to one's job responsibilities.

6. Refers to the celestial abode of Lord Vishnu.

7. In Hinduism, swami is a title assigned to learned and virtuous individuals of large followings.

8. A significant part of the material presented under this heading—particularly that enclosed between parentheses, is drawn from "Once A Blue God" by Ramesh Menon, published by Garutman Pvt. Ltd., 8B Middleton Street, Calcutta-700 071.

PARVA V

LORD KRISHNA AS A MASTER OF SOFT SKILLS OF MANAGEMENT

LORD KRISHNA AS A MASTER OF SOFT SKILLS OF MANAGEMENT

Madhura as a Management Tool

Lord Krishna was born in a prison and his childhood passed in a cowherd environment. Even as a child, He did not allow the enormous constraints of his living environment and lack of schooling, to dampen any of his *mind management capabilities.* His verbal and non-verbal communications had divine superiority. As a child, the little Lord captivated one and all with his innocent antiques and pranks, best known of which were stealing butter and curd. He humbled and eliminated a number of demonic spirits that came to harm him in his early life. It left the cowherd community, in confusing certainty, in regard to the likely presence of an incarnation in its midst

As the Lord grew up, He developed a huge fan following amongst the cowherd boys (gopas) and girls (gopis). His flute play enchanted young and old, humans and animals—and even plants did not escape the magical waves of his music. Right as a young boy, He commenced a planned use of *Madhura* [1] as an influential mode of communication. He could weave webs of magic with his smile, charm, words and the mighty flute.

Employing a divine mix of *Madhura* and logic, the young Lord persuaded the cowherd community to abandon Gokula and move out to settle at Vrindavana. Further, the backward cowherd community, as per his persuasion, discarded a ritualistic worship of Indra, and adopted cow as an economic animal of multiple utilities. Years later, elements of the Lord's *Madhura* approach, spontaneously won over the people of Mathura, after He eliminated the demon Kamsa, his wrestlers and elephants with the ease of a seasoned professional.

Subsequently, as a student at the ashram of guru Sandipani, no one could escape the influence of the young Lord's elements of *Madhura* and grace. He was very popular as a pupil and mastered the sixty-four subjects of science and arts, in as many days of stay at the ashram.

The great migration of the vast Yadava clan, from an established lush environment of Mathura, to an unknown and desolate desert of Dwaraka, over a thousand miles away, was primarily enabled by the wise Lord, through a unique mix of his irresistible logic and *Madhura.* Brother Balarama, elder Ugrasena and other senior Yadava warriors, were under the hypnotic influence of the Lord's irresistible skills of manpower management. In human history, mythological or otherwise, there exists no parallel example of such a huge migration, achieved so smoothly and with such a magnificent success. Establishment of a massive empire on the western coast, at a break-neck speed, and creation of a splendour of a capital at Dwaraka, became feasible, apart from his efficient management of manpower and resources, through the skilful use of *Madhura* technology by the wise Lord, which did not allow any major manifestation of internal disagreement or conflict and speeded up productivity enormously.

Lord Krishna employed *Madhura* with equal ease while dealing with his allies as well as opponents. While handling an angry and abusive demonic cousin Sishupala, at the court of Yudhishtra, where the Pandava brothers had selected the great Lord as a guest of honour after successful celebrations of the Rajasuya yajna, He tolerated the irritant devil with smile and charm, and when the offender exceeded his assigned number of excesses, the swift Sudarshana did the long awaited justice with the flick of a divine finger, and without any trace of remorse. The great job of final disposal of the long irritating devil was performed with immense peace and smile. An unpleasant work was done so pleasantly.

The great warriors, namely Bhishma, Drona and Karna, who were placed on the side of evil Duryodhana, due to provisions of destiny, were handled by Lord Krishna, with a lot of respect and regards. He always respected virtue and merit. As per the intelligent design of the great Lord, these warriors had to be eliminated, before the evil Duryodhana could be dealt with, in a final act of justice. Hence, with these great warriors too, the Lord employed his immense charm to soften their determination to fight against the forces of righteousness. The wise Lord minimized Karna's monumental rivalry with Arjuna, through the tactful use of *Madhura,* by privately informing the gifted warrior that he was the first born of Kunti and hence, the eldest amongst the Pandavas--and that he could gladly come and take his rightful place on the other side. Although, Karna did not accept the Lord's invitation, his commitment to eliminate Pandavas had come under a cloud of confusion, which helped to turn the tide of the battle at Kurukshetra. The charismatic persona of the Lord, fortified with *Madhura*, was capable of altering the mental thought process of whosoever encountered him for favour, friendship or in opposition.

After the great battle that lasted for eighteen days and ended only after the destined end of Duryodhana at the hands of Bhimma, Lord Krishna in company of the surviving Pandavas, visited the blind king Dharitarashtra and queen Gandhari. Here again, the wise Lord applied his well-tested approach of *Madhura*, but the queen mother's grief was so great that the Lord's words had little effect on her, although the grieving king was substantially mollified.

An attempt to summarise Lord Krishna's immensely successful technique of *Madhura Communication* and assess its relevance in the current

corporate work environment, leads one to conclude that this hugely successful and well tested approach of the Lord could be gainfully employed for maximizing the corporate world's competitive efficiency, as it helps in reduction of internal conflict by diminishing manifestations of negative energy and so enhanced team work efficiency would bring results that were not been feasible as yet, even with the best known management tools and technologies. The great ancient oriental wisdom is condensed in this methodology of the great Lord

Respect for Virtue and Merit

A great leader—guru or senior corporate professional, should actively seek and respect virtue and merit; and holder of the same should be honoured and rewarded through words as well as deeds. For people of virtue and merit, there is no better motivation than overt recognition. In life and works of Lord Krishna, pre-Kurukshetra and afterwards, one comes across several examples when he went out of his way, in support of virtue. One striking example was Vidura, son of sage Vyasa, a co-brother of Dharitarashtra and Pandu and an advisor [wazir] to the king of Hastinapura. Vidura was rich with virtues of knowledge of dharma and rectitude and the right ways of conducting business by a king. He was honest, fearless and straightforward in discharge of his duty of wazir to the throne of Hastinapura, He lived a life of austerity and simplicity, in a small dwelling outside the king's palace.

At various stages through which the story of Mahabharata unfolded, Vidura gave ample evidence of his wisdom, courage and sound knowledge of dharma and righteousness needed to be employed in the processes of governance..

Dharitarashtra had declared Yudhishtira as crown prince or heir to the throne. Duryodhana and his bunch of evil makers, feared that the king due to his visual handicap may handover the kingdom to him. Duryodhana did not want this to happen and planed to kill Yudhishtira along with his four brothers and mother. He secretly built a palace of wax and other combustible materials at Varnavarta. [2] He then persuaded the king Dharitarashtra to send the whole Pandava family to Varnavarta, for rest and recreation as a reward for the good work done for the kingdom. Vidura did not want to derail the plan as it was secret and yet he wanted to avert the catastrophic consequences.

As an act of courtesy, Bhishma, Drona and other elders escorted Pandavas, part of the way and then wishing them all the best, turned back. Vidura wanted to have a chance to warn Pandavas. He accompanied them a little further and as soon he could get near to Yudhishtira , he uttered a warning in code language. He said "One who understands his enemy can never be hurt. One should realize that there are sharp weapons, though not of steel, that could strike if one is not watchful. What consumes wood and straw, can never reach a hole; remember that jackal emerges from many outlets underground. The wanderer may know the direction from by the stars and survive by firmness of mind" Yudhishtira understood the warning that saved life of Pandavas.

After the fire of Varnavarta, Pandavas were incognito for some time and surfaced in Panchala where they won Draupadi. When their existence became public, Vidura advised the blind king Dharitarashtra, to invite his nephews along with Draupadi, to Hastinapura. In fact, he took the king's invitation himself to Panchala and was instrumental in bringing back the Pandavas to Hastinapura. A few days after Pandavas arrived at Hastinapura, Dharitarashtra divided the kingdom, and a part known Kandavaparastha, which was almost a desert, was given to Pandavas. On Krishna's active advice and intervention, they accepted their uncle's decision and proceeded to work hard--and with assistance and guidance of Krishna, created a kingdom of matchless beauty and prosperity.

Jealousy in Hastinapura was natural. It was further fueled when Duryodhana and the party of his evil friends witnessed the beauty and prosperity of Indraparastha, during the celebrations of the *Rajasuya* by the virtuous king Yudhishtira and his valiant brothers.

Afterwards, as part of a grand conspiracy, Duryodhana invited Yudhishtira for a game of dice to Hastinapura where the latter lost his kingdom, including his bride. When Duryodhana and his gang of evil makers attempted to molest Draupadi, Vidura attempted to fight their evil acts to the best of his skills. Words of logic and wisdom flowed from his fearless oration. He saw clouds of evil engulfing Hastinapura. He was outspoken and upright and went to the extent of advising the king to arrest and kill Duryodhana, as in view of Vidura, the prince was going to be the cause of destruction of the whole Kaurava clan. His bold defense of civility and dharma was widely appreciated.

Lord Krishna was aware of Vidura's virtuosity and merit .The Lord saw him as an ally in his fight against evil and wickedness that was tormenting the righteous, and often consulted with him. During the long exile of thirteen years that Pandavas went through, Vidura was summoned several times by Dharitarashtra, to advise how to have peace of mind as he was always torn between love for his son Duryodhana on one hand, and regrets for misfortune of Pandavas, on the other. Every time, Vidura advised him correctly and courageously on the consequences of evil actions of the king's eldest son.

Developments during the long exile of Pandavas, were keenly watched by Krishna. He greatly respected virtuosity and merits of Pandavas who were to be employed as the main tools for success of his mission to rid the world of accumulated evil and wickedness.

On expiry of the 13th year, Pandavas surfaced in the Virata country. They wanted to regain their kingdom and Indraparastha, as they had successfully completed their exile. How to regain their kingdom from Duryodhana, was debated at length, after the marriage of Uttarai [the daughter of king of Virata] with Abhimanyu, the son of Arjuna. Krishna was consulted on this vital issue. A priest was sent to Duryodhana's court at Hastinapura with relevant message but he had returned empty handed. It generated another session of intense discussions after which it was felt that, with his skills of diplomacy, Krishna was the most suitable person to go to Hastinapura and convince Duryodhana in respect to the genuine demand of the Pandavas.

Though, the great Lord knew in advance that the mission was destined to fail, He willingly went to plead Pandava's case. Krishna refused to accept Duryodhana's hospitality in view of his unrighteousness, and went to Vidura's humble home for a night's stay. Vidura, as always correct and upright, advised the Lord to be careful of evil and unpredictable Duryodhana. Next day Krishna made a righteous and forceful advocacy of Pandava's case, and despite appreciation by Vidura and other Kaurava elders, the Lord failed to shake away Duryodhana's evil adamancy.

Krishna had also noted Karna's merit as invincible warrior and tried him to see reasons of righteousness and stop supporting evil acts of Duryodhana, but because of his massive indebtedness to the evil Kaurava prince, he was not able to abandon his long-time friend. Further, the Lord was fully aware of virtuosity and merits of Bhishma, the Kaurava grand-shire, who had tied himself with a vow to protect the kingdom of Hastinapura and, as such, was invincible. Guru Drona's skills in technology of warfare were well known and his life time association with Kauravas was another hindrance in the Lord's mission against the evil. As per vision of the Lord, while virtue and merit had to be appreciated and supported but when allied with evil and wicked, the same had to be destroyed as part of the clean up objectivity.

Lord Krishna's divine approach towards respect to virtue and merit has massive applications in the field of modern management. With the practice of genuine approach in regard to respecting the virtue and merit, corporate workers are bound to be more innovative and aggressive towards bettering performance as they will be free from stress and apprehension of one not getting due recognition and reward for the good work done. Thus, freeing the corporate work environment from fear of biased credit and reward distribution can easily be achieved, through practice of the wise Lord's technology of ethicality management.

Ethicality of Management Approach

As per common understanding, ethics refers to moral principles or set of rules that govern human actions and behavior, commercial or otherwise, which do not have to be always in black and white as traditionally expected and accepted ones are equally significant. Primarily, it underscores the righteousness of human actions. Initially, ethicality concentrated on areas of governance and commerce; but presently all spheres of human activity are subjected to the prism of ethics. Depending upon sphere of applicability, terms such as medical ethics, political ethics, social ethics, business ethics and many others, are often employed in relevant communications.

Practice of ethics was present in all societies since time immemorial, whether tribal or non-tribal, developed or backward. Although there is no exception to this rule of presence of practice of ethics in all social groupings, variations and deviations do sometimes occur, creating problems of differential magnitude.

In ancient times, ethics or practice of *dharma* was greatly valued and even for battles and wars, there existed codes or rules and regulations. Kings, princes and all those involved in functions of governance, were traditionally trained in practice of relevant codes of ethics.

During periods of Mahabharata, especially during decades prior to this epic event, righteousness and *dharma* had come under severe pressure from accumulation of evils of various types. Lord Krishna had incarnated specifically for the purpose of ridding the earth of an unbearable load of evils.

At the court of Hastinapura, there were matchless experts of ethics, namely Bhishma and Vidura, whose adherence to dharma or code of ethics had no parallel. On the larger arena, Lord Krishna, the powerful ruler of Dwaraka, was well accepted as a greater expert of ethics in the field of governance and social affairs. Despite active presence of several luminaries of ethics in Hastinapura, conflict between Kauravas and Pandavas could not be averted -- primarily due to unreasonable approach of Dharitarashtra. His excessive love for power and his progeny became the main cause for massive destruction.

During the years preceding Mahabharata and also in course of active battle of Kurukshetra, there were numerous instances when the veil of ethics had either run very thin or was totally unfurled. The notorious game of dice that turned against Pandavas through the cunning Sakuni and subsequent disrobing of Draupadi had an unacceptable high content of unethicality. Further, persistently unwise refusal of Duryodhana and his friends, to restore Pandavas their part of kingdom, too had no justification of any type--except pure obstinacy.

Killing of Abhimanyu, when left alone and unarmed in middle of Kaurava warriors, was another high point of violation of code of ethics of war prevalent at that time. During the long drawn war that lasted 18 days, there were several such instances of violation that shattered many bright reputations. At one serious stage of war, Drona and Dharisthadyumna were engaged in deadly combat. The latter had waited long for this opportunity to avenge the insult that his father had met, several years ago, at hands of Drona. He tried all his weapons and every time Drona's precise arrows disarmed him in nick of time and finally Bhimma had to rescue him from this precarious situation by lifting him out of the combat zone.

On another occasion, the fighting continued even after sunset and Drona was inflicting unacceptable losses on Pandava forces. Krishna watched his activities with despair and said to Yudhishtira, "We must put an end to this terrible warrior; he is invincible and if he goes like this, no one will be left in our camp." He further added that Drona's only weak point was his son Aswathama who by himself was invincible. If an announcement can be made in darkness of the evening that Aswathama was dead, then the old warrior would lose spirit and action. Now, who would go and announce to him that Aswathama was dead. Arjuna refused to take part in this game and no one else seemed ready to do the job while Drona's attacks were becoming unbearable with every passing moment. Sensing urgency of the situation, Yudhishtira gave a serious thought to the matter and took a deep breath. He himself was one of the biggest votaries of ethics of war but safety of Pandava's cause now demanded action and there was no better person, at that moment, to effectively undertake this delicate job. He said, "I will go and speak to Drona but in order to keep a veil of ethics on the matter, let the elephant by the name of Aswathama be killed. After the announcement we shall add that it was an elephant, which in the din of fighting may not be clear to Drona" The trick worked and the old warrior threw his weapons and sat down unmindful of happenings around him. Then, noticing the opportunity, Dharisthadyumna attacked him with a sword, freeing the old guru from the agony of fighting on the unrighteous side, in the great battle.

Similarly, to save Arjuna from self-immolation on his failure to kill Jaidharatha before sunset, Lord Krishna, through his celestial powers created an illusion of sunset as a consequence of which combat ceased. When Jaidharatha emerged from the protective coverings of Kauravas, Krishna employing his superhuman powers lifted the illusion of darkness and exhorted Arjuna to complete the job in one go. Here too, the thin veil of ethics was maintained.

At the end of war when, Duryodhana was left dying on the ground, he accused Lord Krishna of motivating the Pandavas for employing un-ethical means to eliminate several of the Kaurava warriors, who otherwise were considered invincible. To this accusation, the Lord initially replied that when the enemy was excessively powerful or invincible, a little stretching was acceptable in the larger interests of the society. Since, evil forces themselves violate ethics, stretching the same while dealing with them was acceptable in view of the great Lord.

Lord Krishna's concepts of ethicality have immense applicability in modern management, both for superior corporate efficiency and cleaner democratic governance. A corporate worker often takes pride in ethical actions, while in war a soldier is thrown in a different predicament, as he may not live to see and experience results of such acts. Hence, there is no justification for over-stretching the veil of ethicality in corporate work environments. Here, alternatives are available to act righteously and still win.

The evil of corruption in the bureaucratic apparatus of governance, especially in third world countries, has assumed a serious challenge for the respectful continuation of civil societies. How should the stressed citizen of such economies fight the evil of corruption? Should the action shift to streets for fight to finish? Will it be better to equip the generation next, to face and fight this accumulating evil? Action in every home, school, college and all institutions of learning, especially those engaged in management education, seems vital to train the future components of our socio-economic apparatus, to actively resist and fight this evil challenge.

In summary, ethicality of action, especially in governance and commerce, is the only option of practical sensibility, as per teachings of Lord Krishna, for containing the evil of corruption and other undesirable practices. Practice of ethicality improves work environment from the point of employee cooperation and initiative. It also reduces the stress and negativity load of the work environment—pushing productivity beyond expectations. Modern management institutions have a specific responsibility to orient their products for this task of great significance.

Essentiality of Secrecy

Secrecy or confidentiality is a weapon of effective action at the right time. Since time immemorial, it has had apparent significance in conflict and war--while in business and corporate activities its various subtle variations have been practiced, (a) to protect plans and fruits of R&D activities, (b) for production technology protection, and (c) to safeguard strategies to do better than the competition--just to enumerate its major employments. In recent times, advocacy of transparency especially in business and governance, has gained active currency but, in actual practice, only minor variations in wielding of secrecy as a tool of management or mis-management are being allowed to emerge. In the present apparatus of governance or the so-called bureaucracy, secrecy is being employed entirely for anti-public operations to deny righteous citizens basic right to information. It is, in fact, a gross misuse of secrecy. Lord Krishna viewed it entirely in a different manner. With the implementation of the RTI [3] legislative provisions, the needy and righteous members of public may get some relief in the future.

Lord Krishna, during his illustrious life and works, employed secrecy as a weapon of devastating efficacy. He followed the principle of *Time Relevant Disclosures* in order to gain maximum advantage over his competitors and enemies which, as per forces of destiny, He was assigned a substantial number. One significant example of the efficacious employment of the above principle, by the wise Lord, was his knowledge of circumstances of Karna's parentage, that he was the first born of Kunti, prior to her marriage to Pandu of the Kuru lineage. He was left to float in the holy river Ganga, and a charioteer, who was childless, had picked him up and raised with care and affection. Although, Karna was often anguished on his inability to know his actual parentage, Kunti and Krishna kept it as a well guarded secret.

Krishna knew fully well that if this fact became known to Yudhishtra and the other Pandavas, then no one will fight Karna and the whole scheme of things or the wise design of the Lord will fall apart. It would have left Karna as totally invincible and without eliminating him it was not possible to fully and finally get rid of the evil grouping of Duryodhana. After the historic failure of Krisna's abortive yet impressive mission of diplomacy at Hastinapura, towards avoidance of the fratricidal conflict between the Kauravas and Pandavas and on escaping the unwise attempt of Duryodhana to seize and confine him, the wise Lord invited Karna to his chariot and disclosed to him that he was, in fact, the eldest of the Pandavas. He tried to convince him to shift side in the conflict and come and join the Pandavas. The numerous benefits that could have accrued to him as a consequence of such a change, were explained to Karna in an alluring manner. He was offered to lead the mighty Pandava grouping and rule the eventual empire but being truly faithful to his friend Duryodhana, the warrior refused to accept the alluring offer from the mankind's greatest diplomat and communicator. While Krishna was a little disappointed, He succeeded in substantially softening the invincible warrior's animosity towards the Pandavas. In fact, Karna developed a soft corner towards the Pandavas and, a few days after, when Kunti visited Karna to ask for the safety of her sons, he promised her that, at least, five of her sons shall survive the conflict. Even after these developments, Krishna kept the secret to himself while Karna and Kunti had no incentive to disclose the same to rest of the community.

Lord Krishna was privileged of being privy to vital secrets in regards to most of the important participants of Mahabharata, the epic conflict of cousins and in cases where He felt deficient in this regard, He effectively employed his massive intelligence gathering service. He was aware of the origin of Bhishma, Vidura, Sikandi, Draupadi, Dharishtadyumna and several other key players of the time. Further, He could draw at the services of Vyasa and Narada from whom little or no information of vital significance ever escaped.

Origin of Jarasandha and the cause of his invincibility was also kept a well guarded secret and it was disclosed to the Pandavas only at the right time. When Yudhishtra was keen to celebrate the Rajasuya in order to declare himself as a superior ruler, Lord Krishna elaborated on its impossibility in the likely event of the evil forces of Jarasandha camp joining hands with Duryodhana, the permanent sworn adversary of the Pandavas. Hence, He stressed that elimination of Jarasandha at that stage was the most important necessity. And a strategy was drawn to finally eliminate the great evil, employing the very secrets of his origin.

The fact that He had given a word to Sishupala's mother, an aunt of Krishna, to the effect that He would ignore even a hundred insults and abuses from the abnormal evil, too was kept honorably undisclosed. All friends and relations of Krishna were perpetually confused as to why the great Lord tolerated the uncommonly insulting behavior of the evil relative. Only at the right moment when the persistent evil had exceeded his solemnly allowed quota of abuses, insults and pranks, Krishna acted to kill him with the gentle flick of the mighty Sudershana.

The present community of management professionals, irrespective of engagement in business, governance, training or in any other act of significance, stands to benefit substantially from the wise Lord's observance of the vital principle of *Time Related Disclosure* of information of importance. For the purpose of benefiting from the wise Lord's above stated and so effectively practiced principle, it would be necessary for the professionals involved to train themselves in appreciation of value of information and its time related significance.

Humility of Management Approach

Humility is a unique innate capability of some the great people. When it is actively noticed by people who work for or with such a leader, it assumes the form of an effective tool of management and can be employed with significant success. Instead of broadcasting own skills, achievements or greatness, one should leave the same to ones subordinates and peers, to be perceived, accepted and appreciated, in an independent and democratic manner. Such an approach can generate great positive following for superior output at the right time. Only people of evil parakriti are unable to appreciate a truly displayed humility.

Great managers often do not make an exhibition of their achievements or greatness. They should leave it to people, to imbibe, accept and appreciate the same. A great leader's following generates out of gentleness or smoothness of communication that he makes, affording people a chance to evaluate and accept the same. Lord Krishna was a great practitioner of humility of approach in his dealings with people, whether a commoner or a king. He did not let his greatness or Godliness interfere with this practical application of wisdom. He respected his elders and peers a great deal.

On completion of his studies at the ashram of guru Sandipani, as a normal disciple He offered *Gurudakschna* to His revered teacher, and as desired retrieved His guru's long lost son from captivity of the sea God.

Humility of Lord Krishna's approach shined most brilliantly when He welcomed his long lost friend Sudama [4], when the latter came to visit the Lord at Dwaraka with great hesitations and misgivings. He was worried whether his old ashram friend who had now become a great emperor, would recognize him, after passage of so many years. All his apprehensions were however totally groundless. He was received with a lot of love and honour. The great Lord washed his visitor's feet with his own hands, which was an unprecedented example of humility and courtesy.

Another unique example of Lord's humble approach manifested, when without being present at Hastinapura, he responded to the distress call of Draupadi and frustrated the evil attempts of Duryodhana and his evil friends to disrobe her in full public view. By not appearing physically, He avoided direct credit for saving the dignity and honour of a woman in distress. He made no great song and dance story about it as only Draupadi new about the Lord's divine assistance. He avoided claiming any direct credit for it until and unless, sometimes later, the beneficiary herself disclosed it while complaining to her husbands about her great ordeal in court of Hastinapura.

Lord Krishna had a very humble and respectful approach towards elders as well as people of virtue and merit. Handing over the kingdom of Mathura to Ugrasena, after slaying the demon king Kamsa, presents another such great example. Neither the Lord himself, nor his elder brother Balarama, exhibited any direct interest in ruling the liberated kingdom. Instead, both the brothers proceeded to the ashram of guru Sandipani to acquire formal knowledge of scriptures and all that was required to know in the realm of religion, dharma, diplomacy and art of war and defense.

For men of great merit and virtue at Hastinapura, namely Bhishma, Drona, Kirpa, and Vidura, despite their presence on the wrong side of righteousness, the great Lord had a lot of respect and admiration, and always treated them accordingly. He was aware of the origin of Bhishma, his great vows and also his invincibility in time of war as well as in confrontation of logic and erudition. Guru Drona's capabilities and invincibility too was no secret to the great Lord. Vidura's erudition and his fearless defense of virtue and merit too was well appreciated by Lord Krishna. Hence, the great Lord showed exceptional humility while dealing with these great personalities of his times. Through his own study and judgment, Bhishma was aware of Lord Krishna's divine incarnate realities but the latter, as part of his humility of approach, never made an exhibition of the same, except when absolutely unavoidable under force of circumstances.

When a right opportunity arose to eliminate Jarasandha, the great demon king of Magadha, He got the job performed by Bhimma, the mighty Pandava who had the requisite skills and might to wrestle and tear his opponent into two. Lord Krishna did not want to do this job himself and draw avoidable attention. With matching humility, He freed hundreds of kings and princes who were kept imprisoned by Jarasandha, for a sacrificial ritual to please Lord Shiva. Through this great act of diplomacy, the Great Lord earned numerous allies and friends. Further, He claimed no credit for it as the same went to the great Pandava warrior.

Despite being a mighty king of Dwaraka, Krishna offered to make the final attempt of mediation between Kauravas and Pandavas, and went to Hastinapura as the latter's representative, in order to plead their case in the court of Dharishthrastra. Subsequently, when mediation attempts failed and war became the only option available to Pandavas, He became Arjuna's charioteer. There does not seem be a better or greater example of humility available in human history, written or otherwise.

Krishna took great care not to exhibit his greatness or Godliness until and unless it became absolutely necessary. One such situation arose when in the battle fields of Kurukshetra, prior to commencement of the fight, Arjuna got totally depressed and refused to fight, actively arguing that it was not worth killing so many nears and dears standing on the opposite side. Here, the Lord had no option but to reveal his all pervading multilateral Godliness, by allowing his great disciple Arjuna, benefit of a celestial eye. Without active participation of Arjuna, it was not possible to conclusively end the epic battle and free the earth from accumulated evil, for which the Lord had specifically incarnated in human form.

In conclusion, it can be said without doubt that humility is a highly effective tool of management, available to senior leaders and managers, to motivate corporate workers achieve objectives set righteously. Lord Krishna effectively employed this unique tool at numerous occasions in his long and

arduous life—always with bright and memorable results. This unique tool of management has not lost any of its efficacy or shine in the long period of over five millennia. It should be employed as often as possible.

Human Nature as HR Tool

Lord Krishna's understanding of human nature was most profound and perfect. He could read through people like a high powered scanner often from a distance and assess not only their motives and intentions but also their capabilities, active or inherent. While discoursing Arjuna on the battlefields of Kurukshetra, He dwelt upon, amongst others, the vital aspects of human nature, in view of the fact that all actions of human-beings were nothing but manifestations of an individual doer's basic nature. He elaborated that his own "higher spiritual nature" was present as *Self* in all living beings. In course of the celestial dialogue which later came to be known as Bhagavad Gita, He declared this truth thus—"Arjuna, there is nothing else besides Me. Like cluster of yarn-beads formed on a thread, all this is threaded in Me. Hence, there is only one consciousness." He moved further to elaborate that there were three modes of human nature (Gunas)—Sattava, Rajas and Tamas—through which the non-dual consciousness manifests into diversity, apparent to worldly experience. It is for this reason that no two individuals, even when born to same parents, will not be alike as the interplay of Gunas makes a wide-spread variety possible. He added a renowned example to illustrate this phenomenon, the three brothers, Vibhishana, Ravana and Kumbhakarana were so totally different in their nature and consequent actions.

Vibhishana had the predominance of Sattava and, as a consequence, occupied himself in acts of goodness, righteousness and welfare while Ravana, though highly intelligent and erudite, engaged himself in expanding his kingdom and influence without much attention to the righteousness of means employed. So, he parted ways with Ravana when the latter abducted Sita through deceit and deception, and did not concede his wise advice to free her respectfully. While Rajas was dominant in case of Ravana's nature, Tamas dominated the being of Kumbhakarana.

Lord Krishna wisely exploited this human nature differential in effectively managing his colleagues, disciples, devotees and adversaries--for superior results from activities of governance, diplomacy and war. He thoroughly analyzed and understood the basic nature of his important contemporary personalities such as Bhishma, Vidura, Dharishthrastra, Duryodhana, Yudhisthra, Arjuna, Karna, Bhimma, Draupadi and all the other key players in the epic conflict of Mahabharata. He had a clear idea of strengths and weaknesses of each of the key players and how will he or she act in a given situation, was clearly visible on his celestial screen.

Since the basic nature of a human-being so intensely governs his or her thought and action processes, and consequently the responses, it is high time that the modern HR-professionals and senior corporate functionaries take serious note of Lord Krishna's concepts and techniques of human nature management--as described in the Bhagavad Gita. Employing the human nature yardstick of the celestial manager, it should be possible to study, assess and document the nature differential of corporate employees/workers into specific categories and proceed to exploit the same for greater collective/corporate productivity and good.

Clear assessment of the basic nature differential of people should, in principle, facilitate to decide what shall effectively motivate individuals into superior performance. As a matter of principle, Sattavic people may perform better where higher levels of ethics are required or where unbiased performance credit distribution is to be achieved. In other words, where honesty, impartiality and righteousness have a premium, persons of Sattavic nature stand a better chance of superior performance. Senior corporate professionals with predominance of Rajas will be of distinct advantage in situations where leadership for push and performance is in demand where targets and competition are to be effectively tackled. Employees with higher levels of Tamas are likely to be better motivated with incentives that translate into immediate gratification. Higher values of righteousness or matters of greater common good and incentives of long-term benefits shall not go very well with their expectations. These types of people are lost in their *material forest*. Individual and immediate gratification is of pivotal significance for them. Such individuals are likely to require greater intensity of supervision and guidance for producing acceptable levels of output and efficiencies.

In most people, performance energies are distributed in relation to their thought and or action preference or their internal balance in this regard. Predominance of Sattavic elements predisposes a person towards thought warriorism, meaning that where new ideas, schemes, projects and propositions are of primary import, such a person should be of greater utility. Inversely, for action warriors--doing is always more important than thinking-- in other words, the action warriors do not allow or relish elaborate or in depth thinking to become a hindrance in commencement or completion of a task. In general, persons of Rajas dominance are more likely to orient in favor of action warriorism while maintaining a balance with their activities of thought energies.. For the third category of predominance, neither thought nor action are of primary concern—here, the service of self and hence, self-gratification becomes the dominant concern.

Negativity levels of individuals and its practical manifestations in form of cooperation or criticism, initiative or indifference, help or hindrance, interest or disinterest and its numerous other forms, are essentially representation of the basic human nature and its interactions with prevalent factors of work environment. Efficient management professionals especially the HR-experts can definitely better succeed in obtaining best possible outputs from all varieties of employees if they attempt and learn to employ the well tested concepts and technology of human nature differential as practiced by Lord Krishna, the true master of management expertise.

Empowerment as a Management Tool

Empowerment is the process of acquiring or assigning authority or powers to perform. The principle of empowerment states that it is the process of activating creative forces within the doer. In other words, it is the precursor of success-- as on empowerment effective action becomes much faster and rewarding. It can also be said that empowerment is the catalyst for success since it initiates genesis of thoughts and actions for an assigned or assumed goal through interaction of body, mind (intellect) and Atman (Self). The mind or intellect is involved with the process of thought genesis and evaluation while action is primarily a physical function of conversion of thought into work. And empowerment is effected in two different ways;

- self-empowerment or auto-empowerment and
- external empowerment or enabling empowerment.

The first is an internal process initiated and controlled through energies emitting from within the doer while in the second case, the initiative and impetus in infused from outside by the controlling or motivating force, either a superior or a guru. In both the cases, empowerment is a selection process in the first instance, it is selection by the self and in the second, the job is effected by the controlling force.

Self-empowerment is a more complex and demanding process because the whole spectrum of activities involved, right from initiation of thought process to conclusion of karma is managed by the doer and the total responsibility of its speed and conclusion lies on him. There exists no scope for justification for non-action or assigning of inadequate energy or input for the desired results to flow out. Blame apportioning has little or no scope here. This type of empowerment normally sprouts only in beings of superior intellect having Sattvic or Rajasic prakriti and people of the third type are likely to remain devoid of such capabilities. One who successfully handles the process of self-empowerment needs to grapple, among others, with the followings queries;

Who you are? Who they are?

What is a relationship?

What makes you work?

Believe and achieve!

What is the purpose of life?

Now or never—do it now!

What is the supreme power?

From any standard, self- empowerment is not an easy process as it demands a high level of initiative, motivation and determination on part of the doer. The second type or the external empowerment, on the other hand, requires (a) an eager recipient and (b) a capable and committed senior, mentor or guru who is to act as an infuser of ideas, technology or energies necessary for completion of targeted objectives. Here, the need of double direction initiative and commonality of objectives becomes a necessity.

Lord Krishna was an embodiment of empowerment. He practiced both of its forms as per situation specific environment of his times that were heavily burdened with the accumulated load of evil, on part of those charged with the responsibility of governance. As a young boy, He empowered himself with the skills of music, dance, wrestling, games, love, and leadership to the extent that all those, male or female, young or old, who came in his contact, directly or indirectly, could not escape being influenced by his celestial grace and charm. When He got a chance for formal education in the ashram of guru Sandipani, He empowered himself with all the available knowledge of scriptures, astrology, astronomy, biology and sciences and arts of war, diplomacy and governance, in a fast track manner, learning all the available sixty-four forms of specialties available at that time, in as many days. It left his knowledge empowerment agent or guru utterly surprised and immensely pleased.

Through dramatic elimination of the demonic king Kamsa and his whole clan of evil operators-- and handing over the reigns of power to the virtuous Ugrasena, the young Lord empowered himself to the position of a super ruler. Killing of numerous demonic and evil princes and kings, in a ceaseless campaign spread over several years, fully empowered the young Lord into the position of total leadership. Establishment of a unique empire at Dwaraka, matchless in spread and prosperity, and ruling it indirectly as a super ruler through large clan of Yadava warriors, fully completed the wise Lord's process of self-empowerment.

Lord Krishna's exercise of empowering Ugersena, Balarama and numerous other Yadavas was much more extensive than what is normally assessed by students of his life and works because it always got shadowed by the Lord's efforts of empowering of the celestial Pandava warriors. It was only through the wise Lord's celestial empowerment that the Pandavas converted a barren and desolate landscape of Khandavaparastha into the most fertile and prosperous kingdom of its times, igniting an intense spark of jealousy in heart of intolerant Duryodhana. His most dramatic exercise of empowerment related to protecting Draupadi from evil hands of Duryodhana and the bunch of his evil brothers, in a manner that astonished all those who witnessed the unholy act. Having been dishonored beyond tolerance, Draupadi moved a step forward and self-empowered herself to the extent that in the whole episode of Mahabharata, she became a decisive force. She refused to tie her tresses which had come loose when evil Dussasana had tugged at the same to drag her to the assembly of Kauravas. For over thirteen years, this unique act of protest on her part, did not allow the Pandava brothers forget, even for a moment, the humiliation that they had undergone at hands of Duryodhana and evil bunch of his colleagues and brothers. Thus, she had raised herself to such a decisive position that even Lord Krishna, while attempting to cool and console her, had to promise her that the wrongs done to her shall be avenged. Subsequently, Bhimma was forced to enable her in fulfilling her vow of washing her hairs in blood of her tormentors.

As advised by Vyasa, through Yudhishtra during the period of exile, Arjuna had launched himself on a long and arduous exercise of self-empowerment by successfully attempting to acquire celestial weapons that proved useful in the battle of Kurukshetra, to circumvent the elements of invincibility present on the opposite line-up.

In fact, Lord Krishna engaged himself into an endless exercise of empowering the celestial Pandavas because only through them He could complete the major part of his persistent battle against evil and the wicked who were growingly assembling around Duryodhana. The wise Lord could not directly kill them without the risk of totally de-masking his own Godliness. Pandavas were the only potent tool available in his hands for completing this divine assignment. The task to eliminating this unique combination of evil was so great that it could not be achieved even by Pandavas without the mighty Lord's celestial empowerment. The most vital and arduous part this exercise of empowerment, the great Lord had to complete right in middle of the battle of Kurukshetra, when in the process of motivating a disheartened and demoralized Arjuna, who had refused to fight on finding a large assembly of his elders and relations on the opposite side of the battle formation, He delivered the renowned discourse, later called and compiled as Bhagavad Gita or the Song of Wisdom. In this tedious process, He had even to reveal his cosmic form of omnipotence to his insistent and argumentative disciple.

To summarise, it can be said with certainty that Lord Krishna magnificently executed numerous exercises of empowerment in his long and pernicious struggle to rid the earth free of accumulated evil and wickedness. This great task could not have been achieved without this unique attempt in man and resources management. In corporate environment, CEOs and senior professionals should attempt application of this unique tool of motivation and enabling, with care and caution, only with capable and dependable juniors and disciples as undertaken without adequate precaution it has potential to turn into cause of envy and heart- burn.

Master of Measured Responses

Senior management functionaries are often faced with a challenge to come out with measured and calculated responses. Serious phases of negotiations with labour unions or those related to mergers and acquisitions, among others, often throw up such challenges. In such situations, right quantum of response i.e. neither too little nor too much, determines the future turn of events.

Lord Krishna was often faced with difficult situations while dealing with numerous unrighteous princes and kings, and demons and evils, during his long career of over ten decades. The very purpose of incarnation of the Lord on this earth pre-ordained the same. As a young cowherd, He had to get rid of Kalia, the naga king of serpents, who had made life miserable for his fellow cowherds and their cows and other animals. The young Lord subdued the serpent king by ceaselessly dancing on his multi-hooded head and forced it to vacate the holy Yamuna, with whole of his poisonous clan, and move to its original abode in the sea. The kind Lord did not physically eliminate the evil offender as it begged to be pardoned.

Years later, at Inderaparastha in the court of Yudhishtira, Krishna was selected as the guest of honour after successful celebration of "Rajasuya" yajana. There, Sishupala, the prince of Chedi, an evil cousin of the Lord, who had secured a promise of a hundred pardons, was maddened with jealousy. He started a non-stop tirade of abuses against the Lord; who ignored the same with smile and charm. While the offender had lost the count, and as soon as he crossed the assigned number, Krishna spun his magical Sudarshana, and the offender's head rolled on the floor amid the stunned gathering. There was no expression of any anger or regret on the Lord's face as the destined act was unavoidable. Here, such a response was necessary to liberate the soul entrapped in the evil's body.

Another superb example of the Lord's rightly measured response pertained to the incident in Dharitarashtra's court, where as an emissary of Pandavas, He made a valiant effort for an amicable settlement of the epic dispute. Duryodhana, as per his evil design, attempted to arrest the Lord, who in fitness of response, exhibited his multi-dimensional vision supreme Godly stature. It dazzled the assembly to the extent that, for a moment, the blind king lost his blindness and cried out of fear of the events to come. Soon, the Lord assumed his mortal form and walked out of the court. He was bade a respectful farewell by all the Kauravas and elders. Duryodhana was left alone reflecting on his folly and failure. Here again, the divine response was finely measured as per demands of the situation.

Prior to the epic battle of Kurukshetra, both the warring sides wanted Krishna's help for the decisive fight. The complex situation was instantly solved by the Lord through his decision for not wielding any weapon during the battle and stating that one side could have all the forces of mighty Yadavas--and the other, only him alone and that too unarmed. While the unwise Duryodhana was overjoyed to have the renowned forces of Dwaraka, Arjuna was content to have the wise Lord on his side. He knew that in the divine company of the Lord, success was bound to be of the Pandavas.

In thick of the battle, in his own invisible ways, the wise Lord responded to delicate situations in a decisive manner, in absence of which the course of the conflict would have been different. At one occasion, the Lord enabled Arjuna to escape his unwise vow to self-immolate, in event of his inability to avenge slaying of his warrior son Abhimmanyu, by an unequal and unethical ganging up by the Kauravas. He created an illusion of sun-set and when Jaidharatha, the main culprit for young Pandava warrior's death, emerged from hiding, the sun shined again through Lord's celestial powers and noticing the same Arjuna wasted no time in disposing off the targeted enemy. The decisive Lord further intervened, through appropriately measured responses, to ensure that the severed head of the Kaurava warrior fell right in lap of his father who was meditating at that moment, thus saving Arjuna from disastrous consequences.

Karna, the invisible warrior on side of Kauravas was a sworn enemy of Arjuna and, during a close encounter, when he fircd a sure weapon on the great Pandava fighter, Krishna the charioteer pushed the chariot five fingers into the ground, thus saving Arjuna's head.

At the end of the battle, Duryodhana was brutally disposed off by Bhimma, witnessing which, Aswathamma, a long time friend and camp follower of the diseased, was greatly disturbed, who in the darkness of the night attempted total destruction of Pandavas. As per providence, while the all the five Pandava brothers escaped unhurt, their next generation was wiped out and Abhimanyu's son in Uttarai's womb too was hurt. To this delicate situation, the all-powerful Lord responded by re-infusing life into the unborn child. Later on, the child was delivered safely and was named Parikshata.

Without further recounting the great Lord's masterly measured responses that not only controlled but, at several occasions, altered the outcome of the epic battle, it can safely be concluded here that a great leader or guru, irrespective of his field of activity, should attain superior skills in employment of appropriately measured and calculated responses, in order to influence course of events in crucial situations. Practitioners of modern management can benefit a great deal from this time-tested technique of the wise Lord.

Holistic Management Practitioner

A good manager or a great leader is normally endowed with multilateral capabilities as specialists, technocrats or experts, who suffer from limited stretch of expertise, do not go far enough in the highly demanding race of leadership. Perhaps, persons with superior skills in man-management, form the only exception to this cardinal rule. Lord Krishna wanted to reform the whole system of governance to rid the earth of evil and wickedness that operated through unrighteous kings and princes. He was not interested in elimination of only one or two demonic operators and hence planned to handle the gigantic problem, as an efficient holistic manager. Lord Krishna was an incarnate of many bits of strengths and merits stitched together as He was, amongst others

- a great lover, musician, dancer and wrestler.
- a good disciple, warrior, strategist and ruler.
- a good analyst, planner and administrator.
- a good organizer, builder and diplomat.
- a good teacher and a superb motivator.
- a wisdom concentrate of unparallel dimensions.
- a store-house of many other virtues and merits which add up to form a holistic manager.

Lord Krishna had to build his following from a scratch—from the grazing grounds of Gokula and Vrindavana. Right in that difficult environment, He taught his cowherd kinsmen how to work together—to face the great evil threat of Kalia, the mighty and arrogant serpent king who had colonized large water bodies of river Yammuna and nearby ponds, rendering them unsafe for cows and cowherds. Further, there was the problem of depleting food and fodder resources in Gokula and the whole cowherd community had to move to Vrindavana. A very young and illiterate Krishna managed all this and much more. He assumed the leadership of his kinsmen so early and so effectively. His skills as a master manager came into play very early in life.

Through his soft and sweet mannerism, dance and music, successful danger management, anticipation of opportunities and grabbing the same, He established a vibrant mind-body connection with his people, both male and female. All gopicas and gopalas, without any resistance and exception, were ready to respond to his wishes and commands, spontaneously and vigorously. There was virtue in his technology of influencing people and prompting them to perform collectively for common good. Welfare of every one, or whole the community, was the central point of all the strategies and activities of the wise Lord.

Lord Krishna often employed multiple senses amalgam, i.e. an admixture of sound, touch, speech, vision and movement, to influence his followers and co-workers into efficient collective action. Active involvement of people, right people for the right jobs, was forte of the ever-effective Lord. After killing the demonic ruler Kamsa of Mathura, He restored the kingdom to the elderly and wise Ugrasena. In order to equip himself for requirements of the future, along with brother Balarama, the young Lord joined the renowned Sandipani ashram for formal learning. Here, as per his holistic approach, the great Lord learned all that was available to be learnt at that time, in a fast track process of knowledge gathering.

Krishna's approach as a holistic manager was most vividly evident through his most intensive and composite efforts, during his fateful dialogue with his most accomplished disciple Arjuna, in the battlefield of Kurukshetra before commencement of fighting. He challenged the very basic concepts and perceptions of his confused and depressed disciple, in regard to life and death, body and soul, karma and dharma, action and in-action, creator and creations, persons and relations, evil and good, righteous and non-righteous, and many other practicalities in human society, including the supreme Lord's scheme of things.

Lord Krishna as per requirements of the delicate situation, employed a highly effective communication technology, a combination of speech, touch, movement and expression, and finally a 3-D power point presentation--where He revealed his multi-dimensional, omnipotent cosmic form to shake Arjuna out of his doubts, depression and inaction. Finally, after viewing the cosmic form of the Lord of universe, Arjuna accepted non-destructibility of soul, on one hand, and killing in war as non-sinning activity, on the other.

In the field of holistic management, there seems to exist no other practitioner of repute, ancient or modern, than Lord Krishna who operated with utmost efficiency over 5,000 years ago. He was truly a complete manager of uncommon superiority. His discourse to Arjuna, rendered in the

most trying conditions of an active battlefield that later on came to be known as the "Song of Wisdom" or Bhagavad Gita, is the most comprehensive compilation of supreme management thoughts—with applicability in all aspects of life—personal, corporate or religious. A good part of the wise Lord's holistic management concepts and practices have relevance and applicability in today's corporate environment.

Superior Emotion Quotient as a Management Tool

Not long ago, modern management professed high performance managers and CEOs to possess higher I.Q. as an influence of the western management thought. Rethinking, in this regard, was forced by the consistent failure of US and European enterprises to compete, in certain fields, with the companies from the orient, where milder culture and the background of inter-dependency and empathy, encouraged greater productivity. Today, in progressive business corporations, leadership with greater *Emotional Quotient* is more in demand than stiff-neck efficient CEOs with hire-and-fire, and cut-and–dried approach. Softer skills are more in demand for senior managers as it is felt that earning or encouraging cooperation is more productive than demanding or enforcing the same. Some are progressing to the next stage of preference, i.e. the *Spiritual Quotient* as it is thought that superior ethicality in corporate operations, may lead to superior productivity that eventually encourages greater physical and non-physical well-being of the masses.

That Lord Krishna was endowed with superior I.Q. became visible right in his early childhood as He had easily established his leadership amongst fellow cowherds. His initiative and logic had no parallel. On emotional plank too, He was a superior being and hence, a great lover and a great leader. People as well as animals responded to him in whatsoever manner He so desired. Innumerable instances from life and works of Lord Krishna, signaled his divine mix of intelligence and emotional superiority.

The first significant example of the young Lord's high emotional quotient or maturity was witnessed when after killing the demon king Kamsa of Mathura, He did not harm or imprison the dreaded demon's family, despite the inhuman treatment that his own parents had received in the demon's prison. He allowed the two wives of Kamsa, who were daughters of Jarasandha, the mighty demonic ruler of Magadha, to return to their parental home with due dignity and honour.

Years later, when his long-lost and poverty stricken friend and classmate Sudama traveled to visit him at Dwaraka, the manner in which Lord Krishna treated him, spoke volumes of the great Lord's divine *Emotional Quotient* to the extent that it left a unique example for the posterity to remember and quote. The whole royal family and palace workers were amazed at the way He treated a poor friend, some even felt jealous. It broke all constraints of wealth and status, exhibiting a divine bond of love and empathy.

Soon after Pandavas' exile resulting from the cunning and machinations of evil Duryodhana, Lord Krishna visited them in the forests of Kamakya and listened to the woes of Draupadi, who was first humiliated right in presence of her warrior husbands and all seniors of the Kuru-clan in the court of Hastinapura and then had to suffer a miserable existence in the harsh environs of the forest. Her grief and anger was so profound that Krishna had to make intense efforts to calm her. Draupadi's weeping was so inconsolable and intense that it affected Krishna's own composure, touching his heart and soul. Taking her tears washed face in his hands and attempting to wipe the same, the Lord said "Wait a little longer Draupadi. Your tears will not be in vain, when all the Kauravas –hundreds of them and their supporters will be killed by Arjuna and Bhimma. Duryodhana will be lying prostrate with broken thighs and Dussasana's chest will be torn open by Bhimma. Kuru women will weep more than what you are weeping. I promise you that all these things will happen. Nothing can stop it. Just wait a little longer. You will see all the Kauravas dead and those who supported them at that hour of your insult and humiliation will also die. Yudhishtra will be king again." It was a moment of intense feelings for the Lord and it exposed the emotional richness of his divine personality.

Lord Krishna's life was full of acts of high emotional intensities –as He dealt with great number of his relations, kinsmen, friends and followers, under conditions where expression of love and empathy was often unavoidable. For a great supporter and protector of good and righteousness, there was no other viable way out. Narration of all of his acts of empathy is beyond human endeavor and hence can not be attempted.

A very significant event, without narration of which the view about Lord Krishna's emotional superiority will not be adequately portrayed, belonged to the heroic effort that He made for the survival and perpetuation of the Pandava clan, after Ashwathama's attack on the Pandava's family camp fully destroyed their second generation. Uttarai was carrying the child of Abhimanayu and the same was gravely hurt in this attack. She delivered a stillborn child, later named Parikshit. Krishna, through his supernatural powers revived the stillborn child and thus kept the Pandava generation growing. Parikshit grew into a handsome prince and later proved to be a very righteous ruler.

After the ruinous battle of Kurukshetra that saw total destruction of the Kaurava clan, Krishna in company of the surviving Pandavas, as per norms of righteousness, met the grieving Dhritarashtra and Gandhari. The later had lost all her hundred sons and was totally inconsolable. In her anger, on hearing Krishna, she directly blamed him for not doing enough to avoid the bloodshed--and without waiting for any explanation, cursed Krishna to meet a similar fate. He kept quit and said that He was aware of his fate and destiny. It was, indeed, a unique example of emotional richness of Lord Krishna to take the risk of this visit. He could have avoided it under numerous pretexts. He took the risk—did his duty without concern to results and consequences—a very bright example of what He preached to Arjuna, while delivering hid divine message of Bhagavad Gita.

During the long and arduous life, Lord Krishna definitely faced more situations of high emotional charge than any other person, normal or incarnate, in the whole human history, written or otherwise. And most of such situations, He faced very boldly and judiciously. After leaving Gokula and Vrindavana, at a tender age, He never attempted, as part of an intelligent design, to return not even for a visit. He did not desire to be distracted in his larger objectivity as a mission incarnate.

His greatest rather divine act of emotional maturity and balance pertained to his considered decision to eliminate his whole ruling clan of Yadavas which, in the Lord's assessment, had huge potential for evil manifestations after his departure from this world. He did not want to be blamed (a) for leaving the job of evil elimination as incomplete and (b) of impartiality of any manner in dealing with evil or potentially evil elements. What a great instance of practice of what He preached!

From the display of superior management of emotional quotient or emotional richness or balance, in life and works of Lord Krishna, towards its great utility as an implement for promoting actions of righteousness, for acquiring greater cooperation for activities of greater good and implementation of the same, practitioners of modern management can draw a lot of inspirations and guidance. The wave of positive and righteous energy that superior emotional management is capable of unleashing for productive and collective actions is, in deed, substantial. Let today's professionals attempt to practically employ these divine concepts and practices of Lord Krishna.

Superior Ego Management

Ego is a troublesome characteristic of human beings, uncontrolled run of which, often lands people in difficult situations or complicates the already un - comfortable ones. It is defined as an individual's perception or experience of oneself, especially in relation to other people or the outside world, or as part of the mind that can think, feel and act in relation to self. Similarly, egotism refers to the state of mind in which one is always thinking about oneself and what is best for him or her. It is an avoidable preoccupation with oneself. In a related manner, egotism pertains to an individual's practice of talking too much about oneself. It is an expression of selfishness. Uncontrolled manifestation of egotism is particularly evident with people endowed with tamsic prakriti. As per Hindu mythology, most of the demons or evil operators that Lord Krishna had to deal with, especially Kamsa, Jarasandha, Sishupala, Salva, Rukmi and Duryodhana suffered from excessive accumulation of ego. Most of them perceived themselves as invincible and immortal, and hence behaved with untold crudeness and cruelty.

Lord Krishna, right early in life, had a perception of being an incarnation. He was actively aware that several of his acts as incarnate of Lord Vishnu, and his plans for subsequently cleansing the earth of accumulated evil, could be construed as egoistic if not suitably clothed and sweetened. Hence, as a precaution, He equipped himself with superior degree of charm and charisma, the spell of which was highly infective. He could calmly absorb harsh words, insults, insinuations and pranks, and reacted only when necessary, with masterly measured responses (MMR). [5] Normally, his smiles were enough to deflect minor evil intentions. His skills with words were legendry—music at his lips left no one uninfluenced. He could weave a maze of pleasure and happiness with his technology of language. He employed Madhura or sweetness as an instrument to charm people on one hand, and disarm enemies, on the other. It earned him a huge multitude of admirers. He could cloth difficult and unpleasant proposals as gifts of silk and honey.

Escapades of young Krishna with gopis of Gokula and Virindavana, presented a massive deviation from accepted norms of life. Hence, they were packaged with such intense charm that no one could really oppose his unusual acts. He created spells of happiness (Ananda) that blanketed any harsh reaction. He had divine success with females who exhibited enthusiastic or almost slavish submission. In his early life, Krishna uprooted trees, subdued Kalia, killed demons and lifted mount Goverdhana, yet these and many other superhuman or godly performances, never reflected on his persona. Humility, sweetness, smile and courtesy never left his unique personality even in hostile situations. He actively avoided claiming or accepting Godliness. Despite His persistent precaution to avoid exhibition of egotism, there was no dearth of evil and demonic people, even in his own clan and relations who exhibited open enmity towards the divine Lord.

While on way to Mathura on invitation of his demonic uncle Kamsa, miraculously He straightened his deformed female admirer Kabuja and went to her humble abode to enjoy her hospitality. For him what counted most was the quality and intensity of emotions—not the low or high of ones birth. Even at Kamsa's court, He went about the business of destroying "Shiva's Bow" and killing the demon king's wrestlers and elephants with professional ease, without even a trace of ego or enmity. Quietly, He restored the kingdom of Mathura to the virtuous Ugrasena.

Foreseeing his greater role as a ruler and warrior in the next few decades of youth and middle age, the great Lord along with brother Balarama, went to the ashram of guru Sandipani, to officially acquire relevant knowledge of all available arts, sciences, scriptures and warfare. He studied and lived there as a normal student abiding by all rules and regulations of the ashram life. He chopped wood and roamed forests, with his class mate Sudama, collecting whatever was required by his guru and the guru mother. He served his guru with utmost pleasure and happiness.

While withdrawing from Mathura with his total clan and armies to distant Dwaraka, in face of an imminent defeat at hands of evil forces led by mighty Jarasandha, the evil king of Magadha, the great Lord betrayed no trace of ego-hurt. Jarasandha, the head of evil forces after death of demon Kamsa, was protected by a boon that he could not be killed by any incarnate and some of his allies too had unique protections.

Years later, during the swayamwera ceremony of Draupadi, organized by her father king Drupada, Krishna—then the mighty ruler of Dwaraka, remained almost incognito as He awaited emergence of his future allies, namely the mighty Pandavas. He did not flaunt his status and silently persuaded all the five brothers to accept Draupadi as their collective wife—as it was so ordained by the destiny.

At the right opportunity, when Yudishtira the great Pandava king of glorious Inderparastha wanted to celebrate Rajasuya, Krishna pointed out that the same was not possible as long as Jarasandha, the demon king of Magadha, who was the undisputed leader of all the evil forces, remained alive. As per a well thought plan, Krishna accompanied by Bhimma and Arjuna, disguised as Brahmins, went to Jarasandha and when their disguise fell through, He asked for a one to one fight with any one of them. The great Lord showed no trace of ego hurt when Jarasandha called him a cowherd and preferred to fight with Bhimma whom he thought as a better match suiting his stature and reputation. With Krishna's guidance Bhimma killed the mighty demon after a grueling fight spread over 28 days. Krishna, with no expression of any hatred or ego and without any fuss, installed the dead demon's eldest son Sahdeva as king of Magadha. He also arranged release of a hundred princes and kings who were imprisoned by the great demon for a sacrifice after a few days. It earned Krishna and Pandavas immense goodwill and following that helped Rajasurya become a truly grand success.

After celebrations of the Rajasuya, Krishna was chosen for special worship by the Pandavas. Sishupala, the prince of Chedi and a cousin of both Pandavas and Krishna, started a tirade of insults and abuses, on poor choice of a cowherd for this auspicious purpose. The Lord kept quite with divine amusement and no traces of any hurt. He knew that the offender was taking the final advantages of the hundred pardons that were promised by him to Sishupal's mother, an aunt of the Lord. As soon as the offender crossed a count of hundred, Krishna flicked his renowned Sudarshana to do away the demonic manifestation. No expression regret or ego touched the Lord's face.

When poor and emancipated Sudama, a good old friend from the Lord's days at the ashram of guru Sandipani, visited him at Dwaraka, He himself ran to the door and picked up his semi-conscious friend in his lap, laid him on his own royal bed and nursed him to consciousness. The joyous Lord washed his friend's feet with his own hands and served him choicest meals. Later, He relished with abandon of a child, the handful of puffed rice that Sudama's wife had sent the Lord as a gift. The great Lord always exhibited a store of pleasure and the malice of ego rarely touched the divine persona.

Prior to Mahabharata, Lord Krishna volunteered to go to Hastinapura and try to make evil Duryodhna see reason and come to an honorable settlement with Pandavas. Though his mission failed, He did not exhibit ego-hurt of any type. During the epic war of Kurukshetra, He voluntarily served as a charioteer and wielded no weapon of any type. In fact ego display had no place in his "intelligent design" for riding the earth of accumulated evil and wickedness.

In brief, it can safely be concluded that Lord Krishna effectively employed *ego suppression* as a unique tool of management to influence his friends as well as enemies with equal ease and superior results. Practitioners of modern management can take an ever useful leaf from this divine practice of the Lord.

Empathy as a Management Tool

Kindness, compassion and sense of caring and concern for community or greater good, are positive human values that generate immediate impact (feel) within the recipient. Collectively these positive thoughts are grouped as *Empathy*. Actions rich in this virtue have great power for release of positive energy to create goodwill and support which, depending upon right employment, can significantly enhance productivity or efforts to win in a competitive work environment. Many leaders, spiritual, political and otherwise, have employed the tool of empathy to win over situations that earlier looked hopeless or even hostile. The unique force of empathy tends to create a strong bond of confidence between its operator and the target, for a long term association of mutual benefit.

Lord Krishna was indeed a great operator of this unique tool of universal effectiveness. Early in life, as a cowherd leader, He lifted the mount Goverdhana to protect his cowherd community—their cows and animals, from angry outbursts of Lord Indra, a peril of incessant rains. The mass following that an illiterate little Krishna had built, got so strongly cemented by the divine act of empathy that the members of his clan became his ardent devotees and nothing could shake their faith in his greatness and divinity. After this event of celestial proportions, He was viewed a definite incarnate of the supreme Lord and his fame spread like wild fire, earning him a lot more devotees and followers, on one hand, and a large number of enemies, on the other. It sent waves of fear through heart demonic Kamsa who was forewarned of his impending end at hands of Krishna, by the wandering sage Narada.

Another act of empathy that multiplied the tales of prowess of the young Lord, was straightening of back of Kubuja, a deformed young woman who secretly longed for Krishna. The compassionate young Lord corrected her deformity by a mere touch and visited her house to return her love in a memorable manner. Krishna-Sudama episode is well known as an ultimate event of empathy. Mere utterance of Sudama's name by a palace attendant made the Lord of Dwaraka run bare feet to the palace gate. He could not wait for his long lost friend to be brought by attendants. The compassionate Lord lifted the frail and emaciated visitor in his own hands, brought him to his personal chamber, washed his tired limbs and tended him lovingly to consciousness and good health. Through his divine communication He ascertained his friend's needs and without even a hint, bestowed on his friend immense material wealth.

A more significant act of empathy the great Lord performed when He visited Pandavas, after they were exiled, in the forest of Kamakhya. On seeing him, Draupadi, recalling the humiliation and indignity she had suffered at hands of Duryodhana and his brothers, and also the fact that no senior Kaurava came to her rescue, wept inconsolably. Her grief and anger was so great that even Krishna could not escape its impact. He reacted empathetically and promised (or inadvertently disclosed) that the Kauravas will pay dearly for their unpardonable sin of dishonoring a pious woman. Holding her face in his divine hands and tenderly wiping her tears, He said, "Wait a little longer, Draupadi, your tears will not be in vain. The women of Kaurava house will weep even as you are weeping now." His dialogues were long and reassuring and Pandavas became his ardent disciples and followers. They developed a great faith in Krishna's greatness and invincibility.

After the devastating battle of Kurukshetra that had left all the Kauravas dead, except the blind king, Lord Krishna at great risk of being blamed and cursed, visited Gandhari to offer his words of solace. He was cursed by the angry Gandhari but the wise Lord took her lightly, stating that He knew the future well. Thus, the mighty Lord did his duty irrespective of the risks involved Bhishma, the great Kuru warrior, after falling in the battlefield of Kurukshetra, waited for the sun to move to uttrayana [6], for him to decide to leave this world. He was a great devotee of Krishna and also one of the most learned men of his times. Krishna was worried that on Bhishma's death, the vast reservoir of wisdom will be lost for ever and hence, He convinced the apprehensive Pandavas to come with him and visit the dying warrior on his bed of arrows. Bhishma had always recognized the Godliness of Krishna and was very happy to see him come to meet him. When requested, Bhishma gave a detailed discourse to Yudhishtira and other Pandavas in regard to the methodology of righteous governance, including duties, functions and role of king and his ministers. Later, it helped the Pandavas a great deal, in ruling effectively and righteously during the post Kurukshetra era. Lord Krishna's image and popularity grew many folds after this incident.

Almost all leaders, CEOs and senior professionals know the significance of empathy in building effective and productive human relations for strengthening bond of association and generating positive work environment but very few are able to employ this celestial tool for the benefit of more efficient man-management. The primary cause for this deficiency ,on part of even very senior managers, lies in the fact that they are not suitable trained in use of this vital management tool. Often their ego becomes a hindrance. They should strive to learn from the life and works of Lord Krishna to effectively wield this ever effective tool of management.

Flute Play as a Management Technique

The ultimate objective of management is to move people, individually and collectively, to superior planned action. Practitioners of modern management, despite all the benefits of education, training, research, consulting and EDP, have been unable to locate an effective tool to achieve this objective. Always, a mix of approaches and tools are employed for this purpose, with varying results and satisfaction. A Brahmastra for modern management has not yet been discovered or invented.

Sometimes, to overcome his highly difficult to handle enemies, Lord Krishna employed Sudarshana Chakra, a reusable celestial weapon which relentlessly pursued a targeted enemy, finally eliminating the same. Once fired, it never returned without completing the assigned task. On the civilian front or in non-combat situations, He had to attend to numerous challenging tasks, right from childhood though youth, middle age and afterwards, as a warrior, ruler and diplomat. He used superior communication, i.e. *magic of words and song of wisdom*, to influence people, young and old, wise and arrogant, warriors and sages, friends and enemies, gurus and disciples, asuras and devas, with equal ease and efficacy. As a mission incarnate, except on most crucial moments, He had to keep his Godly vision under wraps, he had to keep wearing the mask of human body and, within its limitations, had to achieve the basic mission targets of eliminating the evil and wickedness from face of this earth.

For this purpose, he employed target specific technology, varying from super communication Madhura for friendly and mildly unfriendly humans; for reluctants and non-cooperators, his Song of Logic did the job of washing away the resistance. And for cowherds, his flute did the job of gathering all his cows, calves, gopas and the gopicas, with un-common ease. In fact, all his communication had the virtue and efficacy of his irresistible flute play. With the *Song of Logic*, He persuaded the proud and reluctant Yadavas to abandon their traditional and well established kingdom of Mathura and migrate, all the way, to the unchartered and desert territories of Dwaraka.

As per terms of the division of kingdom offered by Dhritarashtra, Krishna persuaded the reluctant Pandavas to accept the unfertile and almost desert territories of Khandavaparastha, as their part of the kingdom. His logic, in relation to conflict management, could not be resisted. In line of conviction or design, He assisted the mighty Pandavas in converting the wastelands into a highly fertile and productive empire of unmatched riches and effluence, their capital Indraprastha became known even to surpass the celestial Dwaraka in grandeur and magnificence.

Decades later, Lord Krishna, made a supreme effort in exercise of diplomacy and logic, when in court of evil Duryodhana, He pleaded for the cause of conflict avoidance. He extended flawless justifications in favor of the Pandavas' case, quoting from scriptures, detailing all possible formations and injunctions of righteousness. The whole assembly of court luminaries, including the learned Bhishma and Drona and the righteous Vidura lauded the celestial exercise of logical exposition. But it did not break the deliberate adamancy of evil Duryodhana, as he behaved quite possibly in line with the destiny or celestial design. Despite the apparent failure of the divine effort to avert the ruinous bloodshed that followed at Kurukshetra, it succeeded in weakening the support of the invincible warriors who witnessed the Lord's unique diplomatic enterprise. Further, it ensured the righteous side an advance insurance against apportioning of any blame on to it by the posterity, for not doing enough in direction of conflict avoidance.

While returning from this event of decisive magnitude, Lord Krishna had a pre-designed talk with warrior Karna. He explained to Karna the circumstances of his birth, clarifying that he was Kunti's first born and hence the senior-most amongst the Pandavas and that he could, in all appropriateness, come and join the group of the righteousness. He could head the kingdom that the Pandavas were to reclaim soon. Krishna's logical presentation had a lot of positive impression on Karna, his antagonism towards the Pandavas reduced substantially but in justification of his long and fruitful friendship with Duryodhana, he could not so quickly accept the wise Lord's invitation. These two apparent failures, in assessment of various logical observers, were in fact no failure in any manner of the great Lord's divine technology of communication. They were designed to turn that way, as per will of the supreme power.

The most amazing flute play of the Lord Krishna's communication technology evidenced in the battle fields of Kurukshetra, when in the processes of persuading a reluctant and depressed Arjuna, to stand up and do his duty as a warrior, Lord Krishna played his most renowned Song of Wisdom that later on came to be known as the Bhagavad Gita. It was so profound and intense in its flute effect on not only those who heard it but even on those who continue to read and hear it, thousands of years after the epic event. No one escapes its intense impact.

Lord Krishna's system of target specific communication of flute efficiency—including, amongst others, its better known components, namely madhura, song of logic and song of wisdom, offers a lot to learn from, for the modern management community. Through its active employment, various ills and deficiencies of modern work environments can be very easily remedied with substantially positive results.

A Change Agent of Significance

True leaders always tend to act as *Change Agents* and the magnitude of impact largely depends upon the cause of attention elected by the individual and intensity of the subject campaign. They clearly visualize what needs to be done and methodology for implementing the same is worked out well in time. Normally, they are the people who deviate from the normal and exhibit capacity to swim against the flow or the tide in their specific areas of activity. They are focused upon the target that they happen to set for themselves. Those who go along with the change, are known as the followers or the camp followers. They, normally, are the people who either have no choice or do not risk electing to have one. There exists another category of people who are change resisters—the status quo advocates. They are either apprehensive of the uncertainties inherent in change or are envious of the people who spearhead a change.

Leaders (professionals or gurus) shape future or have *Future by Choice.* [7] They first recognize the present, its limitations and demands, and then visualize the future, its shape and scope, and work out ways and means to achieve the same. Lord Krishna was a great Change Agent, probably the greatest, witnessed as yet by the mankind. He was a Mission Incarnate, i.e. the objective of the Lord's taking birth in human form, was decided well in advance. Its need was well justified and the resources needed to effect the target change were also well thought out. Freeing the world from the grip of well fortified evil forces, i.e. the demonic rulers, was an urgent objective. And since the challenge was so great, no lesser change agent (soul or being), than the Lord himself, could perform the job with any acceptable certainty.

Lord Krishna exhibited his immense capacity as Change Catalyst right from early stages of his life. He deviated significantly in his actions and behavior that significantly influenced not only his fellow cowherds and gopicas and his elders and community leaders too could not escape being immensely impacted. He became the harbinger of group activities whether wrestling, swimming, singing, dancing, and organizing dance circles, just to name a few from his vast activity spectrum. The varied and persistent influence of Lord Krishna's artistic activities and perfections is distinctly visible even today, in most of India's dance forms, dramas, art works, temple traditions, and mass festivities and celebrations. It was, in fact, young Krishna, through whose activities, the tradition of intense male-female social and cultural interactions became popular and widely acceptable, and continued so during the times that followed the mankind's most persistent change agent.

As a young cowherd, He effected a great social change by persuading his nomadic rural community to abandon a pernicious practice of ritualistic sacrifice and replaced it with greater care of cow and its progeny as He foresaw in it the potential to act as the economic foundation of the community for many centuries to come.

Destruction of demonic forces such as Kamsa of Mathura, Jarasandha of Magadha, Sishupala of Chedi, Rukmi of Vidharbha, and Duryodhana of Hastinapura, just to name a few, was pursued by Lord Krishna in a relentless manner. Obviously, He must have had a well laid plan for the same. He had to effect a massive change in the methodology of governance—and had planned to replace

- evil and wickedness with practice of righteousness and goodness,

- terror and persecution with development and welfare,
- illiteracy and ignorance with learning and awareness,
- superstition with science and logic, and
- suffering and deprivation with happiness and prosperity.

In pursuance of these objectives of righteousness and good, the wise Lord decided to have Future by Choice at Dwaraka, abandoning the troublesome spot of Mathura and establishing a vast empire of prosperity, happiness, virtue and creativity and assemble resources, capabilities and allies to one day successfully take on the forces of evil and wickedness.

He developed a highly fruitful and complementary partnership with the Pandavas by taking them under his celestial tutelage and protection. They were destined to act as major tools in his scheme of mass scale destruction of evil forces, in a swift and centralized operation. For Lord Krishna, the battle of Kurukshetra was, thus *destruction by choice* or *destruction by design*. He was, in deed, the celestial Change Strategist of the mankind.

Lord Krishna, not only effected masterly changes as per his divine design, He secured the post Mahabharata future of India by (a) convincing Yudhishtra to rule Hastinapura and Indraparastha after the decisive destruction of Kauravas, and (b) by protecting Pandavas' progeny in womb of Uttarai (Abhimanyu's widow) for perpetuation of the rule by the forces of righteousness.

The effects of Lord Krishna's approach as Change Agent or as agent for Shaping the Future still continue to be visible by his growing influence in all major aspects of our social, cultural, religious and philosophical life. In fact, no part of human life in the entire expanse of what is now India, and in certain of its neighborhoods, is free from influence of the changes effected by Lord Krishna's multifarious activities. His ever relevant teachings offered to mankind in form of the Song of Wisdom or Bhagavad Gita continue to influence and guide a multitude of lives all over the world, irrespective of caste, creed, religion, color of skin and or economic status.

Divine Love as a Management Tool

In Bhagavad Gita Lord Krishna emphatically declares that his power is present every where in the cosmos, from the tiny ant to the mighty galaxy. Everything that man seems to have achieved, is actually the result of the Divine Power animating an otherwise inert body. Love is, in fact, a divine power emitting from Atman, the immortal soul, through subtle mind and gross body. Divine love is not what human-beings normally understand this term to mean. Devine love or Prema, is in fact the love that God [8] has for his children or creations, and it is totally selfless--as He expects no returns or favours of any type. Selfless love is a remarkable force that comes from purity of thought, word and action.

Lord Krishna, being a mission incarnate, was endowed with an intense force of Divine Love which He richly employed in his dealings with residents of Gokula, Vrindavana, Mathura and Dwaraka, with mesmerizing effects. He could influence his fellow cowherds, gopicas, the young maidens of Gokula and Vrindavana, cows and bulls that he and his fellow cowherds tended, and also animals of all types, wild or otherwise, with ease of a professional magician, into doing whatsoever He desired irrespective time, place and session. They exhibited no resistance, asked no questions and raised no doubts as the power of divine love was so overwhelming in its spread and intensity. The young Lord had, in fact, established a powerful wireless communication with all of his people and animals. He often employed the unique system with amazing effect and efficiency. He, thus, left very little doubt in mind of his kinsmen about presence of an incarnation amidst them.

In fact, the young Lord was managing people, a multitude of cowherds and nomads, as per his planned design. First, He convinced them to move from Gokula to the more endowed pastures and forests of Vrindavana. Subsequently, in a totally unexpected manner, He convinced them to migrate from a well established kingdom of Mathura, to an unknown desert desolation of Dwaraka, on the western sea coast. It was a massive management of people. It could not have been possible without an intense interplay of divine love of the young Lord and its mystical influence on his people. It was a unique example of employment of the divine love as a massive management tool.

In today's corporate work environment, an effective (selfless) CEO can employ the unique tool of divine love to effectively relate to his constituent workers, white or blue collar, and influence their cooperation into a collective positive action towards achieving planned objectives of productivity. When a corporate worker feels or experiences a positive connection with his/her corporate entity, right results, in quality as well as in quantity, are bound to multiply. Inefficiency, non-cooperation and negative interactions of all type tend to minimize and eventually disappear, leaving behind an unobstructed field for superior productivity. The divine love in corporate context does not mean easy give-outs, either to an individual or a group. In fact, the reference is drawn here in context of flow of greater positive energy in the work environment—its direction primarily being from CEO to constituent workers, right up to the lowest rank. The positive thought process once activated, at the workers level, can smoothen all interruptions, active or potential, in the flow of work productivity.

Divine love is a powerful catalyst with remarkable longevity, a powerful non-monetary tool of motivation that Lord Krishna employed so effectively, first with his people of cowherd community and later with the Yadava clan, at Mathura as well as at Dwarka. The massive community of mighty Yadavas, several constituents of which were inclined towards indiscipline and non-cooperation, was kept united and orderly by the wise Lord, through employment of the irresistible force of divine love. Afterwards ,through various developments of the epic Mahabharata conflict, application of this divine force was attempted by Lord Krishna with devastating efficacy. The very mission incarnate objectivity of Lord Krishna emitted an irresistible fragrance of divine love.

A corporate mission statement, when suitably laced with elements of divine love for the greater good of community, can be a highly effective reminder to the constituent worker to do what is expected of him and also willingly walk an extra mile. It is the consciousness or Atman that acts as the basic source of the positive energy flow, manifesting first in positive thoughts and then into constructive actions, through instruments of active mind and gross body. Once a linkage is established between the positive forces of a corporate leader and his workmen, in right earnest, then productivity and output remain no longer a problem.

When an individual forgets or is allowed to forget his true nature as embodiment of divine, positive values get excluded automatically from life and actions of such a person. Consequences of such value erosion are very serious for a corporate and the society where such a person operates, leading to undesirable effects such as

- wealth acquisition without honest work,
- education without character,
- business without morality and ethics,
- science without humility,
- politics without principles,
- power without responsibility and many more.

To summarise, the message of the wise Lord is that divine love is a powerful management tool for superior workman motivation and to get done whatever is necessary for enhanced productivity on long term basis in a positive work environment where ideas and initiatives for new products and services promptly germinate for sustained growth. Modern professional managers will do well by learning and practicing the ever sure technique of divine love.

Self-realisation as a Management Tool

Thought is the precursor of action. Thought genesis often rises to its peak in solitude when one pushes brain and mind to higher limits to synthesize constructive thoughts/ideas and processes the same logically. Brain storming sessions, with persons of equal or superior capabilities, offer another fertile environment for thought generation. Solitary confinement is often awarded as appropriate punishment to grave offenders of law. For authorities of colonial India, narrow cells of the Cellular Jail in the Andaman islands were the preferred destinations to confine unrelenting agitators of the Indian freedom struggle. In most cases, these confinements were not able to break or dim the resolve of the committed workers of the long struggle. On the other hand, many of them were able to process a rich harvest of new ideas. Reading and recitation of holy scriptures, helped several of such confined individuals to self-brainstorm and churn out valuable thoughts and ideas which, in many cases, served as foundations for incisive actions in situations that followed.

Only strong and sensitive minds survive solitude. To the determined and disciplined, solitude becomes an instrument of self-realisation and often it helps generate gems of thoughts coupled with subsequent actions of matching significance. In fact, self-realisations helps concentrate the vital thought energy into arrows of well-targeted actions. Through this valuable process, enlightened ones can attain right alignment of body-brain/mind and Atman and when such a state is achieved, constructive action becomes an effortless occurrence. Through the brain storming of celestial proportions, Lord Krishna pushed Arjuna into a state of active self-realisation in regard to his duties as a warrior. He stressed, among others, indestructibility of soul, cycle of life and death, and destiny of most of the prominent warriors assembled on the battlefield of Kurukshetera. For the purpose of coxing such a self-realization out of the deeply depressed Arjuna, Krishna had to resort to revealing his Vishwasaroopa (universal vision) and had to assure his celestial disciple that he should not unnecessarily grieve about the fate of his kith and kin as they were destined to die. He added that, in fact, they were already killed by the almighty Lord and that he was to only enact a role-play on behalf of the Master of the Universe. This decisive realization, propelled into the mind of Arjuna, made him fight relentlessly and without any habitation or remorse.

Being a Mission Incarnate, Lord Krishna had attained self-realisation very early in life. Even as a child, He was aware of himself—who he was and what for he had come into this worldly environment, was very clear to him. Hence, the wise Lord did not waste even a moment of his precious time, in doing what He thought fit in a given situation. He thoroughly enjoyed his childhood and enlightened others' lives too, through his energy rich childish acts and pranks. Spread of love and happiness through dance, music and fashion amongst all those nears and dears to him, was the divine one's full time job for a number of years. Only through strengths of self-realization, the young Lord, even at the tender age of mid-teens could develop highly motivated teams of coworkers and devotees and performed superior tasks, the most prominent of that time being the swift elimination of the demonic Kamsa of Mathura, and thus freeing of numerous innocent persons, inclusive of his own parents, from prisons of the notorious asura.

Consequent to unique self-realization of his larger role on the canvas of righteous and corrective governance, He elected to put himself and his elder brother Balarama, through the grueling process of intense schooling and leaning at the ashram of guru Sandipani, mastering all the then available sixty-four disciplines sciences, arts, scriptures and warfare, in as many days. He could not possibly afford the luxury of a more relaxed learning as the newly liberated kingdom of Mathura was intensely besieged by the invincible demonic ruler of Magadha, who was greatly annoyed because of widowing of his two daughters who were married to Kamsa.

Soon, through his distinct superiority of thought and action, the young Lord attained commanding heights of leadership by totally bridging gap between talk and action. He realized the futility of having to repetitively face persistent attacks from Jarasandha who had acquired, in certain manner, immunity against the massive powers of the Yadavas. The right power capable of eliminating this menacing demon had not yet appeared on the action screen of the young Lord. Employing his immense charm and communication skills, He convinced and coerced the proud Yadavas to abandon their prosperous kingdom of Mathura and effect a massive migration to a distant and desolate Dwaraka, on the western sea coast of the Indian land mass. His approach of zero gap between talk and performance was again visible in full blast at Dwaraka where a large and greatly prosperous empire was established with lightening speed. It rejuvenated the reputation of Yadava warriors and the young Lord emerged as the "brightest force of righteous governance" on map of the country. It laid a solid foundation, on which He could base his long and arduous fight against the forces of evil and wickedness.

By now the great utility of the celestial Pandavas, for meeting his overall objectives, had dawned on the wise Lord and he actively strived to bring them under his protective folds. Arjuna became the most potent tool in the mighty Lord's armory against the accumulated evil, a significantly large part of which was destroyed on the battle-grounds of Kurukshetra, through the wise Lord's skillful employment of Arjuna and other Pandava warriors. For the success of the epic struggle, He had wisely managed to ignite the forces of self-realization in

Draupadi, Bhimma, Yudhishtira, Bhishma, Karna, Vidura ,and several other key players of this great game of the Supreme Master. The wise Lord had ,however, failed to attain any success while dealing with the prominent evil elements such as Dharistarashtra and Duryodhana. It was probably so due to the forces of destiny rather than lack of efforts on part of the wise Lord.

In realms of business and governance, immense benefits are bound to accrue when senior managers/ professionals are pushed into the enlightened state of self-realisation by training them to effectively coordinate flow of their positive energies of body, brain/mind and Atman i.e. if they are made to realize who they are (on individual and collective basis) and what for they happen to be there? Such a self-realisation shall free immense positive energies of thought and action, leading to forceful initiative, cooperation and innovation and the resultant team work, right appreciation and correct credit apportioning will create cascades of unexpectedly superior results. Suitable training can be designed and provided to make work environments free of negative energy manifestations and resultant friction and loss of output opportunities. Thought righteousness leads to the righteousness of action and in such a situation superior results always emerge for larger benefits.

Selective Use of Divine Vision

Devine vision is perceived as the capacity to see beyond what is physically visible. Sometimes it is called as *intuition* or the *sixth sense*, and presence of this capability in some endowed leaders and professionals comes handy under demanding situations. Only challenging conditions test true metal of a leader, professional or otherwise, as under normal circumstances routines and systems take care of what is happening and what needs to be done. This capability to see and visualize beyond physical occurrences can protect against unpleasant happenings or help remedy the same well in time. This capacity of intuition, when truly strong, can take the form of *divine vision*.

Lord Krishna was a mission incarnate. He was Lord Vishnu in human form and therefore, had to constantly wear the mask of humanity, to have time and opportunity for remedying the chaotic situations that prevailed on the earth under the concentrated forces of evil. At several occasions, in his eventful lifetime, Krishna gave evidence of his greatness or *Godliness* but the facility of divine vision, He granted only in very specific and demanding situations. On personal plane, it seems certain that the great Lord employed his facility of divine vision very often, to have a wider or more specific look at the world around and to peep into the interesting situations brewing therein.

For mother Yashodha, the child Lord felt the need for her to see and realize what a great being she was to have the opportunity of rearing him as her son. One day, assuming that her mischievous son had eaten some muck and to investigate the matter for herself, she forced open his mouth, and to her wonderment, saw a whole universe in the little mouth, in its all greatness and limitlessness. She fainted and when the little Lord realized the gravity of the situation, He restored her original vision and memory, and when she regained her senses, only a faint residue of what she had seen was left with her. The little Lord enjoyed the slight bewilderment of his mother.

On another occasion, Lord Brahma, the creator of the universe, wanted to see for himself how the great Krishna was doing on the earth? He herded Krishna's fellow cowherds and their cows, and through his celestial powers concealed them in some caves so that Krishna was unable to locate the same. Krishna quickly saw through the game and exhibited total unconcern, making no effort to search and locate fellow cowherds and their properties. To prove that He was present in all creatures and creations, the little Lord created duplicates of all that had been stolen by Brahma. Years passed, and an unnerved and frustrated Brahma, revealed himself admitting his failure to operate the trick. His confusion was further confounded when He could not differentiate between the originals and the duplicates. To help Lord Brahma out of the dilemma, the cowherd Krishna allowed his confused visitor benefit of the *divine vision* and a view of his true form. Transfixed by what He saw through the divine grace of Krishna, Brahma extolled the great Lord.

While in the court of Kauravas at Hastinapura, acting as Pandavas' emissary for a last ditch effort to prevent a disastrous war, Lord Krishna had to frustrate the ill-advised attempt of Duryodhana to seize and confine him by force. Duryodhana was either not sure of the great Lord's incarnate reality or He was an evil beyond redemption. When encircled, Krishna assumed his multi-dimensional form complete with components of cosmos and a ring of Pandavas and other celestial warriors around him. The brightness of the event was so great that even Dharitarashtra's blindness failed to give him a cover. Kaurava elders were dumfounded and profusely apologized to Lord Krishna for the misadventure. Krishna left the scene respectfully and the humiliated Duryodhana had nowhere to look at.

The most dramatic and prolonged use of the *divine vision* was effected when a depressed, disheartened but persistently curious Arjuna was unable to cast away his doubts and the Lord had to permit him a detailed view of his multi-dimensional cosmic form. Krishna revealed himself to Arjuna's undisguised terror, as the ultimate power destroying his own creation, devouring the warriors gathered on the battlefield, and at the astonished viewer's own pleadings, modified his vision and returned to his normal human form.

In a moment, the Lord's great disciple lost all his doubts and weaknesses and was ready to perform his duty as kshastriya and fight for elimination of the accumulated evil, irrespective of who were present on the opposite side. He was now sure that his killing of people, his nears and dears, gurus and relatives will amount to nothing more than the requirement of the destiny.

Professional management, in the present corporate environment, does not possess the benefit of Lord Krishna's divine vision, but when enriched with righteous intellect and intense experience, a capacity for intuition can be strengthened if the divine principles of karma, dharma, anusasana and non-material motivation are employed in a truly righteous manner.

Principle of Total Impartiality

"I look upon all creatures equally; none are less dear to me and none more dear" Bhagavad Gita

This vital statement of Lord Krishna enunciates the great *principle of total impartiality in human resources management*. When this principle is followed correctly in dealing with subordinates, disciples and co-workers;

- in assignment of work as per their capabilities,
- in apportioning credit as per performance and
- in training and guidance for sharpening their potentialities, it creates a flow of positivity in work environment, unleashing the forces of initiative and cooperation that, for sure, leads to higher productivity.

Lord Krishna, right from his early youth, exhibited adherence to the principle of observing total impartiality in dealing with his friends, followers and other members of the cowherd community. Even in the delicate situation of dealing with love infected gopis, his over demanding female friends and lovers, He found a way for total impartiality by multiplying himself into adequate numbers and being physically with each one of them thus granting each one total satisfaction. So, the young Lord well exceeded the principle of impartiality by granting them equality in satisfaction. Hence, his female following in Gokula and Vrindavana never diminished even a little bit and He is continued to be loved even today with increasing intensity and abandon.

Lord Krishna ruled Mathura and later the vast Yadava empire at Dwarka, indirectly, through Ugersena, Balarama, Akura, Sataki and various other warriors of repute, employing principles of management and diplomacy and the *principle of total impartiality* played an important role in keeping the huge Yadava clan happily united and performing.

As a mission incarnate, Lord Krishna destroyed numerous demons and evils i.e. kings and princes who had gone astray and tortured weaker and righteous people and almost all of them were released from worldly bondage and they finally merged into him. Even Sishupala, the evil prince of Chedi and a cousin of the Krishna, who ceaselessly insulted the Lord at all important occasions, met the same gracious and blissful end.

Lord Krishna very wisely employed Pandavas, his celestial cousins, towards completion of his mission incarnate objectives. He respected Yudhistra for his sense of righteousness, Bhimma for his physical prowess and Arjuna for his unique proficiency with materials and techniques of war. They were his specific tools to eliminate such warriors and evils whom, for one or the other reason, the great Lord did not want to tackle himself. The wise Lord assigned them jobs as per their capabilities and strengths and gave them due credits for performing the same. Mighty Bhimma was utilized to tear away Jarasandha, the most powerful and persistent enemy of Krishna because of whom the latter had to vacate his established kingdom of Mathura and earned the nickname of Ranchood.

Despite being in the opposite camp Bhishma, Karna, Drona and Vidura had earned appreciations from Krishna, for their specific virtues and strengths. Bhishma, the grand Kaurava warrior, recognized Krishna as Supreme Being and revered him accordingly. At one point in the battle of Kurukshetra, Lord Krishna, felt so frustrated by the war prowess of the old warrior that the great Lord was almost ready to break his vow of not wielding any weapon during the entire conflict, and only a nick of the time promise by Arjuna to do the needful, saved the situation. Despite the open challenge mounted by the old warrior that almost amounted to humiliation, the kind Lord visited him on his death bed of arrows while the great warrior waited for the right time to depart from this world. The dying warrior praised the Lord and was happily released from the worldly bondage.

In the long and arduous struggle of Lord Krishna towards re-establishing the supremacy of righteousness, the *principle of total impartiality in human resources management* proved hugely beneficial for him in assembling a winning and performing team and sustaining the same at a superior performing level. It won the wise Lord a large following of supporters and admirers, and was very handy in many complicated situations. Senior corporate managers and CEOs, who have the responsibility of keeping people adequately motivated and performing, can effectively employ the wise Lord's well tested and tried principle of impartiality, in dealing with their human resources, along with his other

important management concepts and practices, for continued superior performance

Notes

1. It is a unique communication technology combining the forces of righteous logic, love and charisma that Lord Krishna had employed with devastating efficacy.

2. A tribal location, at that time, about 80 Km. to North-West of Hastinapura

3. Right to Information Act has recently become applicable in India.

4. In the old Indian system of student and teacher relationship, it was a tradition to offer gratitude in some suitable manner.

5. MMR was Lord Krishna's uniquely effective technology of managing people—evil and righteous both.

6. Refers to the period when sun and earth are so aligned that the north of equator faces the sun in a more significant manner—and length of day start growing. Bhishma, the great old warrior had a boon assigned courtesy his father that he could choose the time of his death.

7. For Lord Krishna, it was more of a responsibility, to effect the needed change and it turned him into a "Maker of Time" in true sense of the word.

8. Persons with elements of Godliness or intense Sattvic prakariti tends to exhibit divine love. Several saints and sages or other good souls have been known to exhibit this divine quality.

PARVA VI

LORD KRISHNA AS A DIVINE TEACHER AND A GURU

Guru with a Strong Spiritual Core

A leader, corporate or otherwise, when endowed with a *strong spiritual core (SSC)* [1], serves as a great source of strength to his disciples and subordinates. Lord Krishna had incarnated to serve a higher purpose to curb and finally eliminate evil, especially on part of leaders and rulers. His divine objective was to promote the practice of goodness and righteousness in human interactions so that the life on earth could become peaceful and productive. *Strong spiritual core* of a leader emits positively contaminative forces that influence all those who come in close contact with such an individual. It initiates a chain reaction towards spread of spiritual discipline for greater benefit of the society. When goodness or righteousness leads, spiritual discipline comes into play, negativity of thoughts diminishes and positive actions spurt. Results pore in without clamouring for the same. It empowers a leader with capacity to stand and fight for what is right, irrespective for obstacles, and pave a path for success against forces of evil, exploitation and sin. A person with built-in resistance against evil forces, or one possessing a strong spiritual core, will fight injustice, greed, anger, sensuality, arrogance and jealousy as each of these evil manifestations, as thought and action (in passive and active forms) have potential for derailing a leader/manager from his assigned path and function. Hence, a strong spiritual core is an essential requirement for a leader or professional, to succeed in the long run, especially in an evil infested environment or strongly competitive work situations.

Lord Krishna, as human incarnation, possessed a maxima of spiritual strengths and He employed a judicious situation specific mix of the same, as weapon of invincible efficacy against the array of evil forces that the great Lord had designed to destroy. For Krishna the decision to guide and support Pandava brothers amounted to standing against injustice being perpetuated by one of the greatest assembly of evil forces at that time. Any failure to raise a voice against the anti-Pandava combination would have amounted to indirect support to the evil and wickedness of uncommon intensity. When Krishna spotted the Pandavas at Panchala, on the occasion of wedding of Draupadi to the five warriors, He immediately took them under his protection and tutelage and through his long-term intense association , He became their Guru (friend, philosopher and guide) guiding them in all challenging situations. In the process, particularly after the epic battle of Kurukshetra, He became the undisputed Guru of whole the mankind.

Prior to commencement of the battle of Kurukshetra, in his divine attempts to persuade a disheartened Arjuna to fight and perform his destined duty as a kshatriya, the wise Lord dwelt in detail, on merits of goodness, righteousness, discipline, duty, karma, dharma, gyana(janana), devotion (bhakti), meditation, yoga, prakriti and many other positive values and essentials for hard-core spiritual discipline needed by a great leader, warrior or professional, to succeed in a perpetually rewarding manner. Sometime earlier in court of Hastinapura, in an attempt to persuade an obstinate and evil intentioned Duryodhana, to be fair and return to Pandavas a part of the kingdom, Lord krisnna gave a mighty display of his strong spiritual core. Everyone was left spell-bound by the wise Lord's forceful and spiritually righteous presentation of Pandavas' case, despite the fact that the desired results were not received due to uncommon adamancy of the main evil player.

Superior spiritual core was also significantly visible in words and deeds of virtuous Vidura, grand warrior Bhishma and Balarama but none of them came any where near to the great Lord when it came to its timely and judicious employment towards containment or elimination of evil forces. Lord Krishna's strong spiritual core was also at its brightest display when He welcomed his long lost friend Sudama in Dwaraka and took personal care of all his requirements even without the visitor attempting to voice the same. In fact, the illustrious life of Lord Krishna is adorned with countless instances where his divine SSC repetitively comes into play. To enumerate the same, in any conclusive manner, is beyond human competence. Only sage Vyasa could have done justice to this challenge. For the mortal beings like us, a little essence of the same should be good enough.

Practitioners of modern management can make the corporate life much more pleasant and rewarding for all those involved--directly and indirectly, by cultivating a strong spiritual discipline, in concept as well as in practice. When the spiritual core of an organization is strong, especially in its upper layers of staffing, positive productive actions at individual as well as at collective levels are stimulated, pushing productivity and output to an unexpectedly high levels. Distribution of positions, placements, work and credit becomes more fair and just under influence of strong spiritual core, leading to enhanced positive interactions that finally lead to greater initiative and cooperation, the key requirements for superior performance. Pleasant work environment is a natural fruit of a strong spiritual core of senior management and it easily percolates to the other desired levels. Ultimately, it benefits the society, the rightful recipient all fruits of human endeavour, in an immensely positive manner.

Guru of Rectitude and Alternatives

When Lord Krishna incarnated with the express objective of cleansing the earth of accumulated evils, the concept of *karma and dharma* existed in some form, not properly highlighted and only adequately practiced. On the eve of the great battle of Kurukshetra, Arjuna faced the moral dilemma: should he fight and kill members of his own family and also friend and relatives assembled on the side of opponent Kauravas. Would it not be better to renounce the world, go and beg for alms, and thereby avoid the inevitable bloodshed? There was intense conflict within Arjuna's judicious self, between his duty as a warrior and a son of Pandu, to fight for rights of Pandavas, and the ideal of non-violence (ahimsa) expounded by the renouncer tradition. He refused to be easily convinced by Krishna's logic and arguments. He came out with equally valid logic and arguments. While attempting harder, the wise Lord gave his argumentative disciple an exit valve, the choice in action itself and said, "Arjuna, while killing them you won't be really killing them." Atman can not be killed nor does it kill and regardless of whether you fight or not, your action will not affect the eternal soul of these warriors—as soul journeys from one body to another—from birth to birth in a series of re-incarnations. It was a beautiful situation of alternatives.

The second most important reason for Arjuna to fight, the Lord said was to uphold his own dharma (duty and responsibility) as a warrior to do battle. The Lord added that war was lawful and should be fought to uphold and protect dharma. It was the wise Lord's recipe for *ultimate rectitude* which influenced Arjuna. Since Arjuna was a tough nut to crack—cleansing of his doubts was not easy; he was not sure how all these people (their souls) shall be liberated when killed in battle. Krishna had to finally reveal his divinity to Arjuna with the help of a third eye, the divine vision which the Lord bestowed on him for a few moments. Arjuna saw the Lord's majestic and glorious multidimensional form, entire universe in a microform, with all types of creatures ,objects, galaxies and even gods in it.

Initially terrified and eventually convinced about his duty to fight as a warrior, Arjuna further probed whether there was any other way to achieve liberation or salvation, and the kind Lord explained that there were the following three alternatives (margas or paths) available for this purpose.

- The first and the most appropriate is the path of action (karma yoga) which, as often noted, is detachment from fruits of action. It emphasizes as a way to reconciling worldly commitments with liberation, which forms the central theme in the Bhagavad Gita.
- The second path, i.e. above the path of action, is the path of devotion (bhakti-

yoga) for the purpose of salvation. The Lord added that even women and low castes could achieve liberation through this path. One attains the state of *Brahman* and enters the Lord through his grace.

- Third is the path of knowledge (gayana or Janana-yoga) which, in contrast to the first two, refers to the knowledge of Absolute (Brahman)

As the most profound and the ultimate guru, Lord Krishna gave Arjuna vital alternatives to achieve an objective. He, however, emphasized, as any knowledgeable guru should, that the righteous choice for Arjuna was to follow the path of karma. Through the logical mix of divine arguments employed by the wise Lord, Arjuna's confusion and depression was fully cured, and with his total commitment, he vowed to go through the war that was being waged to protect the validity and supremacy of righteousness.

In any sphere of life, whether teaching, training, business or management, a true guru or professional, for longevity or long-term validity of what he preaches or suggests, it is necessary that alternate paths or approaches are given for achieving a target objective. He could go even further to assist his disciple or subordinate select the most appropriate path as per his or her specific strengths and circumstances. This approach of rectitude and righteousness has a long-term spectrum of validity and acceptance.

A Universal Guru of Perpetual Relevance

Any attempt to study or examine Lord Krishna as a *Guru,* is encountered by the massive heterogeneity and omnipotence of his character in this role because He exhibits essential of a universal guru, a perpetual guru, a righteous guru, and a lovable guru of ever growing relevance in the present, as well as, for the future. His popularity and longevity as a guru primarily stems from the fact that He enjoys a unique appeal amongst people of all ages, children, youth, householders and elderly irrespective of caste, creed or religion. He commands relevance independent of one's erudition, profession or work engagement. The range of his actions as a child and as a youth, i.e. butter thief, cowherd, dancer, lover, musician, warrior and a ruler, just to name a few, was amazingly vast and varied.

In subsequent years, as a diplomat, teacher, builder, preacher, charioteer and as a strategist for war as well as peace, his activities were so profound and diverse that the universality of his appeal and relevance overwhelmed all aspects of human life like the rising turbulence of an ocean. He offers every thing to every one irrespective of limitations of time or age. Every human being, on face of this earth, can pick up some useful pearls from life and works of Lord Krishna, as celebration of the true universality of his celestial relevance. And since, He is independent of the limitations of time and space, his perpetual utility as a guru and as a teacher is fully assured for all generations of posterity.

In Vrindavana, people still believe that every night Radha and Krishna meet and re-enact their *raasa-lila*. In and around Vrindavana, Gokula, Nandgaon, Barsana, Goverdhana and Mathura, Radha and Krishna live in hearts of people, not as a lore or legend, but simply as an unshakable faith. Thousands of pilgrims walk the 22 km trail around mount Goverdhana, with gusto and elation with persistent chant of the names of the celestial lovers on their lips. At Barsana, the Radha's ancestral village, not far from Vrindavana, the entire area is dotted with a variety of sites commemorating her love for the blue God. Here, the celebrations of Holi, the Indian festival of colors, are truly unique in terms of intensities of festivities and their suggestive ruggedness. The spirit of participation and abandonment of these events seems to instantly rub on visitors, tourists, pilgrims, and the locals alike. No one ever seems to get offended when drenched with colours of exceptional variety..

Amateur theater groups enacting the celestial raasa-lila and other incidents from the life and times of the playful Lord, are not only popular all over India, but their intensity seems to grow with the passage of time. For instance, popularity of Janamasthmi celebrations, signifying incidents related to his birth, is to be seen to be believed. Govinda-groups of youngsters train hard for weeks ahead of participation in the final events of breaking pots of curd hanging high, for truly competitive and challenging efforts. And the growing popularity of *garbha dancing,* particularly in the states of Gujarat and Maharastra, seems to exert an infectious influence on young boys and girls ,in a manner that the contours of fashion and festivities are getting truly redefined.

On another platform of colours and imaginations, Krishna definitely holds the position of the most widely painted God, in countless forms and modes. There exists hardly any artist of substance who does not attempt or desires to attempt his or her skills with the celestial form of choice, the most popular ones being butter-thief, flute-player, cowherd, tormentor of gopicas, subduer of Kalia, the serpent king, and charioteer of Arjuna. The unchallenged uniqueness of Krishna lies in the fact that the incidents/ depictions related to his play of pranks such as stealing of curd and butter, and also taking away cloths of gopicas while they were busy taking a river bath, are relished by the masses with express joy and abandon even to rival the popularity of his serious teachings of spirituality and wisdom enshrined in the renowned Bhagavad-Gita.

Further, Krishna is one such guru and God about whom it is most difficult to decide whether He is more popular amongst men or women or amongst young or elderly. Even the limitations of caste, creed or religion do not seem to apply to him. Every one can learn a thing or two from this truly multifaceted personality, to love, dance, sing, paint, steal or elope and still feel good and justified about it. Such a large canvas of freedom or variety of choice is available no where else.

He is said to be the Akila Kaladi guru, the apostle of all arts and expertise and all what is beautiful and delicate. It is believed that all arts emanated from his rigorous dance on head of the evil serpent king Kalia. From his creative rhythm, beauty of frenzied control, subtle balance and vigor of warrior, was born the poetry of movement and sound. In the delicate seduction of movements, He is Natwara [2] and forms the main themes of Kathak, Manipuri and Odissi, the renowned dance forms of India. Yakhagana in Karnataka, Kuchipudi in Andhra, and Bharatnartayam in Tamil-Nadu, have been, primarily, based upon the dancing activities and skills of young Krishna. In fact, there is no region of India where dance, drama, painting, music, poetry, printing, sculpture and almost all other forms and activities of culture and tradition are not deeply influenced by Krishna. In addition, people in all other varied walks of life, not to speak of cowherds, wrestlers, fighters, diplomats, rulers, politicians, priests and common house holders and even thieves, draw active inspirations from the glorious life and works of Lord Krishna. There seems to be no sphere of human engagement that can be said to be devoid or untouched of influence of Krishna's universality. Hence, there is no hesitation in concluding that Lord Krishna is the *Universal Guru of Perpetually Growing Relevance* in the widest possible arena of human engagements, individual or collective and commercial or otherwise.

That Lord Krishna is the matchless Management Guru or guru to learned and professionals, was most unshakably established during his divine discourse that He delivered to the Pandava warrior Arjuna in the battle fields of Kurukshetra. It was, subsequently, immortalized as the celestial Song of Wisdom or Bhagavad Gita.

Despite rigorous efforts, I find no aspect of modern management, western or oriental that could not draw profound relevance and enrichment from the pearls of deep wisdom contained therein.

Several of the vital teachings of Lord Krishna, especially those bearing direct relevance and reference to the currently important aspects of modern management, are briefly dealt with, at appropriate places, in this work. Lord Krishna, the Mater of the Universe is indeed the true Master of Management. There is no aspect of management, ancient or modern, that does not draw relevance to what Krishna preached or practiced. His pursuance of assigned objectivity with divine Thought Warriorism and Action Warriorism was truly unique. The management principles, tools and skills that the great guru applied, in order to complete his assigned or accepted responsibilities of clearing the earth of accumulated evil and

wickedness, are lessons of perpetual excellence. His wise teachings are time-independent: their perpetual relevance and utility for all the time to come, is decidedly ensured.

World's Greatest Management Teacher

Brought-up in a nomadic cowherd household of Nanda and Yashoda, childhood and early youth of Krishna, passed without the normal benefits of schooling and education. The nomadic cattle rearing community of Gokula, at that time, was devoid of the concept and facility of schooling. Krishna, as a charismatic lovely young boy with flute on his lips and cows and Gopis making a bee-line to him whenever and wherever He so desired, enjoyed an overwhelming popularity in his community. Various superhuman feats that the young Lord had performed to slay or subdue the numerous demonic spirits which came or were sent to harm him, had elevated him to an unenviable position of early leadership. He had become a center of power. His kinsmen entertained an almost certain belief that He was a mission incarnate, a God in human form. The backward community of cowherds enjoyed the power that emanated from certainty of presence of a divine force right in its midst.

Soon after completing his early mission of liberating Mathura from cruelties and misrule of the demon king Kamsa, the young Lord with his elder brother Balarama, now part of the great ruling clan of Yadavas, proceeded to join the renowned ashram of guru Sandipani, at a far away locale in central India. It was felt that as young and upcoming princes of the Yadava kingdom, they should be well equipped with knowledge of scriptures, skills of war, art of governance and diplomacy, and all other specialties of learning available at that time. Both Krishna and Balarama were gifted students with total dedication and superior discipline. Along-side sons of poor Brahmins and mighty kings, the great avataras swept simple hutments, chopped fire-wood and gathered fruits and flowers from forests, with total submission to karma and discipline, and gave no chance for complaint of any type.

In class, Krishna was totally absorbed in what was taught, the quietest sishaya [3] of all and his guru loved him for his behaviour and speed of learning. It is said that the two celestial brothers imbibed languages, grammar, astrology, astronomy, vedic rituals, military sciences, occult mantaras, magical weapons etc., with lightening speed, finishing a five years course just in three months. No one had learnt so fast and in such a masterly manner, leaving the great guru astonished and their colleagues dumfounded. The story of the fast learning Yadava princes spread like wild fire to all kingdoms from where other students of the ashram had come.

Lord Krishna's function, as a great teacher, had commenced much earlier to his own formal schooling . As a child and young lad, He had donned the hat of an accomplished teacher of music, dance, wrestling and other martial arts, creating an army of followers and disciples, male and female, and young and old. No one, normal mortal or avatara, ever matched the distinction achieved by Krishna, as an accomplished teacher, so early in life and with such a large following. Further, He achieved the feat of becoming a great teacher so early in life, without any facilities of classrooms or teaching aids as the cowherd environment of his community was not conducive for the same. He was a self-taught teacher of multiple expertise.

Soon after leaving the hermitage of guru Sandipani, Krishna had to engage himself in the great exercise of team building, for strengthening first the Yadava kingdom at Mathura, and subsequently shifting the same to Dwaraka. On the new location, He undertook the rare feat of re-engineering the greatest known empire on the western coast of India. In this process, the great Lord had to continuously resort to teaching *finer aspects man-management* to the team of Yadava warriors, for successfully acquiring new territories through numerous war campaigns. In fact ,He must have designed and implemented a *great management teaching and training program* of all times, for ensuring such uncommon achievements. He practiced and taught, by example, the great state-craft of governance, successfully implementing the system of federalism for governing the vast newly acquired territories. He demonstrated effective governance through righteous delegation.

Lord Krishna excelled the speed of his own learning, while acting as a *cosmic teacher and a guru* to Arjuna, on the battle-fields of Kurukshetra, when He gave the great Pandava warrior a detailed and mesmerizing sermon on wisdom of action, karma and dharma, right and wrong, body, mind and atman, birth and death, creation and destruction, yoga and bhakti, desires and greed, duties of persons of different prakariti, happenings on earth, in heavens and beyond in a quick and crisp manner, while the mighty armies of Kauravas and Pandavas waited for orders to annihilate each other.

Here, Lord Krishna's job was not easy, He was facing his incarnate life's most difficult test and hence, had to access deeper awareness strata of his disciple's mind for it to accept the supper logic of his teachings. An organic approach to encourage holistic learning through establishment of a *mind-body-atman connection* was attempted by the wise Lord. He employed the multiple tools approach of touch, forceful words and expressions as He was aware that Arjuna could not be motivated until and unless all doubts on his mental screen were wiped off. Keeping this in view, the facility of third vision was granted by the Lord to his insistent disciple, for deep penetrative teaching which challenged long held beliefs and prejudices. And finally Arjuna's mental screen was wiped clean and he accepted the wise Lord's logic with folded hands. He was ready for action to do a warriors karma, and left results in hands of the mighty Lord.

Teaching with such a lightening speed, thoroughness and intensity was never attempted earlier to this celestial discourse of the great Lord to his equally gifted disciple. The valuable capsule of wisdom so effortlessly transmitted by the wise Lord, later came to be known as Bhagavad Gita or the celestial Song of Wisdom and it continues to guide millions of people, in all vital areas of life, even after passage of over 250 human generations. When analyzed in depth, no part of this unique Song of Wisdom seems either out of place or out of time, even in the present environment. His teachings seem non-alterable, beyond modification, ever fresh and universally applicable. No better teaching manual has ever been designed. He was not a theoretical teacher: He gifted us a solid basis to rely upon.

On scale of lesser intensity, Krishna attempted to create correct awareness of righteousness of things with Karna, Duryodhana, Dharitarashtra and other key players of Mahabharata, but the great spell of evil that had engulfed them did not permit a deep penetration of the wise Lord's attempted teachings. Possibly, the package of teachings to the perpetrators and supporters of evil, was designed for limited impact only, because any shifting of course by them and coming on board with righteousness, would have left a lot of lesser players of evil un-eliminated. Such a situation was not in conformity with the basic objective of the wise incarnate. It would have left his basic objective incomplete. Lord Krishna was, in fact, the greatest teacher that mankind has ever known and it seems that no superior one shall ever emerge.

Lord Krishna taught management of welfare oriented righteous governance along with effective war management to subdue and eliminate undesirable elements. The canvas of his teachings and trainings was really very vast in terms of content and applicability. Modern management, for training as well as practice, can profit considerably through righteous adoption of his major teachings, should it desire to gain an efficacy edge over the presently followed concepts and practices for producing more efficient managers and unbeatable corporate results.

Lord Krishna as a Supreme Management Guru

Lord Krishna's magnificent discourse to motivate Arjuna into action, delivered prior to commencement of fighting at Kurukshetra, covered most valuable aspects of human thought process interactions-especially governance, and included among others

- life and death, mortals and immortals, heaven and hell.

- creator and creations, birth and rebirth.
- body and soul, karma and dharma, varnas and duties of people.
- action and inaction, various paths for salvation.
- renunciation and renouncement, right and wrong.
- human prakriti and performance.
- janana and devotion ,ethics of war and peace.
- all that was necessary to push Arjuna out of inaction.

Persuasive flow of arguments from the wise Lord resembled a melting iceberg at a mountain top. It was impossible for his celestial disciple to stay unmoved for too long in face of a torrent of persuasive darts of wisdom. Years later, this celestial discourse, through untiring efforts of sage Vyasa and Lord Ganesha, assumed the form of Bhagavad Gita, also called the Song of Wisdom.

Coverage of all vital aspects of life and beyond, in this treatise of wisdom, is so thorough and complete that even after lapse of several millennia, no improvement in any manner is felt necessary or seems feasible.

Lord Krishna was a great guru to Arjuna, even greater than his warrior guru Drona because when what was taught by the latter looked irrelevant, Krishna stepped in to activate the hidden potentialities of this celestial warrior. Supremacy of Lord Krishna rested in the fact that he made Arjuna believe in his capabilities and enabled him to achieve the greatest heights ever possible for a warrior. The wise Lord treated his disciple of apprehension of attracting any sin by killing so many nears and dears in the battle of good against the evil. In addition, Krishna acted as an advisor to other Pandavas too, especially Yudhishtra and Bhimma. The former was alerted about the hindrances that could crop up if the reining leader of evil forces at that time namely jarasandha, the demonic king of Magadha, was not removed from their path prior to observance of the Rajasuya sacrifice. The strategic balance could go hay wire if the demonic forces of Jarasandha camp elected to side with the another great evil named Duryodhana, the perpetual enemy of the Pandavas.

How and why the unique supremacy of Lord Krishna, as a guru, has remained so unchallenged or unmatched for the long period of over five millennia, needs to be understood against the currently accepted yardsticks. The following uniqueness of Lord Krishna, as a guru are truly outstanding and the same seem to have contributed to his perpetual superiority:

- Durability/longevity or in fact the timelessness of acceptability and utility of his teachings, concepts and methods for management of human affairs-for commoners or kings. There seems to exist no scope for improving the wise Lord's teachings of karma and dharma, and relevance of one's duties irrespective of the situation or position one is placed into.

- No other leader or guru in the field of management or religion, any where in the world, has been able to match his important concepts of karma, dharma and nonmaterial motivation which, later on, became the comer stone of the Indian philosophy. They could neither be criticized beyond a point, nor improved upon in any substantial manner. Any discussion on Indian philosophy, irrespective of place and people involved, always ends up in further strengthening of these golden concepts. And the same seems to come true if one browses into his other sayings and teachings-- with requisite depth and desire to seek the truth.

His teachings and concepts provided an evergreen field to poets and writers, sufis and saints, lovers and painters, and worshipers and pujaris, to continuously engage in magnifying the wise Lord's glories and validity of his teachings-in endless forms, methods and media.

Lord Krishna's teachings and concepts have a rich center of ethics: The supremacy of right over wrong, and the final victory of good over evil, have nothing standing as a challenge, ancient or contemporary.

Further, there has been no discontent amongst his followers, in any manner or at "any time, except that from gopis, his childhood female friends who wanted more of him in physical form that the ever loving Lord could not grant due to his mission incarnate responsibilities. Apart from this limitation, his followers were free to worship him in any manner or form, call him by any of his thousands of names, and even celebrate theft of curd and butter. An uncommonly huge range of freedom to love and be loved, is provided and hence, his following continues to grow without limitation of distance, caste and religion. Modes of expressions of his followers too are limitless.

All that He said and preached has suffered no obsolescence and the same continues to be relevant to every one at all places and in any profession. The great Lord enjoys ever growing charisma-with flute in hand, tending his cows, dancing with Radha and gopis, subduing Kalia or wielding his brand weapon--the famed" Sudarshana"

Lord Krishna has not suffered any debunking or backlash that often has been the fate of most of gurus, in fields of religion as well as management, primarily because what He said and did, continues to hold firm grounds and looks very attractive even today.

Meaning and Definition of the Term Guru

The honorable term *guru* as per Oxford Dictionary, originated from Sanskrit to describe some-one who is *weighty, grave and dignified.* In Indian context, it is an ancient term widely used as early as the times of Ramayana and Mahabharata. Honorable and frequent reference to guru Drona in story books, often remains the earliest recollection to all Indians in this reference. The term guru is steeped with respect, honor, expertise and virtue as he is some-one superior and experienced, with a lot to learn from but nothing to match and criticize. The very mention of guru Drona and guru Parsurama, evokes unique feelings of expertise and ethics about their teachings and technologies, and their respectful relevance continues unruffled in the society even after lapse of several millennia from their occurrence.

A deserving guru has a unique status in the Indian society in terms of authority and reverence from disciples and followers-as his words are final on any matter of significance. An intelligent disciple is, however, free to seek clarifications and elaborations but never to criticize and confront. No challenge is ever mounted to the inherent authority of a guru and obedience is often taken as guaranteed.

Upon entry into English language, the term guru has assumed an intriguing status passage (Jackson, 1996). It has entered in general and trivial usage as well, to describe an influential teacher, mentor and pandit. The latter is a term of Indian contribution and refers to some-one who is learned in Sanskrit and in philosophy, religion and scriptures, and follows a code of ethics in day to day life.

In the contemporary context, the term guru is liberally assigned to someone who has acquired a superior level of expertise in any field of human endeavour, technical, managerial, religious or otherwise.

Mass media frequently exposes one to terms such as fitness-guru, investment-guru, diet-guru, yoga-guru etc. Presently, instances of application of this term in an indiscriminate manner and out of context, too are not uncommon. In the corporate world, the term guru or management guru, has only recently been accepted for common usage. References to the term management guru or simply guru in business journals surfaced in mid 1980s. The Financial Times ran a series of articles on this new interesting phenomena, under the title The Guru Factor and show-cased a number of western management experts, practitioners and thinkers, through these writings (Dixon, 1986; Dodsworth, 1986; and Lorenz, 1986).

Subsequently, a number of business writers picked up and elaborated the guru factor or terminology in their writings that finally accorded this divine term, the current acceptability in the modem management, in teaching and practice both. Today this term has wider resonance in management speaks and trainings, and in addition to thinkers and practitioners of substance, encompasses management consultants and writers too. A varied depth of meaning and relevance is assigned to the term guru as per place and context of its usage.

Concepts and practices of management have seen unexpected accelerations and variations in the last 3-4 decades of the last millennium. Many of the earlier accepted ideas, concepts and approaches have been altered, discarded and replaced by newer or catchier ones. This processes has been initiated and sustained by a variety of management related writers, teachers and consultants some of whom, over a period of time, have been honoured by affixing the Guruhood to their names.

Cutterbuck and Crainer (1990) was the first to list contributions of 29 such personalities. In Guide to Management Gurus, Kennedy (1991) identified 33 real guru personalities while R. Gibson (1997) selected only 16 persons to the list of honours in his book Rethinking the Future. The Guru Guide by Boyett and Boyett listed 79 gurus from 1980s to 1990s by reviewing the best sellers of that period. In brief, there is no universally accepted method or criterion to sum up and confirm the number of management gurus, past and present, as their popularity and acceptance continues to change almost on daily basis. In true sense a guru should possess the following characteristics of virtue and merit:

- Originality and uniqueness of ideas, approach and expertise.
- Authority and acceptance—leading to reverence.
- Capacity to encapsulate and communicate.
- Wider acceptance and following.
- Longevity of thought and expertise i.e. sustainability.
- Bright disciples and unique timings.
- Preferably, non-commerciality of approach.

When measured on the above scale, not many out of those listed as management gurus by various writers, shall qualify for this honorable classification. Lord Krishna seems to be the only personality that qualifies for the title of a management guru from all the angles because management does not limit itself to business only. Components of his *song of wisdom* have perpetual positive utility in all aspects of management-whether related to business, war, religion or otherwise. He is the ultimate and inexhaustible store-house of management ideas of superior value. His management wisdom shall never get outdated or irrelevant.

Management Fads and Buzwords

The variety of management gurus; teachers and consultants operative over the past 3-4 decades have created a flood of management terminologies or fads, also sometimes called as buzzwords and silver points-the number of which shall exceed several thousands if attempts are made to list the same in an exhaustive manner. The often employed ones include management by objectives, business culture, corporate culture or organizational culture, natural leader, business re-engineering, crisis management, downsizing, outsourcing, empowerment, TQM, JIT, core-competency, quality circles, lean and mean, hire and fire, bench marking, activity based costing, zero budgeting, value addition, mission statement, customer satisfaction, strategic alliance, self-directed teams, value chain analysis, mass customerization, cycle time reduction, theory-x and theory-y and many others.

None of the above and many other sophisticated terminologies have helped management gurus and consultants to effectively subdue the numerous ills that infect corporate work environments and push down their performances. No set of ever effective non-failing terminologies or technologies has been specified to ensure perpetual superior performance and root out inefficiency and negativity that continue to work as corporate *black holes*.

Fool-proof method to motivate employees for unsupervised continued superior output with zero defect and nil staff attrition, has not been found. Many areas of manpower management continue to be deficient as human work behaviour has not been fully understood. More than ideas and terminologies, methodology to work upon corporate workers' mind for problem free cooperation has been missing from the modem management.

Backlash against Management Gurus

Management gurus and the various fads spawned by them have had no smooth sailing in class rooms and conferences. Commentators from related academics and also writers and journalists have often torn apart all that most of the gurus preached. The most persistent complaint against the gurus, probably for no fault of theirs because implementation often is not in their hands and they never have the right and capacity to remove organizations' intentional resistance to new ideas and approaches. Anti-guru tenor of a section of self-sufficient executives has also been visible. The most relevant of these has been Tom Peter's well publicized capitulation to Dilbert, the satirical cartoon character created by Scott Adams, as America's most important management guru (Fisher, 1997). Further, management gurus have also suffered from effect of time on corporate environment that remains in perpetual dynamism--because its requirements are not absolute but alter under stresses of planned and unplanned obsolescence. It is, however, true that management gurus and their ideas suffer on account of time related loss of charisma which negatively affects their pick and application by the implementing executives.

The management wisdom of Lord Krishna is absolutely free from the variety of deficiencies and problems encountered by the management gurus, because being western in origin, they are basically deficient in operative incentives that propel workers or corporate functionaries to work for common good, with non-diminishing initiative and enthusiasm.

Notes

1. SSC is the invincible merit that a leader or manager can ever attain, as its holder is instantly lifted above the normal.
2. Natwara refers to the celestial dancer of excellence.
3. Sishaya refers to a dedicated and disciplined learner in the in the ancient ashram or gurukul system of education.

PARVA VII

LORD KRISHNA AND SOME FINER ASPECTS OF MANAGEMENT

Superior Energy as Management Tool

Scientists have recently worked out the concept of matter and antimatter. Two American scientists were awarded the 1959 Nobel Prize for Physics, for the discovery of antiproton, proving that matter exists in two forms—as particles and as antiparticles. According to one of the fundamental assumptions of the new theory, there may exist another world, or an anti-world—built up of antimatter. This suspected anti-material world is expected to be consisted of atomic and subatomic particles spinning in reverse direction or orbits to those of the world that we inhabit—and if these two worlds should ever clash or come in contact, they would both be annihilated in a blinding flash. The Times of India of October 27, 1959, carried a news item to this effect, based on a report originating on October 26, 1959 from Stockholm, in this regard.

The likelihood of annihilation of both the worlds, i.e. the matter and antimatter has not yet been ascertained with any dependable degree of certainty although the concept of black holes has often been discussed. On the other side, various Vedic literatures of which the Bhagavad Gita is of central significance, possess reference to material and anti-material worlds. It describes the concept of matter and antimatter in term of two forms of energy. Matter is the energy form which creates the material world and the same energy, in its superior form creates the anti-material or transcendental world. Living entities represent the *Superior Energy* form and it is termed as *para energy,* while the inferior or material energy is called as *apara energy.* These are the two forms of energies described in the Bhagavad Gita. Matter is not self creating; it has no creative powers and can be manipulated and is, therefore, a form of latent energy. As per Bhagavad Gita, Krishna is the manifestation of *para prakriti*, the cosmic energy or superior energy or the anti-material world.. He clearly states there that He is the creator and the creation—He is in everything and everything is in him. He proceeds to explain that the anti-material particle or the vital force or Atman is non-destructible and, as such, it can not be annihilated. Thus, there exists a degree of difference in the present view of scientists and that of Krishna but finally, after a lapse of some more time, the scientific community may progress to confirm what was said by the wise Lord such a long time ago. The science is today, in more ways than one, limited by the depth of its own knowledge, experimentation and verifiability.

Lord Krishna presented multiple manifestations of superior energy at different stages of his human incarnate life. He was a bundle of superior energy and employed it in a very discrete manner. In childhood and early youth, his superior energy manifestation took, amongst others, the form of his divine dances, music, games and dialogues which amazed or unnerved those who witnessed the same. Later on his cosmic energy flashed in his brilliance as a wrestler and a warrior, for defeat and destruction of the evil forces that crossed his way in numerous forms.

Soon after He destroyed the demonic ruler Kamsa of Mathura and his evil associates, His superior energy evidenced in form of a fast-track intense learning marathon, in the ashram of guru Sandipani, when He and elder brother Balarama, mastered the all sixty four branches of knowledge (scriptures, sciences, logic, astronomy, war skills etc.) in as many days, breaking all learning speed records. Analysts have also viewed that the two brother incarnates could not afford the luxury and joy of the normal learning processes, as the newly liberated kingdom of Mathura was being persistently attacked by Jarasandha, the mighty demonic ruler of Magadha whose two daughters married to Kamsa of Mathura, were widowed due to the killing of the latter by Krishna. Jarasandha had vowed to extract a revenge. Hence, he was not leaving any stone unturned to this effect. Although, he failed in redeeming of his vow but significantly enough, made the mighty Yadavas abandon their kingdom and run for the safety and security of Dwaraka, a good over thousand miles away on western sea coast.

The highly challenging situation encountered by Krishna in early youth and the years that followed, expeditiously matured him, amongst others, into a sharp situation analyst, realistic planner, matchless warrior, brilliant strategist, irresistible motivator, great manager and guru, peerless preacher, ardent lover, dependable friend, enviable advisor and celestial builder, his superior energy making dazzling display in all these and whatsoever else He attempted. He earned a large following of devotees and disciples, both male and female, warriors and non-warrior, and kings and commoners. The display and expanse of his superior energy was truly mesmerizing and all encompassing with occasional flashes of *omnipotence and omnipresence.*

Lord Krishna's innovative employment of superior energy, in whatsoever He attempted during his long and arduous life, gifts a highly useful management technology, for today's professional workers, to better their performance of whatsoever they are attempting to undertake and achieve. The key to understand is that every person has certain content of superior energy or cosmic energy that propels a living being and through self-awareness, effectiveness of body-mind and atman interaction can be activated and elevated to superior output of righteous actions. It will amount to acceleration of superior energy emission and will definitely ensure

superior multilateral management performances.

Magnificent Management Theory

Richness of management thought enables a good professional tackle difficult situations—because in a critical situation such a person escapes running into a desert of ideas and way-outs. This is how a strong theoretical base is beneficial for a good performer. Most of the modern management teaching and training institutions lay substantial emphasis on case studies and theoretical content. Capabilities of their output, however, remains deficient as several of their MBAs, in practical corporate environment, feel perplexed when faced with new and complex situations.

Management primarily pertains to development and employment of skills of people-handling for superior results, because all other inputs or factors of production, whether goods or services, are totally people dependents

- all machines are operated/worked by people.
- all materials are handled/converted by people.
- all moneys are invested and managed by people.
- all technologies are developed/utilized by people.
- all products are moved and marketed by people.
- no corporate or non-corporate activity ever occurs without people.

In fact, people are the most crucial component of all corporate or non-corporate activities. Lord Krishna understood, in full depth, the significance of human element for development, governance, war and/ or any-thing else. His management thoughts and practices, centered on manipulation and motivation of human element. The key components of the wise Lord's management thoughts and practices, among others, included

- prakariti or inherent nature assessment of involved individuals.
- human prakariti based capacity/capability analysis.
- prakariti/capacity based work/responsibility assignment.
- prakariti/capability based training and empowerment.
- centrality of objectives— key emphasis on righteousness.
- karma and dharma—the two central planks of emphasis.
- jnanna or gyanna as a useful input.
- non-material motivation for exceptional results.
- renunciation and renouncement.
- effective and well supervised delegation.
- effective mentoring and, if necessary, timely intervention.

- intensive use of divine vision.
- situation specific difficult decision management.
- madhura communication and diplomacy as productive tools.
- intensive information collection and analysis.
- leading by example.
- right credit apportioning and total impartiality.
- efficient internal dispute resolution.

Lord Krishna deeply understood the role of human prakariti as the key determinant for an individual's calibre or capacity to assimilate knowledge and interpret and exploit the same. Keeping this principle in view, the wise Lord selected Arjuna to expound the Gita, because the great Pandava warrior was rich with *Rajasic Prakariti or Rajoguna***.** And it was for the same reason that Bhishma taught the Vishnu Sahasaranama to Yudhishtra who was sattvic in nature. In view of intense tamas or tamoguna of Dharitarashtra, the job of discoursing him was assigned to sage Sanatasujata who had capabilities to handle such people.

Lord Krishna always emphasized that fairness and righteousness was the best hormone for human performance enhancement. It sprouts an environment of positivity, the most fertile ground for initiative and cooperation. Well-being, happiness and prosperity are the by-products of righteousness, and hence it was always the center-point of the wise Lord's emphasis in all of his human interactions. He further stresses that evil has the capacity and potential to suffocate righteousness and reduce output--as energies are wasted in infighting and conflict. His primary objective of incarnation was to reduce and, if possible, eliminate evil from face of the earth. In human society, as no such massive objective can be achieved single-handedly, hence creating and managing a large performing group or alliance became indispensable even for the all powerful Lord. It necessitated the great Lord to propound and promote his wise and most effective thoughts and practices of management.

Lord Krishna discouraged over-emphasis on results and, in fact, it was forbidden in many situations as it tends to reduce initiative and innovation. It was, indeed, one of the central points that the wise Lord emphasized in his famous discourse to Arjuna in the battlefields of Kurukshetra, prior to commencement of fighting between the opposing forces of evil and righteousness, which later on was summarized as Bhagavad Gita by the great sage named Vyasa.

The great beauty of the great Lord's management thoughts lies in the fact that there is little or no gap in theory and practice at his end. This narrow or nil gap between the theory and practice of management by Lord Krishna, also known as the *Zero Gap Approach*, was the main cause for the massive attraction of a large number of supporters and allies who assisted the divine incarnate to achieve the difficult goal of totally subduing the accumulated evil. The wise Lord always followed the principle of *talk after your walk* which means that he never advised what He did not practice. Hence, before giving any suggestion, one should make sure that the same is followed by one's own self. This will enhance the credibility of suggestion giver among members of his team or his followers, motivating them to emulate or even excel.

Lord Krishna's management concepts are, thus, very rich in content. They were very intensely practiced by him and by Pandavas, and also his other disciples and followers for a long time. Many great personalities in human history, saints and rulers alike, imbibed the great Lord's concepts of manpower management and governance, over the past several millennia. Long presence of foreign invaders in India, and their interference in the process of governance, shifted emphasis from the wise Lord's vital teachings. In the past two centuries western management practices had their sway and now that these so called modern management thoughts are exhibiting substantial deficiencies in meeting demands of the time, the great Lord's management concepts and practices shall show the way for multilateral success in the complex situation where human elements shall need a divinely efficient approach for superior motivation and performance. Hence, practitioners and students of modern management will do themselves a lot of good to study and understand the wise Lord's divine ideas and practices of management.

Creative Destruction

In the competitive corporate world, each business entity has to be dynamic and vigorous. It needs to shed what is avoidable and acquire what is desirable-- in pursuance of its specific objectives. *Creative destruction* [1], sometimes confused with selective destruction, is a widely employed corporate practice in modern times. Over half a century ago, renowned economist Joseph Schumpeter (1943) stated that processes and practices constituent to the capitalist society, produce creative destruction-- where innovations or new products destroy and replace obsolete and existing ones, only to be later on assaulted themselves by newer and more efficient breed of the same.

Presently, Creative destruction is a well-accepted management practice necessary for growth and innovation. Companies deliberately kill certain products and processes to promote new ones, more efficient, cost effective and environment friendly. Corporate decisions in regard to implementation of this practice of vital importance are normally based on a lot of statistical and EDP exercises.

Lord Krishna, over 5000 years ago, was well versed in the practice of creative destruction and employed it in a strategic manner, as a vital management tool, in a variety of situations. He destroyed cruel and public unfriendly regimes and replaced the same with more humane and efficient ones. Evil and wicked rulers were hunted with uncommon regularity in preference to the good and righteous—all through as an elaborate intelligent design. The long drawn destructive feud between Kauravas and Pandavas, culminating into the final battle of Kurukshetra, was the brightest example of the wise Lord's practice of creative destruction. It was the largest and fastest destruction of concentrated evil forces, in human history--written or otherwise. After the epic battle that led to massive clean up, a new society with more tolerant and considerate rulers emerged.

Prior to Mahabharata too, the wise Lord engaged himself in a relentless exercise in creative destruction. For several decades, He pursued systematic elimination of evil and wicked, fighting almost every week one or the other demonic or evil force, prominent of which were Kamsa of Mathura, Jarasandha of Magadha, Sishupala of Chedi and Rukmi of Vidharba. All of them were replaced with more tolerant and righteous rulers. Very thoughtfully or by deliberate design, Lord Krishna endowed the new generations with a unique gift, a store-house of code of conduct for the civil society, in form of Bhagavad Gita, which even today finds no equal in the whole world, as a superior moral guide to the mankind for a happy, productive and conflict free life. It provided for a contended and progressive society, following the ever bright active principles of karma, dharma and anusasana which have even today fitting applications for progress, peace and salvation, for all human-beings irrespective of caste, creed, religion and nationality. Rich or poor, illiterate or erudite, all can benefit from the wise Lord's *Song of Wisdom.*

In fact, the creative destruction practiced by Lord Krishna incarnated into *Creative Creation*, as after his principled enlightenment of the basic fundamentals of works and ethics, dharma and karma, life and death, body-mind and atman, and all other relevant matters that an eager and enquiring being desires and requires, nothing superior to the supreme concentrate of Bhagavad Gita has been able emerge or germinate. There is no alternative to the massive superiority of Krishna's *Pearls of Wisdom* which, in addition to spirituality and religion, enjoys a unique and equal applicability to matters of management and governance.

Lord Krishna employed the principle of creative destruction without favour or fear, and with total detachment, in furtherance to his sole objective for which He had incarnated on this earth. He went to the extent of practicing *Preventive Destruction* by enacting the destruction of the mighty Yadavas at Parbhasa, prior to his own departure from this earth. In his divine assessment, the Yadavas had no opponents who could exercise any restraints on them. Since they seemed incapable of self-restraints, their evil potential was enormous. The wise Lord did not want to leave behind such a dangerous force. He implemented a preventive destruction in a totally unbiased manner.

In corporate world too, productive application of this principle requires a wise and dispassionate approach, to timely discard (a) what is unproductive and outdated, and (b) dangerous and obstructive, from the point of view of future productivity and prosperity. It should be replaced with what is more appropriate, productive and environment friendly.

Power of Absolute as a Management Input

Awareness of Self and its relationship with the Supreme Being is intensely stressed by Lord Krishna in Bhagavad Gita. The Lord explained this truth in his own words as under: "Brahman or the Absolute is that which is immutable and independent of any cause but itself. When we consider the Brahman as lodged within the individual being, we call him the Atman. The creative energy of Brahman is that which causes all existence to come into being." The principle of causality, however, does not apply in case of Absolute or Atman. This is an exception to the processes of creation.

Interaction of *Absolute or Atman* with the active thought processes (mind) causes discrimination and differentiates the eternal from the ephemeral. This interaction causes all actions of a being, right or wrong. When in an individual, the Brahman or Atman is not strong or active (jagrat), the forces of mind (logic) may over-rule in favour of selfish or negative actions .All production or corporate action inputs such as capital, materials, machines, labour, and technology are controlled by man in an active manner. Irrespective of the type of worker ,it is his mind that controls all actions and outputs, right or wrong.

Normally, *Atman* within a worker operates in a passive way. Therefore, for correct and productive corporate actions, management should try and strengthen manifestation of their positive inner forces (Atman) through proper training. It will positively affect correct decision taking capabilities of workers.

Training of workers for activating and strengthening their positive action forces, though difficult, can be achieved through application of non-monitory motivational techniques. For this purpose a concerted application of Lord Krishna's following time tested concepts could be made:

- The Principle of Dharma that emphasizes one's responsibility to perform duty with full commitment and devotion.

- The Essentiality of Karma without active concern or preoccupation with results or its fruits as the same are the concern or privilege of the wise Lord.
- Principle of Non-material motivation, in order to diminish concern for rewards for every performance.
- Adequate incorporation of righteousness and virtue, especially in all people related activities.
- Holistic approach to action or work through superior body-mind and Atman coordination.
- Visible application of the wise Lord's approach in regard to commitment appreciation.
- Correct credit assignment to performance.
- Timely and effective guidance in difficult situations.
- Effective internal conflict management.
- Effective use of the principle of ethicality.
- Timely capability enhancement through suitably designed training programmes.
- Effective and well supervised delegation.
- Situation specific empowerment.
- Employment of empathy as a management tool.
- And several other manpower management technologies of the wise Lord, in situation-specific considerations.

Human Prakriti, its three significant divisions, should be employed in assignment of work or responsibilities in light of workers' nature and capabilities. In fact, a person's prakriti is an indirect reflection of his or her Absolute or Atman through the gross body. The physical mask of the body does not fully hide it from discerning and trained eyes. Further, Atman or Absolute works as the occupier of body; it can through the services of intellect and mind, manipulate desired manifestations or performances.

In brief, the power of Absolute can be significantly employed to upgrade human performance from the angle of output volume and its quality (righteousness of work) in a harmonious and cooperative manner.. Through study of Lord Krishna's management technology, the modern management professionals can have a significant harvest of benefits, particularly in difficult or challenging work environments.

Principle of Causality

The principle of causality states that everything that happens must have a cause. In other words, behind every effect or happening there lies a cause. It may or may not be visible or noticed under normal circumstances. Sometimes, the cause may be too difficult for human senses to detect and or to interpret as signals emitting from the same may be too faint to be intercepted or decoded by preoccupied or insensitive beings. Lord Krishna, in Bhagavad Gita, has voiced the relationship of cause and effect at several places. To begin with He states that; "For the protection of good, for the destruction of wicked, and for the establishment of righteousness, I am born from age to age."

Growth of evil or its accumulation, in various forms, becomes the cause for the Lord to assume birth, and re-establish the dominance of right over the wrong. The Lord does not resort to this action for all the small events of evils growth, as the same are left for his various disciples to handle. Only when the situation gets serious, i.e. too difficult to be handled by his disciples or bhaktas [2] and when no other choice remains at his disposal, He incarnates as human being, or in any other suitable form, to rectify the situation. He can not destroy evils by remote control, just on sensing the same, because this recourse shall eliminate incentive for the righteous to struggle in limiting the evil. His intervention is the last recourse.

And when He incarnates as human-being, He subjects himself to all the laws and rules that govern common individuals in the society of the celestial choice. He demonstrates how to cope with the worldly demands—for He has himself undergone the pangs of hunger, thirst, separation, suffering, sorrow and solitude, to impress upon human-beings the code of conduct that makes individuals accountable for their deeds (karmic accounting) [3] and face the consequences (effects) of the same. He even subjects himself to the cause and effect nature of occurrences that attaches itself to all actions and reactions.

As per the cosmic Law of Karmic Balance, all actions generate proportional effect that may or may not be adequate for effecting immediate visibility to the untrained eyes of the doer being. Progressive accumulation of such effect may give rise to delayed visibility and keeping that in view the wise Lord has forbidden a doer to be over- concerned about fruits or results of actions or deeds undertaken; they should not be the doer's worry, particularly when the actions are performed in direction of righteousness. In Lord Krishna's view, that is the area of his concern and responsibility. Karmic accounting occurs automatically and efficiently under this celestial law. The doer being is not to worry if he or she has employed the available wisdom to act in direction of righteousness.

All the events, popular or obscure, that occurred in the life of Lord Krishna, had cause-effect relationship. The most controversial decision of the wise Lords life—namely vacating Mathura and migrating to Dwaraka, with the whole

Yadava clan, had a very valid cause in the invincibility of the demonic Jarasandha of Magadha, whose two daughters were widowed due to Krishna's unavoidable killing of Kamsa of Mathura. Repetitive attacks of the mighty Jarasandha were occupying all the resources and energies of Krishna and Balarama, and no time was being left for any constructive work. Moreover, the wise Lord at that time had no tools to eliminate this persistent threat. There was a real risk of defeat, at hands of the evil forces, which Krishna wanted to avoid at all costs. Hence, the migration was the wisest choice at that time even at the risk of being labeled as one who ran from the battlefield. It was no time for the young Lord to reveal his Godliness. Probably, in his divine assessment Mathura was not the right location to implement his intelligent design of eventually eliminating the concentration of evil and wicked that was progressively assuming larger proportions.

The biggest conflict of all times, namely the conflict of Kaurava and Pandava cousins and the resultant battle of Kurukshetra, had the greed of Duryodhana to claim whole the Pandavas' kingdom of Indraparastha, as the main cause for it to grow to its conclusive stage. The righteous Pandavas were left with no honourable option but to fight and regain what rightfully belonged to them. The principle of causality manifests itself here with immense clarity. The right or wrong depended upon how one viewed the conflict, but all the invincible warriors on side of Kauravas, namely Bhishma, Drona, Karna etc. were killed—as their invincibility in terms of superior weapons, skills of war and boons failed to protect them in face of the wise Lord's attempts to eliminate evil regimes and all those who supported the same.

In terms of conclusion, one can safely state that the principle of causality is always operative irrespective of circumstances and their intensities. From corporate and management angles, it has useful lesions for senior operatives to always keep in view that cause-effect analysis should always be undertaken for all significant events—and the righteousness of the cause as well as of the effect should be examined, before taking a final view of a situation. The tool of cause can successfully be employed to give various corporate events a fruitful direction of long term benefits.

Principle of Superior Communication

Communication is an integral constituent of all collective activities whether related to business, governance, religion or war. In modern times, mankind has progressed significantly from the old practices of message runners, message riders and pigeon messaging to the present ones of SMS, video-phones, e-mailing and much more. And with the continuing progress of science and technology, more efficient means of communications shall continue to emerge. Origin of communication and progress in this field is nothing new. It seems to have commenced with the origin of life itself.

As a matter of principle, all living beings communicate, some do better than others, and consequently, they survive, progress and win better than the rest. The Principle of Superior Communication, which Lord Krishna practiced long time ago, states that in challenging situations only situation relevant superior communication allows us the opportunity to propel ourselves to superior performance. This is the surest way of beating the competition.

In his times, Lord Krishna employed the WUL technology which elaborates to wireless in universal loop. WLL or wireless in local loop, is one of the currently employed cell phone technologies with which one can communicate within a limited circle of distance, with help of equipment, to send/receive words /messages. Lord Krishna was far ahead in the field of communication. He sent and received messages in a far wider areas through wireless in universal loop and that too without any handheld equipment—either at end of the sender or the recipient.

Despite being a long distance away, He instantaneously connected to Draupadi when she was under immediate threat of being completely disrobed in the court of Hastinapura. She prayed intensely and found herself miraculously connected to the helpful Lord who endlessly extended her clothing to the amazement of one and all. She was saved from the indignity of total nakedness. This two way communication took place without any handset or any other device.

Lord Krishna was master of verbal communication with unique expertise in choice and employment of words and tones which enabled him win many friends, on one hand, and dissuade many adversaries from attempting to implement their anti-righteous schemes and plans, on the other. On certain occasions, despite his celestial capabilities, He encountered failure in the effective usage of verbal communication. One significant instance related to his intense advocacy of Pandavas' case that He presented very lucidly and logically in the court of Duryodhana. No argument of justification or righteousness cut any ice with the greatest surviving evil manifestation of that time. It was not because the content or intensity of communication had any deficiency but for the adamancy of the evil superior of the Kaurava clan. Here, the wise Lord's divine communication failed due to a deliberate deficiency on part of the target recipient.

Another great failure of Lord Krishna's celestial communication occurred when through his long drawn verbal dialogue with Arjuna, He could not fully convince him on the validity of the path of action, irrespective of consequences, which the great Lord was wanting the Pandava warrior to follow. Arjuna's questions and arguments were very searching and intense as he did not see any merit in killing so many warriors assembled on the battlefield of Kurukshetra, many of whom were his own relations, elders and gurus. Finding Arjuna's uncommon argumentativeness as the biggest hindrance in his scheme of things i.e. en-mass elimination of a grand assemblage of evil forces, Lord Krishna had to openly and clearly tell his disciple that he was the creator and the creation or master of the whole universe—and that all the warriors assembled there were already killed by him. He elaborated that by physically eliminating them, the Pandava was not going to attract any amount of sin. Further noticing Arjuna's reluctance, He presented to his warrior disciple, his Vishvarupa or the cosmic vision of his omnipotence and omnipresence. Arjuna got the direct exposure to the microcosm of universe including the hell and the havens; it instantaneously broke the inaction and adamancy on his part. It was the Lord's *visual communication in the universal loop (VCUL)*, a technology on which He possesses total monopoly for all the times to come.

Lord Krishna was the greatest expert in the field of communication, visual or non-visual, verbal or non-verbal, and local or universal. Any expert lesser than Lord Krishna, would have definitely failed to convince the great warrior Arjuna whose depth of curiosity was indeed matched to his prowess on the battlefield.

Since the occurrence the celestial dialogue between the two greatest participants of the epic event of Kurukshetra over 5,000 years ago, no communication event of such magnitude has reoccurred and to the informed minds, no likelihood of such a reoccurrence seems possible even in the distant future. Lord Krishna's superiority of communication expertise is unlikely to challenged. It will, however, be wise for the present management community to make the best use of his Principle of Superior Communication as per relevance and requirement of a situation.

Art of Managing the Boss

Managing the boss is a perpetual challenge to most of the people who are engaged in collective work environments. Whether one is working in a corporate house or in a government department, the shadow of boss always seems to curtail one's liberties and happiness or at least generates a perception of the same. The concept of boss is as troublesome and as unavoidable for a white-collar worker as the reality of a mother-in-law in life of a young woman. In both the cases troubles are certain to arise if one fails to understand and appreciate the pecking order. For some people, it is difficult to appreciate the sensitivity of authority (seniority and /or position): Many find it difficult to take orders while acceptance of criticism is unpalatable to one and all. And most bosses do not care to sweetly encapsulate the criticism that they may find essential or unavoidable. Strains of boss-subordinate relationship consequently force many to exclaim, "I hate my boss!" This imbalance in the unavoidable boss-subordinate relationship is superbly dealt with by Bob Weinstein (1998) in his most relevantly titled work.

The un-palatability of managing the boss often arises either from lack of skills of thought and action, on part of the parties involved, or from the innate self that refuses to accept requirements and responsibilities of authority. Minor deficiencies of expression, even body language normally considered inconsequential, tend to complicate the situation. This delicate human relationship primarily rests and feeds on impressions and perceptions. Performance does play an important role but it is secondary in nature; it takes longer time to create the right impact or the bond of trust that is so essential for smooth functioning of this vital relationship. Further, third party inclusions often tend to complicate the matters as work environment always involves seniors, peers and subordinates. Skills of thought, communication and the resultant behaviour are of greater utility then the energies of action.

The challenge of managing the boss diminishes considerably if the boss is endowed with merits of multilateral superiority. Here, respect for authority and merit quickly develops to subdue all other conflicting manifestations. In some cases when boss takes up the function of a mentor, the strains of this relationship miraculously convert into positive forces of synergism. Also, it is not uncommon when juniors, by design or otherwise, take to feeding and fueling insecurities of the boss by carrying information and tales suiting the recipient's taste and orientation. They end up promoting internal politics, which often harm productivity and quality of work environment.

Hating the boss is no solution: It does not solve any problem. It complicates the existing situations, simultaneously creating several new problems. Solution is probably concealed in acceptance of authority and enabling the boss achieve his official agenda. The Purpose for which the boss and subordinate exist in a given situation should be sacrosanct, entirely inviolable. Convincing the boss or getting convinced is the only workable option. Doing as told creates little or no problem--and doing better than that is a far superior alternative. The best solution, however, lies in making the boss say, "What do we do in this case or what do you suggest?" In other words, creating significant dependence of boss on oneself is the best situation to be. But to achieve the same is normally not easy: It necessitates superiority of skills of thought as well as action.

The problem of managing the boss has stayed with the mankind since time immemorial. And it is totally unlikely to disappear in the near future. Despite the prolonged encounter of the best of men and women with it, the *Brahamastra* [4] for management of the boss has not yet been perfected, because the human society continues to evolve ceaselessly and by default, requirements of this demanding function too tend to alter without much advance or timely clues.

Over five millennia ago, Lord Krishna evolved and practiced an effective strategy in this regard. Despite being an incarnate, He had to carry the mask of normal human life. Since He never directly headed a kingdom, both at Mathura and Dwaraka, the challenge of handling the king and elders (Ugrasena and Balarama, in particular) always existed. Orienting their thoughts and actions in line with his own mission incarnate responsibilities of eliminating the evil forces, had to be achieved; it had to be managed with their consent and cooperation. He had to do the king's job without being one; and also discharge functions of a boss without officially being so. It was truly a challenging situation, in fact more challenging than simply managing the boss. Despite intricacies of the situation, the Divine Manager of Impossibilities (DMI) performed the job superbly; keeping the king and elders happy and often making them do what He wanted. For this, He employed a unique strategy comprising of the following inputs.

- Creating dependence—for survival as well as growth.
- Exhibiting superiority of thought as well as action.
- Total commitment adherence i.e., delivering beyond commitment
- Unique management of critical phases (crisis management).
- Strategic attention diversion.
- And solving situations of invincibility.

Lord Krishna liberated the Yadava clan from the torturous grip of the demonic Kamsa, thus giving them an opportunity to again live with honour and righteousness. For them, Kamsa represented a situation of invincibility. He had managed to be born as king Ugrasena's son through an act of deception perpetrated by a Gandharva on the unsuspecting queen. Yadavas were not able to get rid of him and for a long time had to tolerate indignities and exploitation by his cruel apparatus of governance. Krishna freed them from this invincibility. Further, He protected them from repeated attacks from the equally cruel Jarasandha of Magadha. He was father-in-law of Kamsa: He was incensed due to killing of his son-in-law by the cowherd Krishna. Jarasandha repeatedly attacked Mathura, almost every year; and his each attack progressively grew in severity. Krishna had become indispensable for safety of the Yadava kingdom. From the Sandipni ashram located at Ujjain, where Krishna and Balarama had enrolled as students, they had to rush to Mathura for its defense from the demonic Jarasandha.

The invincible Jarasandha had secured celestial boons to the effect that he could not be killed by any avatara. [5] And no other Yadava was in a position to face him effectively. Hence, the whole Yadava clan had agreed to migrate to Dwaraka, as per Krishna's suggestion, despite having acquired the not so flattering distinction of running away from a battle. The new location, as was promised by Krishna, proved lucky for the uprooted Yadavas; they were able to craft out a great empire and a divinely splendorous capital at Dwaraka. Thus, Krishna delivered more than what was promised. Later on, the divine master was able to break Jarasandha's invincibility with the help of Bhimma, the mighty Pandava warrior.

At Mathura and Dwaraka both, Krishna presented a unique management of the two critical phases in life of the Yadava clan. In his absence, the illustrious Yadava clan would have definitely gone on the totally ruinous path under the tyranny of its own demonic Kamsa.

Krishna employed a unique methodology in handling his seniors: Balarama, being immensely powerful and not very ambitious, was sometimes a difficult nut to handle. To manage him effectively, Krishna used a divine mix of madhura and diversion. Since he did not often agree with Krishna's methodology of achieving his goals, prior to the battle of Kurukshetra, he was persuaded to go on a long voyage of religious places. He returned only after completion of the great massacre of the evil forces at Kurukshetra, as per design of the divine master of impossibilities. And Krishna did not, using tact and persuasion, allow him to inspect the site of the great killings. The tool of persuasive diversion was employed with desired efficacy.

Acquiring skills superior to those of the boss in some selected areas, or even performance better than promised or expected, is not a non-failing Brahamastra if the same is not combined with madhura and humility. A little spike of arrogance or superiority is definitely bound to negate the whole benefit with unmanageable complications. Performance alone is not enough! It has been experienced by the author in numerous situations.

Unified Concept of Management Performance

Management or modern management, in essence of reality, represents sophisticated delivery of *Common Sense,* often aimed at productive action. Common sense (CS) [6] encompasses all positive energies of thought and mind that are essential or required for desired action, individually or collectively.

Common sense is mother of management as it emerged from the former, right when the first group of human beings developed on face of the earth, as consequence of procreative activities of Adam and Eve. The need to gather food or hunt for the same, and to ensure safety from wild beasts and harsh elements of weather, necessitated coordinated thought and action regarding leadership, initiative, threat assessment, division of labor, work assignment and hierarchy, just to enumerate a few. With the passage of time, as requirements multiplied, thought and action processes (TAP) responded to meet emerging challenges, initiating a chain reaction of management developments and their applications. The beauty of the situation was that these primary innovators were neither conscious nor aware of the developments that they were initiating.

Being a social animal, man did not lose much time in appreciating and assimilating the utility of collective action, i.e. to cooperate and act in common good. Collectively, it was easier to collect food and hunt more effectively. Safety and security too needed collective action. Thus, the concept of cooperation and team work originated very early on the developmental path of mankind. Hence, the roots of management are very old. Despite the antiquity of management practice, progress in the field of management development has neither been easy or smooth, as man's faculty of mind, and the resultant argumentative nature, assigned it the capacity to differ and deviate. As a result of it, man has always been struggling to improve or perfect his team-building and management skills and practices. Earlier, it included, among others, shouting and gesticulation, on part of propagators of opposing views while today, the modern professionals have acquired various inputs, tools and skills for this purpose. However, we are still far away from acquiring the *ultimate output efficiency (UOE)* [7] in team management. Other areas of the modern management also do not present any better picture. The magic tool of perfect decision making and the *Brahamastra of motivation* are yet to be discovered or invented.

Purpose of corporate activities, all over the world (irrespective of scale of operation) is uniform—namely, to enhance productivity of human actions, collective or otherwise. Hence, it is governed by a common set of formulations—called the *Unified Concept of Management Performance or UCMP,* the major components of which are as under:

(a) Unity at Absolute Level: At the absolute micro level, i.e. atomic and subatomic, all production or management inputs are fully unified and identical. All of them constitute of the same atomic and subatomic units which are held together by the same forces of attraction and repulsion. The living inputs, in form of human beings, constitute the totality of management action. In the interaction processes of management inputs that lead to productivity or output, the living inputs or the human factor plays the vital catalytic and controlling role. The crucial energy of action is provided by the human factor.

Management is a dynamic organic process which is performed by man (as the main reactant) through interaction of the living (knowledge and blue collar workers) with the non-living reactants (namely materials, capital, machines, and technology etc.) vide the controlling and actualizing force of logic and commonsense.

(b) Critical Unitary Force of Man: The unified concept of management performance or UCMP is depicted by the following equation--which clearly establishes the critical unitary force of man, in all management actions and interplays:

me = (K^{m^2})en

Where

me = management performance or management energy,

K = karma or action,

m = man (mind and Atman),

en = work environment (inputs and policies).

The seed of action or work lies in human mind where thought processes sprouts and grows. All actions emanate from mental energy balance or thoughts – generated in mind ,through charge of consciousness (Atman). Hence, the role of man is shown here as m2, the deciding or determining force.

Thus, management performance or efficiency, is firstly *thought-centric* and then *karma-centric*. Work environment or corporate environment, represented by 'en', has an encompassing influence on the whole process of management performance or output..

Today, the major job of corporate management is primarily to manage people, through whom, all the other inputs of production or value addition, are manipulated in desired form or direction. Hence, as per the unified concept, man or the human factor, is identified as the key component of management. For superior results, this key component should be trained or enabled to perform planned or assigned karma or actions, with full positive energy without worry for results. [8] The freedom from worry for results (detachment) is the key for effective karma because it allows the vital energies of the doer/worker to be fully operative in the desired direction, without distraction or disturbance. Results and consequences or subsequent credit apportioning is the job of seniors.

Hence, for superior performance, it is required to train the subject worker or individual (his Atman through brain) and positively re-orient his mental energies. The vital function of senior management pertains to provide the right work environment for the productive manifestation of positive human energies. Efficiency of enterprise, thus, is determined by the propulsion of work force into planned action (karma or action) through energies of motivated minds i.e. collective release of the (+) work impulse. And the chain reaction so commenced can be self-sustaining and contiguous.

(c) Centrality of Karma: As per Lord Krishna's message, rendered to the mankind through the renowned Bhagavad Gita, karma is most central to the whole human interaction and enterprise. Since management is entirely man dependent, karma by default becomes central to all management functions. Without input there is no output—hence, cause and effect automatically comes into play. There are four types of yogas that affect human action and output:

- karma yoga—which is selfless/ worry-less work or action.
- janana yoga—the work that is performed through knowledge and intelligence.
- bhakti yoga—refers to love and devotion or commitment towards work at hand.
- kirya yoga—is transformation of inner energies.

While the karma yoga plays a central role in management functions, its inter-play does not manifest effectively without transformation of inner energies of mind (thought) and consciousness (Atman) into a creative stream. And without love and devotion to what one is doing, nothing substantial gets achieved. In other words, for karma to be really effective, bhakti yoga, which is more a function of mind and consciousness, has to be resorted to, by the subject individual. Hence, in the equation for management performance (me), importance of man (mind and Atman) is depicted with greater/deciding significance. Innovation and superior efficacy manifestation occurs when a knowledge worker concentrates on his or her assigned karma, in conjugation with the other three supporting yogas, with right emphasis assignment.

(d) Quantum Movement of Work: Business or any other work for that matter, moves in bits and lots (quanta)—it is never a smooth or uniform flow because in the equation of management performance, as given above, the key factor m^2 is never uniform for participants of a team or work force.

- Cumulative + energy balance of a team leads to work
- More +energy balance leads to more work.
- Fall in −energy balance or increase in energy release leads to output fall.

Thoughts of positivity or cooperation, or concern for collective welfare, leads to productivity momentum, and consequently output enhancement is effected. Conflict of thought leads to reduction in + energy balance and hence output drop becomes unavoidable.

Frederick W. Taylor, who is considered as father of scientific management, in his work *The Principles of Scientific Management*, stressed that work should be analyzed into small motions—it should also be organized into series of motions—which, in fact, is reflexion of quantum movements of productive action. With greater motivation, i.e. more +energy release, any trend towards output drop can be arrested

(e) Energy Balance and Action: Human mind always operates as per double thought process; positive and negative thoughts germinate and dissipate at regular/ irregular intervals and the process is never uniform or static. Thought genesis and dissipation is a consequence of interaction of consciousness (the absolute or Atman) with the environment through the medium of mind. It involves transfer of energy, in form of electrons, during the biochemical reactions taking place in the human body.

As an innate characteristic, an individual being tends to act more in interest or in favour of self than the society or the nation. It is probably a trait acquired in the early stages of the evolution process when survivals had a great premium—environment being very inhospitable and competitive. This instinct, in due course, acquired gemone specificity, and in some cases, even got intensified over generations. We call it *negativity*. As man could not survive and grow alone, in isolation, he had to be part of a group or family. He simultaneously developed a tendency to work collectively i.e. to service interests of others too, first the family and then his clan. This innate characteristic of feeling for welfare of others or tendency to cooperate or be useful, is called as *positivity*. It comes from the inner self, the consciousness or Atman, under the influence of righteousness. Mind always forms and dissipates + and – thoughts and depending upon the balance, action or inaction initiates.

(f) Prakarti and Thought Balance: Each individual is endowed with specific genetic material component called *gemone* which determines all individualistic features and characters. In addition to physical features, an individual's mental make-up and also his or her thought process and characteristics are governed by the same. Whether one is a person of – or + thought dominance, too is determined by the gemone. In the Bhagavad Gita, three types of gemone based prakritis of people have been described, and the same are supposed to determine individuals' functional responsiveness and suitability.

- Sattvic—Righteous and positive thought balance predominates in persons of this nature.
- Rajsic—In persons of this nature—thought balance swings between negative and positive.
- Tamsic—Mostly suffer from negative thought balance.

Thought balance of a person, positive or negative thought flow, not only determines his output and cooperation, but also decides what will motivate or de-motivate him in reference to his job responsibilities. A worker with significant negative thought balance is likely to respond to material incentives of immediate nature. Strict disciplining too is likely to be effective in such cases.

Douglas Mc Gregor proposed the Theories of X, Y and Z in reference to workers, work output and motivational responses, which on deeper examination seem to depend upon the negative or positive thought balance of people involved. Elton Mayo in his work The Social Problems of an Industrial Civilization, stressed that the roots of work satisfaction is non-economic. In his opinion, man's desire to be continuously associated with work is strong, if not strongest, human characteristic. He further stated that there were differences between a group and a team and left us with the phenomenon of *Howthrone Effect* which signifies the change in behavior and morale of employees that results from management taking an interest in them. His thesis, on careful examination ,seems only partly true as it emphasized only the positive aspects and fully missed the negative thought balance which is equally, and sometimes, even more important in determining workers' behavior. Peter Drucker, the great management guru, opined that Mayo's human relationship prescription was rarely practiced.

Peter F. Drucker put great stress on human factor, as emphasized here in the equation of management performance. His emphasis on knowledge worker is significant in view of the fact that such workers can not be productive without significant flow of positive thought energy within them. Empowerment and leadership which this management thinker often talked about, are fully dependent on role of the human factor(man-mind and Atman), which is very central in the equation of management performance.

In addition, views of the other significant management thinkers and writers, as listed below (and also many others), are also fully explainable by the equation of management performance—a consequence of thought balance.

Peter Senge:	Learning organization/collective knowledge,
F. Hertzberg:	Job enrichment principles, motivation-hygiene theory,
John Arugyris:	Immature-mature theory.
Victor Vroom:	Sustaining motivation, expectancy theory.
Warren Bennis:	Leadership and manager.

Most of the concepts, principles and theories of management, old or new, are perfectly integral or compatible to the concept of thought balance.

(g) Scientific Compatibility of UCMP: The fact that UCMP is compatible with the modern as well as ancient concepts of science and management, is born out of a deeper look at the path breaking work of Einstein, the greatest scientist of the 20th centaury. He had explained the basic relationship between mass and energy, the two forms of the same thing. It is the basis of the unity of all production inputs, living and non-living, at the absolute micro-level, as also stressed under the Unified Concept of Management Performance or UCMP.

Einstein, in his famous Theory of Relativity, in fact as a foot note to it, had added the renowned equation;

$E=mc^2$

Where E stands for energy, m for mass and c for speed of light (i.e. the universal constant.

This equation asserts the fundamental equivalence, or more precisely, the inter-changeability of matter and energy.

Deepak Chopra, a popular writer and consultant, too emphasized the similarity of all things at the atomic and sub-atomic level.

Much before all the scientists and thinkers, Lord Krishna had explained in the renowned Bhagavad-Gita, the unity of all beings and matters, as absolute or Atman, the final non-destructible form of matters and beings. He said, "I am in everything and everything emanates from and merges into me."

Like the Einstein's famous equation, the UCMP too is expressed through an equation.

$me= (K^{m2})en$

During his divine discourse with Arjuna, the Lord emphatically stressed the crucial role of karma and its relationship to thought/mind and Atman. Resorting to selfless karma i.e. action without much concern for its fruits or results, is the greatest tool for motivation. Hence, the overwhelming impact of man and mind on karma is depicted as m2. Rest of the elements of corporate environment, for its over all impact, are collectively represented as 'en' in the equation of UCMP.

The present crop of professionals is well equipped to benefit from Lord Krishna's divine strategy of managing the boss and seniors and achieving, through and with them, his mission incarnate objectivities. A little effort is required to study and understand his divine life and illustrious works, and finding ways and means to employ the same, in a progressive manner, to handle the challenges encountered in the current collective work environments. Benefits, without doubt, are likely to be immense.

Notes

1. Creative destruction is the natural process of creating space or opportunity for the new or more efficient. Lord Krishna made a very innovative use of it in innumerable situations in order to meet his mission incarnate objectives.
2. Bhakta is an ancient Indian term meaning devotee.
3. Karmic accounting is the system of automatic credit or discredit apportioning under the celestial law of Karmic Balance.
4. Refers to a celestial weapon of non-failing accuracy.
5. In Hindu mythology avatara refers to incarnation of God in human for a specific purpose.

6. CS is the one of the first innate intelligent capability development responses of human-beings in realms of thought and action coordination which is the root-stock of all developments—social, religious or commercial.

7. UOE will always continue to elude human-beings since it tends to shift its very perception and goal posts. Commonly agreed yardsticks in this regard are also unlikely to emerge on account of the basic argumentative nature of human-beings.

8. This is one of the key teachings of Lord Krishna enshrined in the Bhagavad Gita.

PARVA VIII

LORD KRISHNA'S OMNIPOTENT TECHNOLOGY OF MANAGEMENT

Brahmastra of Management

Brahmastra, as per common understanding, is the weapon of Lord Brahma, which is sure to be effective under all challenging situations. Modern management does not possess any thing that could be viewed as decisively effective in all truly challenging situations. As of today, it is besieged with numerous problems, deficiencies and deficits, in relation to its capacity to handle human component of corporate action, the key ingredient of operational management. Its methodologies, tools and technologies to motivate corporate workers, particularly the white collar ones, into perpetually high levels of productivity or to reactivate them, if and when they run into depression and delusion on account of non-satisfaction either with their working conditions or the remunerations earned are significantly deficient. The material or monitory incentives, so actively employed today as a key tool for motivation, are proving utterly insufficient for keeping high performers in their jobs for long enough durations--as active and self motivated doers.

Lord Krishna, as per his mission incarnate responsibilities, had to clear this earth free of evil and wicked, some of whom were very powerful, well entrenched and had even acquired certain troublesome invincibilities. He encountered them at every stage of his life in childhood, in youth and right up to the very end of his stay as a mortal in this world. His personal weapons, namely Sudarshana chakra, Kaumodaki mace, Sariga bow and Panchanjaya conch were truly unstoppable and no evil of any type could escape the destructive impact of the same. But as a great leader and an effective manager, it was not advisable for him to eliminate all the evil and wicked rulers and demons of that time, with his own hands. The dangers of over-exposure were truly great and, indeed undesirable, for the celestial head of a divine mission. He had to have a performing team to do the job, as desired or directed. He was not on a simple killing mission. The impact and influence of long-term evil and wicked manifestations at large scale, had to be removed from a suffering and oppressed society. Hence, He had to teach, preach and reform the rulers as well as the ruled, in addition to the direct cleansing activity.

For this purpose, a truly effective team of colleagues and associates (workers, administrators, rulers, warriors and technologists) was required. So, He had to apply truly effective systems of management, for efforts on fronts of education, training and development, along with the long-term war efforts spread over several years. He had to transform a long suffering Yadava [1] community into an invincible fighting force—as in initial years of his campaign in support of righteous and virtuous, Yadava warriors were to serve as his main performing assets. Additionally, the problems and challenges offered by the invincible Jarasandha of Magadha, the greatest leader of the demonic forces of that time, had to be tackled. And the impressive warriors lineup on the Kaurava front, under the great and intractable evil Duryodhana, had to be handled. For this purpose, he had to galvanize the celestial Pandava brothers into an unstoppable fighting machine. All this required supreme management efforts in the fields of planning, organizing, leading, motivation and control. And for each of the truly difficult situations, he had to devise and assemble, a set of management tools, technologies and approaches. There was no scope for failures on part of this divine mission incarnate.

Lord Krishna was omnipotent yet in order to complete his mission objectivity, He had to devise winning teams, gather winning resources, develop winning technologies and effectively assess and evaluate his adversaries. In order to handle the numerous invincible demons and warriors, He had to find out ways and means to neutralize their arrogance and invincibilities. And most of these objectives, he had to attain through his colleagues, juniors, disciples and devotees. It was neither a simple nor an easy job. It needed a massive management exercise and for that purpose He had to evolve and employ some truly potent combinations of management tools as management Brahmastras. All possibilities of failures had to be effectively plugged. The fact that the wise Lord never ruled directly though He was called Dwarkadhesh, sometimes complicated situations for him. It created a need for greater skills of tact, diplomacy and motivation on his part. He had to get things done without directly being the final authority. The need to carry along his elder brother Balarama and the Yadavas' ruling head Ugrasena, for all complicated and arduous missions, was truly great. Special skills of mind, heart and communication were needed to handle temperamental seniors. Hence, He acquired all that was necessary and ruled through significant superiority of thought as well as action.

A study of his divine life and works reveals that in most of the challenging situations, He employed varied combinations of the following approaches, tools and techniques, most of which resulted into management Brahmastras, producing desired and/or planned results with minimum deviations.

- The Doctrine of Karma, which extols preferability of action over inaction.
- Action without concern for or attachment to results or rewards—freeing action energy from shackles of expectation.

- Energizing action through energies of mind and soul.
- Empowering action through righteousness and virtue.
- Directional co-ordination of body-mind-intellect and Atman.
- Essentiality of upholding Dharma in actions of management and governance.
- Effective alternates of Janana and Bhakti for liberation.
- Employment of human prakriti for effective work assignment and deployment.
- Non-material motivation as a non-failing tool of management.
- Madhura technology of irresistibly effective communication.
- Efficient talent recognition for building high performance teams.
- Supervised and enabling delegation.
- Unbiased credit apportioning—employing the principle of total impartiality.
- Dignity of work through self-example.
- Work as a play—through self example.
- Intense rapport with key performers.
- Oneness of thought and deeds—thought and action balance.
- Excellent failure and crisis management.
- Masterly change management.
- Delivering despite limitations of the system and times.
- Unique JIT accessibility to devotee and disciples in need of help and/or guidance.
- Active management of intangibles.
- Masterly measured response.
- Employment of superior emotion quotient.
- Superior ego management; assigning sanctity to objective—keeping method and means as subordinate to end.
- Empathy as a management tool for strong human alignments.
- Flute as a management tool.
- Divine love for effective human control.
- Employment of divine vision.
- Intuition and foresight as a tool of trouble avoidance.
- Creative destruction as a management tool.
- Productive anger management.
- Effective employment of dialogue.
- Active application of the concept of management energy.
- Divine mix of qualities of a superior leader, manager and guru.

- And managing through Purushottama.

All the above tools and technologies of management employed by the divine Lord, at various stages of his life, have been discussed in this work; their relevance to modern management environment too has been examined. Enlightened readers will be able to locate greater relevance and applications of Lord Krishna's divine management technology to their own work environments.

Lord Krishna always attempted to apply the above enumerated tools and technologies, and possibly many more, in need based righteous combinations, to subdue foes and attract friends, collaborators, disciples and devotees. Most of such combinations always turned into well defined and rightly directed Brahmastras.

Right in early stage of his divine life on this earth, He made a winning team with Balarama and Mahamaya, to deceive the demonic Kamsa into a frantic killing of all the newly born babies of Mathura and its neighborhoods, as a futile attempt to ward off the celestial warning of his eventual death at hands of the 8th child of Devaki and Vasudeva. It put all the suffering Yadavas against the demonic ruler, though no one had the courage and resources to openly stand up to the might of cruel Kamsa.

Even as a little child, Krishna made the fullest use of his uncommonly strong intuition and foresight, to subdue and eliminate numerous evils and demons who came in clever disguise to harm the little Lord. At that stage, his divine intuition and perception were the only components of Brahmastra. A few years later, when his little cowherd colleagues and their cattle were threatened by the menacing naga king Kaliya, He demonstrated the principle of work as a play and leading by example, in the most impressive manner. He ordered Kaliya to immediately vacate the waters of Yamuna, which were most vital for survival of the cowherd community of Gokula, and move out to his original abode in the sea. When the arrogant Kaliya mocked at the little Krishna, the latter jumped into the pool and climbed on to Kaliya's head and danced there with celestial abandon, unmindful of the dangers involved and regours of the ceaseless dance. He compelled the devil to plead for pardon, mouthing repetitive assurances to do as ordered by the little Lord. It was an example of supreme initiative and leading by example. Little Krishna showed no signs of stress or exhaustion and, in fact, enjoyed the act, turning it into a unique example of work as a play. Another example of treating work as play related to lifting of the mount Goverdhana by the little Krishna, for protection of his fellow cowherds and their animals from the revengeful act of incessant cloud-busts initiated by an irritated Lord Indra, the practice of whose worship was abandoned by the cowherd community on advice of their little saviour.

All applications of the wise Lord's employment of Brahmastras of management are detailed at appropriate places under different chapters of this work. Hence, re-elaboration of the same is being avoided in interest of appropriate utilization of readers time and energy. However, the most important aspect of the divine Lord's application of Brahmastra, in the field of management needs re-emphasis. It pertained to the non-material motivation of Arjuna, to do the Lord's bidding of eliminating all of his relatives and gurus who, by ignorance or design, had elected to support the demonic Duryodhan, despite the active resistance of the Pandava warrior to avoid the same. Through divine discourse, Lord Krishna was able to break the delusion and the consequent adamancy of Arjuna, in favour of action. All arguments of the Pandava warrior, judicious and logical in their own merit and relevance, were of no avail in face of the divine righteousness of Krishna's presentation of facts of life and death , body and soul, life and afterlife, birth and rebirth, and the ultimate futility of relationships and relations. The divine Lord's justification of action as against inaction – irrespective of logic of non-violence, compassion, grief, and possibility of attraction of sin, prevailed, becoming a perpetual source of inspirational guidance for all times to come. The great Lord achieved almost an impossible feat of persuading a righteous and reluctant Arjuna, to kill all his relations, gurus , friends and colleagues who were present in the opposing line-up of warriors and supported the illogical and greedy Duryodhana.

Lord Krishna gave nothing material to the Pandava warrior nor was any great promise made. This Brahmastra of non-material motivation became feasible only through deeper extolling of the body-mind-intellect and Atman relationship, by the wise Lord, to a confused and deluded Arjuna. He lifted action beyond the limitation of result or reward expectation or attachment of any type. Lord Krishna had Saraswati on his tongue; hence, words of wisdom and janana flowed effortlessly. Friends or foes, none was left uninfluenced. The wise Lord was also rich with Bio-magnetism that attracted all living beings, reorienting them with active or potential desire to be of some service to the celestial Master.

The wise Lord was also gifted with madhura of communication, making irresistible honey coated words flow to overwhelm friends and foes with equal ease. He easily turned any reluctance on part of colleagues and coworkers into active co-operation.

On proper search and effort, the present day management practitioners can always locate a right combination of management tools from the inexhaustible store-house of Lord Krishna's divine wisdom. Just a little effort and interest is necessary on part of the seeker. Solutions to all problems and challenges can emerge from his divine store of management wisdom.

Mahatma Gandhi, while attempting to overthrow the mighty British imperialism with the help of non-violent means, often ran into disappointing and confusing situations. In most of such events, he browsed through the renowned Song of Wisdom, a priceless gift of the wise Lord to the mankind. And the Mahatma always found solutions irrespective of how challenging was the situation. Hence, there is no reason why modern professional managers can not locate management Brahmastras appropriate to their situations and challenges, in the divine store-house of management wisdom that the great Lord left for the posterity.

Note

1. The Yadava warriors community suffered a great deal under the demonic rule of Kamsa of Mathura.

PARVA IX

LORD KRISHNA'S NECTAR OF MANAGEMENT WISDOM

Lord Krishna was a mission incarnate. He took human form with a specific purpose. He had worked out for himself a specific agenda. In true sense of the term, He was a *Professional with a Manifesto.* His life and works profusely stress significance of clearly set objectives if one is to make any significant contribution in his or her selected field of operation. It has significant bearings in field of professional management.

Those who enjoy their assigned work are destined to perform better. Your own resistance to work, or your dislike for the person who assigns work to you or one who is expected to supervise or assess the same, diminishes output and quality both. Work is best done when it is taken as a play. Lord Krishna was the most efficient practitioner of the *work-play concept.*

Several incidents from the event-intense life of Lord Krishna proceed to stress that all acts of work or karma, whatsoever difficult, should be performed with a smile on face of the performer. It improves work environment and enhances impact on those who witness the action; it creates wider acceptance and appreciation, reducing work tensions and negativity. This practical aspect of Lord Krishna's personality and works, offers a great opportunity to modern professional managers for stress free performance acceleration on continuous basis.

Work is the most important aspect of human-life. In this *Sansara* work is as vital to all humans as food and entertainment. It is equally important to a king and a commoner. The type of work may differ from person to person but its significance remains the same. Irrespective to one's origin or place in social order, he or she has to engage in some productive work, to earn or otherwise. It is necessary to maintain balance of body, mind and the living environment.

The Lord said, "You have the right to work, but to work's sake only. Let not the fruit of action be your object or motive in working. Neither you should yield to inaction." The value of Lord's advice lies in both the performance of action and in the right attitude and spirit behind the action. Total commitment to action and need to relinquish any desire for fruit of action are the key watchwords. Irrespective of the nature of work, whether mundane or spiritual, extent of involvement and degree of commitment is the key of Karma Yoga. Conscious avoidance of action or half-hearted involvement is not permitted.

The most important task is to train oneself or to condition one's mind to fully align with whatsoever one does. It is an internal command that should enables work without craving for fruit or reward. Thus, the *right mental work mode* is the most vital part of Karma Yoga.

Assessment of reality of a situation, or facts that prevail, is an important management function. Whether it is necessary to proceed in a pre-set direction or stop, reassess and alter the course of action, to avoid failure or to succeed fully or partially, is decidedly of critical significance. Great leaders, CEOs or commanders have a unique capacity for quick and correct assessment of reality, and assume corrective or most appropriate line of action. They assume full responsibility for uncommon decisions taken under challenging situations. Lord Krishna's teachings proceed to instruct modern managers that if an unpalatable decision becomes necessary under challenging situations, it must be taken *promptly without fear of criticism. Long-range validity of a decision is more important than its* immediate perception by people. False prestige should not be allowed to stand in the way and reality of situation should be respected in most appropriate manner.

Lord Krishna was a unique leader of men, in fact, of all living beings. He never wanted any one to do what He did not do or was not himself prepared to do. He always led his people, disciples and devotees though his own illustrative actions. To re-stress the *leading by example* aspect of Lord Krishna's management, it would suffice to say that today's professionals could benefit a great deal by remembering that:

- knowledge and expertise is necessary for any good worker.
- preaching without practice is not advisable.
- an example set by a senior or the boss has multilateral utilities.
- humility, despite knowledge and prowess, is essential for good following.

Corporate managers and also those involved in activities of governance, can benefit a lot from the golden rule of *leading by example,* as followed by the wise Lord—the principle being that one should first sharpen/improve one's own knowledge/expertise before advising others to follow. Be grateful to those who help or guide you in such learning. It will help a lot in smooth running of the corporate train.

It is necessary for successful managers or leaders to precisely understand *prakriti* of his key people, as their reaction or interactions to challenging work environment are bound to be governed by the same.

For minimizing negative energy/action manifestations, senior management should promote positive energy flow in the work environment. The policy of righteousness, correct credit apportioning, capability based work assignment, performance based rewarding, training for merit refinement, and emphasis for non-material motivation, as practiced by Lord Krishna, are highly productive in promoting greater flow of positive energy in an organization or work environment. His technology of manpower management, thus, can be highly useful in improving corporate performances in the present competitive work environments.

Lord Krishna always led through Prushottama which, in fact, is the only truly great way towards non-failing leadership. Purushottma, in fact, is the manifestation of positive energies, its basic elements being goodness, justice and empathy, application of which in any human endeavour, business, governance or otherwise, invariably leads to better work environment and enhanced productivity. Its positive energies annihilate the anti-work elements, at the levels of thought as well as action, liberating the positive forces of initiative and cooperation. Senior management professionals can definitely benefit by actively incorporating the basic elements of Purushottama in their daily work schedule and bring immense dividends to all concerned, i.e. the employer, employees and also the general public.

For any collective activity, corporate or otherwise, people constitute as the most important component or input. Success of all efforts, in collective work environment, depends upon (a) the quality of people selected and (b) the way they are managed. People management is, thus, the most important aspect of collective human action play irrespective of work relevance or type of activity. A good practitioner of management or a *management guru* should perform this crucial function better than his or her competitors or adversaries, not just to qualify for the title but also to continuously hold on to the same.

Lord Krishna, the great master in judging people and an expert of man management, has left a rich scroll of examples, all practical and effective, which the present day senior corporate managers can benefit from, in their ever frustrating engagements to move people do what is desired of them. His method of sharp observation, decisive analysis, productive engagement, right credit apportioning, active mentoring, madhura technique of communication and non-material motivation, just to recount a few, are particularly of current relevance.

A great leader, guru or senior corporate professional, should actively seek and respect virtue and merit; and holder of the same should be honoured and rewarded through words as well as deeds. For people of virtue and merit, there is no better motivation than overt recognition. Lord Krishna's approach towards respect to virtue and merit has massive applications in the field of modern management. With the practice of genuine approach in regard to respecting the virtue and merit, corporate workers are bound to be more innovative and aggressive towards bettering performance as they will be free from stress and apprehension of one not getting due recognition and reward for good work done. Thus, freeing the corporate work environment from fear of biased credit and reward distribution can easily be achieved, through practice of the wise Lord's technology of management ethicality.

As per teachings of Lord Krishna, ethicality of action, especially in governance and commerce, is a valuable option of practical sensibility, for containing the evil of corruption and other undesirable practices. Practice of ethicality improves work environment from the point of employee cooperation and initiative. It also reduces the stress and negativity load of the work environment, pushing productivity beyond expectations. Modern management institutions have a specific responsibility to orient their products for this task of great significance.

Value of commitment or to honour what is said, orally or otherwise, has great significance in human relations. In corporate world commitment adherence is as valuable as in the field of religion and spirituality. It determines the long-term dependability of a leader, on one hand, and ability of followers to abide by what is said or commanded, on the other. Value of commitment rises further when it comes from a senior person in an organization. Lord Krishna exhibited a very high value to commitments made by him at various stages of his life.

Lord Krishna meticulously fulfilled all commitments irrespective of the cost or efforts involved. For him commitments had a divine value: they were, in fact, one of the most important tools of management available to him to manage people and events both. Commitment adherence was his divine way of attracting and aligning the forces of righteousness with his own apparatus of fighting the evil and wickedness. Commitment appreciation or adherence also has immense utility as a modern management tool and the present day professionals should attempt to find ways and means for maximum use of it in improving all-round productivity and quality of performance.

Lord Krishna not only possessed the capabilities of a Super Power Thinker, but also was able to employ the same to alter course of thoughts and actions of great personalities of his times and assign a unique course to key events, through the unique power of logic and play of words. Neither friends nor foes could escape the magic of his personality and communication. He employed elements of *madhura* with decisive efficacy. Corporate leaders, management teachers and gurus can learn a great deal by imbibing and employing the great Lord's techniques of influencing people and events, to further their corporate as well as personal agenda.

Professional managers are expected to delegate part of their responsibilities. They have to keep track of various projects and developments and decide when to intervene or render help to a subordinate or a coworker if there are signs of unexpected deviations. Intervention at the right time, often termed, as *strategic intervention* is necessary, if inconvenient results are to be avoided. Lord Krishna was an expert at *strategic intervention*. He often delegated critical jobs but knew exactly when to intervene, if the involved coworker was faltering or if the assigned job was beyond his capacity. His timings and extent of intervention were well measured in right quantum and just in time.

He had to attempt strategic intervention to ensure needful support to his disciples, supporters and co-workers, for meeting his basic commitment as a "mission incarnate". He was, in deed, the most successful manager known to mankind and the numerous superior management techniques evolved and employed by him so decisively and fruitfully, continue to hold total validity even in today's work environment. His ancient wisdom is available to one and all, to learn, copy and benefit.

Most of the collective activities, whether managed through project teams or task forces, tend to run into unexpected roadblocks. In many such situations, analytical or discrimination energies of the managing team may not be adequate or suitably oriented to automatically throw up a solution, adopt the same and arrive at the assigned target. Multiplicity of opinion within the team and consequent lack of direction often precipitates a situation of indecision. Normally, a team leader should be capable or well trained to undertake a correction course but in practice such normalities are often missing. The role of problem solving, de-bottlenecking or the *task of facilitation* is an important one and hence, should not be underestimated in reference to outcome relevance.

The task of facilitation, especially in a difficult situation, may be a very demanding one. An efficient facilitator should ideally possess long experience, relevant superior skills and charisma laced with faculties of communication and diplomacy. One has to be not only capable of providing the right corrective inputs but the manner of such provision should generate wide and enthusiastic acceptance. The catalytic interaction so generated should precipitate a forceful group action. The concepts and practices of success facilitation as employed by Lord Krishna, the Supper Celestial Manager are of great practical utility to the present day corporate professionals—and if the same are practiced in right earnest, the performance of business teams shall improve a great deal and the vital senior-junior work relationship will become highly productive and totally stress free.

Lord Krishna's skills of crisis management were truly unique. In fact, there exists no other example of such magnificent achievements in the field of crisis management in the whole written or oral history of mankind that could come somewhere rear to the Lord Krishna's performance in this field of uncommon expertise. His supremacy in this field remains unchallenged; and, as such, it should be a matter of great benefit for management professionals to learn something from this unique oriental heritage in this field of specialties. The highly inspirational examples of crisis management from the life and works of the wise Lord should serve as most appropriate case studies for management training institutes to rely upon, in furthering excellence in this field.

Re-engineering, when undertaken correctly, can be a powerful tool for implementing positive change, depending upon its objectivity orientation. For example, it can be an effective instrument for pushing responsibility and accountability down to the level where it genuinely belongs or where empowerment can effectively take place. But when implemented erroneously, it becomes a game of Tuglakian failure and discredit apportioning.

Lord Krishna's successful shifting of the whole Yadava community to Dwarka and developing the same into a magnificent and prosperous empire, was a truly illustrious work in the field of re-engineering. Modern professionals while attempting re-engineering in their corporate environment could draw upon the life and works of Lord Krishna, for pleasant consequences of such attempts.

All through his life of high event intensity, Lord Krishna displayed uncommonly superior performance of multi-tasking where every thing attempted was performed with utmost perfection. His life and works illustrate that multi-tasking is not a myth, it can be a high performance reality, provided requisite expertise are acquired by the person involved and the same are invested in a right mix and volume. Lord Krishna pioneered and perfected the practice of out-sourcing. Management professionals who encounter a need for this unique instrument of globalization will do better if they expose themselves to the superior skills of Lord Krishna in this field.

Chaotic situations are often encountered in business, politics and war, always offering dual opportunities to those who command the situation at relevant moment. To the wise and energetic, there comes an opportunity to take leadership initiative and manipulate the mass of chaos to his own advantage and to the incompetent and lethargic, a safer chance to flow with the chaotic mass. Lord Krishna's illustrious life and works are of immense utility for professional managers to grow profits and success out of chaotic situations. It will indeed be a true advantage to learn his unique technology of productively managing such situations.

Normally, an out-of-box or unconventional approach is not easily appreciated. There is no dearth of those who either resist such an approach or forecast failure of the same. There is often a tendency to travel the beaten path or prefer the certainty of known to the uncertainties of an unconventional approach. But, difficult or abnormal situations demand unconventional or out-of-box solutions which only truly efficient managers are able to attempt and implement. Such professionals of caliber can draw a lot of support and guidance from the life and works of Lord Krishna who never hesitated from taking the out-of-box approach to problem solving.

Change is the only reality of permanence in this world, perpetually re-occurring without any gap or pause. All living and non-living entities suffer change, some visible and some invisible. Normally, living beings tend to resist change because uncertainties, as inherent in change, are always uncomfortable. Present (time) is often viewed as hard and uncomfortable, because survival and growth take efforts. To complicate the situation, competition and conflict creep in uninvited. Most of the people are uncomfortable with the thought of future because unforeseen and unexpected, invariably causes apprehension and anxiety. It generates fear of unknown, severely undermining one's ability to face and manage the phenomenon of change. But, change must always be faced as it arrives uninvited, there is no escape, neither for man nor any other living being. Hence, it is always better if one faces the inevitability of change with understanding and resolve and still better, if it is done with some enthusiasm. In the business of management and governance, change is not only a constant challenge but also a factual necessity for continuity as well as growth. Practitioners of modern management, irrespective of their area of specialization, can draw immense benefits from Lord Krishna's concepts and practices of change management, the most important teaching in this regard being, that it is often futile to resist change and in fact, to the extent possible, one should welcome and invite change. Once it is accepted enthusiastically, it always works for the benefit of people involved.

Lord Krishna was a true practitioner of intense rapport with his co-workers, disciples and devotees. It was only his intense rapport and interaction with Arjuna that gave birth to what is today known as the Bhagavad Gita or the Song of Wisdom.

The productive bondage of intense rapport always ensures

- fulfillment of expectations from both the sides,
- instant co-operation and eventual performance excellence, and
- total fulfillment of objectivity of a given situation, without creation of any feelings of obligation or indebtedness.

Therefore, it would be always beneficial to actively employ the tool of intense rapport, so effectively wielded by Lord Krishna, in all fields of human interactions, including the modern corporate management.

"I look upon all creatures equally; none are less dear to me and none more dear" Bhagavad Gita

This vital statement of Lord Krishna enunciates the great principle of total impartiality in human resources management. When this principle is followed correctly in dealing with subordinates, disciples and co-workers:

- in assignment of work as per their capabilities,
- in apportioning credit as per performance, and
- in training and guidance for sharpening their potentialities, it creates a flow of positivity in work environment, unleashing forces of initiative and cooperation that, for sure, leads to higher productivity.

Humility is a unique innate capability of some the great people. When noticed by people who work for or with such a leader, it assumes the form of an effective tool of management: It can be employed with significant success. Instead of broadcasting own skills, achievements or greatness, one should leave the same to ones subordinates and peers, to be perceived, accepted and appreciated, in an independent and democratic manner. Such an approach can generate great positive following for superior output at the right time. Only people of evil parakriti are unable to appreciate a truly displayed humility.

Great managers often do not make an exhibition of their achievements or greatness. They leave it to people, to imbibe, accept and appreciate the same. A great leader's following generates out of gentleness or smoothness of communication that he makes, affording people a chance to evaluate and accept the same. Lord Krishna was a great practitioner of humility of approach in his dealings with people, whether a commoner or a king. He did not let his greatness or Godliness interfere with this practical application of wisdom. He respected his elders and peers a great deal.

Lord Krishna's understanding of human nature was most profound and perfect. He could read through people like a high-powered scanner, often from a distance and assess not only their motives and intentions but also their capabilities, active or inherent. While discoursing Arjuna on the battlefields of Kurukshetra, He dwelt upon, amongst others, the vital aspects of human nature, in view of the fact that all actions of human-beings were nothing but manifestations of an individual doer's basic nature. He elaborated that there were three modes of human nature (Gunas)—Sattava, Rajas and Tamas—through which the non-dual consciousness manifests into diversity, apparent to worldly experience. It is for this reason that no two individuals, even when born to same parents, will be alike as the interplay of Gunas makes a widespread variety possible. He added a renowned example to illustrate this phenomenon, the three brothers; Vibhishana, Ravana and Kumbhakarana were so totally different in their nature and consequent actions.

Hence, in professional environment, assignment of work and placement of workers, particularly the white-collar ones, should be done in accordance with their prakriti, in addition to the other considerations of qualifications and experience.

The present community of management professionals, irrespective of engagement in business, governance, training and/or in any other act of significance, stands to benefit substantially from the wise Lord's observance of the vital principle of Time Related Disclosure of information of importance. For the purpose of benefiting from the wise Lord's above stated and so effectively practiced principle, it would be necessary for the professionals involved to train themselves in appreciation of value of information and its time related significance.

Most CEOs and managers suffer from *information distance malady* where there is so much distance from customers and people who contribute to the corporate kitty that there is no information except from cronies who hang around the top-man. They seem to know every thing and advise the boss on all matters of vital importance. For healthy and vibrant corporate functioning, connectivity with customers, suppliers and other key people, whose contribution counts for health of its bottom and top-lines, should always remain available and unhindered.

The life and works of Lord Krishna vividly illustrated the fine principle of timely management accessibility to key performers and its utility, in superior discharge of a professional's responsibility. In that regard, there exists a lot for the present generation of professional managers to learn from Lord Krishna, the ancient world's most efficient management expert.

Lord Krishna often employed immensely successful technique of Madhura Communication. This hugely potent and well-tested approach of the Lord could be gainfully employed for maximizing the corporate world's competitive efficiency, as it helps in reduction of internal conflict by diminishing manifestations of negative energy and so enhanced teamwork efficiency would bring results that were not feasible as yet, even with the best known management tools and technologies. The great ancient oriental wisdom of maximizing co-operation is condensed in the ever-effective communication methodology of the great Lord.

Kindness, compassion and sense of caring and concern for community or greater good, are positive human values that generate immediate impact (feel) within the recipient. Collectively these positive thoughts are grouped as *Empathy*.

Actions rich in this virtue have great power for release of positive energy—to create goodwill and support which, depending upon right employment, can significantly enhance productivity or efforts to win in a competitive work environment. Many leaders, spiritual, political and otherwise, have employed the tool of empathy to win over situations that earlier looked hopeless or even hostile. The unique force of empathy tends to create a strong bond of confidence between its operator and the target, for a long-term association of mutual benefit. Lord Krishna was indeed a great operator of this unique tool of universal effectiveness.

Empowerment is the process of acquiring or assigning authority or powers to perform. The principle of empowerment states that it is the process of activating creative forces within the doer. In other words, it is the precursor of success as on empowerment, effective action becomes much faster and rewarding. It can also be said that empowerment is the catalyst for success since it initiates genesis of thoughts and actions for an assigned or assumed goal through interaction of body, mind (intellect) and Atman (Self). The mind or intellect is involved with the process of thought genesis and evaluation while action is primarily a physical function of conversion of thought into work. And empowerment is effected in two different ways:

- self-empowerment or auto-empowerment and
- *external empowerment or enabling empowerment.*

The first is an internal process initiated and controlled through energies emitting from within the doer while in the second case, the initiative and impetus in infused from outside by the controlling or motivating force, either a superior or a guru. In both the cases, empowerment is a selection process in the first instance, it is selection by the self and in the second, the controlling force affects the job. Lord Krishna was master of effective empowerment for enhancing efficacy of his disciples, devotees and collaborators.

Senior management functionaries are often faced with a challenge to come out with measured and calculated responses. Serious phases of negotiations with labour unions or those related to mergers and acquisitions, among others, often throw up such challenges. In such situations, right quantum of response, i.e. neither too little nor too much, determines the future turn of events. Lord Krishna was often faced with difficult situations while dealing with numerous unrighteous princes and kings, and demons and evils, during his long career of over ten decades. He had fine-tuned the art of Masterly Measured Response for right effect in all demanding situations. Learning a little of this man-management technology will do a lot of good to the present day managers.

In the field of holistic management, there seems to exist no other practitioner of repute, ancient or modern, than Lord Krishna who operated with utmost efficiency over 5,000 years ago. He was truly a complete manager of uncommon superiority. His discourse to Arjuna, rendered in the most trying conditions of an active battlefield that later on came to be known as the Song of Wisdom or Bhagavad Gita, is the most comprehensive compilation of supreme management thoughts, with applicability in all aspects of life, personal, corporate or religious. A good part of the wise Lord's holistic management concepts and practices have relevance and applicability in today's corporate environment.

Thinking ahead, or long-term planning, is an essential attribute of any effective management activity. Its significance in regard to corporate management is of fundamental nature as any negligence or inadequacy of thought or action may lead to loss of market and or revenues. Lord Krishna rigorously followed the principle of thinking ahead and consequent long-term planning. In order to benefit from the divine applications of Long Range Planning, as practiced by Lord Krishna, modern management professionals should emulate the same in vital departments of a business enterprise and review and update the same at regular intervals for (a) sustained growth and (b) to avoid negative surprises in business progression.

An effective manager is supposed to get work done, through and with people—whether subordinates or otherwise. Nothing much can be accomplished if he attempts to do every thing himself. Corporate managers are often hesitant to assign important work to their subordinates, even when the latter have necessary skills and expertise to perform the job. Sometimes, when little delegation is effected, requisite guidance is not volunteered, as the objective often remains to find faults in the event of failure.

In case of Lord Krishna, even a miner glance on his life and works, renders it brightly visible that the wise Lord made an effective use of the Principle of Effective Delegation or performance enhancement through motivation.

- Why did He not take up arms in support of the Pandavas?
- Why did He not destroy Duryodhana and his group of evil makers when an attempt was made to arrest him in the court of Hastinapura?
- Why did He not himself eliminate the super demon Jarasandha?

These and many other questions from the Lord's life are best explained with the fact that He firmly believed in empowering his colleagues and supporters through effectively planned delegation. He actively followed the principle of Participative Management.

Lord Krishna's campaign against evil forces was successful simply because of the great Lord's ability to recognize and assemble a great combination of talents in one camp—deploy, motivate and manage the same into a truly invincible force. He was truly a master in talent management—and kept all components of his assemble of talent well motivated, trained, deployed, counseled, and provided for--without any trace of dissatisfaction or dissension despite the highly trying conditions through which He operated. He employed his uniquely efficacious technology of talent management enriched with non-materials motivation and madhura to keep the every tool of useful or potentially useful talent, well sharpened and ready for employment as and when opportunities arose. Practitioners of modern management, corporate or otherwise, will do well if they could read through the wise Lord's life and works and pick up, even a few invaluable pearls of management wisdom--in regard to talent management and beyond. Corporate success will accelerate to a surprising pace when even a little of Lord Krishna's management wisdom is imbibed and practiced.

Performance energies of thought and action become significantly available through a team only. Lord Krishna was fully aware of this fact and He employed this principle of performance enhancement to the maximum limits of its feasibility. Despite limitations of the ancient times, He attempted to assemble a dream team of virtuous and brave, in view of his specific objective of removal of accumulated evil and wickedness from face of the earth, for which He had incarnated. He succeeded a great deal in his efforts for acquiring the desired team, through innovative employment of Superior Team Management Technology (STMT), the seven components of which are discussed in detail under the relevant heading in this work.

Entirely unpredictable or very difficult to predict situations can lead managers to abandon the analytical choice of the traditional planning process altogether and base their strategic decisions primarily on the *gut instinct*. On the other hand, risk-averse managers who do not trust their gut instincts may suffer from decision paralysis which, in most situations, can be substantially damaging. Normally, the managers who are either basically deficient in *energy of thought and mind* or suffer from job related skills deficiencies, respond in this manner. Persons with excessively negative tendencies too may land corporate bodies into such sticky situations.

Lord Krishna, in various phases of his life and works, encountered situations of intense uncertainties. With his superior skills of situation analysis, He was able to employ the "intensity of uncertainty" as tool for effective determination of options and alternates for each demanding situation. Several incidents from the divine life and works of this great manager and decision maker, illustrate the fact very clearly.

Not long ago, modern management professed high performance managers and CEOs to possess higher I.Q. as an influence of the western management thought. Rethinking, in this regard, was forced by the consistent failure of US and European enterprises to compete, in certain fields, with the companies from the orient, where milder culture and the background of inter-dependency and empathy, encouraged greater productivity. Today, in progressive business corporations, leadership with greater *Emotional Quotient* is more in demand than stiff-neck efficient CEOs with hire-and-fire, and cut-and-dried approach. Softer skills are more in demand for senior managers as it is felt that earning or encouraging cooperation is more productive than demanding or enforcing the same. Some are progressing to the next stage of preference, i.e. the Spiritual Quotient as it is thought that superior ethicality in corporate operations, may lead to superior productivity that eventually encourages greater physical and non-physical well-being of the masses.

Lord Krishna was a great applicator EQ and SQ in management of human resources and he achieved unparallel success through these non-failing applications.

Ego is a troublesome characteristic of human beings, uncontrolled run of which often lands people in difficult situations or complicates the already uncomfortable ones. It is defined as an individual's perception or experience of oneself, especially in relation to other people or the outside world, or as part of the mind that can think, feel and act in relation to self. Similarly, egotism refers to the state of mind in which one is always thinking about oneself and what is best for him or her. It is an avoidable preoccupation with oneself. In a related manner, egotism pertains to an individual's practice of talking too much about oneself. It is an expression of selfishness. Uncontrolled manifestation of egotism is particularly evident with people endowed with tamsic prakriti.

Lord Krishna, right early in life, had a perception of being an incarnation. He was actively aware that several of his acts as incarnate of Lord Vishnu, and his plans for subsequently cleansing the earth of accumulated evil, could be construed as egoistic if not suitably clothed and sweetened. Hence, as a precaution, He equipped himself with superior degree of charm and charisma, the spell of which was highly infective. He could calmly absorb harsh words, insults, insinuations and pranks, and reacted only when necessary, with masterly measured responses (MMR). Normally, his smiles were enough to deflect minor evil intentions. His skills with words were legendry—music at his lips left no one uninfluenced. He could weave a maze of pleasure and happiness with his technology of language. He employed Madhura or sweetness as an instrument to charm people on one hand, and disarm enemies, on the other. It earned him a huge multitude of admirers. He could cloth difficult and unpleasant proposals as gifts of silk and honey.

There is great need for ego management amongst the present day managers and they can productively benefit from the wise Lord's approach in this regard.

I prefer to define motivation as a process of positive thought acceleration, resulting into action or readiness for action. It starts from thought genesis and culminates into action. If the process remains incomplete, stopping at thought itself, then one ends up becoming only a Thought Warrior. For any action, active thought should first convert into active desire and then into need, for action to emerge. A good motivator, in addition to being a thought warrior, should also be a superior "Action Warrior"; only then he will be able to initiate and direct a positive thought process in the target beings, i.e. subordinates and/or coworkers, to a desired and conclusive extent.

Lord Krishna was a fascinating mix of thought and action warriorism. He cultivated the unique technology of non-material motivation (NMM) through employment of which on Arjuna and personalities of his times, He achieved almost impossible results. The technology of NMM operates through effective linkage of body, mind, intellect and Atman. The expertise of NMM, even when available in small volumes on part of manager or leader, will free him from deficiencies of the modern day motivational methodologies that are exclusively centered on material incentives. NMM was one of the most important components of Lord Krishna's Brahmastras of man-management, which He so efficiently wielded through various phases of his challenge intensive life.

While delivering the renowned Song of Wisdom to Arjuna, Lord Krishna deliberated in detail on Time and its importance, in respect to individuals, organizations, kingdoms, regimes and all that falls under the umbrella of universe. He stressed the omnipotence of time, its all-pervading influence on all happenings and occurrences. He elaborated that the wheel of time always moves, it is never static and that time is most powerful as it encompasses all changes into itself. He was the divine maker of time and used it most effectively in completing his mission incarnate objectives. A little grounding of today's professionals in his divine time management technology will do wonders with their performance output.

"Business is Karma—and consequence of Karma!

Karmic balance determines the degree and direction of success!!"

Lord Krishna rightly emphasized superiority of action (Karma) over inaction, as a significant part of his Song of Wisdom is devoted to it. He emphasized action that is free from desire or concern for its fruits or results. This disconnection between action and results frees lot of positive energies of the doer for much superior performances. His divine doctrine of Karma, a major component of his management Brahmastras, is capable of solving all major ills and deficiencies of modern management. His divine life and works are in deed, a true gold mine of management ideas and solutions.

Lord Krishna efficiently married the principle of Karma with the concept of Dharma or righteousness. Its application significantly lifts the quality of action to levels of superiority, imparting new energies of action to the righteous doer. In today's corporate work environment, the Principle of Dharma, when suitably explained and communicated, can be a highly effective motivational tool for pushing employees and workers of all types do their assigned jobs with superior results.

Kindness, compassion and sense of caring and concern for community or greater good, are positive human values that generate immediate impact (feel) within the recipient. Collectively these positive thoughts are grouped as *Empathy*. Actions rich in this virtue have great power for release of positive energy to create goodwill and support which, depending upon right employment, can significantly enhance productivity or efforts to win in a competitive work environment. Lord Krishna was a matchless master in employment of the tool of empathy in motivating people to superior level of actions and performances.

Lord Krishna had a difficult agenda to work upon. In his times it was not an easy task for any human being, incarnate or otherwise, to successfully encounter all the accumulated forces of evil and demonic rulers. As per needs of the times and his mission incarnate objectives, He resorted to working and managing by intelligent design. Despite difficult and often invincible situations, He succeeded magnificently in meeting his mission incarnate objectivity. For the practitioners of the modern management, Lord Krishna's management by intelligent design offers an invaluable lesson that a truly intelligent design, when prepared and implemented with due diligence and care, irrespective of the field of its relevance, is bound to ensure planned results. Hence, one should always pay due attention to it.

In every work environment, one can always encounter some difficult to handle people. By default, such people turn out to be difficult to work with as well. They represent, in a way, a concentration of negative intentions and attitudes, primarily non-conducive for smooth working, in collective work environment. Most managers find it distressing and distasteful to manage people of such uncooperative nature. Lord Krishna encountered more than his share of such difficult to handle people. He developed a unique technology to managing them successfully. His technology in this vital field of manpower management will be highly useful in today's corporate work environment that is excessively rich in negative interactions.

The most amazing flute play of the Lord Krishna's communication technology emerged in the battle fields of Kurukshetra, when in the processes of persuading a reluctant and depressed Arjuna, to stand up and do his duty as a warrior, Lord Krishna played his most renowned Song of Wisdom which, later on, came to be known as the Bhagavad Gita. It was, in deed, profound and intense in its flute effect on not only those who heard it but even on those who continue to read and hear it thousands of years after the epic event. No one escapes its intense impact.

Lord Krishna was a seasoned Master of Dialogue. He was gifted with a divine capacity for effective employment of words and language, anointed with the right mix of expression and action. His intense education and training, at the ashram of Guru Sandipani, transformed him into a truly efficient and, in deed, a divine dialogue master. He had acquired a unique technique of madhura communication that could easily disarm even a very ardent and determined opponent.

The morale of the divine dialogue that took place between Lord Krishna and his celestial disciple Arjuna is that:

- even very serious and fundamental issues can be settled through dialogue,
- dialogue is essential to create lasting understanding and acceptance(U/A),
- and when such U/A is achieved-- fully committed action should emerge.

Since U/A is an essential requirement for any collective action, the significance of dialogue as a management tool is automatically established. Hence, the modern management professionals, whether in business or governance, can significantly benefit from the Lord Krishna's example of effective dialogue. They should not shy away from an honest, intelligent and intense dialogue and like the wise Lord, it is always the responsibility of the senior of the dialogue participants to keep it on track in a polite and constructive manner and take it to logical conclusion.

Lord Krishna respected the centrality of objective of his mission, all through his activities as child, youth, warrior, ruler, diplomat and saviour. What was righteous and virtuous had to be supported against all odds. Hence, modern managers will do well if they learn to respect their assigned objectives for sustained performance.

Energy is the main cause of all productive actions, management being no exception to this rule. It is energy that separates performer from non-performer, doer from lazy, strong from the weak, young from the old and living from the dead. Energy animates both body and mind. It enables a body to grow, a finger to lift and mind to think and direct a being into various life related activities. Lord Krishna managed to align himself with high energy of mind (thought) as well as body (action) in right mix suitable for his target objectivity. He infused high energy levels into the Pandava warriors so that they could perform in line with his objectives of cleaning the earth free of the evil and wicked.

As practiced by Lord Krishna, management of business and governance requires wise employment of energies of thought and action, not only on part of CEOs but also on part of their associates and coworkers. Positive energies have to be kept centered in direction of the pre-set objectives so that the desired levels of initiative and co-operation, on part of key action warriors, are constantly maintained. Regular attempts are necessary, as practiced by the wise Lord, for minimizing negative energy manifestations on part of those involved in the collective effort, in absence of which non-cooperation in the work force or action warriors may ruin the whole plans and expectations. As exemplified by the wise Lord, the energies of thought have almost limitless possibilities as actions are always designed on the foundation of thoughts. Simultaneously, it is also important to keep in view that thoughts alone are not enough, they are no substitutes for acts or karmas and hence actions must follow thoughts in right measure and earnest. Undoubtedly, the corporate world, through appropriate thought and action energies management of the people involved, like the wise Lord, can come out with much better outputs, the key being maximization of positive energy in the active work environment.

Encounters with failure are often unavoidable in every one's life. They get significantly amplified in case of leaders whether political, corporate, religious or otherwise. Despite best intentions, efforts may fall short of creating stresses necessary for genesis of target results or the combination of opposing forces may be too strong for a desired orientation to develop. Failures can take a variety of forms, often unexpected ones. Lord Krishna too encountered failures but He had devised a technology for converting the same into magnificent successes. The modern management community, students, teachers and its professional practitioners, irrespective of their place and nature of engagement, have a minefield of fully tested lessons buried in the life and works of Lord Krishna, in regard to tackling and management of situations of failures.

A great part of the Lord Krishna's Song of Wisdom delves on Anusasana detailing importance of rituals, worships and their proper performance, in other words the methodology of conduct of a king or a commoner. Anusasana assumes a wide canvas of significance in today's corporate work environment. If workers are devoid of anusasana, irrespective of being white or blue collared, all other inputs of business stand to lose their significance or capacity to deliver results.

The role of anusasana in work environment of governance is even of greater criticality. And in war, particularly when the opposing forces represent evil and wickedness, its significance grows much higher. Lord Krishna was acutely aware of all the criticalities of anusasana or discipline, and the need to scrupulously adhere to the same. His divine business was to sweep the earth, to a very significant extent, clear of the accumulated evil and wickedness and for the purpose, He made the fullest use of the element of anuasana, through his disciples, devotees and colleagues.

Relevance or practical applicability of Lord Krishna's work or business philosophy, as detailed in the great book of wisdom, the Bhagavad Gita, with its prime emphasis on the following four elements, is ever green and ever growing, with the universality of time and space.

- Karma—the all important action without witch nothing could happen.
- Dharma—one's duty or need for righteousness.
- Anusasana—the discipline in performance of the above.
- Non-material motivation—advice against excessive expectation of fruits of action.

In the area of vitality of his work and business philosophy, Lord Krishna has really no parallel or comparison amongst ancient or modern gurus as He is ancient and modern both at the same time.

Indirect management or being effective in consulting and service roles is more difficult than line functions. He never ruled directly. Despite absence of direct control, He excelled in converting the Yadavas as well the Pandavas into invincible forces and employed them with astonishing results towards his mission objectivity. Lord Krishna's great consultancy and advisory operations offer lessons of unique significance to the modern management community. He proved beyond any doubts that with merits of skills and righteousness, it is possible to be effective even when one does not have direct executive powers to solve problems. The force of merit and virtue is of great utility in productive management of affairs of governance, whether related to business or war.

Faced with difficult to handle or invincible situation, Lord Krishna persuaded the mighty Yadava community of Mathura to abandon their well-established kingdom and march all the way to a distant Dwarka. He employed the Long March as a management tool and demonstrated that no adversity, whatsoever great or menacing, should be viewed as totally hopeless from angle of possible improvement and/or reversal of fortunes. Situation specific management tools can always be located and employed for desired results. Employing adversity for fortune reversal is a great management lesson left by the wise Lord for the benefit of posterity.

A leader, corporate or otherwise, when endowed with a strong spiritual core(SSC), serves as a great source of strength to his coworkers and subordinates. Lord Krishna had incarnated to serve a higher purpose to curb and finally eliminate evil, especially on part of leaders and rulers. His divine objective was to promote the practice of goodness and righteousness in human interactions so that the life on earth could become peaceful and productive. Strong spiritual core of a leader emits positively contaminative forces that influence all those who come in close contact with such an individual. It initiates a chain reaction towards spread of s discipline for greater benefit of the society. When goodness or righteousness leads, spiritual discipline comes into play, negativity of thoughts diminishes and positive actions spurt. Results pore in without clamouring for the same. It empowers a leader with capacity to stand and fight for what is right, irrespective of obstacles encountered. Maintaining a strong spiritual core or the core of righteousness is of great benefit for corporate work environment.

One of the important arguments extended by Lord Krishna, while attempting to persuade Arjuna to fight, was that the Pandava warrior should uphold his own dharma (duty and responsibility) as kshatriya to do battle. The Lord added that war was lawful and should be fought to uphold and protect dharma. It was the wise Lord's recipe for ultimate rectitude which influenced Arjuna. Protection of dharma or righteousness is a vital hormone at disposal of management professionals for enthusing workers on the path of collective productivity.

Despite being a Guru of Rectitude, Lord Krishna found it necessary to offer to Arjuna, alternative paths for liberation, i.e. the path of Janana and Bhakti, along with the path of Karma, which was the superior one in view of the wise Lord. Hence, it is necessary that in corporate work environment too, alternate paths or approaches are given for achieving a target objective. He could go even further to assist his disciple or subordinate select the most appropriate path as per his or her specific strengths and circumstances. This approach of rectitude and righteousness has a long-term spectrum of validity and acceptance.

Lord Krishna taught management of welfare oriented righteous governance, along with effective war management to subdue and eliminate undesirable elements. The canvas of his teachings was really very vast in terms of content and applicability. Modern management, for training as well as practice, can profit considerably through righteous adoption of his major teachings, should it desire to gain an competitive edge over the presently followed concepts and practices for producing more efficient managers and unbeatable corporate results.

Lord Krishna's magnificent discourse to motivate Arjuna into action, delivered prior to commencement of fighting at Kurukshetra, covered most valuable aspects of human thought process interactions especially governance, and included among others

- life and death, mortals and immortals, heaven and hell.
- creator and creations, birth and rebirth.
- body and soul, karma and dharma, varnas and duties of people.
- action and inaction, various paths for salvation.
- renunciation and renouncement, right and wrong.
- human prakriti and performance.
- janana and devotion ,ethics of war and peace.
- all that was necessary to push Arjuna out of inaction.

Lord Krishna's technology of comprehensive mix of persuasive inputs (CMPI) has a lot of practical utility for the present day managers for evolving a situation specific package of inputs that ensures effective manpower management.

Presently, Creative destruction is a well-accepted management practice necessary for growth and innovation. Companies deliberately kill certain products and processes to promote new ones, more efficient, cost effective and environment friendly. Corporate decisions in regard to implementation of this practice of vital importance are normally based on a lot of statistical and EDP exercises. Lord Krishna, over 5,000 years ago, was well versed in the practice of *creative destruction* and employed it in a strategic manner, as a vital management tool, in a variety of situations without any obstructive feelings or emotions.

A corporate mission statement, when suitably laced with elements of divine love for the greater good of community, can be a highly effective reminder to the constituent workers to do what is expected of them and also willingly walk an extra mile. It is the consciousness or Atman that acts as the basic source of the positive energy flow, manifesting first in positive thoughts and then into constructive actions through instruments of active mind and gross body. Once a linkage is established between the positive forces of a corporate leader and his workmen in right earnest, then productivity and output remain no longer a problem.

When an individual forgets or is allowed to forget his true nature as embodiment of divine, positive values get excluded automatically from life and actions of such a person. Consequences of such value erosion are very serious for a corporate and the society where such a person operates, leading to undesirable effects such as

- wealth acquisition without honest work.
- education without character.

- business without morality and ethics.
- science without humility.
- politics without principles.
- power without responsibility and many more.

To summarize, the message of the wise Lord is that divine love is a powerful management tool for superior workman motivation and to get done whatever is necessary for enhanced productivity on long term basis in a positive work environment where ideas and initiatives for new products and services promptly germinate for sustained growth. Modern professional managers will do well by learning and practicing the ever sure technique of the great teacher.

Lord Krishna has made it very clear in his Song of Wisdom that it is not easy to overcome desire and its associated manifestations such as greed and anger, the force of desire being such that it is never fully eliminated, and enjoyment of one set of objects leads to genesis of desire for others. In order to achieve some success in this field, attainment of Oneness of Thought, Word and Deed or OTWD in brief, is required. When mind is subdued (undesirable thought is curbed with weapon of logic) words and deeds fall in line i.e. harmful words are not uttered and good deeds are initiated. On attainment of such an integration of thought, word and deed, one's capacity for productive work output is enhanced in a manner that indecision and friction are minimized below harmful levels. ONTD, thus, has potential to become a great output acceleration tool.

Tangible inputs or the physical assets of business do not work by themselves. It is the thought capital or intellectual capital of the people involved, especially the knowledge workers that releases human potential in form of more efficient products, processes and services. As compared to economists and accountants, stock markets seem more efficient at recognizing future value which accounts for the apparently high multiples of market value to the book value. The recent spurts in value of financial assets much beyond the physical assets, signifies the decisive value of intangibles in the economic growth. The fact that intangibles often play a more significant role in wealth generation than physical assets, has been empirically established. Accountants and accountancy have, however, often succeeded in overshadowing the intangibles by not quantifying their critical contributions, not reflecting the same in balance sheet in some suitable manner.

Lord Krishna always paid great attention to intangibles and similarly, modern day professional will do much better if they assigned due attention to these vital factors in their day to day activities.

Richness of management thought enables a good professional tackle difficult situations because in a critical situation such a person escapes running into a desert of ideas and way outs. Modern corporate management professionals have not yet fully grasped the centrality of human factor in production and value addition processes. Lord Krishna understood, in full depth, the significance of human element for development, governance, war and all other human interactions, amongst themselves and with their environment. His management thoughts and practices, centered on constructive manipulation and motivation of human element. The key components of the wise Lord's management thoughts and practices, when studied properly can serve the modern management a great deal, enabling it to successfully come out of its current mess of failures and deficits.

Lord Krishna often employed *mind management technology,* in reference to his disciples, friends and foes. He could read through mind and body of a person who faced him irrespective of distance involved, and worked on him or her from within, if so required. From his long carrier, numerous instances are known where He effectively employed this ever- effective tool of *mind management*, to either motivate people to cooperate, or scare them away into change or confusion.

While delivering the Song of Wisdom, He tells Arjuna that one who has a good mind is dear to him. "He who hates no creature, and is friendly and compassionate towards all, who is free from the feelings of 'I and mine,' even-minded in pain and pleasure, forbearing, ever-content, still in meditation, self-controlled, and possessed of firm conviction, with mind and intellect fixed on Me—he who is thus devoted to Me, is dear to Me." The wise Lord explained to his foremost disciple, the vital relationship between *body, mind and soul,* stating that soul or the Absolute is the owner occupier, body like various physical and material assets and facilities of a corporate, viz. factories, depots and branches, and mind as the controlling CEO. In this vital tripod, the first is Me or part of Me, it finally returns unto Me and at my direction. The last two are only mortal manifestations. Modern day corporate managers hence have to learn the mind management technology as practiced by him as it is capable of delivering them out of their collective mess of performance deficits.

Richness of management thought enables a good professional tackle difficult situations because in a critical situation such a person escapes running into a desert of ideas and way-outs. Management primarily pertains to development and employment of skills of people-handling for superior results, because all other inputs or factors of production, whether goods or services, are totally people dependent as:

- all machines are operated/worked by people.
- all materials are handled/converted by people.

- all moneys are invested and managed by people.
- all technologies are developed/utilized by people.
- all products are moved and marketed by people.
- no corporate or non-corporate activity ever occurs without people.

In fact, people are the most crucial component of all corporate or non-corporate activities. Lord Krishna understood, in full depth, the significance of human element for development, governance, war and/ or any-thing else. His management thoughts and practices, centered on manipulation and motivation of human element. Professional managers need to study and understand his technology of human element management.

Lord Krishna actively appreciated the utility of action and thought warriorism –and practitioners of these attributes. Throughout his long and eventful life, Lord Krishna rigorously attempted to practice a right mix of thought and action warriorism, as per demands of his role as a mission incarnate and at no point, He allowed any adversity to hinder his righteous mix of work emphasis. He judiciously analyzed all of his kinsmen, colleagues and disciples for their preference in terms of thought and action emphasis(skills, strengths and balance of the same) and utilized each one of them in the most appropriate and rewarding manner. Today's management professionals and CEOs can learn a great deal from life and works of the wise Lord and improve working of their respective organizations by suitably employing the thought and action warriors in their work force, for most rewarding results.

The principle of causality states that everything that happens must have a cause. In other words, behind every effect or happening there lies a cause. It may or may not be visible or noticed under normal circumstances. Sometimes, the cause may be too difficult for human senses to detect and or to interpret as signals emitting from the same may be too faint to be intercepted or decoded by preoccupied or insensitive beings. Lord Krishna, in Bhagavad Gita, has voiced the relationship of cause and effect at several places. To begin with He states that, "For the protection of good, for the destruction of wicked, and for the establishment of righteousness, I am born from age to age."

As per the Law of Karmic Balance, all actions generate proportional effect that may or may not be adequate for effecting immediate visibility to the untrained eyes of the doer being. Progressive accumulation of such effect may give rise to delayed visibility and keeping that in view the wise Lord has forbidden a doer to be over-concerned about fruits or results of actions or deeds undertaken; they should not be the doer's worry, particularly when the actions are performed in direction of righteousness. Application of this principle in the present work environment is capable of unleashing strong energies to accelerate productivity beyond expectations.

Thought is the precursor of action. Thought genesis often rises to its peak in solitude when one pushes brain and mind to higher limits to synthesize constructive thoughts/ideas and processes the same logically. Brain storming sessions, with persons of equal or superior capabilities, offer another fertile environment for thought generation. To the determined and disciplined, solitude becomes an instrument of self-realization and often it helps generate gems of thoughts coupled with subsequent actions of matching significance. In fact, self-realizations helps concentrate the vital thought energy into arrows of well-targeted actions. Through this valuable processes, enlightened ones can attain right alignment of body-brain/mind and Atman and when such a state is achieved, constructive action becomes an effortless occurrence. Through the brain storming, Lord Krishna pushed Arjuna into a state of active self-realization in regard to his duties as a warrior. He stressed, among others, indestructibility of soul, cycle of life and death, and destiny of most of the prominent warriors assembled on the battlefield of Kurukshetra. Modern managers stand to benefit a great deal from the instrument of self-realization.

Devine vision is perceived as the capacity to see beyond what is physically visible. Sometimes it is called as intuition or the sixth sense, and presence of this capability in some endowed leaders and professionals comes handy under demanding situations. Only challenging conditions test true metal of a leader, professional or otherwise, as under normal circumstances routines and systems take care of what is happening and what needs to be done. This capability to see and visualize beyond physical occurrences can protect against unpleasant happenings or help remedy the same well in time. The force of intuition, when truly strong, can take the form of divine vision.

Lord Krishna was a mission incarnate and was gifted with uncommonly superior faculties of intuition, which He employed with astonishing results. His methodology of intuition applications could be a great performance enhancing input for modern management.

Purpose of corporate activities, all over the world (irrespective of location and scale of operation) is uniform, namely to enhance productivity of human actions in a collective manner. Hence, it is governed by a common set of formulations called the Unified Concept of Management Performance or UCMP. At the absolute micro level, i.e. atomic and subatomic, all production or management inputs are fully unified and identical. All of them constitute of the same atomic and subatomic units which are held together by the same forces of attraction and repulsion. The living inputs, in form of human beings, constitute the totality of management action. In the interaction processes of management inputs that lead to productivity or output, the living inputs or the human factor plays the vital catalytic and controlling role. The crucial energy of action is provided by the human factor.

The unified concept of management performance or UCMP is depicted by the following equation which clearly establishes the critical unitary force of man, in all management actions and interplays:

$$\mathbf{me = (K^{m2})en}$$

Where

me = management performance or management energy,

K= karma or action,

m = man (mind and Atman),

en = work environment (inputs and policies).

The seed of action or work lies in human mind where thought processes sprout and grow. All actions emanate from mental energy balance or thoughts – generated in mind, through charge of consciousness (Atman). Hence, the role of man is shown here as m2, the deciding or determining force.

Thus, management performance or efficiency, is firstly thought-centric and then karma-centric. Work environment or corporate environment, represented by 'en', has an encompassing influence on the whole process of management performance or output.

ATTACHMENTS

MAHABHARATA: A BRIEF INTRODUCTION

Mahabharata is one of the two great ancient epics of India, another being the Ramayana. It is the story of conflict between two branches of a ruling warrior family; more precisely, descendents of the great king *Bharat*, after whom the country took the name of *Bharata, which* still perpetuates. King Santanu's son Devavarata, born from his first wife Ganga, had taken a difficult vow of total celibacy and perpetual service to the throne of Hastinapura, in order to enable his father marry a fisherman's daughter named Satyavathi. As a consequence, he was called *Bhishma* and had acquired the unique boon of being able to decide the time of his own death.

King Santanu's two sons from Satyavathi, named Chitrangada and Vichitravirya had died without leaving any male claimant to the throne, endangering continuation of the great Kuru dynasty. After Bhishma's curt refusal to accept the queen mother's proposal to enable the two widows of Vichitravirya, to have sons from him, the resourceful mother arranged the same through sage Vyasa, who was her first born from the eminent rishi Prasar, prior to her marriage with Santanu. Thus, three sons were born into the Kuru family; a blind one to Ambika—later named as Dharitarashtra, a pale one to Ambalika, later called Pandu, and a bright and intelligent one, named Vidura, to a female attendant of Ambalika. Afterwards, the sequence of events proceeded as under.

- Dhritarashtra grew up under the care of Bhishma who arranged him to be married to Gandhari, the princess of Gandhara.
- In time, Pandu grew into a matchless warrior who added several new territories to the kingdom and acquired two wives, Kunti and Madri. On account of elder brother's visual handicap and his own valorous and just nature, he was crowned as ruler of the kingdom of Hastinapura. Dharitarashtra, though apparently happy, did not really like this development and seeds of a great conflict were sown.
- Pandu, however, died young as consequence of a curse slapped on him by a celestial being who was killed by the warrior king, while engaged in an intimate love game with his mate.
- Kunti was blessed with special powers by sage Dhurvasa, to be mother to godly children. Employing these unique powers as persuaded by her husband, she had produced three godly sons: Yudhishtira from Yama, Bhimasena from Vayu, and Arjuna from Indra. She also gave the mantra to Madri who produced Nakula and Sahadeva from Aswins.

- On the other hand, a pregnant and jealous Gandhari, produced one hundred sons and a daughter, benefiting from the tissue culture technology of sage Vyasa. Her eldest son Duryodhana, an evil concentrate, was predicted to be cause of great destruction. Vidura, the wise and righteous of the family, advised destruction of this new born evil, but his counsel was ignored. While this brood of Dhritarashtra was called the Kauravas, the progeny of Pandu came to be known as Pandavas.
- Right from childhood, Duryodhana grew very jealous of the talented Pandavas. Arjuna's matchless talents with bow and arrows, guru Drona's fondness for him, and the pranks that Bhimma played on the multitude of Kauravas, prompted Duryodhana's jealousy and enviousness to explode in form of schemes and plans to damage, and if possible, even to totally destroy the Pandavas.
- With the grace of Surya, the Sun God, prior to her marriage to Pandu, Kunti had a son who was born encased in an armour and was adorned with unusually large earrings. To avoid a scandal, Kunti had floated the baby in a basket down a river, wherefrom he was picked up by a charioteer's wife who, being childless, raised him with a lot of love and care. He came to be known as Karna, a great expert with bow and arrows, and grew very envious of Arjuna. With the objective of finding an antidote to the Pandava warrior Arjuna, Duryodhana assigned some land areas to Karna and declared him as the king of Anga. He became a life long friend of the evil Duryodhana, and being guru Parsurama's disciple and an invincible expert on astras, was one of the main causes of the his friend's arrogance and evil manifestations.
- Being elder and talented, Yudhishtira was declared as the crown prince. He discharged his duties very diligently and righteously, earning the praise of one and all, except the pair of envious Duryodhana and his blind but scheming father who dreamt of his evil son to eventually ascend to the throne of Hastinapura.
- Presenting as a reward for the good work done, the blind king, on prodding of his evil son, persuaded Yudhishtira to go, with his whole family, to Varanavata, a tribal locale at edge of the kingdom, and enjoy the festivities. With total secrecy, a magnificent palace of combustible materials was built there, in which Duryodhana wanted to burn the Pandavas, as a permanent solution to his jealousy and hatred towards them. With secret guidance from the just and vigilant Vidura, and a little luck on their side, the five Pandavas and their mother escaped unhurt.
- Though apparently mourning the loss of their cousins, Kauravas, in their

hearts greatly rejoiced on quick riddance of their sworn enemies. Charred remains of a woman and five men had served as confirmation of their objective. The blind king too was very happy, except that occasionally he suffered pangs of conscience. Vidura was aware of the great escape while Bhishma and other elders grieved over the loss of the talented branch of the Kuru family.

- The Pandava family moved incognito in the forest, totally unsure of their future, and bearing the hardships with great fortitude. Bhimma was very angry at turn of the events, often ground his teeth and swore vengeance on his kinsmen. Once he killed a ferocious rakshasa who used to make a meal of people or animals coming that way. The rakshasa's sister, named Hidimba fell in love with the mighty Pandava and adorning human form, she born him a mighty son named Ghatotkacha, who always came to his father's aid in any crisis and played a great part later in the battle of Kurukshetra.
- One evening, their great grandfather Vyasa, the great sage and the island-born son of Satayavati, appeared unannounced and told them the right path and advised them to go to the town of Ekavarata, for temporarily spending a safe and quite life. He advised them to live and behave like Brahmins. He assured them that they would have victory for their principles and that after some time they would again live in their palaces, perform grand sacrifices such as Rajasuya and Aswametha.
- Through the good offices of Vyasa, they secured peaceful residence with a Brahmin family at Ekavrata. Yudhishtira helped them keep calm through his philosophy of resignation and hope. As Brahmins, they begged for alms and passed their time as best as they could.
- Soon, the host Brahmin family was faced with a crisis as part of a local arrangement to keep peace with demon Bakasura, it was their turn to send a member of the family with a cartful of food to the ferocious demon who normally, along with the food, also polished away the person as well his bullocks which pulled the food cart. Kunti, as a matter of gratitude to the family and to save it from the crisis, sent Bhimma to kill the troublesome demon. While it solved the town's problem, the Pandavas faced the danger of exposure of their identity for which it was not yet the right time.
- In the meantime, a traveler came from Panchala and informed that the king Drupada there planned to organize the sawayamwara of his daughter, and that prospective bridegrooms from far and wide, were invited to assemble on a specific day. The Pandavas, as per the guidance given earlier by the sage Vyasa, decided to move out to Panchala where they took residence in a

potter's lane.

- Drupada had suffered defeat at hands of guru Drona's disciples and was determined to take revenge some day. He had performed prayers and sacrifices for the purpose and in the process had a son who was born bearing arms and encased in armour, giving all indications of one day becoming a great warrior. He was named Dhrishtadyumna, meaning one born with courage, arms, and ornaments. And a dark and beautiful daughter born was called Draupadi or Panchali.
- In a bow stringing and target shooting contest, Arjuna won the hand of Draupadi and as a result of an unintentional comment by mother Kunti, all the five Pandavas married her in a glittering ceremony. Kauravas, who were present as a large contingent, were not happy on losing the chance of grabbing a prestigious bride. They attempted to grab the bride by force but were beaten back by the mighty Bhimma.
- Krishna, the king of Dwaraka, was present in the assembly along with elder brother Balarama, and had recognized the Pandavas despite being disguised as Brahmins. Later on, He helped them in handling the morality aspect of a woman marrying five men, as he knew that Draupadi was not an ordinary woman and that she was destined for such a role.
- On hearing about the reappearance of the Pandavas, a confused Dhritarashtra consulted with wise and learned men inclusive of Vidura, and finally sent the latter to Panchala to bring back his nephews and their bride. Here again, Krishna played a crucial role in convincing the confused and reluctant Pandavas to return to Hastinapura as per invitation of their uncle. In fact, He accompanied them on their journey back home.
- In order to camouflage his guilt, the blind king warmly received the returning warriors and their bride, despite opposition from Duryodhana and his bunch of evil friends. A few days after, he divided the kingdom, giving to Pandavas the infertile wasteland of Khandavaparastha, which on Krishna's advice was accepted by the reluctant Pandavas.
- Led by Krishna, the Pandavas proceeded to Khandavaparastha which, on arrival, they found nothing more than an expanse of desert. Counseled by Krishna, they were finally happy to have something of their own.
- After completing the necessary purificatory ceremonies, the industrious Pandavas plunged into constructional and developmental activities under the celestial guidance of Krishna who willingly provided them the services of the renowned architect Vishvakarma. The name of the city was changed to Indraparastha since it matched the splendour of the city of God. Many traders

and citizens from Hastinapura shifted to benefit from the prosperity of a new capital city.

- When they were just settled in the new capital, sage Narada paid a visit to Yudhishtira and, among others, advised him to work out a foolproof system of sharing the common wife so as to avoid any complication in this delicate affair. When she was possessed by one, others had to avoid all thoughts of her and never to disturb privacy of the couple. Exile of twelve years was prescribed for any violation of the arrangement. Once Arjuna, per force of circumstances, could not avoid disturbing the privacy when Yudhishtira was in company of Draupadi and as decreed, Arjuna had to endure an exile of twelve years for the lapse. During this period, the great Pandava warrior married Ulupi, a princess of serpent world and also Subadhara, the sister of Krishna and Balarama.
- The fame and prosperity of the Pandavas created a lot of active jealousy in heart and mind of Duryodhana. Celebrations of Rajasuya and the massive gathering of all mighty kings and princes at this occasion further fueled the state of Duryodhana's discomfort and he was in constant consultation with his shroud and cunning maternal uncle Sakuni in this regard. He advised the evil Duryodhana not to entertain the idea of war, as he foresaw no chance of a win against the mighty Pandavas. But he promised his brooding nephew that he would come up with some other way-out.
- Soon after, sage Vyasa visited Yudhishtira and left with a prophecy that the next thirteen years shall be of critical significance for him and at the expiry of that period the entire race of kshatriyas shall be annihilated and that you would be the main cause of the same.
- Despite the warning, Yudhishtira fell to the cunning scheme of Sakuni and Duryodhana, and accepted an invitation to play the game of dice, lost whole of his kingdom, and suffered the terrible humiliation of attempted disrobing of Draupadi, when only the invisible force of Lord Krishna partly saved the situation. Obscene gestures of Karna, Duryodhana and Dussasana left a non-erasable mark on the psyche and persona of Bhimma who took terrible vows of revenge at the right time.
- As per terms of the game of dice, Pandavas were to be sent for a long and arduous exile, in the beginning of which all of them were highly dispirited and gloomy. A learned man Saunaka and Yudhistira's official priest Daumya attempted to console and advise them. As advised by the wise Daumya, Yudhishtira prayed to the Sun God who was kind enough to gift him a copper bowl when held by Panchali, it produced all desired meals and foods in

requisite quantity.

- Wise and fearless, Vidura berated the blind king on his excessive love for his children, especially the Duryodhana, and his bias against the Pandavas. He went to the extent of even advising that the king should cast away his evil eldest son. It, however, brought no solution.
- The evil combination of Sakuni, Duryodhana and Karna even planned to do away the Pandavas in the wilderness of the forest, least the fickle and the blind king calls them back from the exile. The sage Vyasa came, smelling their terrible plans, and advised the king not only to thwart the same, but to push his sons to go and make peace with the exiled Pandavas. He warned the king that if his advice was not heeded to, then terrible consequences were to follow after the expiry of the thirteenth year.
- Sage Maitreyi too attempted to make Duryodhana to see reason and appreciate the consequences that were likely to follow. Duryodhana's reaction was totally cynical, slapping his thigh and kicking the ground in gestures of evil defiance.
- Kriskna too came to visit them in the forest and was greatly moved by Draupadi's tears. While consoling her, He promised that Duryodhana, his brothers, Karna, and the evil genius behind them all, Sakuni, all of them will be punished and that their blood shall stain the dust. He added, "You will see Yudhishtira installed on the throne."
- After Krishna left, an angry Draupadi questioned the wisdom, manliness and the kshatriya origin of Yudhishtira who took all of it peacefully. She did not understand his stupidity of losing his kingdom, whole of his wealth and also the entire family. She did not curse him and except that said all that an excessively angry woman is capable of saying. Bhimma too was very unhappy and terribly hurt at the insults and humiliation which were heaped upon the whole group but he did not have the language skills of a woman, to adequately express his frustrations.
- But more than Draupadi, Bhimma's bitter words pained Yudhishtira a great deal. He pleaded for patience and said that he had given word and it was not wise to plunge into active conflict before expiry of the period of the exile. His logic and righteousness, however, did not influence any of the grieving and brooding five.
- Patiently, Yudhishtira argued that it was not the right time for a direct fight because the opposing side had invincible warriors namely Bhishma, Drona, his son Aswathama, Kirpa and Karna, and that the kings who were mishandled at the time of Rajasuya might also side with them. I see no

capability of winning a direct fight. "We must gather strength", he added.

- At the moment Vyasa arrived, and said, "Yudhishtira, I read what passes in your mind, and I am here to dispel your fears. There will come a time, be assured of it, when Arjuna will slay all your foes in battle. I will impart you a mantra called Pratismriti, and that will help you. You will impart it to Arjuna, and let him go forth to meet Gods in their worlds and receive from each of them a special weapon. After he obtains them he will be invincible. Don"t despair." He received the mantra as per the right procedure and understood how it was to be transferred to Arjuna. As suggested by Vyasa, the Pandava group moved from Dwaitavana to Kamyakavana, as the latter offered better and safer environment. On and auspicious day, Yudhishtira imparted the mantra to Arjuna and instructed him to go to Indra, Varuna, Iswara and other Gods for the specified purpose. In Vindhaya mountains, he meditated and soon Lord Shiva appeared and blessed him with astra called Pasupatha. Subsequently, Varuna, Yama, and Kubera came and gave him respective weapons that assured him victory against the Kauravas.
- Then, being the son of Indra, a celestial chariot took him to Amaravathi where he was received with all the courtesy and care. In due course, Indra imparted to him the secret of his weapons and further arranged for him to learn the art of music and dance from a gandharva named Chitrasena. During the period, a celestial courtesan Uravasi fell in love with Arjuna and, with Lord Indra's sanction, wanted to marry the great warrior. But Arjuna politely refused her saying that to him she was equal to mother Kunti and Madri. She felt spurned but Arjuna explained to her that he was under an ascetic vow at that time in order to receive certain arms and could not view her nothing less than a mother. She did not see the logic and cursed him to become an eunuch for some time. Later, Lord Indra told him, "You have surpassed even the most austere rishis in exercise of self control. Urvasi's curse will bear fruit in the thirteenth year of your exile, when you will find it actually to be a blessing."
- After finishing pilgrimage of all important places as advised by the sage Narada, Yudhishtira's entourage reached the Himalayas at the end of the twelveth year of their exile where Arjuna joined them, well equipped with weapons of invincibility and that raised the spirits of the long suffering group.
- The word of Arjuna acquiring celestial weapons reached Hastinapura, where Dhritarashtra felt uneasy on account of conflicting feelings, but Sakuni could see through the problem that a better equipped Arjuna was to create in the future. But he was confident that Yudhisthira would not go back on his

commitment even if the king sends for him to return. He advised Duryodhana to establish a camp near to the Pandavas' abode in the Kamyaka forest and tempt them with the royal pomp and glitter. Their scheme did not succeed as they were intercepted by an army of gandharvas who arrested Duryodhana while his friend Karna ran away from the scene.

- Hearing about the episode, Yudhishtira instructed Bhimma and Arjuna to go and free Duryodhana, arguing that with all said and done, he was one of them. Duryodhana thanked the Pandavas for the help, wound up his camp and returned to Hastinapura, sadder and wiser. This episode was organized by Lord Indra to teach the arrogant Kauravas a lesson.
- Soon, the twelfth year was over, and for the thirteenth year which the Pandavas had to pass incognito, they selected the Matsya kingdom and planned their individual disguises and facades with a lot of thought and care. Yudhistira planned to pose as Kanka and give king Virata company and contribute to his amusement through the game of dice. Bhimma coined the name of Vallabha and said that he would offer to work in the royal kitchen. Arjuna said that it would be hard for him to hide the bowstring marks on his arms. Hence, he proposed to adorn himself with a stack of conch bangles, a long braid and brilliant earrings and dressing as a neuter, planned to pass like a woman. He added that he is destined to live like an eunuch as per the curse of Urvasi, a celestial dancer in service of Lord Indra. Nakula looked forward to work in the royal stable and call himself Granthika. Sahadeva said that he would take care of the cattle of the king, as he knew all about cows, their maintenance and management. While the brothers looked happy with their plans, Yudhistira was worried about Draupadi as she was delicate and unaccustomed to drudgery. But she had already planned to work as handmaid to royal ladies and planned to call herself as Sairandhari.
- Afterwards, they consulted their loyal priest Daumya who selected the auspicious time for reaching the capital of Matsya kingdom. He advised each of them on the risks involved and precautions to be observed. He was particularly worried about Yudhishtira, as giving company to a king for long hours on daily basis was not going to be easy and hence, a very detailed code of behavior was specified for the eldest Pandava.
- It was not difficult for them to secure the respective jobs, except for Draupadi as the wise queen was apprehensive that her great beauty and looks might invite trouble from men of the household. But, somehow, Draupadi convinced the queen assuring that she would take every care in this regard. Life was smooth for all of them until the beauty of Draupadi brought her to the active

attention of Kichaka, brother of the queen and also the commander of the royal forces.

- She discussed the matter with her husbands and only Bhimma offered to help. As per plan, she lured Kichaka to the dance hall in middle of the night where Bhimma was waiting in disguise and he throttled the love smitten offender with bare hands. As natural, Kichaka's death created a sensation in the country as he was a powerful man, in addition to being chief of the army. This incident unnerved the king and the queen, but Draupadi skillfully explained that her gandharva husbands were enraged at her mistreatment and that they had killed the queen's brother and his soldiers. Stating that she was not at fault, she begged to be permitted to stay for a few days more.
- Duryodhana and his friends were feeling uncomfortable on their inability to locate the Pandavas during the period of disguise and the story of Kichaka's death compounded their confusion and worry. Susurman, the Trigartan king, an ally of Duryodhana, too was looking for an opportunity to have a go at the Virata king, at whose hands he had suffered repeated defeats. Intensive consultations took place and while Karna and Dussasana exhibited eagerness to immediately attack the Matsya kingdom and force the Pandavas to emerge, Drona cautioned against the haste. Knowing that only a man of Bhimma's caliber could kill Kichaka in the manner described by his spies, Duryodhana was very keen that the Pandavas be exposed before expiry of the stipulated period of their exile.
- Kauravas and the Trigartans attacked forming two columns, the one headed by Susurman went first to attack the Matsya capital and due to presence of Bhimma in disguise with the Virata forces gave Susurman a bloody nose. He was, however, set free on intervention of Yudhishtira who was giving company to the king. But in the meantime the march of the Kaurava forces from another side created panic in the Matsya capital. Prince Uttara was the only man present to protect it against the mighty forces. He did not know the gravity of the challenge and in the beginning was very boastful. On advice of Draupadi, Uttara took Brihannala (Arjuna in disguise) as his charioteer and, while on way to meet the advancing Kaurava forces, the young prince developed cold feet and wanted to run back. And as per force of circumstances, Arjuna took over the job of the fear stricken prince, who with the first testing of his newly acquired celestial weapons, rendered all the mighty Kauravas, including the boisterous Karna, unconscious on the battle ground. Uttara was made to collect part of the garments of the stricken warriors as proof of his victory, to show to the ladies of the royal household.

- While returning from the battle, Arjuna put back his weapons on the tree in the cremation ground and instructed the prince to assume the place of warrior on the chariot, himself acting again as the charioteer. Back home the king was jubilant as messengers reached early to announce the victory of the prince over the mighty Kauravas. When Kanka (Yudhishtira) persisted in explaining the effect of Brihannla's presence, the king got irritated and hurled a dice at the Kanka who started to bleed from the forehead. Draupadi, noting the bleeding with concern and afraid of the consequences of even a single drop falling to the ground, placed a vessel to collect the blood. In the meantime Uttara reached and was aghast to see what the king had done. He could not restrain himself from disclosing the whole episode. The king severely repented his action and wanted to correct the wrong done to the Pandavas. He offered to marry his daughter Uttarai to Arjuna, who saying that she was his disciple and like a daughter, accepted her hand for his son Abhimanyu.
- Defeated and soiled, the mighty Kauravas returned to Hastinapura, blaming each other for the episode and not being sure of what had truck them. They waited for some news of emergence of the Pandavas with utmost impatience which got confirmed only with the marriage of Uttarai, in absentia, with Abhimanyu.
- An unexpectedly large number of kings and princes participated in this wedding. Krishna, with a large force came from Dwaraka and on the sidelines of the auspicious occasion, intense consultations and discussions took place amongst those assembled as how to proceed in direction of recovering the Pandavas' lost empire, from the evil Duryodhana.
- Krishna took the control of the great assembly of the kings and princes. He made a long and impressive speech listing various options and scenario. Balarama spoke but sounded caution as he expected Duryodhana to be adamant and non-cooperative. Finally, it was decided to send a messenger of suitable learning and merit to put forward the Pandavas' claim with right impact and emphasis.
- Simultaneously, action started on the alternate front, as not many thought that Duryodhana would relinquish his hold on any part of the kingdom which he had exclusively enjoyed for long years. Messengers were dispatched to over fifty kingdoms, in all the four directions, to obtain commitment for support in the event of an armed conflict. Krishna prepared to return to Dwaraka and while leaving He advised, "Let us try to maintain a friendly relationship, but if Duryodhana spurns us, call me first, and then summon our allies. Then the Gandiva and all our other weapons can go into action".

- The mission of messenger that was sent to Hastinapura failed miserably due to adamancy of the evil Duryodhana—and the return visit of Sanjaya, as emissary of the blind king Dhritarashtra was of no use –and the Pandavas were left with no option but to prepare for the war. Even the Pandavas' proposal to give them only five villages was turned down with utmost disregard for justice.
- The cunning Duryodhana understood the might of the Yadava forces and immediately reached Dwaraka to ask for support. Arjuna too happened to reach there almost at the same time. They waited patiently on two sides of the royal bed as the Lord of Dwarka was asleep at that moment. When Krishna opened his eyes and on hearing the visitors, offered to one side whole his mighty army and himself alone and unarmed, to the other. Duryodhana was happy to receive the Yadava army while Arjuna was satisfied to have the unarmed Lord, knowing well that his presence itself was a big guarantee for the final victory. Balrama refused to take part or side in the war and said that he planned to proceed on a long pilgrimage.
- When the mighty king Salya, father of Madri was coming to meet Yudhishtira, Duryodhana cunningly organized a grand reception, which he mistook as arranged by the Pandavas and as a consequence, had to support the wrong side in the war. When he met Yudhistira, on the request of the eldest Pandava, he promised to be helpful if ever an opportunity arose for one to one combat between Karna and Arjuna.
- Wise counsel of Vidura, Bhishma, Drona, Vyasa and also the ancient rishi Sanat-suja fell on the deaf ears of the blind king. He could see the cloud of destruction developing but he was also handicapped in the faculty of rational or righteous thinking. Duryodhana's evil adamancy and Karna's blind hatred towards Arjuna pushed the situation in the direction of destined destruction.
- In the heat of arguments on the combined strengths of Arjuna and Krishna, and Karna's boasting of Brahma-Astra in his armory, Bhishma reminded Karna of what had happened a short time earlier on the outskirts of the Matsya capital when all the six mighty warriors of the Kaurava side were lying in the dust for a long time, just in one simple encounter with Arjuna, that too when he was in disguise. Hugely slighted, Karna vowed not to fight as long as Bhishma was alive.
- Now, preparations for the war were well advanced but Yudhishtira and Bhimma were developing stresses of conscience. Lord Krishna offered to go Hastinapura and make a last ditch effort on avoidance of the war. Everyone, except Sahadeva and Satyaki, wanted him to be polite with the villainous

Duryodhana—and take enough care of his own safety. Draupadi was bitter on the non-kshatriya softness of the four of her five husbands. She broke down and wept bitterly. Krishna consoled her and reassured that the wrongs done to her shall be fully avenged and that the time when the Kaurava women will weep more than what she did was not far away. Kauravas had intelligence reports on Krishna's mission and planned to give him a grand reception. Various omens en-route were indicative of failure and hostility. Being a mission incarnate, Krishna knew better and his objective was to ensure that afterwards, no one blamed either him or the Pandavas that adequate last ditch efforts were not made to avert the war.

- On Dhritarashtra directions, Krishna was received with all pomp and show and all courtesies due to a great visitor were extended but He refused to accept Duryodhana's offer for a royal dinner with him and went, instead, to Vidura's modest abode. His explanation for the refusal did not please the master of evils, in any manner. Vidura explained the evil Duryodhana's schemes and his over confidence in the invincibility of the main Kaurava warriors. He cautioned Krishna about his own safety, in the wicked assembly planned for the next day.
- Unmindful of the fears expressed by wise Vidura, Krishna next day appeared in the great Kaurava assembly and made an impressive appeal for justice to the Pandavas, also detailing the devastating consequences of war. Duryodhana not only ignored all that and attempted to put the blame on the Pandavas. Finally, he declared that as long as he was alive, land not even enough to cover a needlepoint shall be given to them and that was final. The demonic usurper showed utter hostility and disregard to advice of his own elders assembled there—and also the warning of mother Gandhari who was called in to exert some influence on her evil son. Exhibiting utter disregard to the great assembly, Duryodhana and his bunch of evil supporters ran out, hurriedly consulted the evil genius Sakuni, and decided to forcibly arrest Krishna as they had concluded that without him, the Pandavas would be rendered totally incapable of any action. The malevolent attempt brought in unexpected consequences. Krishna presented a multi-dimensional vision of his stature and personality, surrounded with the Pandavas and all the gods, and all the great armies of the world. It was impossible to touch any part of him—and it is said that the brightness of the celestial flash was so strong that even Dharitarashtra lost his blindness for a moment to behold the grand vision. He begged to be left sightless again so that later on he did not see the destruction of his own race. Everybody was left dumbfounded and

speechless. The great Lord assumed his human form and prepared for return to Upapalavya.

- Krishna signaled Karna to come into his chariot, explained to him the mystery of his birth and how he was the eldest of the Pandavas. He even nudged the glittering warrior to return to his rightful place in the righteous camp. Stressing his long-term commitments to Duryodhana, he politely turned down the offer. His enmity to the Pandavas and the resolve for a tough fight was, however, greatly weakened. It was decidedly part of a celestial plan to defeat the great assembly of evils under the leadership of Duryodhana.
- Krishna and his entourage soon returned to the Pandava camp. Preparations for the great war were completed at breakneck speed. The time and place of the great armed conflict that left millions dead and irrevocably crippled the forces of evil and wickedness, was decided with mutual concurrence.
- What happened on the battle fields of Kurukshetra, from beginning to the end and also (a) what motivational technology the great Lord employed to push a reluctant, confused and deluded Arjuna to finally fight and win, (b) how difficult questions raised by an argumentative Arjuna regarding the intricate aspects of body, mind and soul or Atman , life, death and rebirth; karma , dharma, janana and bhakti; conscious and subconscious; bondage, liberation/salvation, renunciation and renouncement; relation and relationships; senses, desires and maya; mortal and immortal; asuras and evils; human prakartti and its effect on actions and responses; killing and being killed; violence and non-violence; earth, sky, heaven and universe and all that concerns humans and non-human beings in this life and beyond, were answered and how that celestial dialogue formed the great and renowned store-house of wisdom—known to the posterity as *Bhagavad Gita or the Song of Wisdom,* (c) how invincibility of the great Kaurava warriors namely Bhishma, Drona, Karna and Duryodhana, was circumvented, even employing the means which in opinion of some commentators, were not fully in line with the code of war and ethics prevalent at that time, (d) how the non-arms wielding charioteer of Arjuna effected the magnificent management of the great and intense war lasting eighteen days, and (e) how the post war activities were managed to perpetuate the rule of righteousness and good, for which the Lord had incarnated in human form, has been detailed at appropriate places in this work which feebly attempts to highlight (a) the supper management concepts, (b) management skills and technologies practiced by the great Lord and (c) and how the present day management professionals could benefit from the same.

- Hence, re-narration of the events that took place during the massive war which eliminated the major part of the evil load from the face of the earth, is not attempted herein. This summary of the great epic is primarily based on the work of R.K. Narayan (1988) and the readers interested in greater details have wide option of rich literature on this topic of perpetual interest, some of which are listed under the references section.

NOTES ON PERSONS AND PLACES MENTIONED IN THE WORK

Abhimanyu Arjuna's son from Subhadra (Krishna's sister); great young warrior who had learnt war skills while still in his mother's womb, from his father's talks now and than; was brought up and trained in Krishna's guidance.

Airavata Indra's four-tusked elephant of white colour.

Akrura A Yadava lord and Krishna devotee; was sent by Kamsa to fetch Krishna and Balarama, with secret design to kill them.

Amaravati Indra's heavenly city; also spelt Amaravathi.

Amba A princess of Kashi who along with her two sisters was forcibly abducted by Bhishma for marriage with a Kuru prince, to take revenge on Bhishma, was reborn as Sikandi.

Ambika A sister of Amba and mother of the blind king Dharitarashtra.

Ambalika Another sister of Amba and mother of Pandu.

Ananta Sesha The cosmic serpent on which Lord Vishnu rests.

Anusasana Ancient term referring to discipline.

Arista The demonic bull.

Arjuna The third son of Kunti (also the third Pandava), the invincible warrior of that time; a disciple and devotee of Krishna; played the most crucial role in Mahabharata, eliminating a number of invincible warriors of the Kaurava side. He was son of Indra.

Ashram A hermitage

Astra An unearthly weapon.

Asura Demon.

Asvamedha Horse sacrifice, also called Aswametha.

Aswathama Son of guru Drona, and an invincible warrior and a friend of Duryodhana.

Ataman Individual soul; also spelt as Atman; the eternal part of the living-being.

Avatara An incarnation.

Bakasura A demon.

Balarama Elder brother of Krishna; an incarnation of Ananta Sesha; was most powerful man of his time; trained Bhimma and Duryodhana in mace fighting: had great knowledge of earth sciences.

Bhagavad Gita The Song of God; emerged as summary of the discourse that Lord Krishna gave to Arjuna on the battle fields of Kurukshetra, in an effort to convince the latter to do his duty as a warrior and fight.

Bhagavad Purana The most reliable ancient text dealing with the life of Lord Krishna.

Bhakti One of the yogas denoting devotion or worship.

Bharat/Bharata Ancient Indian king after whom the country assumed the name of Bharata.

Bhimma Also as Bhima or Bheema; the second Pandava warrior, Kunti's son from Vayu; played a vital role in the struggle of Mahabharata.

Bhishma A Kuru patriarch; Son of king Santanu from Ganga. His first name was Devavarata who facilitated his father's marriage to the boatman's daughter Satyavati, and in the process took the most difficult vow of lifelong celibacy and also life long service to the throne of Hastinapura. He was Parsurama's disciple and had mastered Vedas under sage Vashista; was a devotee of Krishna.

Brahma One of the Hindu Trinity; The Creator.

Brahmin A priestly caste, also called Brahmina of Brahman.

Brihaspati An ancient sage or also known as guru of devas.

Chakravyuha A wheel-like battle formation, mastered by Arjuna from guru Drona. Abhimanyu had learnt only how to break it and gain entry, not how to break it and come out, and was killed collectively by Kauravas, in Arjuna's absence and it had greatly agitated the latter.

Chatakasura A cart demon who was killed by the baby Krishna.

Chitrangada Son of king Santanu from Satayvathi.

Chitraratha A gandharva king.

Dantavakra Crooked-teeth; Krishna's cousin and enemy.

Daruka Krishna's charioteer.

Deveki Kriskhna's biological mother. She was sister of Kamsa of Mathura who had married her to Vasudeva, a Yadava chief.

Dharma Righteousness-also employed to depict duty.

Dharitarashtra The son of Ambika from Vyasa; blind king of Hastinapura.

Dhurvasa A temperamental sage who was well cared for by Kunti when he visited her father and being pleased, he in turn blessed her to be mother to godly sons.

Drona The guru of the Kaurava and Pandava princes. He was a disciple of Parsurama and like his guru, had acquired invincibility. He very much liked his ablest disciple Arjuna.

Drupada The ruler of Panchala and father of Draupadi. She was born along with her brother Dharishtadyumna, as a result of great prayers and sacrifices performed by her father who desired to avenge the insults that he had suffered due to Drona.

Duryodhana The eldest of the 100 sons of Dharitarashtra who were born as result of the tissue culture technology attempted by the sage Vyasa in order to the prophesy he had made earlier; an embodiment of evil and an ardent enemy of Pandavas.

Dussasana The second son of Gandhari and Dharitarashtra. He was responsible for attempt to disrobe Draupadi.

DwaparaYuga The third great Age, at end of which Mahabharata took place.

Ekavarta An ancient town.

Ghatotkacha Bhimma's son from Hidimba, he always came to his father's aid in time of need, played a crucial role in the battle of Kurukshetra by forcing Karna to use a celestial weapon which he had reserved for attack at Arjuna.

Gandhari The princess of Gandhara, married to Dharitarashtra against her will, she had vowed to continuously blindfold herself and not to have a look at the world like her master.

Gandharva Unearthly being, a race of heavenly musicians.

Garuda Lord Vishnu's vehicle, an eagle.

Gokula An ancient cowherd location near Mathura.

Gopa A cowherd, also called Gopala.

Gopala Another name-one of thousands used for Krishna.

Gopi Cowherd woman, also called Gopika.

Govinda One of Krishna's names.

Guru Preceptor, master or teacher.

Hastinapura Capital city of Kurus; about 100 Km from Delhi.

Hidimba A female rakshasa who assumed human form when fell in love with Bhimma.

Ikshvaku Ancestor, a race descending from Sun is named after him.

Indra King of devas. He was considered father of Arjuna.

Indraparastha Pandavas' capital city, raised with Indra's help at Krishna's instructions, and was considered as beautiful as Indra's own abode.

Jaitra Krishna's magical chariot.

Jambavan An ancient king of bears from Lord Rama's time.

Jambavati Jambavan's daughter and Krishna's wife.

Jara A hunter who was responsible for Krishna's death. As a favour, he was liberated and sent to heaven.

Jarasandha Demonic king of Magadha, an ardent enemy of Krishna; was father-in-law of king Kamsa of Mathura. He attacked Mathura eighteen times to avenge the widowing of his daughters at hands of Krishna.

Jaydaratha A Kaurava ally; son-in-law of the blind king. During Mahabharata he was considered responsible for the death of young warrior Abhimanyu, in an ethically unsound manner.

Kalayavana A black supporter of Jarasandha; an enemy of Krishna.

Kali Yuga The 4th and the darkest of the four Ages.

Kamadhenu The sacred cow of wishes.

Kamsa The demonic king of Mathura, an uncle of Krishna. He had ascended to the throne of Mathura at an early age by dethroning his father. He had become the principle leader of the evil forces of that time.

Karma Action, duty, also fruits of the actions of past.

Karna A hero of Mahabharata; fights on behalf of Duryodhana as he does not know his origin; in fact, he was the first born of Kunti from sun God.

Kanka A court attendant for pleasing a king, Yudhistira disguised himself as one in the court of Virata.

Kaumodiki Krishna's mace.

Kauravas Sons of the blind king from Gandhari, a100 of them.

Khandavaparastha The unproductive part of the kingdom that the blind king assigned to the Pandavas.

Kichaka Brother of the queen of Virata who was killed by Bhimma for troubling Draupadi.

Kirpa Another guru of the Pandavas and Kauravas; his sister was married to Drona and he had introducer the latter to Bhishma for further training of the princes.

Kshatriya A warrior caste.

Kubera Lord of wealth.

Kubja A hunchback devotee and lover of Krishna who straightened her.

Kunti Pandavas' mother; Krishna's aunt.

Kuru Descendents from an ancient king of that name; Pandavas and Kauravas were its two branches.

Madri One of the two wives of the king Pandu. She had committed sati on death of Pandu and her two sons were reared by Kunti

Mahabharata The great war that took place some 5,000 years ago between the Kauravas and Pandavas.

Mahamaya The goddess of illusion; Krishna's sister and helper.

Manu The ancestor Law giver.

Mathura The ancient city of the Yadavas which was also ruled by the demonic Kamsa.

Maitreyi A sage of that time who was assigned by Vyasa to advise the confused blind king.

Maya Illusion or cosmic illusion.

Muchukunda A king from ancient times who had powers to burn whosoever disturbed him while at rest or in sleep.

Mustika A demonic wrestler of Kamsa of Mathura who was readied to fight and kill Krishna.

Naga Great serpent, also mythical serpentine race.

Nakula One of the Pandava brothers, son of Madri.

Nanda Foster father of Krishna; a gopa chief.

Narada Lord Brahma's wandering son and rishi; a devotee of Vishnu or Krishna.

Natwara One of the numerous names of Krishna. Also means a great dancer, the distinction acquired by young Krishna by ceaselessly dancing on head of Kalia, the serpent king, who was forced to vacate the waters of Yamuna.

Panchala The kingdom of Draupadi's father.

Panchanjaya Krishna's conch of magical powers.

Pandavas The five warrior sons of the Kuru king Pandu, three from Kunti and two from Madri.

Pandu The son of Ambalika from Vyasa who was crowned as king of Hastinapura, elder brother being blind.

Parsurama The greatest Brahmin warrior who almost eliminated or subdued all the kshatriya warriors of his time.

Paundraka The false Vasudeva, an enemy of the Lord.

Paradyumna Son of Krishna from Rukmani, he is Kama incarnate.

Parikshit Son of Abhimanyu and successor of Yudhishtira.

Prakriti Nature, the earthy principle that decides the nature of every being.

Pundit A knowledgeable person, particularly one with erudition in texts of Hindu religion.

Putana A demoness who attempted to kill the baby Krishna, on instructions from the demonic Kamsa of Mathura.

Radha A gopika, Krishna's first lover.

Rajarishi A royal seer, a king who is a sage.

Rajasuya A great sacrifice of emperors.

Rajas The second guna in nature of beings. It has a balance of righteous and non-righteous and capacity to differentiate.

Rakshasa A denon.

Rama A previous incarnation of Lord Vishnu.

Rig Veda The first Veda.

Rishi A sage.

Rukmi Rukmani's brother and Krishna's enemy.

Rukmani The princess of Vidhabha who secretly loved Krishna and the latter, after forcible abduction, married her.

Sahadeva One of the two sons of Madri, the youngest Pandava.

Sakuni The evil genius price of Gandhara, maternal uncle of the evil Duryodhana. He was annoyed at Bhishma for forcibly marrying sister Gandhari to the blind king and had vowed to avenge the insult.

Salva An evil king and enemy of Krishna.

Samba Krishna's son from Jambavati.

Sanjaya A commentator of excellence and a full-time companion of the blind king.

Sandipani Guru Sandipani's ashram was located in the ancient city of Ujjain which now falls in the state of M.P. It was the most prestigious centre of learning at that time.

Sansara Refers to the mortal world: Samsara also employed for the same.

Sarandhari Draupadi's name while in disguise in the Virata capital.

Saringa Krishna's bow.

Sasurman The Chief of Trigarthan and friend of Duryodhana; he had prompted the Kauravas to attack the Virata kingdom where Pandavas were in hiding.

Satyaki A Yadava Chief, Krishna's companion and charioteer and an ardent supporter of the Pandavas.

Satrajita A Yadava who possess the Saymantaka jewel.

Sattva The first and the purest guna of the nature.

Satayabhama Krishna's wife and Satrajita's daughter.

Sikandi Amba reborn as a warrior to be the cause for death of the invincible Bhishma.

Sishupala Krishna's cousin, his ardent enemy, Lord of Chedi. He was to marry Rukmani but she was forcibly secured by Krishna. He often insulted Krishna as the latter had promised his aunt, the mother of Sishupala to ignore a hundred of pranks/insults from the perpetual offender.

Siva Or Shiva, the third God of the Hindu Trinity; the destroyer.

Sudama A student time friend of Krishna.

Sudershana Chakra The rotating and flying wheel weapon of Vishnu or Krishna.

Suka A disciple of Vyasa; the narrator of Puranas.

Sunnaka A learned person who came to the Pandava when they came out on exile.

Swayamvara A rite at which a princess selects her bridegroom.

Tamas Third and the grossest guna of nature.

Tuglakian Refers to behaviour of a Muslim ruler of Delhi who had unsuccessfully attempted to shift his capital to central India without any feasibility study and had to quickly come back.

Ugersena The king of Mathura who was dethroned by his demonic son Kamsa.

Urvasi A celestial courtesen who fell in love with Arjuna—and wanted to marry him.

Uttara The Virata prince, his sister was known as Urrarai and was married to Abhimanyu.

Vaikuntha The celestial abode of Lord Vishnu.

Varnavata A tribal town of that lime located about 100 Km from Delhi.

Vasudeva Vishnu, also Krishna's father's name.

Vichitravirya The second of Santanu from Satyavathi, who died without producing a son for the throne of Hastinapura.

Vidura The wise and righteous Kuru, the youngest brother of the blind king, born from a female attendant of Ambika through Vyasa.

Vishvakarma A celestial architect who helped to build the Indraparastha for Pandavas.

Vrindavana Literally forest, *Forest of Vrinda*. Vrinda was a lover of Vishnu and was born as a forest for Krishna to roam about.

Vivasat	An ancestor.
Vyasa	Son of rishi Parasar and Matsayagandhi, later known as Satyavathi; great poet and composer of Puranas and also the Bhagavad Gita.
Yama	The God of death.
Yashodha	Foster mother of Krishna.
Yudhishtira	The eldest of the Pandavas; son of Yama born to Kunti.
Yoga	Union, union with the self or with God.
Yogi, Yogin	One who is united with his or her higher self, or the God.
Yuga	The Age: any of the four ages in the duration of world, each of which lasts for 3000 celestial years (one celestial year is equal to 3600 years of human time) and possesses special character of good and evil.

YADAVA DYNASTY: A NOTE

Yadavas are considered as having descended from Yadu, son of king Yayati of the lunar race. Prior to Krishna's entry into this race, on express request from Mother Earth, the Yadavas were ruled by a righteous king known as Ugrasena of Mathura. The great asura Kalenemi managed to be born as Kamsa into Ugrasena's family, through cunning deception of his young queen by Dramila, a gandharva who had assumed the exact form of the king. At a young age, Kamsa dethroned his own father and became the demonic ruler of the kingdom at Mathura.

Krishna and Balarama, the 7th and 8th incarnations of Vishnu, who came with the specific purpose of freeing the earth from an intolerably huge accumulation of evil and wickedness, became part of this illustrious family of kshatriya warriors. In addition to Ugrasena, Vasudeva (Krishna's father), Kuntibhoja [1], Akrura (a devotee of Krishna) and several other elders of the clan suffered a great deal, at hands of the demonic Kamsa. Devaki (Krishna's mother) and Kunti (mother of Pandavas) too were part of this warrior dynasty. Sataki, Satrajita (who possessed the Symentaka jewel), Uddhava (a great devotee and disciple of Krishna) and Daruka (Krishna's charioteer) were the other, often mentioned, contemporaries of Krishna and Balarama. Prominent amongst the next generation of Yadavas included Pradhyumna [2] (Krishna's son from Rukmani), Shambha [3] (Krishna's son from Jambavati) and Anirudha, the grand son of Krishna (through Pradhyumna).

Per force of unique circumstances, the mighty Yadavas had to endure the humiliation of having to vacate Mathura, their established ancestral kingdom, as they could not eliminate or convincingly defeat Jarasandha of Magadha, a powerful leader of demonic forces. His two daughters were widowed as a result of Kamsa's slaying by Krishna and he had vowed to extract a revenge for the same. He attacked Mathura seventeen times, almost at predictable frequency, causing great devastation and misery. Though Krishna and Balarama were able, each time, to defend Mathura but he could not be decisively defeated so as to refrain from attacking again and again. Seventeen of his attacks were successfully beaten back by Krishna and Balarama. On the eighteenth occasion, he was joined by the vicious forces of Kalayavana [4] and Krishna saw chances of sure defeat at hands of the evil forces. A unique boon protected Jarasandha against Krishna and Balarama and the Yadava combine had no other warrior who could eliminate this evil. Krishna did not want to face defeat at hands of evil forces so early in his career. He explained the grim scenario to the proud Yadavas and persuaded them to accept the fact that it was preferable to have another day to tackle the evil menace than sacrificing everything. Krishna's wise counsel was heard and the Yadavas migrated to a distant and desolate Dwaraka, where with the passage of time, they established an impressive empire.

After Mahabharata, Yadavas as a combined fighting force, grew into a truly invincible military might. With Krishna's reputation on their side, their fame and influence extended well beyond the land and sea boundaries of Bharata. Krishna was well aware of the negative implications of the invincibility of the Yadavas who had started exhibiting certain symptoms of eventual evil implications. Since the major manifesto of Krismna's presence on this earth was elimination of evil and wicked (active or potential), He did not want to leave behind, after his own departure from here, seeds of invincible evil with a potential to overtake the whole world. Hence, He planned and effected, at Parbhasa, total destruction of his own clan, in a fully judicious and impartial manner. Only after the clean completion of his *Mission Incarnate* assignment, He left the earth. It remained as a place of peace and justice for a long time to come.

Notes

1. A Yadava chief and father of Kunti.
2. An incarnation of Kama and was renowned for his physical charms.
3. Also spelt, at places, as Samba.
4. A foreign fighter with a huge army of mlechchas.

KURU DYNASTY: A NOTE

ATTACHMENTS

The Kuru dynasty originated from the great ancient king Bharata who ruled a great landmass which came to be known as Bharata. Starting from king Puru (a descendent of Manu through Ila who married Budha, the son of Chandra), it grew in a long span of 90 generations up to the king Santanu. Hence, it is also known as the Puru-Bharata-Kuru dynasty (Kochhar 2000). King Santanu was a popular descendent of the Kuru dynasty, with Hastinapura [1] as the capital of his kingdom. Kings of this dynasty were also called Chandravansi, being descendents of Chandra.

Santanu married a lovely maiden, in fact a celestial being, who had put a condition that she had to be totally free to do whatsoever she wanted, and if the king objected to any of her actions, then she would immediately desert him. Santanu, being deeply in love, had accepted the condition wholeheartedly. In course of time, she gave birth to seven sons, one after the other and each time after birth, she drowned the child in the nearby river. The king did not like her actions but being bound to a commitment, he raised no objection. After birth of the 8th child, when the king noticed her carrying the new born to the river, he could not refrain from raising an objection and cried, Stop it. The queen replied calmly, "Yes, you have broken the condition of our marriage, I will spare this child but will leave you immediately." Before disappearing, she declared that she was Ganga, the deity of the river. She also explained that she took human form with the purpose of freeing the eight vasus [2], who in their earlier life had stolen the sage Vasishta's renowned cow Nandini, and as a punishment, they were cursed to be born on earth (Narayan, 1978). Here, no better person than you cold be found to father them. This eighth child that I am holding now, was the leader of the culprits, and hence, he has to stay alive for completing the punishment as per terms of the curse. Though, his existence on earth shall be extremely brilliant, he is condemned to a life of total celibacy. And while departing, Ganga said, "I will carry the child now but will restore him to you after he is grown up." The king's questions of when and where were ignored.

Years later, Ganga reappeared with a handsome young boy and told the king, "Here is your son; his name is Devavarata and he has mastered Vedas under sage Vasishta himself; he will be a great warrior, an expert in use of astras and matchless with mental and spiritual capabilities." The king was very happy to have a grown up warrior son.

Four years later, the king while on a hunting expedition, came across a beautiful girl, daughter of a fisherman. Her father, when approached, put a very difficult condition for allowing the king to marry her. The king could not fulfil the condition and consequently ran into depression and sickness. The young prince came to know of his father's condition and cause for the same. He approached the girl's father and enquired what he wanted for marrying off his daughter to the king. The fisherman was very shrewd and said, "I want my daughter's children to be the sole claimant to the throne." Devavratha assured that there was no problem for this to happen. But the truly farsighted fisherman said, "Who will be the king after my grandson?" To this, the young prince replied, "Of course, his son!" In order to fully clear the fisherman's anxieties, the price added, "Don't worry, I hereby promise that I shall live and die totally celibate. This is a firm vow." Noticing the fisherman's satisfaction, the prince told the girl with due politeness, "Come, get into the chariot, henceforth you are my mother." Devavartha, from that time came to be known as Bhishma, meaning one with a difficult but firm vow.

The name of the young queen was Satyavathi. Earlier, she was called as Mastagandhi, as strong fishy smell emanated from her body. She was cured of this problem by an eminent rishi named Parasar, from whom she had produced a son called, Island-born, later named as Ved Vyasa, a great sage in his own life time. In the process, she was cured of the offensive smell and was endowed with a perpetual pleasant fragrance. No one, except the rishi Parasar and herself, was aware of this event as her virginity was miraculously restored.

In time, Satyavathi bore the king two sons named, Chitrangada and Vichitravirya. The elder one was killed in battle with a gandharva king. The young Vichitravirya was installed as the successor, with Bhishma acting as the regent, at request of queen mother Satyavathi. Bhishma, being anxious not to allow the dynasty to fade away, forcibly secured the three daughters of the king of Kashi, at the time of their sawayamwara, for being married to the young prince. The elder one called Amba, was not happy as she had already set her heart on the king of Salwa. While Ambika and Ambalika were married to Vichitravirya, Amba was sent respectfully to the king of Salwa who refused to accept her. She returned heart broken and insisted that Bhishma should marry her but the latter, bound by a strict vow of celibacy, did not yield to her insistence. On the advice of some sages, she approached Bhishma's guru Parshurama for pressurising the celibate warrior to marry her. After intense arguments ,a fight took place between the guru and the disciple, which turned out to be inconclusive. Subsequently, through hard penance, she secured a boon to be born as a man and be able to kill the celibate warrior, as a revenge. As a consequence, she was born as Sikandi in the family of king Drupada of Panchala and played a decisive role in the battle of Kurukshetra.

For seven years of marriage, Ambika and Ambalika lived happily with the young king Vichitravirya but were unlucky not to have any child. He died of an untreatable wasting disease, leaving no claimant to the throne. Satyavathi approached Bhishma to help the young widows to have children but the celibate warrior politely yet firmly reminded her of his vow which was inviolable. Having no alternative, she disclosed to Bhishma that she had another son and that she could call him at will. Bhishma encouraged her to go ahead, as that was the best alternative. Vyasa, her island born son, appeared as commanded by his mother and on her explaining the problem, agreed to do the needful.

Ambika found the sage Vyasa somewhat repulsive or dreadful and closed her eyes while submitting to him and from this union, as was predicted by the sage himself, a blind male child was born. He was named Dhritarashtra. Ambalika who had turned pale when approached by Vyasa, gave birth to a pale looking child later named Pandu. He turned out as a brave and just warrior king. Another child was born to Ambika's female servant who grew to be a very intelligent, righteous and outspoken man and was later named as Vidura. All the three young Kurus were well trained under the able guidance of Bhishma. Being brave and righteous, Pandu was crowned as the king but the same was silently resented to by his blind elder brother who never stopped cursing his disability and the bad luck. When the boys came to youth, the blind prince was married to the princess of Gandhara, named Gandhari, a bit against her wishes. In order to register her protest or to gain a point, she took a vow of lifelong darkness and kept herself fully blindfolded. Pandu was married to Kunti, the daughter of a Yadava chief called Kuntibhoja. He took another wife named Madri—and both the ladies had a good rapport among themselves.

Pandu's enthronement received all round appreciation. He proved valorous and just, and, in a short time, enhanced the prestige of the Kuru kingdom a great deal. After several martial excursions, he sought relaxation in a forest camp in company of his two wives. One day while hunting, Pandu killed a celestial being who had disguised himself as a deer and was engaged in love game with his mate. While dying, he cured the young king to meet the same fate. Pandu, thus, was in a quandary as both of his young wives had no issues by that time. And the king was greatly aggrieved on this account. His elder wife, Kunti had been granted special powers by the sage Dhurvasa, to call any God at will and grant her a child. She had once experimented with these powers by calling the Sun God, from whom a son was born to her, well encased in armour and wearing large earrings for protection. Being unmarried at that time, she had discarded the newly born child in a well cushioned basket which was left to float in a river. The child was picked up and reared by a childless charioteer. He grew into an invincible warrior named as Karna.

Pandu was keen for Kunti to try her capabilities and encouraged her to attempt the same. He told her to first call Yama, the God of death and ultimate justice--and from this union was born a unique child, later named as Yudhistira. A heavenly voice had claimed that the child would grow into a great man of reason ,thought and courage. At Pandu's further inducement, Kunti produced a mighty being called Bhemsena, by calling the all powerful Vayu, the God of wind. Later on, she had Arjuna with the help of none other than the Lord Indra. He grew into a great warrior and the key character of Mahabharata. Madri picked up the mantra from Kunti and gave birth to the twins. Soon after, Pandu died on account of his inability to resist the charms of his younger wife Madri. While Madri became sati with the body of Pandu, Kunti returned to Hastinapura, with all the five uniquely endowed sons of Pandu.

On hearing the news of Kunti giving birth to her first son, Gandhari had become desperate. Sage Vyasa had informed her that she would be mother of a hundred sons. She, however, delivered only a stillborn lump of flesh and seeing her desperation, sage Vyasa, employing tissue culture technique, converted the same into eventual birth of a hundred sons and a daughter. Gandhari and the blind king were, however, not happy on account of two facts; (a) Kunti's son had become the eldest in the family, and (b) at the time of birth of Gandhari's first son, inauspicious sounds and related happenings had predicted that this child will be the cause of the total destruction of the Kuru clan. Sage Vyasa and Vidura, along with the other well wishers of the dynasty, had advised immediate destruction of Gandhari's first born but their advice was ignored by the blind king.

Gandhari eldest son was named as Duryodhana (the invincible) and right from beginning, he developed a very intense rivalry and hatred towards the sons of Pandu. His feelings and behaviour of naked hostility towards the sons of Pandu, who came to be known as Pandavas, further intensified when under the tutelage of Guru Drona, the Pandavas out-performed the Kauravas (the sons of the blind king). Duryodhana spared no effort or trick to destroy the Pandavas, with the covert or overt support of the blind king who somehow wanted only his progeny to rule the kingdom of Hastinapura.

Vidura, through his righteous approach, mostly supported the sons of Pandu and the same was not liked by the blind king. Bhishma was bound to his destructive vows to support the kingdom of Hastinapura, irrespective of who headed or controlled it. On account of refusal of guru Drona to accept Karna as his disciple, the latter developed an intense rivalry with Arjuna, which subsequently grew into a blind commitment to support the evil Duryodhana.

They became inseparable friends and co-authored several schemes and plans, to damage and destroy the Pandavas.

Finally, the conflict of the two lines of the Kuru dynasty, the Kauravas and the Pandavas, became the main cause of the battle of Kurukshetra, where the entire Kaurava clan, except the blind king, his wife and only one of his sons (who was neutral in the conflict) survived. On the Pandavas' side, the whole second generation was eliminated in the conflict and their blood line survived only through the grace of Lord Krishna who had revived the stillborn son of Uttarai and Abhimanyu. He grew up into handsome and just prince and took over the governance from Yudhistira. He was named Parikshit.

Notes

1. Hastinapura, the ancient Kuru capital is located approximately. 100 km from Delhi (Indraparastha). It was reportedly established by king Hastin, another ancestor of the dynasty. There are varying opinions amongst experts on ancient Indian locations, as some of them expected the Kuru capital being somewhere near to the river Sindhu.

2. Attendants of Lord Indra.

REFERENCES

REFERENCES

A. Fisher (1997), "Tom Peters: Professional Loudmouth," Fortune 136, 12: 237-276.

Arvind Sharma (2005), "Modern Hindu Thought," Oxford Press, New Delhi.

B.G. Jackson (1996), "Guru's Line Is It Any Way? An Exploratory Geneology," SCOS Network 14, 1:12-16.

Bhagavan Das (1990) "Krishna: A Study in the Theory of Avararas", a Vidya Bhavan publication, Bombay, India.

Bob Weinstein (1998), "I Hate My Boss," McGraw-Hill, New York.

C. Arugyris (1957), "Personality and Organization," Harper and Row, NY.

C. Kennedy (1991), "A Guide to Management Gurus," Business Books Limited, London.

C. Lorenz (1986), "The Guru Factor: Europe Warms to Business Punditry," Financial Times, July 2:18.

D. Clutterbuck and S. Crainer (1990), "Makers of Management," Macmillan, London.

Deepak Chopra, "Every Day Immortality", Random House, London.

Eric J. Sharpe (1985), "The Universal Gita: Western Images of Bhagavad Gita," Duckworth, London.

F. Herzberg, et al., "Work and Nature of Man", World Publishing.

Frederick W. Taylor (1911), "The principles of Scientific Management," Harper and brothers, NJ, 44.

G. A. Akerlof (1970), "The Market for Lemons: Qualitative Uncertainties and the Market Mechanism," Quarterly Journal of Economics, 84, 488-500.

Guy Brown (2000), "The Energy of Life", The Free Press, 1230 Avenue of Americas, New York, NY 10020.

Henry Fayol (1949), "General and Industrial Administration," Pitman, NJ, 20-41.

H.H.N. Stevension, "Do Lunch or Be Lunch" by Harvard Business Press, Boston, Missachusetts.

J.B. Kripalani (2004), "My Times: An Autobiography," Rupa and Co, Ansari Road, New Delhi.

J. Chang and J. Halliday (2005), "Mao: The Unknown Story," Jonathan Cape, London.

J.H. Boyett and J.T. Boyett (1998), "The Guru Guide," John Wiley, New York.

J. Nash (1950), "Equilibrium Points in N-person Games," Proceedings of the National Academy of Sciences, 36, 48-9.

Joseph Schumpeter (1943), "Capitalism, Socialism and Democracy," by Allen & Unwin, London.

K.M. Munshi (1988), "Krishnavatara," Vol. II "The Wrath of an Emperor", Bombay, India.

M. Dixon (1986), "The Guru Factor; Ancient Wisdom with a Novel Twist," Financial Times, July 17:14.

M.E. Porto (1980), Competitive Strategy: Techniques for Analyzing Industries and Competitors, Free Press, NY.

Mayo (1949), "The Social Problems of an Industrial Civilization," Routledge and Kegan Paul, London.

Mc. Gregor (1960), "The Human Side of Enterprise" McGraw Hill, NY.

Pawan K. Verma (1995), "Krishna: The Playful Divine," Published by Panguin Books, Nehru Place, New Delhi.

Peter R. Drucker (1946), "Concept of the Corporation," John Day, NJ.

Peter Senge (1998), "The Strategy Leader," Backwell, Oxford.

R. Gibson (1997), "Rethinking the Future," Nicholas Brealey,

R.J. Aumann (1959), "Contributions to the Theory of Games," Volume IV, Princeton University Press, Princeton, NJ.

R. Kochhar (2000), "The Vedic People," Oriental Longman Ltd, Asaf Ali Road, New Delhi, 110 002.

R.K. Narayan (1978), "The Mahabharata," by Vision Books Pvt. Ltd., New Delhi, 110001.

Ramesh Menon (1993), "Once a Blue God," Garutman Pvt. Ltd. 8B, Middleton

Street

S. Radhakrishna (1927), "The Hindu View of Life," George Allen & Unwin, London.

—1948, "The Bhagavad Gita," With an introductory essay, Sanskrit text, English translation and notes: George Allen & Unwin, London.

—1953, "The Principle Upanasads," George Allen & Unwin, London.

—1960, "The Brahma Sutra, "George Allen & Upwin, London.

Swami Sawanada (1990), "Selections from Complete Works of Swami Vivekananda," Advaita Ashrama, Mayavati, Pithoragarh, Himalyas.

T.C. Schelling (1960), "The Strategy of Conflict," by Harvard University Press, Cambridge, MA.

T. Dodsworth (1986), "Why America is Just Wild about Wisdom, Financial Times, July 14:14.

V.S. Murlidharan (2006), "Intelligent Manager," Ane Books India, Ansari Road, New Delhi, 110 002.

Varoon Victor, H. and Arther, G. Jago, Decision Making as a Social Process: Normative and Descriptive Models of Behavior, Decision Sciences, 5(1974) 743.

W. Bennis (1989), "On Becoming a Leader," Business, Books, London.

INDEX

INDEX